The Chinatown Trunk Mystery

THE CHINATOWN TRUNK MYSTERY

Murder, Miscegenation,
and Other Dangerous Encounters
in Turn-of-the-Century New York City

Mary Ting Yi Lui

PRINCETON UNIVERSITY PRESS

PRINCETON AND OXFORD

Copyright © 2005 by Princeton University Press
Published by Princeton University Press, 41 William Street, Princeton, New Jersey 08540
In the United Kingdom: Princeton University Press, 3 Market Place, Woodstock,
Oxfordshire OX20 1SY

Second printing, and first paperback printing, 2007
Paperback ISBN-13: 978-0-691-13048-4
Paperback ISBN-10: 0-691-13048-5

The Library of Congress has cataloged the cloth edition of this book as follows

Lui, Mary Ting Yi, 1967–
The Chinatown trunk mystery : murder, miscegenation, and other dangerous encounters
in turn-of-the-century New York City / Mary Ting Yi Lui.
p.   cm.
Includes bibliographical references and index.
ISBN 0-691-09196-X (cl. : alk. paper)
1. United States—Emigration and immigration—Government policy.   2. Immigrants—
New York (State)—New York—Public opinion.   3. Chinese—New York (State)—New
York—Public opinion.   4. Interracial dating—New York (State)—New York—Public
opinion.   5. Murder—New York (State)—New York—Case studies.   I. Title.

JV6483.L85 2005
364.152'3'097471—dc22

                                                                        2004044252

British Library Cataloging-in-Publication Data is available

This book has been composed in Sabon

Printed on acid-free paper. ∞

press.princeton.edu

Printed in the United States of America

10   9   8   7   6   5   4   3   2

To the people of New York City's Chinatown

Contents

List of Illustrations　　　　　　　　　　　　　　　　ix

Acknowledgments　　　　　　　　　　　　　　　　　xi

INTRODUCTION
"Find Miss Sigel Dead in Trunk"　　　　　　　　　　　1

CHAPTER ONE
"Terra Incognita": Mapping Chinatown's Racial and
Gender Boundaries in Lower Manhattan　　　　　　　17

CHAPTER TWO
Beyond Chinatown: Policing Chinese American Male
Mobility in New York City　　　　　　　　　　　　52

CHAPTER THREE
Policing Urban Girls' and Women's Mobility and Desires　　81

CHAPTER FOUR
Playing the "Missionary Game"　　　　　　　　　　111

CHAPTER FIVE
Chinese American Interracial Couples and Families
in New York City　　　　　　　　　　　　　　　143

CHAPTER SIX
"The Most Remarkable Get-away in Police History"　　175

CHAPTER SEVEN
"Disgrace on the Whole Body of Our People"　　　　198

Epilogue　　　　　　　　　　　　　　　　　　222

Notes　　　　　　　　　　　　　　　　　　　227

Bibliography　　　　　　　　　　　　　　　　277

Index　　　　　　　　　　　　　　　　　　　293

Illustrations

Maps

1.1. Chinatown and Five Points area in lower Manhattan   23

2.1. Key locations in the Elsie Sigel murder case   53

2.2. Manhattan's elevated train and subway system in 1905   57

2.3. Distribution of Chinese laundries throughout
     Manhattan in 1893   58

Figures

1.1. Lulu Shu, the white wife of a Chinese man, 1909   19

1.2. "New York City – The Opium Dens in Pell and
     Mott Streets – How the Opium Habit Is Developed," 1883   29

1.3. Opium dens pictured in a Chinatown guidebook, 1908   31

1.4. "High-class" Chinese restaurant in Chinatown, 1909   39

1.5. "Doyers St., 1909"   40

1.6. Chuck Connors, "Mayor of Chinatown," 1908   42

1.7. Chinese and white businesses on Pell Street, ca. 1900   43

1.8. "The Conversion of the Spider," 1909   44

1.9. "The Real Yellow Peril," 1909   45

2.1. "Chop suey" joint, 1909   66

2.2. "Converted!" 1909   79

3.1. The first floor "recreation room" of the Chinatown
     Settlement for Girls, 1908   105

3.2. "Mission Where Elsie Sigel Met Her Slayer," 1909   108

4.1. Hy. Mayer, "Just Supposing," 1909   112

4.2. Robert Carter, "The Infernal Question," 1909   114

4.3. "Christianized?" June 23, 1909   115

5.1. W. A. Rogers, "A Wedding in the Chinese Quarter, Mott Street, New York," 1890   148

5.2. Chinese family at 34 Mott Street, 1908   151

6.1. Published photographs of the missing suspects, Chong Sing and Leon Ling, 1909   177

6.2. Nelson Harding, "The Chinese Jekyll and Hyde," 1909   181

6.3. Hy. Mayer, "A Raid in Chinatown Puzzle Find the Guilty One," 1905   189

7.1. Chong Sing arriving in New York City, 1909   202

7.2. Police detectives in Chinatown during the Fourth of July holiday, 1909   209

Acknowledgments

I have been fortunate to receive the generous support of family, friends, and colleagues throughout the research and writing of this book. First and foremost, this book would not exist without the invaluable work experience at the Museum of Chinese in the Americas, formerly known as the New York Chinatown History Project, situated in the heart of New York City's Chinatown. While working on the museum's exhibition on early Chinatown history I stumbled across the long forgotten Elsie Sigel murder case and was quickly inspired to investigate further. I did not know at the time that this after-hours sleuthing would one day lead me to write this book. Many thanks go to my former colleagues at the museum, who not only encouraged me to research the murder but also to pursue full-time graduate work in Asian American history. In particular, I wish to thank Fay Chew Matsuda, Maria Hong, Lamgen Leon, William "Charlie" Chin, Adrienne Cooper, and Charles Lai.

I am deeply indebted to my graduate dissertation advisors for their initial enthusiasm and expert tutelage in developing this project. Gary Okihiro, my dissertation advisor and mentor, quickly recognized the importance of the Elsie Sigel case and granted me the opportunity to develop the necessary tools to turn this sensational tale of murder and miscegenation into a serious work of historical analysis. Sunn Shelley Wong and Nick Salvatore were equally important for enlarging the book's analysis to incorporate the themes of geography and social history respectively.

I am also grateful to fellow historians and friends K. Scott Wong, John Kuo Wei Tchen, and Dorothy Fujita Rony who directed me to key archival sources and taught by example the importance of reexamining the turn-of-the-century experiences of Chinese immigrants on the East Coast. My discussion of the problems of racial identification at the turn-of-the-century in chapter 7 was greatly improved as a result of my participation in a collaborative research project on the history of fingerprinting and the Chinese Exclusion Act with Simon Cole. My thanks go to him for his knowledge and friendship. I am grateful to Edward Rhoads for making available his research on Charles Sing and the North Adams Chinese shoemakers. Thanks also go to Ian Lewis Gordon for sharing his research on the murder case.

This book has also benefited greatly from the meticulous reading and thoughtful comments from a number of scholars whose work I greatly admire. Friend, colleague, and fellow traveler Moon-Ho Jung, has provided constant critical commentary, invaluable editorial support, and camaraderie throughout the various incarnations of this project from dissertation to book. I have also been fortunate enough to participate in an Asian American women's writing group with a remarkable group of scholars from a range of academic disciplines: Evelyn Ch'ien, Shirley Lim, Sanda Lwin, Suzette Min, Mae Ngai, Shuang Shen, Sandhya Shukla, Lok Siu, Cynthia Tolentino, and Lisa Yun. I am particularly grateful for their comments on chapters 2 and 4. I am also grateful for the comments provided by Crystal Feimster, Ginetta Candelario, Deborah Thomas, and Cheryl Hicks on chapter 4.

Since arriving at Yale, I have been fortunate to receive the enthusiastic support of peers, and graduate and undergraduate students. A number of colleagues from my home departments of history and American Studies have provided insightful suggestions for improving particular sections of the book: Sanda Lwin, Dolores Hayden, Laura Wexler, Matthew Jacobson, and Aaron Sachs. I am also greatly appreciative of the assistance provided by Yale's Social Science Statistical Laboratory (Statlab) and Steve Citron-Pousty in the use of GIS software to generate maps for the book.

Like other historians, I am extremely beholden to the attentive assistance I received from the staff of various archives consulted during the course of my research. In particular, I wish to express my gratitude to Kenneth Cobb, Director of the New York City Municipal Archives; and Wayne Kempton, Archivist of the Episcopal Diocese of New York; and the archivists at the National Archives, northeastern regional branch in New York City. These archivists went beyond the call of duty to suggest and locate materials they felt would be pertinent; the book would certainly have been a lesser product without their contribution. I also wish to thank the Church of the Transfiguration for allowing me access to their baptism and marriage registries. I am grateful to the National Endowment of the Humanities, Williams College, and Yale University for their financial support of some of the research and travel expenses incurred.

Ten thousand thanks go to Thomas LeBien, whose editorial expertise and unflagging commitment to the project have been invaluable from the moment I began the arduous process of revising for publication. It has been my good luck to have such a thorough and committed editor. I also wish to thank Brigitta van Rheinberg for continuing the process of shepherding the book to its completion. I am also grateful for the assistance of Mark Bellis, Dale Cotton, Alison Kalett, and Dimitri Karetnikov for their fine work. I have been especially fortunate to have the manuscript reviewed by historians Timothy Gilfoyle and Henry Yu, who strongly endorsed the project from the outset and made numerous insightful suggestions for revision. Additional thanks go to Timothy Gilfoyle for generously sharing his expertise on turn-of-the-century New York City history and pointing out additional sources for consideration.

Most importantly, I wish to acknowledge the constant support and love of my family. My parents, Pok Sang Lui and Fung Shim Chan Lui, have waited a long time to see the conclusion of this project, but have never doubted its completion. Since joining the Balbarin family, Corazon and Eduardo Balbarin have been an equally important source of encouragement. It has often been said that cats make the perfect writing companions; this is certainly true of our companions, Oscar and Dexter. To my partner, Vincent Balbarin, who has brought laughter, music, and technology into my life, I am forever grateful for your limitless patience and good cheer for making this possible. Now that the book is completed, we move together toward a new chapter of our lives as parents to our son, Mateo. Let the adventure begin.

The Chinatown Trunk Mystery

"Find Miss Sigel Dead in Trunk"

SEVERAL DAYS PASSED before Sun Leung, the proprietor of a "chop suey" restaurant at 782 Eighth Avenue, decided to report the disappearance of his cousin, Leon Ling. The two men lived in separate fourth floor apartments above the restaurant, and for nearly a week Sun Leung knocked repeatedly on his cousin's door but received no response. A foul odor emanating from the room finally convinced Sun Leung that he had to go to the police.[1] On the afternoon of June 18, 1909, he walked from his restaurant to the West Forty-seventh Street police station and filed a report with the policeman on duty. The station promptly dispatched Officer John Reardon to accompany him to Leon Ling's room. With the assistance of a locksmith, Reardon managed to open the door. On entering the men immediately noticed a large bound trunk left in the center of the room and set about untying the thick rope to reveal its contents. Instead of finding Leon Ling's body as the policeman and Sun Leung had anticipated, to their astonishment they recovered the corpse of a woman with a piece of rope around her neck.[2]

Reardon lost no time sending word of his discovery to Captain Post back at the West Forty-seventh Street police station. After rushing to inspect the scene, Captain Post notified the Detective Bureau at police headquarters and duly turned over the investigation to Captain Arthur Carey of the Homicide Bureau.[3] By the end of the day, the coroner and several police officers and detectives had inspected the crime scene and the entire building, and interrogated its occupants. Police arrested a number of Chinese men who were present in the building when they arrived on the scene: Yee Kim, manager of the restaurant; Chin Sung, who also lived in the building; and Dong Wing of 10 Pell Street in Chinatown. Unable to provide the police with any information about the murder, all three men were eventually released on bail.[4]

While searching the crime scene police found a number of letters, written by various American women, addressed to the missing Leon Ling. Among them were thirty-five letters signed "Elsie," which led police to suspect that the victim was nineteen-year-old Elsie Sigel of 209 Wadsworth Avenue in the Washington Heights section of New York City, who had disappeared on June 9th while en route to visit her grandmother.[5] Their suspicions were confirmed that evening when the Sigel family members recognized the clothes and jewelry found on the corpse.

With her identity confirmed, police set off to apprehend the chief murder suspect, Leon Ling, who by Sun Leung's recollection had about a week's head start. Also absent for some time and wanted for questioning was Chong Sing, who lived in the room adjoining Leon Ling's. As the city's police force launched their manhunt, detectives worked to establish a motive to tie the chief suspect to the murder. More importantly, they sought to explain how her body came to be found in a room rented by a Chinese man. The rumor that she had been a Protestant missionary working with the city's predominantly male Chinese immigrant population, seemed to provide the necessary explanation.

Overnight, the city's and nation's newspapers quickly publicized the news of the dramatic discovery of the murdered "girl missionary." The coverage of the Sigel murder investigation remained in the front pages of New York City newspapers for at least a week after its initial reporting, and follow-up stories continued intermittently for several months. In other parts of the country, area newspapers provided detailed coverage of the New York investigation and reported on the extent to which local communities were also deeply affected by the Sigel murder and police investigation. To make sense of the murder, journalists also focused their attention on Protestant missionary activities and the city's Chinese immigrant population, presenting portraits of individuals and Chinatown daily life.

By 1909 newspaper articles and stories about the activities of the "heathen Chinee" were not unknown in New York or other parts of the country.[6] A glance through some of the city's major newspapers—*New York Herald*, *New York Times*, *World*, *New York Tribune*—and popular magazines reveals that period's sensationalistic reporting of Chinatown life as defined by sordid underground vice activities or exotic cultural peculiarities. Reports of tong wars, prostitution, gambling dens, and opium joints mixed with accounts of social events involving the more "respectable" members of the community such as Lunar New Year celebrations, picnics and suppers sponsored by the city's Protestant missions, and announcements of weddings and births. While stories about Chinatown's vice activities occasionally made front-page news, lengthy follow-up stories seldom appeared. Judging from the constant level of press attention focused on this case, Elsie Sigel's murder had taken the city and country by surprise. Readers throughout the nation eagerly followed the developments of both the police and investigative journalists in their efforts to apprehend the Chinese fugitives and resolve the many questions surrounding the murder, the nature of Sigel's relationship with Leon Ling being the most important.

In most murder mystery novels, readers eagerly turn the pages to follow the intrepid investigator's attempts to outwit and apprehend the murderer. Dangled clues and red herrings tease and heighten readers' anticipation of the final revelation of the killer's identity. In the classic "whodunit," the criminal is unmasked and explanations of unseen motives and behind-the-scenes plotting are laid out in this eagerly anticipated moment. Historical accounts of real-life murder cases have much to share with these mystery novels. Through the meticulous search for clues and evidence left in the archival record, the historian painstakingly reconstructs the details of the crime, placing it within the historical backdrop of a bygone era. The reader follows the drama of the police investigation that often leads into the final courtroom trial where all secrets are divulged. In retelling the courtroom drama, the historian weighs each piece of testimony and evidence entered into the court record, showing us the flaws and strengths of both prosecution and defense before presenting each party's final arguments and the long-awaited jury verdict. Whether served outside or within a court of law, at the book's conclusion the historian and reader might pause to ponder whether justice has been served before bringing closure to the episode.[7]

The Chinatown Trunk Mystery departs from this narrative structure. Leon Ling, the chief murder suspect, in the end eluded all attempts to bring about his capture; for both New York's police and all subsequent historians, Leon Ling disappeared into thin air. Without him, there would be no courtroom drama to put to rest the many circulating rumors and thus bring a satisfactory sense of judicial closure to this case. Instead, the murder remains a tangle of bizarre tales intermingled with some indisputable facts, just as it did in the hours, days, weeks, and months that followed the grisly discovery of Sigel's body. Nearly a century later, the case remains unsolved and forgotten.

There is certainly a mystery here that commands our attention, but it is not about revealing the murderer's identity or establishing a motive. These were not the questions that gripped early-twentieth-century New Yorkers or the country at large when a nation of newspaper readers became thoroughly engrossed in the details of the murder and its investigation in the summer of 1909. Indeed, for the general public, the identity of the murderer was no mystery. It was Leon Ling, a Chinese Sunday school pupil who had become infatuated with a young white missionary and murdered her in a fit of jealousy when he learned of her growing affections for another Chinese man. As far as the public was concerned, these were the facts of the case and they were not in dispute. The modern day historian faces a mystery far more compelling than the effort to seek out evidence that conclusively damns or exculpates Leon Ling. The historical mystery, the mystery warranting our attention and this book, has at its core the public's obsession with the details of the ensuing murder investigation. In particular, readers needed to understand

Sigel's motivation for befriending Chinese men such as the murder suspect, and more importantly, the place of Chinese immigrants in New York City and the nation at large. These questions ultimately mattered more to readers than proving the murderer's identity and motive.

What fascinates now is not Sigel's unresolved murder, because its causes and meanings were indeterminate from the beginning. Rather, the mystery to unravel involves understanding why New Yorkers and the nation at large should become so fascinated with this particular unsolved murder. New Yorkers in this period were after all, hardly strangers to tragic and unexplained deaths. This could also be said for the rest of the nation. On the same day that Sigel's death was reported, the *New York Herald* reported several mysterious deaths, including a Pennsylvania man and his wife who died under odd circumstances that suggested the possibility of a double poisoning.[8] Within weeks following the murder, a *World* headline announced in typical sensationalistic fanfare that the Elsie Sigel case was only the latest among "112 Unsolved Murders in Manhattan and Bronx Alone Since Jan. 1, 1906."[9] The shocking discovery of the victim's body and her relationship to New York's Chinese community were two obvious reasons for the public's excessive fascination with this case. The yellow journalism genre of this period sensationalized the story further. These reasons alone do not fully explain the shaping of the murder narrative around specific sets of images and stories that had little bearing on the murder itself. Indeed, what immediately strikes the historian when looking at this period's discussion of the Sigel murder is how the public seemed less concerned with finding out what truly happened than affixing a particular set of narratives to explain the murder—that would remain in accordance with turn-of-the-century popular views on race, class, gender, and sexuality.

The stories—official and unofficial—emerging out of the murder investigation ruptured New Yorkers' perceptions of not only Chinese immigrants in their midst but also the place of white working-class and middle-class women in a city undergoing rapid industrial and commercial expansion, and unprecedented population growth. Occurring when the city's physical terrain and social relations were changing—with the arrival and settlement of new immigrant groups and with cleavages between various socioeconomic classes—the murder warned that past attempts to maintain social order through the regulation of racialized, gendered, and sexualized borders were failing and that the consequences would be devastating. Apprehending the vanished suspects and resolving the nagging questions about Elsie Sigel's involvement with Chinese residents quickly became instrumental for New York police, social reformers, journalists, and residents in regaining the social and spatial order that had been disrupted. In the aftermath of the murder, this translated directly into the surveillance and investigation of the spaces typically inhabited by Chinese immigrants: homes, houses of worship, places of business, and the Chinatown neighborhood itself. Likewise, popular depictions of these spaces and of the murder itself—through imparting moral and social lessons for readers—also worked to reassert social and spatial boundaries by restraining the physical and social movement of Chinese men and white women of all socioeconomic classes while reaffirming mobility as a white male privilege. Despite these efforts, the reinscription of such boundaries into New York City's rapidly changing landscape proved difficult. Surprising revelations emerging from the murder investigation and the actions of the people being policed continued to challenge the contemporary racial and gender ideologies upon which these boundaries were erected.

READING AND MAPPING TURN-OF-THE-CENTURY NEW YORK CITY CHINATOWN

Revisiting nineteenth- and early-twentieth-century published texts that purport to describe accurately the everyday lives of the city's Chinese immigrant population presents great difficulties for the modern day historian. Authors from the 1870s to the early 1920s usually promoted their respective side of the debate concerning the passage of exclusionary Asian immigration and naturalization laws. Put into effect beginning with the passage of the 1875 Page Act and the 1882 Chinese Exclusion Act, such federal legislation not only aimed to deny Chinese laborers entry into the United States, but also to contain socially, politically, and economically those who entered by not extending the same legal protections and rights guaranteed to U.S. citizens. This period's published accounts of "Chinatowns" in the United States often assisted in the project of Chinese exclusion by transforming these urban neighborhoods comprising ethnically diverse populations into both cultural and spatial constructs that reinforced and reproduced Euro-American notions of racial and cultural superiority against an immoral and vice-ridden Chinese immigrant community.[10] Although the majority of the city's Chinese immigrants did not reside or work in Chinatown, these racialized images of Chinatown vice continued to accompany Chinese immigrants in their attempts to settle and work in neighborhoods throughout the city. The fear that Chinese homes and places of work served as conduits for Chinatown vices such as opium smoking, which threatened to undermine white womanhood, seriously challenged Chinese male laborers' efforts toward permanent settlement and physical and social mobility.

These accounts also reveal the importance of contemporary gender relations in the making of New York City Chinatown's imaginary and physical landscape. Popular Chinatown narratives that portray white womanhood under assault, such as those appearing after the Elsie Sigel murder, echoed this period's concerns with the physical and social mobility of different urban populations. As has been shown with the Jack the Ripper stories in London, Victorian narratives of sexual danger were attempts to redraw that city's social and spatial boundaries. The rapid social and economic changes that emerged in nineteenth-century London left open possibilities of social and spatial transgressions by different groups of people—particularly middle-class women and working-class men and women.[11] In New York City, narratives of racial and sexual danger worked to refashion spatial and social boundaries disrupted by the settlement of Chinese throughout the city. Changing gender roles and sexual mores granted urban women such as Elsie Sigel increased physical and social mobility. To many readers this tragedy began with the arrival of Chinese businesses into white neighborhoods such as Washington Heights, where the Sigel family first encountered the murder suspect Leon Ling. Sigel's decision to leave the protection of her comfortable, white middle-class surroundings in upper Manhattan and accompany Leon Ling to explore the immoral and criminal underside of Chinatown in working-class lower Manhattan ultimately led to her undoing.

These press accounts of Sigel's wanderings reaffirmed the division of the city's neighborhoods into a distinct moral geography of territories of "daylight" and "darkness" that had been popularized by tourist guidebooks, newspapers, and magazines. While white middle- and upper-class neighborhoods were consistently bathed with sunlight and open air, the neighborhoods of non-whites, the poor, and working-class immigrants were enshrouded in darkness, disease, and criminality. Descriptions of Chinatown's hidden moral and physical dangers—in the form of subterranean opium dens and illegal gambling halls—neatly situated this neighborhood within the territories of "darkness" that encompassed other notorious poor and working-class slums of the Sixth Ward. At the same time, writers suggested that Chinatown's exoticness brought about a clear physical and social separation from its European immigrant neighbors.

Representations of Chinatown were not only marked by a peculiar racial otherness, they were also gendered in that these images projected a rough, working-class male space that included both Chinese and white men. While these men were able to move through the area unhindered, white women could not enter unescorted without fear of grave risk to their person at the hands of Chinatown's predominantly male laborer population. To the general public, female social and religious reformers could neither reform those they targeted nor properly guard against a dangerous Chinatown environment that threatened their own piety and morality. The image of the young missionary in the trunk became a potent reminder of the consequences of such <u>unmonitored racial and gender trespassing</u>.

DECIPHERING THE WOMAN IN THE TRUNK

Elsie Sigel, the young woman found inside Leon Ling's trunk, was hardly a typical New Yorker but instead the granddaughter of a well-known Civil War general in the Union army, Franz Sigel. After the war, Franz Sigel settled in New York City, where he continued to be a prominent public figure in New York social circles. He made an unsuccessful bid as the Republican candidate for secretary of state of New York, but in 1871 he was elected Registrar for New York County. In 1885 President Grover Cleveland appointed Sigel to be the New York City pension agent for the U.S. government, a position he held until 1889.[12] When Franz Sigel died on August 22, 1902, more than 25,000 people gathered to pay their respects at his funeral held at the Melrose Turnverein Hall in the Bronx.[13] In 1907, to honor his memory, the city dedicated a large statue of him in Riverside Park.[14]

The fact that the murder victim was the granddaughter of this illustrious figure, as well as the namesake of his beloved wife, impressed upon the public both the personal and <u>national dimensions</u> of this tragedy. The press further alleged that the victim at a young age had been introduced by her mother to Protestant missionary work among the city's Chinese inhabitants. Mrs. Sigel had taught at the Chinese Sunday school affiliated with St. Andrew's Church on 127th Street and Fifth Avenue for many years.[15] But Elsie's family members including her father, Paul Sigel, disapproved of his wife and daughter's affiliation with the Chinese and urged them to stop their missionary activities. The press frequently played up this angle of the tragedy, emphasizing that despite her family's concerns, <u>Elsie continued to devote herself to the selfless task</u> of *Saintlike* <u>Christianizing and educating the city's heathen Chinese population.</u>[16]

Newspapers claimed that it was during the course of their missionary activities that mother and daughter had met Leon Ling four years earlier, when he had operated a Chinese restaurant on Amsterdam Avenue near 191st Street. At that time, the Sigels resided at 188th Street, within the restaurant's vicinity. Mrs. Sigel, as part of her missionary work, occasionally called upon Chinese working in the laundries and restaurants of her neighborhood to encourage them to attend church services or Sunday school classes.[17] The visits, it was reported, were reciprocated.

According to press interviews with the Sigels' former neighbors, Chinese and Japanese men frequently visited the Sigel family at their home. The *New York Herald* reported that some neighbors even went so far as to claim that "Chinese and Japanese boarders were accommodated at the residence. It was stated further that on frequent occasions girls in that neighborhood were seen in company with young men of those nationalities."[18] Neighbors frowned upon the Sigels' relationships with these men and found their visits to be scandalous. In an interview with the *New York Tribune*, Elsie Sigel's cousin and confidante Mabel Sigel, attempted to defend her aunt's actions and explained that Chinese men often visited her aunt at their home with requests for assistance. She, however, firmly denied that they were allowed to stay as houseguests.[19]

By several newspaper accounts, Leon Ling was one of these regular visitors on familiar terms with the Sigel family. He was said to accompany both mother and daughter to church services and invited to call on them at their home.[20] As the murder investigation progressed, the press reported that the relationship between Leon Ling and Elsie Sigel went beyond cordial. Aside from visiting the Sigel home, he also took mother and daughter on trips to Chinatown that included on at least one occasion a visit to the infamous Chinese Theatre on Doyer Street.[21] The theater had become well known throughout the city as a site of occasional shootings between rival Chinese fraternal organizations known popularly as "tongs." The association of Leon Ling and the Sigels with one of Chinatown's more notorious sites impressed upon readers the physical and moral dangers posed by his relationship with them.

The police's discovery of a packet of thirty-five "love letters" written by Elsie Sigel to Leon Ling proved to the police and reporters that the two were engaged in a serious love affair.[22] Clearly, they had overstepped the line separating student and teacher, but this transgression was of lesser concern than her crossing of racial, gender, and class boundaries. First, she undermined racial borders by treating Leon Ling as though he were a "white man," as one reporter claimed, meaning that she saw him as a social equal. Second, she expressed the types of sentiments and endearments reserved for properly engaged or married women. By doing so she acted not as one possessing the feminine virtue ascribed to unmarried, respectable middle-class women of her station and calling, but behaved in the brash manner of urban working-class women who were targeted by that period's social reformers. In other words, Sigel acted less like a missionary/reformer than one who needed to be reformed herself.

The newspapers' attention to the illicit romantic relationship between Sigel and Leon Ling further fueled public speculation on the activities of Chinese missions and their suitability for young, white middle-class women. Following the murder numerous editorials on this question flooded newspapers across the country, openly challenging female missionaries' and their institutions' legitimacy as a force for urban moral and social reform. The deviousness of the Chinese men posing as converts to meet young white women, for these writers, was matched by the sentimentality and naïveté of the white female missionaries. Not surprisingly many of the city's writers and cartoonists portrayed Chinese men as hypersexualized creatures posing legitimate threats to white female missionaries, when they discussed Chinese male participation in the city's Protestant missions. While some writers acknowledged that not all Chinese students were insincere or lascivious, most remained convinced that the risk of tragedy was too great to allow white women to continue teaching Chinese men.

The debate over the effectiveness of Christian missionary activities among the Chinese was not brought on by this murder. Discussions over whether or not Chinese could be Christianized had been present since the establishment of American Protestant missions in China in the early nineteenth century, and it continued in this country as part of the larger Chinese exclusion debate throughout the latter half of the nineteenth and early twentieth centuries. The devastating accusation that these missions were in actuality a vehicle for miscegenation, however, demanded the regulation of the mission on gendered and spatial terms. Employing turn-of-the-century notions of femininity that saw women as overly sentimental and lacking in calm, rational thinking, these critics argued that the only way for further disasters to be averted was to bar middle-class white women from this work and only hire men to teach the Chinese. In the aftermath of the murder, white female missionaries' responses to these attacks on their moral authority vividly revealed the clash over how to define proper gender roles and maintain racial borders in the American Protestant missionary movement.

As the police and reporters moved quickly to reconstruct Elsie Sigel's movements prior to her disappearance, they made even more troubling discoveries about her past associations with Chinese men. According to several friends, Sigel had also been seen in the company of Chu Gain, the Chinese manager of the Port Arthur Restaurant at 9 Mott Street, a favorite restaurant among white middle-class sightseers visiting Chinatown. The police lost no time bringing Chu Gain into custody, and during intense examination by the police he admitted having "known Miss Sigel intimately."[23] The police immediately arrested Chu Gain and held him for further questioning. While searching his living quarters above the Port Arthur, police found a similar collection of letters written by Elsie Sigel to him.

From the press's accounts, under questioning Chu Gain told police that Leon Ling had verbally threatened him a few months earlier because he was jealous of Chu Gain's growing friendship with Sigel. A few weeks prior to the discovery of Elsie Sigel's body, Chu Gain received an anonymous letter warning him to desist in his attentions toward her. Chu Gain did not at first report the incident, but suspected the sender to be Leon Ling. With this information in hand, the police quickly concluded that Leon Ling murdered Sigel out of jealousy.[24] While the discovery that Sigel was on intimate terms with two Chinese men provided the police with a motive and prime suspect for murder, it was nonetheless a troubling conclusion because it greatly challenged the image of the virtuous girl missionary as put forth in newspaper accounts. It was indeed difficult for the victim's friends and family as well as the press to explain how it was possible for a supposedly unworldly and pious nineteen-year-old to behave in such an openly coquettish manner.

The press attempted to track Sigel's movements to Leon Ling's room to reveal the truth about her moral character. According to the *New York Times*, Captain Carey put forth the theory that she may have met him in her neighborhood that Wednesday morning and "he induced her to go to his oriental den on Eighth Avenue." Carey also alleged that Leon Ling often visited Sigel when her father was away; "he would wait for her at the Subway entrance at 181st street and St. Nicholas Avenue and they would go downtown together."[25] The captain was not alone in believing that Leon Ling tricked Sigel into going to his room. Indeed, family members and friends firmly believed that she had not visited his room before that fateful day. Yet, the description of the deceased purposefully deceiving her disapproving father in order to visit Leon Ling continued to call into question her virtue and moral character.

The press's discussion of the relationship between Sigel and the two Chinese men forced into the open the larger topic of interracial marriage and sexual relations between Chinese and whites in New York City. The press provided sketches of several Chinese-white couples questioned by the police as potential witnesses. The presence of interracial couples is not surprising given that New York City did not have anti-miscegenation laws. Unlike many states on the West Coast and in the South, the New York state legislature never succeeded in passing similar anti-miscegenation laws. Nor was interracial marriage a taboo subject for nineteenth-century New Yorkers, as newspaper and journal articles depicting Chinatown life frequently included discussions on Chinese-white intermarriage or sexual relations. With few exceptions, these articles construed these relationships as symptomatic of larger urban social problems that plagued a city undergoing rapid industrialization and unprecedented labor immigration: poverty, intemperance, opium addiction, and white slavery. By correlation, those white women who chose to marry Chinese men were described as poor immigrant or working-class women whose economic deprivation led them to engage in socially deviant behavior that threatened the urban moral order.

These narratives of interracial sexual liaisons circulating in popular culture worked to construct categories of sexual and moral deviance and helped in the absence of anti-miscegenation laws to support other institutional forms of policing these relationships. The *New York Times* reported that Captain Galvin of the Elizabeth Street station in the Chinatown area used the Sigel murder to justify and garner further support for "his crusade against the white women in Chinatown" that he had begun in May of that year.[26] In early July Captain Galvin boasted to the press that within two months he had forced as many as two hundred white women to vacate Chinatown with the result that only six remained; these women were allowed to stay only because they possessed marriage licenses.[27] Such measures restricted the social and physical mobility of white teenage girls, women, and Chinese men and reinscribed social and spatial borders in areas of the city where these groups overlapped.

Sigel by contrast did not fit the press's stereotypical portrait of the poor, European immigrant woman married to or cohabitating with a Chinese man. The usual reasons given for these relationships—drug addiction, economic necessity, white slavery, etc.—did not hold in this case. The public's vigorous response to the murder illustrates their uneasiness with the idea that a respectable white woman belonging to a family with sound economic means could be attracted to a Chinese man. A closer look at Sigel's relationships with Leon Ling and Chu Gain illuminates the experiences of interracial couples in Chinatown. Until recently, historians writing on late nineteenth and early-twentieth-century urban Chinese American communities in the United States have not studied fully the subject of interracial marriages, sexual relations, and family life.[28] Historians frequently point to the effects of exclusionary immigration laws beginning with the 1875 Page Law and the 1882 Chinese Exclusion Act in creating heavily skewed Chinese male-to-female ratios in this country.[29] As a result, we have come to see nineteenth- and early-twentieth-century urban communities as comprising mainly single Chinese male laborers living in transnational households apart from their wives and families who remained in China.[30] The few Chinese women in these communities are identified mostly as either prostitutes and servants or members of established merchant families.[31] Based on a conceptualization of Chinatowns as insular "bachelor societies," these studies present a historical narrative that implies ethnic and racial homogeneity and solidarity as the basis of community life, erasing those members of the Chinatown community who were neither of Chinese descent nor of mixed parentage.[32] But a reexamination of the history of interracial couples and families through other archival sources—such as *sources* [handwritten annotation]

federal census schedules, court records, and immigration files—suggest the importance of such relationships for Chinese living in Northeast cities such as New York. Such an inquiry will also help to explain the context in which Sigel established her relationships with Leon Ling and Chu Gain.

Tracking the Elusive Leon Ling

The disappearance of the two major suspects—Leon Ling and his friend and neighbor Chong Sing—prior to the discovery of Elsie Sigel's body, led to the mobilization of a massive manhunt spearheaded by the New York Police Department (NYPD) and assisted by police and civilians in major cities across the country and throughout the world. From major metropolitan newspapers, such as the *Boston Globe* and the *San Francisco Examiner* to small town publications such as the *Binghamton Press and Leader*, stories concerning the Sigel murder case could be readily found.[33] Many of the nation's major newspapers carried the NYPD's official descriptions and photographs of the two suspects, allowing readers to assist in their identification and capture. The day following the discovery of Sigel's body, New York City newspapers reprinted the wanted circular issued by Police Commissioner Theodore Bingham to police departments in major metropolitan areas across the United States. This description of Leon Ling—emphasizing his good looks and "Americanized" dress and manners—formed the general public's perception of the prime suspect. Leon Ling, also known as William L. Leon, was unlike the typical "Chinaman" with queue and traditional Chinese dress as popularly depicted in this period's press. His flashy clothes and jewelry, facility with the English language, and ease in moving in and out of Chinatown, made him appear to fit more accurately other familiar urban social types, such as the "dandy" or the "sport."[34] Further examination of the press's discussion of Ling and his character reveals not so much a fear that Chinese immigrants could not assimilate into American urban life, but that Chinese men like Leon Ling appeared to be succeeding all too well.

The heightened visibility of Leon Ling profoundly impacted the lives of other Chinese men also perceived by the larger public as "Americanized." This included community leaders such as merchants, interpreters, and ministers, as well as university students and diplomats. Because these men spoke English fluently and familiarized themselves with American cultural and legal practices, they often felt secure in their interactions with white Americans and played important intermediary roles between Chinese residents and white American social and legal institutions. The tremendous amount of negative publicity generated around the "Americanized" Chinese ultimately placed these men under intense public scrutiny, making them vulnerable to attacks and harassment by police and civilians alike.

The national and international manhunt for the prime suspect and the widespread publicity generated by the press combined to draw police and ordinary citizens throughout the country into the search for Leon Ling. Within a few days of the discovery of Elsie Sigel's body, reports of policemen and ordinary citizens claiming to have captured the fugitive flooded NYPD headquarters. These arrests included Chinese men from many different parts of the country, such as Tien Bow Leo, a student, taken into custody in Middletown, New York; Jun Ling, a Chinese laundryman, picked up while riding a street car in New Jersey; and many others. Several Japanese men were also falsely arrested, including Marshal Kobayashi, a lecturer residing in the Bronx. In Morristown, New Jersey, a Japanese butler for an American family was also mistakenly arrested when police thought he resembled the missing neighbor, Chong Sing.[35] In most cases, the men were arrested after ordinary citizens matched them to the published descriptions and photographs of the missing suspects. In addition to these arrests, numerous private citizens claimed to have seen or interacted with the murder suspects. The nationwide media coverage of the murder ensured that the residents of major cities and small towns alike could participate in this national and international manhunt. As a result, the daily lives of Chinese and non-Chinese throughout the nation became enmeshed in the national drama created by the Sigel murder investigation and newspaper coverage.

In any U.S. city with a noticeable Chinese population, the murder's impact was deeply felt by its Chinese residents as well as white women of all socioeconomic classes who came into regular contact with these men. Throughout the country, Americans responded to the Sigel murder by investigating and monitoring in their hometowns the same spaces chiefly identified as occupied by Chinese workers—homes, Protestant missions, "chop suey" restaurants, and hand laundries—that New York police, reporters, and social reformers were targeting. As with New York, the residents in these areas grew alarmed by the permeability of supposedly established boundaries separating Chinese men from the general population.

The *Chicago Daily Tribune* ran its story on the murder on the front page, prompting an investigation into the Chinese missionary activities within its own city. Reporters interviewed several of Chicago's Chinese missionaries to reassure readers that their city's missions differed from their New York City counterparts.[36] Another article that appeared one week into the murder investigation reaffirmed these claims: "In

Chicago, at least, the folly of allowing young and inexperienced women to attempt conversions among Chinese men is committed rarely if at all. The feminine influence is strong, to be sure, but, as it has been expressed, these women workers have 'sanity, good taste, and understanding.'"[37] Such assurances, however, did not prevent the closing of a Chinese Sunday school run by Dr. Minerva A. Kline in the basement of her 6446 Drexel Avenue building in the Woodlawn neighborhood of Chicago. Evidently, Dr. Kline's neighbor, Timothy Barett of 6447 Drexel Avenue, took advantage of the Sigel murder to rally his neighbors and Chicago's police and public officials to shut down the school. On June 27 a building inspector called in by the police examined the doors of the school and found them to swing inward instead of outward, a violation of the city's building codes. Half an hour later policeman John Kane of the Woodlawn station entered the school and demanded that the school be closed immediately.[38]

In Pittsburgh, police made a series of arrests as part of Police Superintendent McQuaide's crusade to close down the city's two Chinese Sunday schools. On July 3 the police arrested Sarah Crew, a seventeen-year-old Sunday school teacher, and Yee Fulk, one of her students, at the latter's business establishment, a Chinese restaurant. The two police officers believed the place to be a "Chinese resort" that was a "restaurant and gambling den" and forced their way into the back to arrest the two. Crew vehemently protested her arrest stating that she had done nothing wrong. She claimed to have gone to the restaurant to thank Yee Fulk for a fan that he had given her as a gift.[39] Despite Sarah Crew's complaints and her wealthy and respected businessman father, the two were held overnight without bail and McQuaide planned to have her "lined up in the morning with the usual grist of Saturday-night drunks."[40]

In a public statement to the press McQuaide defended his actions as warranted because of what he believed to have been inappropriate, if not dangerous, behavior on Crew's part. Not everyone agreed with McQuaide's fears that Chinese missions posed a moral threat, and his initial efforts to dissuade white middle-class families from allowing their daughters to work in Pittsburgh's Chinese missions met with many rebuffs. In response McQuaide announced his draconian plans of surveillance and arrest "to stop the evil" by "shadowing" every young female Sunday school teacher in the city. If a teacher was caught visiting a "Chinese dive" he planned to raid the place and put the teacher and Chinese under arrest. "It doesn't make any difference to me whether their parents plead and protest, these girls will be treated as common criminals, until they learn that I mean to protect the womanhood of Pittsburgh against the inroads of the 'yellow peril' in its vilest form."[41] By treating their socializing with Chinese men as a criminal act, McQuaide categorized these women as potential sexual and social deviants similar to prostitutes or promiscuous working-class girls. It is not hard to understand why the teachers' parents disliked the superintendent's tactics and viewed their daughters as the innocent victims of brutish police harassment. Nonetheless, fearing further trouble from the police, Rev. Dr. Warren G. Partridge, a pastor of a church with a Chinese Sunday school, issued the order that women would no longer be allowed to teach Chinese students.

Chinese Americans quickly mounted numerous protests against the ongoing harassment resulting from the increased police and press presence in their communities across the United States. By looking beyond mainstream newspaper coverage and delving into archival sources that give voice to different segments of the diverse Chinese immigrant community, a range of personal and collective protests can be found. A study of the Chinese Legation's correspondences regarding the case, along with accounts published in Chinese-language newspapers such as the San Francisco-based *Chung Sai Yat Pao* also known as the *Chinese Daily Paper*, for example, reveals the various strategies employed by Chinese Americans. In spite of their political disempowerment as aliens ineligible for citizenship, Chinatown merchants and laborers consistently voiced their demand to safeguard their persons, communities, livelihoods, and public image at various levels of the U.S. and Chinese governments. Their vigorous and sustained responses reveal the extent to which Chinese Americans expected certain protections and rights regardless of their lack of legal recognition as U.S. citizens.

Despite the months of unrelenting local and national publicity surrounding the murder investigation, public memory of these events has not survived into the present. A proper understanding of Chinese immigrants' attempts to strive for physical and social mobility in turn-of-the-century New York has been replaced by the more popular view of Chinese American working-class urban neighborhoods as "Chinatowns" with fixed ethnic and racial borders predicated on residents' desires to maintain ethnic solidarity and homogeneity. Seldom do today's writers make the effort to examine the spatial boundaries of America's Chinatowns and understand their creation as shaped by historically situated social, cultural, and economic processes of segregation connected to the broader history of Chinese exclusion.

By bringing our attention back to this forgotten episode, we have a rare opportunity to witness how the contemporaries of Elsie Sigel and Leon Ling struggled to make sense of the shocking murder and the place of Chinese immigrants in New York City and the nation at large. Indeed, for most New Yorkers, the real mystery lay in the cross-racial movements and relations that, to their surprise and horror, had occurred unnoticed in their city. Through their responses we see and hear attempts to restore urban moral and spatial order by investigating and remapping the proper social and physical spaces and boundaries for both the city's Chinese and white, and male and female, populations. Their motives and actions allow us to understand the historical making of New York City's Chinatown as a recognizably racialized and gendered territory at the turn-of-the-century.

Revisiting the Elsie Sigel murder reveals more than just how Chinese Americans struggled to build and sustain livelihoods, families, and communities during the Chinese exclusion era. Their daily routines also brought them into contact with immigrant and native-born, working-class and middle-class, white women who were similarly exploring their own potential for social and physical mobility in a city readily differentiated by race, class, and gender. In an industrialized city that promised women increased opportunities for work and commercial leisure, these groups met one another and explored the limits and possibilities for their social interaction. Poised at the dawn of the twentieth century, New Yorkers worked to redefine themselves and their city according to new visions of modernity. Yet, as they experimented with new forms of social and cultural interactions, they also scrutinized and regulated those encounters that allowed the crossing of racial and class boundaries, and ultimately established new social and spatial borders among its diverse populations to contain those forms of mobility that threatened to disrupt the urban moral order. The grisly details of the Sigel homicide, replete with titillating rumors of interracial sex and exhaustive accounts of the dramatic manhunt for the missing Chinese male fugitives, provide a wealth of material for understanding this process of urban cultural, social, and spatial transformation. To begin this historical inquiry we must return to the moment when New Yorkers encountered the unsettling discovery of a murdered Sigel locked inside a "Chinaman's" trunk, sparking what would become known as the "Chinatown Trunk Mystery."

Goals:
- to examine the social role of Chinese in NYC, ditching chinatown stereotypes
- discuss how urbanization + industry changed urban living for women
- how social + spatial spheres are shaped by an event that speaks to race, class, gender.

"Terra Incognita": Mapping Chinatown's Racial and Gender Boundaries in Lower Manhattan

DESPITE THE FACT that the victim and chief suspects neither lived nor worked in Chinatown and that the murder itself did not occur in Chinatown, the press and police nonetheless connected the murder to this part of the city. Newspapers such as the *New York Evening Journal* referred to the murder as a "Chinatown mystery."[1] Before long, the murder became identified as the "Chinatown trunk mystery," which also became the title of a 1910 play about the murder.[2] The public quickly concluded that the case was another example of Chinatown vice and immorality. The association of Chinatown with the Sigel murder was hardly an accident; it was, instead, clearly shaped by prevalent middle-class concerns over the seemingly unfixed place of women and Chinese immigrants in a rapidly changing commercial and industrial metropolis that rendered geographical borders and spaces less intelligible. To New Yorkers, Elsie Sigel's death resulted from the increasingly unencumbered mobility of white middle-class women throughout a city that included working-class immigrant neighborhoods such as Chinatown. The linking of the murder to this part of Manhattan worked to contain discursively and physically the movements of these groups by creating and reaffirming the gendered borders of racialized territories such as Chinatown.

Journalists urged New Yorkers to take closer looks at their Chinese neighbors and their community in lower Manhattan's Sixth Ward. Echoing earlier descriptions of Chinatown as "terra incognita," they suggested that the general public's failure to comprehend fully the distinct social, cultural, and political institutions of the Chinese in their city contributed to the death of Elsie Sigel.[3] The editor of the *Cosmopolitan*, in his preface to a lengthy article on the Chinatown neighborhood published two months after the murder, alerted readers to the dangers of Chinatown and its Chinese residents. "It is a shock to the law-abiding people of this country to learn that in nearly all our great cities there are settlements of Orientals who are with us but not of us, who administer their own affairs according to their own conception of what is right and wrong, who never subscribe to or heed either our laws or our customs, and even arrogate to themselves the power of life and death over the people in the community.[4] The editor's claim of a shadowy Chinatown, and the ensuing article by police reporter Charles Somerville, promoted the idea that the Chinese and their communities would always remain foreign. Acknowledging the different European groups that had immigrated to the United States, Somerville concluded that for the last century America had been "a mighty crucible in the welding of a new people" but impressed upon his readers that the Chinese, unlike other immigrant groups, simply did not mix.[5]

In the same month *Munsey's Magazine* published an article, written by journalist William Brown Meloney, emphasizing Chinatown's inscrutable terrain and mystical allure as grave threats to white womanhood. Describing his nocturnal adventures in Chinatown with a slumming party and its police escorts from the nearby Elizabeth Street station, he aimed to offer "a glimpse into the sordid underworld of the Mott Street quarter, where Elsie Sigel formed her fatal associations" to explain why so many young white women were attracted to Chinatown.[6]

Employing the popular narrative convention of rural innocence corrupted by urban vice, Meloney wrote that during the course of the evening "two young women—fresh-faced country lasses"—came perilously close to being ensnared in Chinatown's web.[7] During their visit to an opium den, he believed that the ambient smoke worked its way into the women, lowering their guard and affecting their behavior even after they had left the room: "They talk loudly; they laugh without occasion. Most of them fail to pull in their skirts now as the Chinese go jostling by them on the narrow sidewalk."[8] The party then headed past a shop window displaying lingerie for sale, and the two women tried to bargain with the Chinese storekeeper. Slipping into pidgin English, asking "how muchee," they haggled with the Chinese storekeeper and pointed "unashamed at an article of feminine finery." Though the women eventually left the store without purchasing the garment, the exchange deeply disturbed Meloney and Captain Michael Galvin, their police escort.

Captain Galvin noted that the exchange they had witnessed could very well become the beginning of the women's descent into immorality. "'That's the way and that's the kind,' says Galvin, looking after the girls. 'There is always a to-morrow for one or two of every slumming party, who have not seen enough the night before. Did you catch the pidgin English? I'll bet those girls were never in a Chinatown in all their lives before to-night!'"[9] The ease with which these women could slip into this racialized speech demonstrated the potential for racial and cultural contamination Chinatown posed to unsuspecting white female visitors. Galvin then instructed one of his plainclothes detectives to look out for the two women and keep them out of the neighborhood in case they returned to Chinatown the next evening.

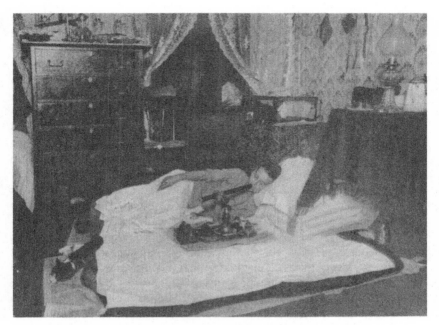

Figure 1.1. A Chinese man's white wife trapped in Chinatown, as described in William Brown Meloney's article on Chinatown shortly following the Elsie Sigel murder. The original caption read: "A room on the second floor of a tenement-house on Pell Street—'a coop with a wire-meshed window'—in which Lulu Shu, one of the white wives of Chinatown, has lived for eighteen years." *Source*: William Brown Meloney, "Slumming in New York's Chinatown," *Munsey's Magazine* 41 (September 1909): 825. Courtesy of Yale University Library.

Having taken leave of the slumming party, Meloney then headed off under the escort of various plainclothes detectives from the Elizabeth Street station to visit several white women married to Chinese men to provide readers with a more intimate exploration into what attracted these women to this neighborhood. In recounting this part of the trip, Meloney devoted considerable attention to his encounter with a young woman named "Elsie," who had married Chu Wing, a prosperous Chinese laundry owner, in St. Louis seven years earlier. The coincidence of her name and Meloney's emphasis on her education and respectable middle-class family origins made her appear to resemble Elsie Sigel.

At first Meloney described this Elsie as appearing to be content with her current life, but later revealed that she actually felt desperately trapped in Chinatown. In a sense she fared only slightly better than Elsie Sigel, whose racial trespassing had led to her entombment in Leon Ling's trunk. "No chains, no barred doors hold us here! But there is a wall! You cannot see it; you cannot even imagine it; but it is there! I can see it! I have dashed myself against it and been hurled back!" Elsie continued by adding that she only knew of "but one white woman to get over that wall and back to our own kind," and that was only through the help of a newspaper man who had come across her while working on a story.[10] The man worked incessantly to persuade her to leave with him so that she could "see real rainbows and green trees and grass" outside of the fake ones she experienced while in "poppyland." She eventually left Chinatown and took up typing and stenography and worked in the same newspaper office as her rescuer. Only through the intervention of a white male hero, such as this journalist, could women such as Elsie hope to escape the trap posed by Chinatown and pass through those invisible "walls" to regain respectability by becoming part of their "own kind" again. Yet, the woman in Elsie's story did not experience the "happy ending" expected of working-class heroines. She never married, suggesting that a complete social redemption was impossible even though she had left Chinatown. By recounting the stories of Elsie and this unnamed woman, Meloney provided a cautionary tale of the hidden dangers of Chinatown to his white middle-class female audience: women who dared to engage in such sexual and racial transgressions would either become trapped or remain permanently tainted by their association.

The Making of the Chinatown Space

Chinatown's rise as a site of cultural interest for middle-class New Yorkers occurred as the city experienced the rapid urbanization and expansion that brought an end to the walking city and saw the rise of new class-stratified residential, financial, and manufacturing districts. This period of growing urbanization in America instilled new fears of social fragmentation resulting from industrialization and deepening class divisions. The growing waves of new emigrants from southern and eastern Europe, along with smaller numbers of workers from Asia and the Middle East, also brought increased cultural and religious diversity that challenged the moral authority of the city's Protestant religious institutions.[11] In response to these perceived problems, middle-class social reformers in the late nineteenth and early-twentieth-century Progressive era sought to cure the ills of the city by focusing on what they identified as sources of social decay and moral corruption. Places like Chinatown, thought to be an enclave of vice and a danger to white womanhood, could not be ignored and social reformers sought not only to reinforce social and geographical boundaries to contain these threats but also undertook campaigns to "cleanse" Chinatown through the organizing of religious missions and anti-vice crusades.

Turn-of-the-century New York City writers, in turn, attempted to impose social and moral order onto the newly emerging modern cityscape by investigating and depicting life in different parts of the city. The writings of journalists like Meloney and Somerville helped to map out new class and gender boundaries on the city's shifting residential and commercial geographies. As these popular narratives on Chinatown make clear, the policing of these borders was not so easily accomplished, and residents, including the city's Chinese male and white female populations, continued to transgress them with alarming frequency.

The publication of tourist guidebooks, for example, enabled visitors to move through city neighborhoods that were once considered foreign and inscrutable because of the rapid settlement of new immigrants. The guidebook similarly worked to demarcate neighborhoods and bring order to the increasingly chaotic and spatially fragmented city. By cataloguing, naming, and describing these locales, such books rendered each neighborhood's hidden dangers visible, allowing nonresidents to traverse the terrain unharmed. The following description of New York City's Chinatown, listed under "Chinese" in the 1879 edition of *Appleton's Dictionary of New York and Vicinity*, depicted the neighborhood in a manner that exemplifies the usual entries found in most New York City guidebooks of this period:

> New York has now quite a large Chinese population, which is mainly engaged in the laundry business. The laundries are scattered all over the city, but the Chinese quarter—in so far as it can be said that there is one—is in the neighborhood of the Five Points, especially in Mott st. [sic]. It is there that the Chinaman may be found disporting himself in ill-smelling, squalid apartments, smoking his favorite opium pipe—to the sale of which several shops are devoted—or gambling at his peculiar game of cards. The best day to see him here "at home" is Sunday, when the laundries are closed, and John takes things easy after the manner of his "Melican" customer. There is a Joss house one corner and then to gamble in another. A Christian mission occupies a building near it, where the first step in the work of proselytism is to teach the English language.[12]

This description, one of the first to appear among the city's many guidebooks, helped to locate the neighborhood and render visible its main physical features that made it distinct from the rest of lower Manhattan: Joss house, gambling den, opium joint, etc. Such descriptions not only worked to guide readers to identify the physical markers that would indicate their arrival into the neighborhood but also warned of the potential moral and bodily risks involved.

The mention of Five Points by *Appleton's Dictionary* also clearly linked Chinatown to lower Manhattan's working-class neighborhoods, further evoking images of urban poverty, disease, and immorality. Since the late 1820s the clearance of the Five Points slum area was debated by city officials, land developers, and city proprietors.[13] The infamous cholera epidemic of 1849 was popularly rumored to have originated in this area;[14] Charles Dickens's descriptions of the wretched living conditions of the inhabitants of the Five Points neighborhood in his *American Notes* augmented the area's notoriety in national and international circles.[15] During the mid-nineteenth century, buildings such as the "Old Brewery" located on Park Street near Worth, was rumored to have been the most densely populated building with as many as 1,200 inhabitants at one time, and became a frequently cited example of urban poor overcrowding.[16]

The Sixth Ward, which housed the Five Points area, was equally infamous in the minds of New Yorkers as the "bloody sixth," so described because of the history of reputed violence there between rival working-class gangs. Since the 1820s, gangs with colorful names such as the Forty Thieves, Chichesters, the Roach Guards, the Plug Uglies, the Shirt Tails, and many others fought each other for neighborhood dominance.[17] Aside from the problems of overcrowding and gang violence, social reformers in the Sixth Ward also lamented the profusion of grog shops visited by the destitute in the area. The November 1871 issue of the *Five Points Monthly Record*, the official organ of the Five Points House of Industry established by Rev. Lewis M. Pease in 1851 to administer to the needs of the neighborhood poor, claimed that on one 25 × 100 ft. lot "shanties" sheltered 286 people and "that the inhabitants may not lack for poison, there are 270 rumholes to supply it, and some of them of the most wretched character."[18]

In contrast to the apparent social and economic stagnation of the Sixth Ward, the city in the mid-nineteenth century was rapidly transforming from a mercantile port city to a major industrial, financial, and retail center. In the 1860s Manhattan above Twenty-third Street was still undeveloped, but a fashionable residential district began to develop above Fourteenth Street, marking the first distinctly middle- to upper-class residential district in the city's history. The area south of Fourteenth Street remained the commercial, financial, and retail center of the city. Residents in this area were mostly limited to the immigrant and working poor who could only afford to reside in this area's densely packed tenement-style buildings.[19] Even with the rise of public transportation, poor and working-class immigrants tended to reside on the periphery of the downtown central business district where the majority of employers of unskilled to low-skilled laborers were located. Long

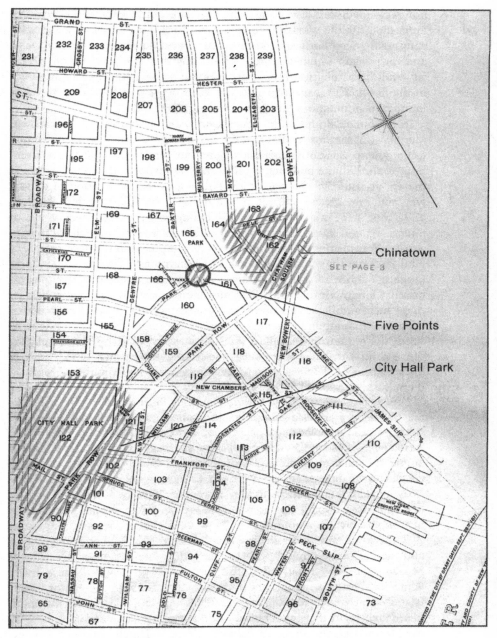

Map 1.1. Chinatown and Five Points area in the Sixth Ward of lower Manhattan.
Source: Board of Taxes and Assessments, *The Land Map of City of New York*, January 1,
1892, Section 1, Blocks 57-239. Courtesy of Map Collection, Yale University Library.

hours coupled with low wages usually made costly, extended commutes unfeasible for the working poor.[20] New York City's distinct geography comprising neighborhoods more readily based on shared ethnicity, class, and race began to emerge after 1875.[21] By the 1880s, economic necessity and discrimination forced the Chinese to establish their community in the Sixth Ward, an area that had been populated by the poorer and immigrant populations since the antebellum period.

In the financial and retail districts immediately outside of Chinatown, the physical features of the modern city could be seen. The first elevated train system was completed and opened for service in 1878.[22] Construction of the Tribune building at the corner of Spruce and Nassau streets in the 1870s, and the Western Union building at the intersection of Broadway and Dey streets, spurred on the trend of vertical growth.[23] Between 1892 and 1897 the number of tall buildings rose from twenty-five to ninety-six, and most of these newer buildings reached a height of twenty stories. Fourteen of these buildings were completed in the area near City Hall Park within walking distance to Chinatown.[24] The seemingly "premodern" allure of the four-, five-, and six-story tenements that comprised Chinatown on Mott, Pell, and Doyers streets was heightened by these surrounding scenes of vertical construction and rapid commercial growth. Contemporary writers in describing Chinatown further emphasized this modern/pre-modern division in their work by further eliding the exotic with the pre-modern, describing Chinatown as a "strange little section of Pekin that is to be found within five minutes' walk of New York's City Hall."[25]

Nineteenth-century New Yorkers had long been familiar with the commercial display and consumption of Asian commodities and peoples—silks, porcelains, spices, teas, acrobats, and cultural oddities. The motley assortment of living Chinese on display in antebellum New York, for example, included the famous "Siamese twins" Chang and Eng, as well as lesser-known figures. In the 1830s, a Chinese woman known as Afong Moy appeared as a parlor display in various New York theaters, attracting audiences hoping to catch a glimpse of the grotesque spectacle of her impossibly tiny, bound feet. New York's most famous impresario, P. T. Barnum, also offered his own "Chinese lady," Miss Pwan-Yekoo, and her "Chinese family" in a similar parlor-like setting at his Chinese Museum at 539 Broadway.[26] By the turn-of-the-century, these living Chinese tableaus were enacted on a grander scale with the rise of Coney Island's amusement parks. Visitors to the Luna amusement park, for example, delighted in their experience of recreated exotic attractions from all over the world, including an Eskimo village, a Dutch windmill, Chinese theater, Japanese garden, and a reproduction of the Durbar of Delhi.[27] But a visit to the Chinatown district, an actual neighborhood in lower

Manhattan rather than these commercially staged recreations, promised a more intimate and "authentic" experience.

Increasingly, white male journalists like Hutchins Hapgood longed to escape the artifice of the rapidly developing modern city by purposely venturing into New York's immigrant, working-class neighborhoods. Hapgood described the role of the urban reporter as the "man-about-town" whose work involved searching out the real city hidden beneath the modern façade of rapid development and commercialism.[28] In contrast to the city's bourgeoisie, whom he abhorred, Hapgood described the inhabitants of the rough-and-tumble Lower East Side as "authentic" and a true "aristocratic" class whose life experiences were unmediated. William Norr sought to similarly employ the reporter's keen eye to depict the people he encountered in his *Short Stories of Chinatown: Sketches from Life in the Chinese Colony*. Norr boasted that his journalism background and direct experience made him an expert: "I am probably better qualified to write upon the subject than any other newspaper man, having for years 'hit the pipe' in Chinatown and possessing an intimate acquaintanceship with the Chinese and whites of the colony."[29] Through interactions with the inhabitants on forays into working-class ethnic neighborhoods, these writers attempted to experience the "real" city, proclaiming themselves to be manly, intrepid explorers possessing expert knowledge of these uncharted areas. Their claims of real first-hand experience separated and elevated them from their white middle-class readers or guidebook-dependent sightseers who were only capable of having mediated experiences at best.

Another journalist, Louis J. Beck, wrote a book on New York City's Chinatown in 1898 to help "reach a fair and just conclusion" to the vexing "Chinese question." Beck, however, did not live up to his claim. He not only failed to challenge prevalent cultural and class biases, he also reproduced the same racial and cultural hierarchies present in the works of others writing about Chinese communities in the United States during this period: "That there is the most radical difference between the civilization of the Orient and that of Western nations needs no affirmation. It is manifest at a glance. These people have been born and educated under that form of civilization which has prevailed in the Chinese empire for thousands of years. Our civilization is the outgrowth of a few centuries. Theirs is the most ancient form of any surviving nation on earth; ours the most modern."[30] Here, the binary oppositions of East versus West—as social backwardness against progress—worked to shape the constructions of Chinatown as the cultural other for modern middle-class New Yorkers and other non-Chinese readers.[31] Instrumental in supporting this construction of a pre-modern, non-American neighborhood was Beck's description of Chinatown's historic formation.

Beck attributed the beginning of the Chinatown settlement in New York City to a merchant by the name of Wo Kee, who opened a store on Oliver Street near Cherry. "About it naturally gathered the few Chinese then in the city. The store was moved soon afterwards to Park street, the growing colony following it. Park street gave it shelter but a short time, and then it was moved to 8 Mott street where it still remains, the center, as it was the foundation, of the Chinatown to-day."[32] Like moths drawn instinctively to a flame, the development of Chinatown was described by Beck to be a natural process where Chinese, through an innate clannish sense, gathered and followed their countryman, Wo Kee, to establish an ethnically and racially homogeneous residential and commercial district.

Such a description, however, obscured the earlier settlement of Chinese in the multiethnic port district located in the Fourth Ward. Documented by historian John Kuo Wei Tchen, this port area was "an international district in which cultures from around the world intermixed, forming a hybrid, creolized New York culture."[33] The nature of port districts and the socioeconomic standing and experiences shared by Chinese and Irish immigrants also provided conditions for intermarriage between Chinese men and Irish women. Tchen writes that a number of Chinese began to establish homes and businesses in the Sixth Ward during the third quarter of the nineteenth century: "This ward went from having no Chinese in 1850 to listing 38 adult residents in 1870 and well over 100 in 1880."[34] An increase in occupational diversity also occurred along with the population increase, and by 1880 Chinese worked in a variety of occupations: cigar makers, stewards, sailors, cooks, laundry workers, grocers, storekeepers, clerks, bookkeepers, merchants, peddlers, candy makers, and boarding house operators. Tchen also found a doctor, barber, interpreter, and opium dealer residing in the ward.

Contrary to Beck's assertion, well before Wo Kee established his Mott Street store, Chinese had begun to move away from the seaport district and into that neighborhood. For Chinese merchants, whose business and social institutions formed the core of Chinatown, settlement in the Sixth Ward also made sense because their import/export businesses required them to remain in close proximity to the waterfront and central business district of downtown Manhattan. By the 1870s the rise of Irish ethnic-based politics in the city, coupled with Irish immigrants' push to be included in Anglo-Saxon racial discourse and accepted as "white," led to the drawing of racial boundaries in the multiethnic port community; a culturally and racially mixed neighborhood would no longer be tolerated.[35] The opening of Wo Kee's store coincided with the decline of this multiethnic port community as well as with the increase in the Chinese population following the completion of the transcontinental railroad in 1869, the rise of anti-Chinese hostility in the western states, and the importation of Chinese laborers to the East Coast.[36] Concurrently a fast-growing manufacturing sector, spurred on by the expansion of markets in the American West, led to further development of industrial loft and warehouse spaces throughout lower Manhattan.[37] Manufacturers' needs for cheap factory and warehouse spaces gave many Chinese little choice but to settle in the Sixth Ward.

In 1875 the state Census Bureau registered 157 Chinese in the city and by 1880 the federal census showed more than a three-fold increase to 587. Although the Sixth Ward clearly had the highest concentration of Chinese residents at 117, nearly double the next highest number of 62 in the Tenth and Nineteenth Wards, the majority of the Chinese population remained scattered throughout the city.[38] Aside from having the largest concentration of Chinese in the city, Chinatown also contained major Chinese American social, cultural, and political institutions such as the Chinese Consolidated Benevolent Association at 6 Mott Street and the Chinese Theatre at 5–7 Doyers Street. But this visible concentration of Chinese residents and ethnic institutions comprised only one of the recognizable markers of Chinatown's foreignness identified by writers and journalists.

Containing the Opium Contagion

Aside from cataloguing visual signs of Chinese occupation of the neighborhood, writers such as Louis Beck also took care to enumerate distinctive smells emanating from the quarter. In describing these odors, Beck quoted an assertion made by Reverend Otis Gibson, a well-known American missionary who had worked among the Chinese in both China and California, that a particular smell could be attributable to all Chinese settlements:

> The Chinese smell is a mixture and a puzzle; a marvel and a wonder; a mystery and a disgust; but nevertheless a palpable fact. The smell of opium, raw and cooked and in the process of cooking, mixed with the smell of cigars and tobacco leaves, wet and dry, dried fish and vegetables, and a thousand other indescribable ingredients; all these toned to a certain degree of what might be called a shippy smell, produce a sensation upon the olfactory nerves of the average American, which once experienced will never be forgotten.[39]

Odors were not just a cultural curiosity for Beck, but also signaled the spatial boundary of Chinatown from the rest of the city. The particular composition of the odor, based on a mixture of opium and exotic foods, posed a potential social and moral threat to the city's other inhabitants. Within the larger context of social reformers' efforts toward tenement house reform and concern over ventilation in overcrowded ethnic and working-class neighborhoods, concentrated odors smacked of human congestion that bred disease and contagion in the city's slums.[40]

Similar to the constant fears of tuberculosis and cholera outbreaks in working-class neighborhoods, the strong smell of opium smoking, described as emanating from the area's "opium dens," marked Chinatown's boundaries as much as threatened to spill over and contaminate the rest of the city. An 1884 account of the emerging opium problem stated that opium could be "smoked, eaten, drank in various preparations, and even injected into the circulation," but then specifically singled out the smoking of opium in "joints" as the most "debased and wretched practice" of all. Although the article specifically discussed opium smoking as a problem predominantly among the city's Chinese population, it also suggested that the practice posed a threat to whites because the presence of opium dens within the city "stimulated the curiosity of that large class of people who are ever on the lookout for a new sensation."[41] In particular the author worried that "the lower order of theatrical people, variety actors, dancers, and many of the demi-monde," who nightly entered the neighborhood in search of cheap amusements and thrills, would too easily succumb to opium's allure. While making clear that Chinese immigrants first brought opium to the city, the author nonetheless rejected popular rumors of "Chinamen dragging young girls into their dens and stupefying them with the drug," as depicted in an 1883 *Frank Leslie's Illustrated Newspaper* drawing purporting to show "how the opium habit is developed."[42] Although opium, rather than the Chinese residents, posed the real moral threat, the association of Chinese immigrants with opium smoking ultimately supported the images captured in the sketch.

In 1890 social reformer Jacob Riis published his most famous work, *How the Other Half Lives: Studies among the Tenements of New York.* Riis, the intrepid social worker/reporter of the slums, took his middle-class readers through New York City's treacherous working-class neighborhoods to bring to the surface the difficult living conditions of poor and immigrant peoples residing in the underbelly of the city: Chinese, Irish, Italian, Jews, and others. He largely linked the social deviance of European immigrants to detrimental environmental influences such as substandard housing and industrial exploitation, but believed the depravity of Chinese workers to be innate. Riis warned that the immorality of the Chinese residents threatened other city residents: "The Chinaman smokes opium as Caucasians smoke tobacco, and apparently with little worse effect upon himself. But woe unto the white victim upon which this pitiless drug gets its grip!"[43] The drug's allure for the city's non-Chinese population, above all among white women, was particularly alarming to reformers such as Riis because the seeming spread of opium smoking created female addicts who would

Figure 1.2. Such cartoons depicting a combined threat of miscegenation and opium addiction reminded readers of the dangers of allowing unaccompanied white women to travel into Chinatown. *Source*: Frank Yeager, "New York City—The Opium Dens in Pell and Mott Streets—How the Opium Habit Is Developed," *Frank Leslie's Illustrated Newspaper*, May 19, 1883.

choose to reside in Chinatown as the common-law wives of Chinese men. In his description of an "opium haunt" in Chinatown, Salvation Army Commissioner Ballington Booth similarly cautioned that "hundreds of women in this city before this night is past will have allowed themselves to come beneath its baneful, demoralizing influence."[44]

Despite the popular depictions of opium as linked to the city's Chinese population, opium and its derivatives could be found in a range of commonly consumed patent medicines and tonics prescribed for a wide range of ailments, including gastrointestinal distress, food poisoning, parasites, anxiety, and pain. The smoking of opium, however, was an activity specifically attributed to the politically disenfranchised Chinese immigrant population and was thus easier to target for regulation.[45] Government attempts at limiting the availability of opium were met with stiff opposition from the U.S. medical and pharmaceutical establishment. But the 1909 ban on the importation of opium for smoking passed easily through Congress because it was publicly perceived as mainly affecting the Chinese community. The ban thus threatened neither the economic interests of patent medicine manufacturers nor the authority of the fledgling American Medical Association and the American Pharmaceutical Association who depended on the continuing availability and distribution of opium and its derivatives.[46] As a result, the criminalizing of opium smoking produced a sociolegal hierarchy whereby it was considered a morally debased act, whereas other types of opium consumption were dismissed as benign or approved as medically beneficial.[47]

The period's differing attitudes toward opium smoking as practiced by whites versus Chinese can also be seen in two separate depictions of "opium joints" in a 1904 tourist guidebook. One caption read "OPIUM JOINTS. Ah Fun, belle of Chinatown, showing the layout used in indulging the national habit of smoking opium. Here the vice is exhibited in attractive form. In the dive shown above the degradation of opium victims is depicted."[48] This carefully staged presentation of Ah Fun, clothed in traditional Chinese silk garments and seated by her opium-smoking paraphernalia, made her appear to the reader as a living exhibit wholly transplanted from the Orient.

In contrast to the neatly staged display of Ah Fun, a photograph (fig. 1.3) of white women and Chinese men sharing the same smoking implements in a real "opium den" projected a spatially chaotic and disheveled image. Whereas nothing had connected Ah Fun to the lower Manhattan dwelling where the prior photograph had been taken, the starkness of the walls and the poor state of the room in figure 1.3 are reminiscent of this period's photographs of tenement dwellers popularized by urban reformers and journalists such as Jacob Riis. The Chinese female opium addict, safely domesticated and contained as a purposefully arranged commercial display for sightseers, was not seen as degraded but

Figure 1.3. Opposing depictions of opium smoking in the guidebook.
The "degraded" victims of a dive are shown in the picture on top. The staged
opium den of "Ah Fun, Belle of Chinatown" is shown in the picture below.
Source: *New York's Chinatown: Ancient Pekin Seen at "Old Bowery" Gate*
(New York: King's Booklets, 1908), 21. Courtesy of the Museum of Chinese in
the Americas.

"attractive." However white women, who "hit the pipe" particularly in the company of Chinese men, were clearly labeled as "degraded." Opium, seen as a drug facilitating racial and sexual transgressions, posed a tremendous social threat. Rather than suppress the fact that whites and Chinese mixed freely in these opium parlors, guidebooks and news stories created a social hierarchy to sustain the bourgeois moral order; white female addicts were condemned, but if solely practiced by the Chinese opium smoking could be condoned as both quaint and exotic.

The smell of opium was not the only marker of Chinatown's boundaries. The strange sounds of the Chinese language being spoken, the bizarre visual sights of building ornamentations, and the noticeable absence of Chinese women in the community also worked to transform this particular set of streets into a distinctly Chinese "colony." Louis Beck's tour of Chinatown's stores and places of business made Chinatown appear as a self-contained environment where all material, cultural, and spiritual needs could be met by the Chinese residents themselves. Any type of service could be rendered by the area's various Chinese tradesmen. Theatrical amusements, such as opera or acrobatics, were furnished by Chinese performers. Gambling could be found at a number of Chinese operated "policy" or illegal lottery gaming rooms. Food was provided by Chinese farmers who grew Chinese vegetables on their farms located outside of the city that were then sold by Chinese grocers or itinerant peddlers. With the important exception of finding gainful employment in the "chop suey" restaurants and laundries scattered throughout the city, Chinese residents did not need to set foot outside of Chinatown. The sociocultural life of the community was said to be self-contained and set apart from the rest of the city.[49] Chinatown, then, was in New York, but not of it.

This popular view of Chinatown as distanced from the rest of Gotham was reinforced and legitimized through the work of an emerging professional class of social scientists at the beginning of the twentieth century. In a 1902 article titled "Social Assimilation," for example, author Sarah E. Simons described the assimilation of non-white races—"Chinese, negroes, and the Indians"—to be different from European immigrant groups. Speaking specifically about the Chinese, she stated: "*Socially*, however, the Chinese always make a class apart in whatever social group they enter. They constitute an element which does not readily assimilate with the other parts of the population. They are, therefore, a hindrance to the complete socialization of the group. Indeed, the Chinese may be regarded as practically non-assimilable with western races."[50] The proliferation of this view in social scientific discourse gave further legitimacy to Chinese exclusion and the popular idea that the Chinese and their community, even with the intervention of social reformers, was not and could not become a part of American society.

A CONTESTED SPACE IN LOWER MANHATTAN

The cultural and geographical boundaries that supposedly separated Chinatown from the rest of the immigrant neighborhoods of lower Manhattan were in actuality neither as rigid nor as impermeable as these writers suggest. Contemporary census data, and newspaper and magazine articles reveal that Chinatown's population was neither racially nor ethnically homogeneous. Despite these writers' attempts to draw rigid sociospatial boundaries dividing the area's Chinese and non-Chinese residents, Chinatown was by no means removed from the other European immigrant working-class neighborhoods in lower Manhattan. Instead, the transformation of these blocks into an exclusively Chinese space involved decades of clashes among the area's ethnically diverse inhabitants, social reformers, and police.

Between 1880 and 1920 the ethnic and racial geography of lower Manhattan changed dramatically as new waves of emigrants from southern and eastern Europe settled into this part of the city. Over seventeen million immigrants entered the United States through New York City in these decades; by 1910, over one million or 47 percent of Manhattan's population were identified by the U.S. Census Bureau as foreign born.[51] The majority of the city's Jewish immigrants—from Russia, Poland, Austria-Hungary, and the Balkans—settled into the Lower East Side while Italian immigrants concentrated around Mulberry Street, forming the neighborhood of Little Italy. The geographical borders separating Chinatown from these European immigrant neighborhoods become increasingly blurred when examining late nineteenth and early-twentieth-century census schedules for this area of Manhattan. In 1880, when the area occupied by Mott, Pell, and Doyers started becoming known as Chinatown, Chinese residents comprised a minority of the neighborhood's residents. Even as late as 1910 many native-born whites and European immigrants continued to reside in the area designated on maps and guidebooks as Chinatown. At 15 Mott Street, supposedly the heart of the Chinese quarter, five Chinese households and nine Italian households lived in the same building. Next door, 13 Mott Street was home to the Lee, Wong, Chin, Barocco, Tittula, Molassi, Bernieri, Scrovani, Cappelini, Pierri, Perillo, Perelli, and Barrone families.[52] Around the corner at 25 Pell Street, So Ling Lung and his partner, Lee Lung, rented rooms to four lodgers: Yen Quong, Frances Miller, Look Wong, and Hing Lee. At 15 Doyers Street, Chung Wing lived with his wife, Marie Fernando, who was born in Cuba of Spanish descent, and their boarders: Charles Welch, Wah Quong, One Lim, Kee Lien, and Wu Fong. Another mixed-race couple, Ung and Saidie Chu, also lived in the building with their four Chinese boarders. Aside from the several apartments occupied by Chinese men, 15 Doyers Street was also home to Ambrose and Margaret Reynolds and their boarders, and William and Bertha Clayton and their son.

Since the 1870s a popular restaurant owned by Wing Sing, at 3 Doyers Street, had a staff solely comprising Chinese workers who cooked and served American dishes found in "ordinary restaurants" ranging from "ham and eggs to turkey." Frequented by a racially mixed clientele of Chinese and whites residing in the neighborhood, the menu was written in both Chinese and English. According to Louis Beck's description of Wing Sing's establishment, the restaurant was small with a seating capacity of twenty-eight persons, but it did a handsome business of $500 per week. Two other Chinese-owned restaurants located at 12 and 22 Pell Street also specialized in American cooking, catering to both Chinese and non-Chinese customers.[53]

Far from being a self-contained and self-governed neighborhood, the city's policemen, social reformers, and Chinese and non-Chinese residents daily contended for dominance over the Chinatown space. The actions of the police often conflicted with the interests of the local Chinese residents. For example the enforcement of the Sunday laws that required the closing of businesses in observance of the Christian Sabbath pitted the area's Chinese residents against the police and some of their non-Chinese neighbors. Because of the large numbers of Chinese living and working outside of Chinatown, many limited their visits to the neighborhood to Sunday, usually the only day in the week when Chinese laundries throughout the city were closed. For sound financial reasons many Chinatown businesses clearly preferred to remain open on Sundays. In 1877, George F. Miller of 43 Mott Street lodged a complaint with the Mayor's office. "The Chinese who inhabit the larger part of Mott street, between Chatham square and Pell street, pursue their legal and illegal avocations, especially on Sunday without interference. This is the cause of attracting hundreds of Chinamen, from other parts of this city and neighboring cities, who stand on the sidewalks for hours, and in such dense crowds, that passers by and Christian residents of the neighborhood have to take the middle of the street."[54] Miller's letter also attacked the local police, whom he perceived as turning a blind eye to ongoing violations of the Sunday laws.

In response to Miller's charges Captain John McCullagh submitted a report to Alex S. Williams, Inspector of the First District, stating that his patrolmen actively prosecuted Chinese who violated the Sunday laws. Some of these shops may appear to be open, McCullagh explained, because Chinese workers often lived in the stores and received visitors there. In the past McCullagh had dispatched plainclothes patrolmen to visit these stores, but "they would not sell nor offer for sale in their presence, any goods."[55] After receiving Miller's complaint McCullagh sent another five police officers to visit a number of Chinatown shops on a Sunday. After visiting several of these Chinese-owned grocery stores, the police reported that they found only one violation. At 50 1/2 Mott Street, police officer William McGinnis arrested Joe Jon after witnessing a sale of groceries to a Chinese customer.

In their efforts to enforce the Sunday laws in the neighborhood, police particularly targeted the Chinese Theatre at 5–7 Doyers Street. Similar to Chinatown's storekeepers, the proprietors of the Chinese Theatre also depended on the patronage of these Sunday crowds of Chinese laborers. Rather than operate illegally the proprietors applied for the exhibition license enumerated in section 1998 of the Consolidation Act, allowing them to hold musical performances on the Sabbath. The theater under the ownership of Arthur F. Kerr in 1893 had no difficulty securing the license. In his review of Kerr's application, Captain Alexander S. Ward of the Sixth Precinct submitted a favorable report to Police Superintendent Thomas Byrnes, stating that Kerr's reputation was "good" and "vouched for by respectable people" and that the customers were "Chinese of seemingly good character."[56]

Once ownership of the theater was transferred to a group of Chinese men, however, the exhibition license was no longer so easy to obtain. In April 1895 the new Chinese manager, Chu Fong, was at first able to renew the license. To convince the mayor's office that the theater would not violate Sunday laws, he wrote the following explanation: "The premises to be used for sacred concerts and religious functions of the Chinese on Sundays." The license, however, was later revoked by the police and Chu Fong was "convicted and fined $500 in the Court of General Sessions for violation of the Sunday Laws in giving Theatrical Plays on Sunday, and as proven in the trial 'immoral plays.'"[57] Contemporary descriptions of the theater and its performances, however, suggest that the plays were probably not "immoral" in their content. Louis Beck, for example, described the plays as "generally represent[ing] some historical train of events, extending through the reign of a dynasty, or an interesting national epoch."[58]

Chu Fong and his associates did not give up. A year later, the Chinese proprietors made another attempt to obtain an exhibition license but were once again denied. Before rendering the decision, the mayor's office directed the police department to collect information regarding the character of the Chinese proprietors—Lee Quay, Chu Fong, Ung Mon Wie, Quan Hop Chone, and Chong Him Yee—and that of the theater's patrons. Aside from reporting that the license had been revoked under Chu Fong's management, Captain Young of the Sixth Precinct also presented an unfavorable description of one of the owners, Lee Quay. "With regard to Lee Quay," Captain Young began, "I would state that he is connected with gambling and lottery games at 32 Mott Street."[59] The captain added further that the theater's audience was Chinese and accused many of being gamblers and feared that allowing the theater to remain open on Sunday would benefit neighborhood gaming interests.

The fight for control over the Chinese Theatre also involved white Protestant missionaries situated in the neighborhood. A mission located at 17 Doyers Street, a few doors down from the theater, had lodged several complaints with the local precinct over "the great annoyance caused by the discordant music in the theatre." With the theater closed on Sundays, missionaries in the neighborhood would no longer have to contend with the noise; and even more importantly, they would not compete with the more popular Chinese Theatre to attract Chinese immigrants to the mission. To Captain Young the closing of the theater on the Sabbath represented an act of reclaiming a geographical area that had been lost with the settlement of Chinese in this part of the city. "The closing of this place on Sunday has been beneficial in compelling those people who are not citizens to respect our Sunday laws, and also a check to the gambling interest prominent among which is the syndicate now making application through Lee Quay for permission to give Sunday performances."[60]

Occasionally the efforts of the police and social reformers were strategically aided by some Chinese Americans when the needs of these different groups converged. Hoping to exact extra leverage over the local tongs in their attempt to gain control over the area, in 1887 Protestant Chinese leaders J. C. Thoms, Huie Kin, and Guy Maine petitioned New York City Mayor Abraham Hewitt for assistance to close gambling establishments in the Chinatown area. Supported in their efforts by the Society for the Prevention of Crime, the men disguised themselves as laborers and entered a number of gambling houses to gather evidence for prosecution. The men then submitted to Mayor Hewitt a lengthy list of Chinese proprietors of gambling houses and their location on Mott Street.[61] The mayor's office passed the list along to Captain McCullagh to pursue. Shortly thereafter Captain McCullagh used the information to make several raids on gambling houses along Mott Street and arrested the Chinese proprietors and some of their Chinese customers.[62] For at least a year gambling in Chinatown receded.[63]

These demonstrations of police and municipal power in the neighborhood reminded Chinatown residents of the dominance of these institutions in shaping the lives of residents and visitors. Such acts of police authority often involved keeping a tight watch over the movements of white women of all socioeconomic classes in the neighborhood. A number of local non-Chinese residents were clearly bothered by the presence of such women in this area, especially if they resided with Chinese men. An 1887 letter signed, "A disturbed neighbor," written to Mayor Hewitt, named several places as disorderly, including 11 Pell Street, a tenement occupied by "Chinese and white girls," and a "candy and ice cream saloon."[64] An investigation by police in the Sixth Precinct, however, disputed the writer's claims. The police report stated that the building was "occupied by Chinamen Cigar makers, and people of other nationalities; some of the Chinamen are married, while others have women living with them."[65] In addition, the police claimed that the "ice cream and confectionery saloon" was not in violation of the Excise Law. Two weeks later Captain McCullagh revisited the building and remained convinced that the charges against the occupants were unfounded: "[N]o evidence could be obtained of any disorderly house, or opium joint being kept or maintained, and I here positively state that there is not now nor has there been any such place at No. 11 Pell St. since May 29th."[66]

In September 1888, police investigated the complaints made in a letter signed by James O'Leary, Edward O'Toole, Joseph Wright, Michael O'Rourke, and Jere. O'Connor, that "girls are going in an out all day long and night" at 10 and 16 Doyers Street.[67] However when police from the Sixth Precinct attempted to investigate, they could not locate Joseph Wright or Jere. O'Connor. No one in the neighborhood appeared to recognize these two individuals. Furthermore when police finally found and questioned the remaining three men about the charge, they claimed to have neither signed the letter nor authorized the use of their names. In fact they told police that they did not harbor any complaints against the named occupants. Regardless the police investigated 10 and 16 Doyers Street and found the building to be occupied by Chinese men and their white wives and did not uncover any evidence suggesting disorderly conduct. In the end the police concluded that "[i]t may be true that these women are visited at times by their female friends," but found no evidence that the rooms were used for "assignation purposes."[68] If police used their authority to discourage white women from entering or taking up residence in the area, the same did not hold true for their male counterparts.

The Making of a Working-class Masculine Space

Contemporary writers frequently commented on Chinatown's overwhelmingly male "bachelor" population, emphasizing the absence of Chinese women in the neighborhood. Descriptions of the few Chinese women who did reside in the area, as wives or servants in merchant families, were accompanied by extensive commentaries on their trapped and invisible existence based on Chinese social practices that forbid women to walk the streets. Discussions of traditional Chinese cultural customs, such as foot binding and child slavery, further explained why

Chinese women were such a rare sight. According to Beck, a small number of white, black, and Chinese boys and young men comprised an intricate network of runners to serve the neighborhood's captive Chinese and white female population.[69] This image of women hidden within Chinatowns' buildings in contrast to the free circulation of boys and men in the neighborhood's streets further accentuated the image of Chinatown as a predominantly masculine space.

Nightclubs or saloons along Mott, Pell, and Doyers, such as the Chatham Club and the Mandarin Tea Garden, filled with "tough" American working-class clientele spilled over from the neighboring Bowery. The concentration of working-class leisure establishments in this part of the city often attracted the attention of the city's social reformers, who saw these establishments as "notorious" and popular hangouts for local gangs.[70] The Mandarin Tea Garden was described as the "hang-out for the worst type of criminals in the world. Headquarters of remnants of the Monk Eastman, Paul Krug and Five Point Gangs."[71]

These establishments were not necessarily for whites only, as patrons and workers reflected the ethnic and racial diversity of the neighborhood. A saloon and dance hall at 41 Mott Street, owned by a Chinese man by the name of Lee Chung but managed by a white American who went by the name of "Patty," catered to predominantly white, working-class customers. One investigator described the saloon as a "hangout for crooks of the Italian type."[72] Another anti-vice investigator reported that McNally's saloon at 12 Chatham Square catered to a racially mixed clientele, stating that he witnessed "a Chinaman there drinking, American girls dancing with pimps, as I was informed they were."[73]

Commercial slumming expeditions brought numerous white middle-class visitors into this part of lower Manhattan on a nightly basis. The rise of tourism in the 1890s helped fuel the rapid development of a tourist-based economy revolving around restaurants catering to non-Chinese visitors. These more upscale restaurants specifically aimed to cultivate a respectable middle-class clientele with claims of authentic haute Chinese cuisine and colorful decorations. In 1890 Louis Beck identified seven such restaurants, noting that all bore Chinese names such as Hon Heong Lau at 11 Mott Street. By the early twentieth century Chinatown restaurateurs more aggressively fashioned their establishments to appeal to white middle-class consumers by choosing names that would be more recognizable to New Yorkers such as the Tuxedo, Savoy, Chinese Delmonico, Port Arthur, or the Oriental.[74] No doubt some of these proprietors chose to appropriate the names of famous New York restaurants such as the Delmonico to signal to customers a more upscale and refined dining experience. Beginning in the late 1820s the Delmonico had defined high-class dining for New Yorkers; originally situated in downtown Manhattan, it

Figure 1.4. A racially diverse clientele dines in a "high-class" Chinese restaurant in Chinatown. Journalists and police warned that such places, by fostering interracial mixing, caused the tragic death of Elsie Sigel. *Source*: William Brown Meloney, "Slumming in New York's Chinatown," *Munsey's Magazine* 41 (September 1909): 822. Courtesy of Yale University Library.

drew from European, especially French, culinary traditions to create the ultimate gourmet dining experience for the city's elite.[75] Despite their middle-brow aspirations, the city's social reformers and police also routinely monitored Chinese-owned restaurants of this class for signs of vice activities. These regular inspections, however, generally confirmed that these were orderly establishments with respectable middle-class customers.[76]

A visit to the Chinatown area promised white middle-class sightseers not just an interesting culinary experience but also the thrill of encountering unknown dangers. Tourist guidebooks and sensational newspaper and social reform reports frequently linked Chinatown's topography to the various vice activities in the area. Doyers Street for example was described in the 1904 tourist guidebook, *New York's Chinatown: Ancient Pekin Seen at "Old Bowery" Gate*, as "the crookedest in [the] city, making half a dozen turns in its short stretch from Chatham Square to Pell St." Crooked streets, though a common feature of lower Manhattan, came to

Figure 1.5. "Doyers St., 1909." Despite guidebooks' and journalists' emphasis on the immoral Chinese character of "crooked" Doyers Street, establishments such as the Mandarin Tea Garden were popular hangouts for the local white, working-class Bowery toughs. *Source*: Library of Congress, Prints and Photographs Division, George Grantham Bain Collection, LC-USZ62-69696.

reflect the immorality and hidden criminal nature of the neighborhood and its residents. The guidebook made clear that Doyers Street served as the main site of illegal activities occurring within Chinatown, because the street's bends and folds made perfect hiding places for the quarter's tong wars and vice activities. In case the reader did not make this connection, the book states that the street's turns had been the site of many a tong war and which the mainstream press has dubbed the "'bloody angle,' so known from the clashes of the Hep Sing and Ong Leong Tongs, in their long feud which ended in a treaty of peace on February 2, 1906."[77] The picture's (fig. 1.5) composition revealed to the reader that only a short segment of the street could be seen before the bend prevented looking further. Criminal activities, if hinted, were just around the bend in the street.

Local white working-class male residents like the "Bowery Boys" took advantage of the rising middle-class interest in Chinatown as a sightseeing destination. Using their familiarity with Chinatown's Chinese residents and businesses, men like "Chuck" Connors played the part of the "lobby-gow" or tour guide for middle-class slummers who wanted to experience the seamy and exotic side of Chinatown life. Seen as street-smart and knowledgeable about the Chinese, contemporary writers revered these white experts of the neighborhood who could make sense of Chinatown's "crooked streets" and not succumb to their hidden dangers.[78]

Connors's ability to engage in Chinatown life was said to be so great that he was popularly identified as "the real Mayor of Chinatown, whose word is law, whose sparkling wit is decorated with a curious lingo, and who is quite as interesting to visitors as the Joss House or the opium joints." His reputation led him to become the subject of a 1903 short film titled "Scene in a Chinese Restaurant," consisting of a staged scene of Connors expertly employing chopsticks while sharing a Chinese meal with two Chinese men. The introduction to his autobiography published in 1904 noted that he had escorted cultural and society celebrities, including European royalty, actors, and the playwright Israel Zangwill, "through the Chinese quarter, with which he is more familiar than any other man in that section of the city." Under the protection and guidance of Connors, white middle-class sightseers believed that they too could learn about the peculiar ways of the Chinese and deftly maneuver through the twisted alleyways of Chinatown. As active participants in Chinatown's daily activities, Connors and other Bowery Boys served a double role as both a cultural mediator/guide as well as an object of interest for the middle-class sightseer. Correspondingly, guidebook's such as *New York's Chinatown* called attention to Barney Flynn's saloon and Nigger Mike's, reputed hangouts of Bowery toughs, along with Chinese-owned businesses such as the Chinese Delmonico restaurant that occupied the Chinatown area. So synonymous was Chuck Connors with sightseeing in Chinatown that upon his death the city's journalists noted that a phase of Chinatown tourism died with him. His passing signaled the decline of the Bowery Boys and their unofficial authority as the area's guides and cultural mediators. In their place, organized commercial leisure ventures such as "rubberneck wagons" or sightseeing cars took over the task of escorting middle-class sightseers through the neighborhood.[79]

Connors and other Bowery men exhibited the tough working-class masculinity that was admired by the professional middle-class men who wrote about them. Living and working in an increasingly corporate urban society, middle-class men envied the seeming independence of the Bowery men while their own autonomy became increasingly challenged by the bureaucratization of the professional workplace.[80] Stories about Connors drew upon other depictions of tough working-class masculinity by describing his former boxing career and highlighting his strength and ability to pull off dangerous stunts. Physical prowess and athleticism reflected enhanced moral restraint and self-control in middle-class men.[81] Traveling through the seemingly dangerous sections of the city, such as Chinatown, men who possessed physical prowess, street savvy, and self-restraint remained untouched by the dangers that seemed to threaten vulnerable white

Figure 1.6. Chuck Connors, "Mayor of Chinatown," guiding sightseers in a Chinese curio shop. *Source: New York's Chinatown: Ancient Pekin Seen at "Old Bowery" Gate* (New York: King's Booklets, 1908), 21. Courtesy of the Museum of Chinese in the Americas.

women of all classes at every turn. In contrast, the white working-class wives of Chinese men were often depicted as morally or physically weak and enfeebled as a result of their terrible addiction to opium and their prolonged exposure to Chinatown. In the aftermath of the Elsie Sigel murder, Chinatown exposés such as William Brown Meloney's article in *Munsey's Magazine* reminded readers of the plight of these desperate women residing in Chinatown whose own moral weaknesses were reflected in their worn-out physical and mental states.

Despite the fact that white female journalists, missionaries, and social reformers also traversed this terrain during the course of their work, they were not portrayed as capable as their male counterparts of penetrating and participating in the hidden life of Chinatown. Instead, the press coverage of the Sigel murder, by emphasizing the image of the female body in the trunk, worked to confirm and reinforce those longstanding descriptions of the unseen dangers of Chinatown that threatened to entrap naïve and unsuspecting white women. A cartoon published by the New Orleans *Daily Picayune,* "The Conversion of the Spider," shows

Figure 1.7. Working-class saloons such as The Pelham, Mike Salter's establishment, could be found among the Chinese-owned businesses on Pell Street. *Source*: Library of Congress, Prints and Photographs Division, NYWT&S Collection.

Chinatown to be a spider's web, ensnaring white female missionaries, the embodiment of Christian "good intentions."[82]

In the weeks following the discovery of Sigel's body, the *World* enlisted writer Marguerite Mooers Marshall to demonstrate to New Yorkers the perils experienced by white female missionaries and social reformers working in ethnic working-class neighborhoods of lower Manhattan. Marshall accompanied a young female Salvation Army worker, Lieutenant Thayer, on her nightly rounds of the saloons and restaurants of different ethnic working-class neighborhoods situated between Chatham Square and Houston Street. Marshall described the young lieutenant as a "slum angel" who looked "exactly like a little German maidchen, pretty as a wildflower, and looking fully as out of place as one on 'de Bowery.'"[83] As the intrepid Thayer introduced Marshall to the many lonesome souls inhabiting the dives of these neighborhoods, Marshall's admiration for Thayer's faith and tenacity increased. Most impressive to Marshall was Thayer's seeming ability to walk through the toughest white working-class saloons unmolested, protected by nothing other than her innate moral goodness.

Figure 1.8. The word "Chinatown" written across the spider's web, represents the Chinatown neighborhood as an unforseen trap that ensnared unsuspecting young white female missionaries, the embodiment of Christian "good intentions." *Source*: "The Conversion of the Spider," *The Daily Picayune*, July 1, 1909.

Upon reaching Chinatown however, the last part of the night's tour, the terrain suddenly shifted. Marshall learned that Thayer and other workers could not gain access to many of the area's establishments. Unlike the working-class saloons for whites they had visited earlier, these were considered truly dangerous places. Rather, they could go only to the restaurants Marshall found to be quite tame, though she spotted scenes of white women mixing with Chinese men in them. In contrast to working-class saloons for whites, the truly threatening parts of Chinatown, then, remained unreachable for white women such as Thayer and Marshall. Their sense of a sudden lack of autonomy was further magnified by a feeling of being captured by the gaze of the men in the neighborhood: "The men [in Chinatown] didn't verbally insult us—they only looked, but—well, I think

THE REAL YELLOW PERIL

Figure 1.9. This cartoon posited that the West Coast emphasis on Chinese economic competition as a threat to white manhood ignored the threat Chinese men and the Chinatown space posed to white womanhood, which this author suggested by the title was the "real yellow peril." *Source*: Robert Carter, "The Real Yellow Peril," *The World*, June 21, 1909.

both of us felt safer in the saloons."[84] Unexpectedly finding themselves trapped, the two women gladly took their leave of the area.

Following the Sigel murder police increasingly lost patience with those female reformers who dared to venture unescorted into Chinatown's streets and tenements. In May 1912 Rose Livingston, a self-described Chinatown missionary, was attacked at a tenement on Doyers Street when she tried to save a young white girl from the clutches of her "cadet."[85] A physician's report stated that Livingston had experienced severe bodily injuries: "In this assault serious and permanent damage was done to the face in a fracture of the alveolar process of the upper jaw bone which caused severe neurities [sic] with persistent neuralgic pain both day and night with much loss of sleep and impairment of health, the fracture and subsequent inflammation likewise causing the loss of all the teeth of the upper jaw on one side of the face."[86] The attack created a public outcry and New Yorkers petitioned Mayor William J. Gaynor to prod the police to offer better protection for female missionaries and reform workers in Chinatown. The police commissioner disputed the complaints of civilians however, responding that "[c]onditions in Chinatown have never been better than they are at present, nor is any portion of the City as heavily policed as this section."[87] Furthermore, the commissioner claimed that police records did not indicate any report of Livingston having suffered such an attack. Satisfied that the police had handled the situation properly, Mayor Gaynor concluded that "[t]he police are entirely capable of taking care of Chinatown. If Miss Livingston is in any danger there she may very easily withdraw."[88] For female missionaries and reformers to justify their work in Chinatown, they could not appear to be physically weak. Clearly such an admission made them vulnerable to the charge that women should not be allowed to venture into Chinatown.

REINFORCING CHINATOWN'S RACIAL AND GENDER BOUNDARIES

In July 1901, while making his investigative rounds for the Committee of Fifteen,[89] a short-lived anti-vice organization begun by the city's business elites the previous year, J. Mayers observed that the three-story tenement at 9 Pell Street was occupied by Chinese men and white girls. He accused the women of engaging in prostitution. J. Reiswirth made a similar report on the five-story tenement building a few doors down at 13 Pell Street. He believed that three apartments in the building were occupied by disorderly white women while the rest were occupied by Chinese residents.[90] Both reports noted that Chinese-owned businesses— a grocery store and dry goods store—occupied the ground floor of the buildings. Though the presence of legitimate businesses may have indicated respectability, the inspectors warned that they served only to disguise the immoral activities of the Chinese and whites residing in the building. The Committee of Fifteen lacked the means to enforce violations, and mainly filed reports indicating the breakdown of racial and gender boundaries in the area. Prosecution and border reinforcement depended on the willing intervention by the police and courts.

In May 1909, Captain Galvin of the Elizabeth Street police station began a "crusade" to remove all unmarried white women residing in Chinatown. The discovery of the Sigel murder a month later allowed Galvin to intensify the campaign as well as gain widespread support for additional policing activities in the neighborhood. He boasted that by July 4 he had succeeded in "cleansing the quarter."[91] By July 5 he claimed that only three white women were left in Chinatown, because they produced marriage licenses that sufficiently proved that they were married to Chinese men. A reporter for the *World* claimed to have witnessed Galvin personally warning these women to leave the neighborhood by the following day. "At noon to-morrow I'm coming around," threatened Galvin, "If you haven't packed up and got out of here I'll send you to the Island."[92]

In addition, Galvin also justified the closing of a number of Chinatown businesses and "questionable resorts" as part of the Sigel murder investigation. Yet Galvin also admitted that the campaign fit neatly with his original intention of getting rid of Chinatown. The "shutting up of the fantan resorts and the dispersion of white women from Chinatown might result in the breaking up of the entire Chinese community there because it did away with the chief attraction for out of town Chinese."[93] By the end of July Chinatown's merchants reported that the combined murder investigation and anti-vice campaigns had wreaked economic havoc on the Chinese immigrant community. "Many stores have closed and the proprietors have moved away during the last six weeks. As compared with other vacation periods very few persons have visited the district this summer."[94] Although the campaigns managed to close temporarily the "dives" in Chinatown and along the Bowery, by October settlement house workers reported that "when one is walking about many of the girls are to be met with on the streets, and many are still living in hiding in Chinatown and in the nearby streets, in tenements where families and children live ..."[95]

The commercialization of the Chinatown space made the task of reformers and police maintaining gender and racial borders increasingly difficult. Extralegal and intrusive forms of policing needed to be employed. While police conducted periodic campaigns in the area, private anti-vice organizations such as the Committee of Fourteen, formed in 1905, operated independently from the city's police and employed their own investigators and means to enforce anti-vice legislation. In particular the Committee of Fourteen aimed to suppress prostitution by targeting the city's Raines Law hotels, saloons whose back rooms or upper floors had been hastily converted into sleeping quarters for let.[96] Committee investigators nightly toured the city's neighborhoods, including Chinatown, in search of prostitution activity. To halt prostitution at a particular establishment, the Committee went beyond alerting the police to directly contacting liquor distributors and requesting that deliveries to those places stop. The threat of losing access to their liquor distributors compelled proprietors to end prostitution in their establishments.

In August 1910 the Committee of Fourteen began to focus their attention on Lee Chung's establishment at 41 Mott Street as part of a larger Chinatown anti-vice campaign. Although not a Raines Law Hotel, the committee was clearly concerned with the establishment; it allowed dancing on the premises. Because dance halls were a particularly popular form of commercialized leisure for working-class women, Lee Chung's establishment attracted both a male and female clientele. Investigator Stockdale reported to Walter G. Hooke, executive secretary of the Committee of Fourteen, that he arrived at 41 Mott Street at 1:23 A.M. and stationed himself at the bar of the saloon. Hooke described the establishment as "a clean looking place" and that the "occupants of place were different class being neater dressed and orderly."[97] He left after a half hour because he saw nothing to lead him to suspect solicitation was taking place. A report by another investigator, however, noted that it was the "hangout for crooks of the Italian type. Guerillas, vaps, procurers and young dissolute women."[98]

By September the Committee decided to designate Lee Chung's establishment as disorderly and contacted his beer supplier, Joseph Doelger's Sons. The lager beer brewer agreed to assist the Committee and replied that in the event that Lee Chung "fail[ed] to comply with your instructions in conducting said place, we hereby agree that upon your request we will withdraw our support therefrom."[99] Faced with the possibility of losing its distributor Lee Chung capitulated, signing a letter stating that "that no women will be allowed in my place, #41 Mott Street and that all music and dancing will be discontinued."[100] Similar pledges were extracted from other saloon owners in the Chinatown area.[101] Reformers enacted these bans to ensure that these establishments would no longer attract female customers and provide opportunities for mingling between the sexes or races. Instead the establishment would return to being a saloon—a leisure space reserved for working-class men. Such transformations, however, may have been short-lived without the official intervention of the police as saloon keepers learned to hide their activities from plain view. Less than a year later patrolmen received a complaint of a disorderly saloon at 41 Mott Street, but on subsequent visits "were unable to observe any violation of law thereat until March 14th 1911, when we observed that some one was in the rear room of said bar at 1:30 A.M."[102]

The intense press coverage on Chinatown during the Sigel murder investigation enticed even more curious white visitors to the area. One reporter observed, "the 'Seeing New York' automobiles did a rushing business, the guides handing out a long line of talk in front of each of the missions, especially at No. 10 Mott Street, where Mrs. Sigel and Elsie were accustomed to visit Mrs. Florence M. Todd, one of the resident workers and who was the first to identify the body of the girl."[103] A group of beauty pageant winners from Pennsylvania visiting New York City en route to Bermuda reportedly planned to visit Coney Island's renowned amusement parks and the city's department stores. When they expressed a strong desire to visit Chinatown due to "their interest having been aroused by the Elsie Sigel case," they were strongly urged to give up their plans.[104]

Alarmed by this increasing popularity of Chinatown as a tourist site for middle-class thrill seekers, police officials stepped up surveillance activities in the neighborhood. On the evening of October 23, 1910, New York City Police Commissioner James C. Cropsey and First Deputy Police Commissioner Clement C. Driscoll led a group of policemen from the Elizabeth Street precinct through Chinatown to inspect the various tourist attractions in the neighborhood, targeting "opium joints" and "chop suey" restaurants. In addition police aimed "to determine what white people remained in the Chinese section after midnight and to learn what business they had there."[105] Though the campaign was described as a broad attack on vice activities in Chinatown, a closer look at the targets of their attack reveals that the campaign was an attempt to reinscribe and enforce both racial and gender boundaries in the neighborhood.

The police specifically selected places they perceived as associated with white women: "a fraudulent 'opium joint,' where tourists were taken to be shown a white woman rolling opium pills in company with a decrepit Chinese. Another was a 'chop suey' restaurant, where white girls ate in company with Chinese residents of the neighborhood." To the police these places posed a great social danger precisely because they allowed gender mixing and threatened to lure more innocent female sightseers to become regular inhabitants of these places. Explaining to the *New York Times* the impetus for their campaign, the first deputy police commissioner pointed to the many complaints he had received about Chinatown's vice activities: "Some were complaints from women that friends who had gone to Chinatown in slumming parties had gradually made their visits more frequent, and had finally passed under the control of white loungers." Police planned to close these fake opium dens and arrest those men or the "white loungers" who made their living by exploiting and exhibiting these "degraded women." As for restaurants frequented by Chinese and whites, the police informed proprietors that "hereafter parties comprising women who visited the restaurants regularly were to be discouraged."[106]

To ensure that sightseers would not be tempted to stay in the neighborhood, the police instituted a midnight curfew and forcibly removed non-Chinese found in the neighborhood after that hour. Concerned that sightseeing businesses in the area would not comply, Driscoll, along with Captain William Hodgins of the Elizabeth Street station and Inspector John Daly, called a meeting with the five automobile sightseeing companies in New York that organized late-night excursions to Chinatown. Under great pressure the operators agreed to end their midnight trips to Chinatown.[107]

During their campaign police were not only concerned with guarding sightseers and patrolling those public spaces designated as tourist attractions, but they also turned their attention to the area's residents, again targeting the neighborhood's white female population. Patrolmen noted the addresses of those buildings where Chinese men and white women resided together and planned to turn over the addresses to tenement house inspectors to investigate for possible violations of the Tenement House Law.[108] Sections 150–156 of the Tenement House Law of 1901 dealt specifically with the use of a tenement house for the purposes of prostitution. The law not only punished the prostitute, but also authorized the Tenement House Department to pursue civil action against the tenement owner.[109] Although the police explained that the search for tenement law violations was meant to force the buildings' owners to take responsibility for their tenants, the strategy meant legitimizing the harassment of Chinatown's mixed-race couples.

The campaign quickly proved disastrous for Chinatown's tourist economy, particularly for the area restaurants and other businesses that relied on the nightly sightseeing traffic.[110] In response a group of Chinatown merchants led by Lee Lok, an associate of the store Quong Yueng Shing at 32 Mott Street, submitted a petition protesting the "issuance of an order by the police department which deprives them of their business and will eventually throw them into bankruptcy."[111] The petition countered the police's charges of disorderly "chop suey joints" by emphasizing that the restaurants represented by the group were "honorable and respectable businesses, catering to a respectable class of people only." With investments for each restaurant ranging from $50,000 to $75,000, these "chop suey" restaurants were considerable financial undertakings by the community's businessmen. Although these restaurants were open from 10 A.M. to 2 A.M., the majority of customers arrived in the evening between the hours of 8 P.M. and 2 A.M.; forcing the restaurants to close during their peak hours was financially devastating for the local tourist economy. Through these much publicized campaigns to expel whites from Chinatown, police and social reformers not only worked to contain the Chinatown space and its residents socially and economically, but also reinforced the area's racial and gender boundaries by attempting to turn the area into a strictly Chinese neighborhood.

Elsie Sigel's death disrupted these popular narratives of Chinatown as impenetrable, unmasking middle-class New Yorkers' fears that Chinatown's borders, in actuality, were not so rigidly fixed but were easily transgressed by Chinese men and non-Chinese women alike. As a result Chinatown's racialized, gendered, and sexualized boundaries could not be taken for granted but had to be constantly watched, reinforced, and maintained through the combined efforts of the city's journalists, police, and social reformers. Contrary to the guidebook and journalist accounts that Chinatown grew out of the innate clannish instincts of the Chinese residents, the making of this area of lower Manhattan into a specifically Chinese space resulted mainly from the ongoing containment efforts of the local police, social reformers, and journalists to make Chinatown a place of residence for Chinese only.

In their attempts to map out boundaries to contain the city's Chinese population and reconfigure the city's rapidly modernizing, shifting racial terrain, Chinatown not only became a racialized space marked by a peculiar otherness but a gendered one as well. These descriptions of Chinatown worked to create an accepted rough working-class male space populated by men like "Chuck" Connors and his Bowery cohorts, the city's gritty policemen, and adventure-seeking male journalists and writers. With their perceived innate abilities to exercise moral and sexual restraint, these men could enter and exit the neighborhood at will and not endanger their manhood in the process. Rather, these men's ability to venture into such a neighborhood commonly perceived as dangerous and unexplored terrain made them even more manly.

For women, however, Chinatown was a different story. The comments of journalists and social reformers showed that working-class and middle-class white women—whether as prostitutes, wives, social reformers, or sightseers—also visited or resided in the neighborhood, but their presence in Chinatown more often created both public concern and outrage. By representing Chinatown as a landscape full of hidden moral and sexual threats, writers, reformers, and police erected distinctly gendered spatial boundaries that worked to exclude "respectable women" from a legitimate role in the community. The gruesome image of Elsie Sigel trapped inside a "Chinaman's trunk" demonstrated this point viscerally for New Yorkers. Although her body was discovered in midtown Manhattan, not in Chinatown, the murder evoked the same racialized narratives of sexual danger easily explained as the consequences of unchecked white middle-class, female mobility among the city's Chinese male immigrant population.

CHAPTER TWO

Beyond Chinatown: Policing Chinese American Male Mobility in New York City

CHINATOWN'S INADEQUATE RACIAL and gender borders granted women entry into this part of the city and allowed Chinese men such as Leon Ling to move beyond its physical limits. After all newspaper reports alleged that Leon Ling and Elsie Sigel first encountered one another in upper Manhattan, far away from the confines of the Chinatown neighborhood. His quick disappearance following her murder similarly signaled his ability to maneuver socially and physically throughout the city, if not the nation at large. Maintaining a close watch over the Chinatown area and setting up strict border patrols at its edges, then, were insufficient in containing an already mobile urban Chinese immigrant male population. Aware of the proliferation of Chinese–owned businesses and residences throughout the metropolitan area, the city's police force continued to search for ways to monitor and restrict the movements of Chinese American men in the hopes of capturing Leon Ling and restoring urban moral and spatial order.

During the first few weeks of the Sigel murder investigation, police throughout the greater metropolitan area stepped up surveillance of Chinese workplaces and homes throughout the region. Concerned citizens provided assistance by scrutinizing the daily activities of their Chinese neighbors, quickly alerting police of anything deemed out of the ordinary. On June 26, in Newark, New Jersey, a number of Chinese men visited Joe Wong's laundry at the southwest corner of Central Avenue and Tenth Street, arousing the suspicions of his neighbors. One white storeowner became so convinced that one of the men was the missing murder suspect that he kept a careful watch of the laundry throughout the stranger's twenty minute conversation with Wong. But when later questioned by a local reporter, Wong, who spoke English fluently, dismissed the allegation that the man was Leon Ling.[1]

Police responded even more vigorously to reports of white women seen in the company of Chinese men. A police raid ensued at a 309 West Forty-seventh Street laundry after a man notified police that he saw a white female enter, but not exit, the laundry. The recent Sigel murder in their jurisdiction hastened the officers of the Forty-seventh Street police station to the scene. The police suspected that the laundry, owned by Louis Suey and his wife, Josie, a white woman, was merely a front for an opium den. Upon their arrival, the police found another woman, Grace Hudson,

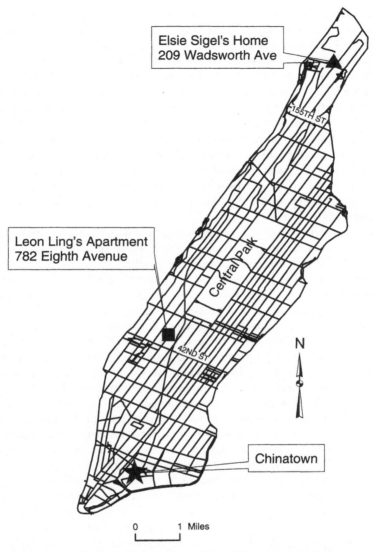

Elsie Sigel's Home
209 Wadsworth Ave

155TH ST

Leon Ling's Apartment
782 Eighth Avenue

Central Park

42ND ST

N

Chinatown

0   1 Miles

Map 2.1 From south to north, locations of the Chinatown area in lower
Manhattan, Leon Ling's apartment in midtown, and the Sigel family residence
in Washington Heights.

inside a basement room outfitted with "two bunks and a complete equip-
ment of pipes, bowls, needles, and morphine."[2] The magistrate, however,
later released Hudson after determining that she had not been smoking at
the time of the raid. Josie and Louis Suey, who were accused of running an
opium den, were also discharged because of a lack of evidence.[3]

Such stories of opium dens disguised as laundries, along with the revelation that Sigel's murder had occurred in a midtown Manhattan building
with a "chop suey" restaurant and rooms occupied by Chinese laborers
reaffirmed popular fears that the proliferation of Chinese businesses and
residences had brought Chinatown's moral and sexual dangers out of the
Sixth Ward to the general populace. The sudden awareness that the city's
Chinese immigrant male population was not geographically contained
within Chinatown, but freely dispersed across the metropolitan area, provoked demands for closer monitoring of these men as they went about
their daily activities. In the week's following the murder the city's police
force, social reformers, journalists, and lay citizens maintained a strict
watch over the many places where Chinese men lived and worked. Of
particular concern were those locations where Chinese workers came into
contact with mainstream residents.

To the public's surprise, the city's small Chinese immigrant population
had become well integrated into many aspects of modern urban life.
Although Chinese Exclusion laws greatly restricted the flow of Chinese
immigrants into the nation, the city's Chinese male laboring population
continued to rise and spread along with the city's physical expansion, con-
founding the city's racial and gendered geographies. The racial exclusion
of Chinese laborers from industrial work compelled the labor mobility of
Chinese men, leading them to seek out work in the service sector as
servants, hand laundry operators, and restaurant workers. New Yorkers'
patronage and reliance on these domestic services allowed Chinese laborers
to enter white middle-class and upper-class homes and neighborhoods.
The rise of popular commercial amusements such as Coney Island and
Times Square generated new forms of leisure and social mixing among
New York's teeming masses, which offered further opportunities for
the city's small Chinese American population to interact with the general
populace. Yet, the movement of Chinese men in and out of private homes
and public spaces often continued to be viewed by many with suspicion
and apprehension. The broad-based efforts at regulating the public
social interactions between Chinese Americans and whites of different
socioeconomic classes demonstrate the ongoing concerns and problems
with remapping gender and racial boundaries in the rapidly expanding
commercial city that seemed to undermine these borders.

LOCATING NEW YORK'S CHINESE AMERICAN POPULATION

While popular accounts suggest that clearly defined racial and geographical boundaries demarcated the Chinatown neighborhood from the
surrounding southern and eastern European immigrant neighborhoods,

single Chinese men and families also resided in these areas. For example, a report from the New York Probation Association noted that the tenement house at 22 1/2 Catherine Street, situated within the Lower East Side area, was the home of "Chinese and white women. Respectable families with children living on the premises."[4] At 57 Bayard Street, among the building's predominantly Russian Jewish residents were a few Chinese men, including William Hook and his white wife and a Japanese man and his white wife.[5] A few doors down at 53 Bayard Street, the majority of the residents were the families of Chinese merchants.

More significantly, the majority of the city's Chinese American population at the time of the Sigel murder lived and worked outside of the Chinatown area. The permeability of the neighborhood's borders not only allowed white men and women of different socioeconomic classes to enter the area, the city's Chinese immigrants also circulated beyond lower Manhattan. Unlike the popular depiction of the "Chinaman" who naturally clustered with his countrymen in ethnically homogeneous neighborhoods and was afraid to step foot outside of the Chinatown area, the city's Chinese inhabitants regularly traversed the city's streets. Similar to the men residing or working at 782 Eighth Avenue, who were arrested and questioned during the course of the Sigel murder investigation, Chinese workers lived throughout the New York metropolitan area in rooms situated above or behind the "chop suey" restaurants and hand laundries where they labored. The long hours required in these service occupations, coupled with the length of time necessary to commute daily from their place of work in one part of the city to Chinatown in lower Manhattan, made it impractical for most of the city's Chinese workers to reside in that neighborhood. Instead, workers commonly shared available housing resources throughout the city to shorten travel times between their places of work and residence.

By the late 1870s Chinese laborers had already begun to take up residences outside of lower Manhattan's wards. Between 1870 and 1880, as local and national agitation by white labor effectively curtailed the entry of Chinese laborers into industrial work, the percentage of the city's Chinese population engaged in cigar making dropped from 31 to 12 percent.[6] New York's Chinese population turned to service jobs as domestics, laundry workers, or restaurant operators. Laundries quickly became the primary source of employment for the city's Chinese residents. An 1876 city business directory specifically listed fifty-six laundries under the heading "Chinese laundries" and by 1880 roughly 75 percent of the city's Chinese population was concentrated in this single profession.[7] The Chinese American writer Wong Ching Foo observed in 1888, "Many an able-minded man as well as skillful mechanic who came to America to better his condition may be found wielding the polishing-irons in a New York

Chinese laundry."[8] Renting and setting up a typical storefront laundry required little capital, roughly $75 to $200.[9] In addition, one could easily open a store after spending less than a month to learn the trade from another Chinese worker, which allowed their numbers to multiply quickly throughout the greater metropolitan area.

In *New York's Chinatown*, journalist Louis Beck estimated that approximately 4,000 Chinese, or less than one-fourth of the 1898 Chinese population of New York City, lived in Chinatown. The remaining 13,000 Chinese in the city were described as "scattered throughout the metropolitan area."[10] The Third Avenue train, built in the 1870s as part of the elevated railroad system owned by the Manhattan Elevated Railroad, provided a station at the intersection of Bowery and Pell, allowing Chinese workers to travel quickly from other parts of the city into the Chinatown area for food or laundry supplies. In the 1880s, many of the city's pioneering Chinese laundry owners took advantage of this convenient transportation corridor to set up their businesses along Third Avenue stretching from lower Manhattan up to 125th Street. By the 1890s, Chinese hand laundries had proliferated along every major transportation corridor in the borough.[11]

Laundries were not simply places of work because they often doubled as residences, with owners and workers erecting makeshift sleeping quarters or permanent homes in their stores. The 1880 federal census and New York City business directory noted that over 55 percent of Chinese working in laundries either lived in or near their place of employment.[12] During their days off from work Chinese laborers took advantage of the growing urban public transportation system of elevated trains and streetcars to make weekly journeys from their workplaces to Chinatown or other parts of the city. Because of the instability of the laborers' work and residences, many preferred relatives to send their mail to more established Chinatown businesses that shared their clan or village connections. Even if the worker's new position took him outside of the city limits, his mail would still go to the same reliable location in Chinatown. Chinese grocery stores, such as Quong Yuen Shing at 32 Mott Street, became one of these "post offices" for the city's Chinese laborers.[13] A laundry supply store owned by Kaimon Chin's father at 59 Mott Street similarly served workers from Chin's village or clan. Kaimon Chin, who was born in New York's Chinatown and then as a teenager worked at the store, recalled the important social functions this place of business served for the Chinese living and working outside of the neighborhood.

> For years and years we were getting their mail in the store. Naturally, when they come for the mail they would gather and talk a little bit, so it was like a meeting place, so not only was it a place of business. That part my father

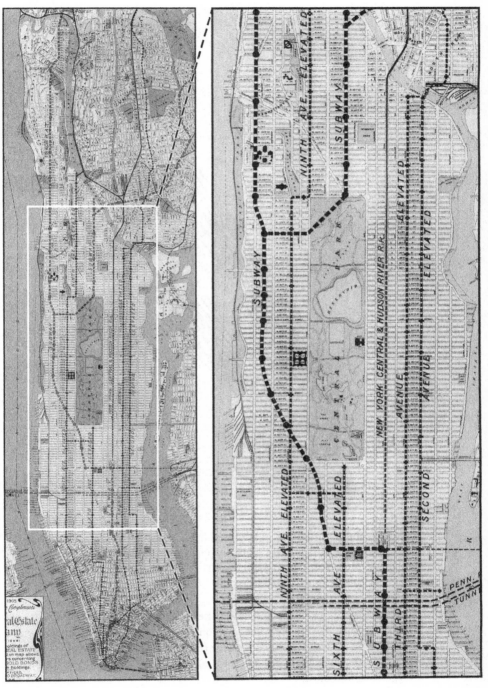

Map 2.2. The map on the left illustrates the elevated train and early subway systems that connected Manhattan in 1905. The map on the right provides a detailed look at these transportation lines running through midtown Manhattan. *Source*: American Real Estate Company, January 1905. Courtesy of Map Collection, Yale University Library.

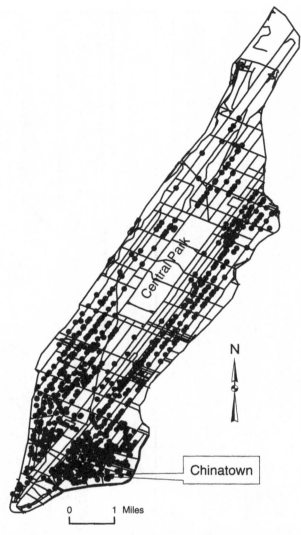

Map 2.3. 1893 Distribution of Chinese laundries throughout Manhattan. Note the establishment of laundries along major transportation corridors provided by the city's elevated train system. *Source*: Based on 1893 *Trow Business Directory of New York* (New York: The Trow Directory 1893).

enjoyed very much. He would have coffee with relatives and cousins he would only see once a week or sometimes once a month. But at least that was a contact, and it was a good contact for the people living outside of Chinatown because they'd have some place to go after they shopped for their fresh vegetables and meat.[14]

Customers also asked Kaimon to prepare mailing envelopes by writing in the address of his father's store. Workers then mailed these envelopes back to relatives in the village to ensure that future mail would be delivered properly to the store. In this manner these Chinatown social and business institutions remained vital in connecting Chinese living throughout the city to one another as well as to relatives abroad.

Chinese immigrants did not take their physical mobility for granted but understood the potential bodily risks that accompanied movement through spaces not allotted to them. The geographical dispersion of the Chinese population exposed proprietors and laborers to verbal and physical attacks in their daily lives. On Sunday, April 24, 1881, three Chinese laundry workers were attacked by a small group of white workingmen on Spring Street not far from the Bowery. Similar to other Chinese laundry workers, on a Sunday the three men—Lee Teep, Ah Sin, and Kwong Tong—attended a Christian Sunday school on Twenty-third Street between Seventh and Eighth avenues, and then visited a store on Mott Street in Chinatown. Upon returning to where they lived and worked at a laundry located at 142 Spring Street, they met a group of white workers on the street. One of the men decided to knock off Lee Teep's hat as the two groups passed each other. Surprised, Lee Teep responded by asking why the man had done that. The ruffian then delivered a couple of quick stab wounds to Lee Teep's chest before fleeing the scene. Unfortunately for Lee Teep the wounds were fatal and he died a few days later. His companions later identified a suspect, but the man was acquitted at trial.[15]

In their workplaces Chinese workers were often the victims of robbery or vandalism. The breaking of windows of Chinese-owned businesses had become so commonplace that insurance companies reportedly refused to insure against such damage.[16] Chinese laundry owners had become so wary of theft or property destruction by local hooligans that most took to putting wire screens on the outside of their windows as a necessary precaution;[17] such measures may not be difficult to understand as robberies could turn violent. On May 18, 1910, two Chinese men, Wong See and Wong Que, were killed while trying to thwart a robbery at the restaurant where they worked. Nathaniel J. Motley, who was described by the police as "colored," was later arrested and convicted of assault in the second degree.[18]

The forms of harassment encountered by Chinese proprietors and workers throughout the city can be seen in Guy Maine's account of a typical workday as the superintendent of the Chinese Guild or *Bao Niang Hui* sponsored by St. Bartholomew's Parish. Established in 1889 at 23 St. Mark's Place, the Chinese Guild acted as a social welfare and legal advocacy organization for the city's Chinese immigrants. In the Guild's 1900 annual report, Maine emphasized the widespread distribution of the Chinese population in the greater New York metropolitan area to explain the urgent need to install a telephone at his home in Jamaica, Long Island. The following description also suggests the breadth of interactions the Chinese population had with their non-Chinese neighbors.

> A boy was arrested at about 7.30 in the morning for assaulting a member; the Superintendent was informed of the fact by telephone and by 9 o'clock was on hand at the fifty-seventh street Magistrate Court to look after the member's interest.
>
> Three Italians were arrested for robbing a member at midnight; the superintendent was notified, and in due time, early in the morning, was in Jefferson Market Court to see that the men were properly arraigned.
>
> There are many early calls, but the earliest was from Jersey City, N.J. It came at 4.30 in the morning and requested the superintendent to be at the Jersey City Police Station by 8 o'clock, as a ruffian, without any apparent cause, had battered a Chinaman's face nearly beyond recognition.[19]

During the course of his normal work day, Guy Maine came to the aid of Chinese living and working throughout New York City, Long Island, and northern New Jersey. Maine's command of the English language and generally good reputation among the city's reformers and political figures made him a valuable resource for Chinese laborers who contended with physical and verbal harassment as part of their daily interaction working and living among a diverse population of immigrants and native-born whites and blacks.

The city's Chinese immigrants could also turn to the Chinese Consolidated Benevolent Association (CCBA) or the Chinese Legation in the mediation of legal or financial disputes among members of the Chinese American community or between Chinese and non-Chinese residents in the city.[20] Nevertheless these immigrants did not depend solely on established Chinese immigrant institutions for survival in the city; they regularly took it upon themselves to petition New York's social service and governmental bureaucracies for assistance. Despite their ineligibility to citizenship, Chinese residents often expected the same rights and protections granted to other New Yorkers, frequently taking their complaints to city officials. In 1884, Wah Sing experienced ongoing harassment from "mischievous small boys" who had broken the windows of his laundry at 300 First Avenue. Wah Sing reported the incident to the police who later arrested two local boys, Frank Kane and Joseph Byrnes, for disorderly conduct. The boys were later discharged, and a dissatisfied Wah Sing took the bold step of writing a letter of personal protest to Mayor Franklin Edson. It is unclear if additional help was forthcoming, however. In his report to the mayor, Captain William Clinchy of the Eighteenth Precinct, dismissed Wah Sing's complaint, stating that "While I have no doubt that Wah Sing is considerably annoyed, yet I believe that his counsel has overdrawn his troubles."[21]

Even in cases involving their fellow countrymen, Chinese frequently looked outside of established community channels such as the CCBA to the city's courts for legal justice. In 1898, Won Han, believing that his friend Li Hong was planning a return trip to China, asked him to take a sum of money to his wife who remained in their village. Li Hong, however, never left for China and kept the money. Won Han retaliated by having Li Hong arrested and charged with grand larceny in the second degree.[22] In 1901 To Non Cue, a laundryman, became the victim of a fraudulent business scheme when four Chinese men attempted to sell him a laundry at 493 Franklin Avenue in Brooklyn for the sum of $200. After paying the men, To Non Cue discovered to his dismay that the men were not the actual owners. He then filed a complaint with the police and had the men brought to trial.[23] *Although not citizens, expect rights*

The city's Chinese residents also on occasion turned to their non-Chinese neighbors and acquaintances for assistance. Shortly after renting and setting up his laundry at 387 Bleecker Street, Yong Fong Yee became the target of harassment by some Chinese men. The previous owner had abandoned the laundry following a fire, but later demanded its return. When Yong Fong Yee did not comply the former owner arranged to have him arrested on a false charge that he had stolen $185 from another Chinese man. Yong Fong Yee's landlord, John H. Timm, quickly intervened by asking his son to write a letter of support on the defendant's behalf. William C. Timm, a lawyer by profession, submitted a brief letter outlining the case to District Attorney William Jerome, summing up the situation as "only a trumped-up charge to get Jung out of the way, so that the prior tenant could get the store."[24] In closing Timm asked that Yong Fong Yee's bail be reduced from $500 or have his case quickly brought to trial. The assistance provided by the Timms, respectable middle-class whites, worked in Yong Fong Yee's favor as the Grand Jury later dismissed all charges.

By the time of the 1909 Sigel murder, Leon Ling was clearly not the only Chinese man in New York able to maneuver outside of Chinatown and navigate the city's different neighborhoods and legal and social institutions. In the early decades of the Chinese exclusion era, New York City's Chinese small business owners and laborers challenged and negotiated their socioeconomic status and sought legal protections on both an individual and collective basis. On September 22, 1892, nearly two hundred English-speaking Chinese from the East Coast gathered at the Cooper Union in the East Village to form the Chinese Equal Rights League to contest the legality of Chinese exclusion, particularly the Geary Act, passed that May. The Geary Act extended the original 1882 ten-year ban on Chinese labor immigration as well as required all Chinese living in the United States to register their residency with the collector of internal revenue in their respective district.[25] Sam Ping Lee, a Philadelphia merchant, became the president

↓ more than exclusion

while Wong Ching Foo took the position of secretary. The group drafted and published a public appeal, stating "as residents of the United States we claim a common manhood with all other nationalities, and believe we should have that manhood recognized according to the principles of common humanity and American freedom."[26] Not always successful in these endeavors, these efforts nevertheless point to the extent to which Chinese immigrants in late-nineteenth-century New York disputed legally based racial exclusion and actively participated in the life of the city and nation.

THE PROBLEM OF CHINESE MALE MOBILITY IN NEW YORK CITY

Similar to the many European immigrants eager to experience the sights and sounds of the modern city, Chinese New Yorkers also learned to take advantage of the many commercial leisure opportunities increasingly available at the dawn of the twentieth century.[27] Whether as workers or patrons, Chinese men's participation in the formation of New York's modern consumer culture further widened their geographical mobility. A 1909 study of Cantonese Merchants who resided in Chinatown by John Stewart Burgess, a Columbia University masters degree student, noted the range of leisure activities available to this group. Similar to other writers in this period, Burgess discussed the popularity of establishments in the neighborhood such as the Chinese Theatre on Doyers Street and the proliferation of saloons, houses of prostitution, opium dens, and gambling parlors. But Burgess also recorded that many residents ventured out of the immediate neighborhood to explore the seemingly endless variety of cultural amusements found in the city. A twenty-year-old Chinese man who had arrived in the United States at the age of twelve and attended the neighborhood public school, P.S. 23, for a few years was described as having more middle-class aspirations including a college education. He had traveled uptown for a more edifying and highbrow pursuit—a visit to the Metropolitan Museum of Art. Other merchants with families enjoyed going to the opera, making excursions to Staten Island to picnic, or taking walks in the city's parks.[28]

More popular among Chinese male laborers and merchants, however, was the city's impressive variety of commercial amusements. Movie theaters along Third Avenue, playing the latest films and frequented by the neighborhood's European working-class immigrants, were also described as regularly "crowded with Chinese." A number of Chinese in the city had also taken up bowling and two bowling alleys located within a Presbyterian Chinese mission located in midtown on Thirty-first Street regularly drew large crowds two nights weekly. A twenty-two-year-old clerk at a Chinese restaurant, who had learned a fair amount of English during his three years in the United States, reported that he often visited Coney Island.[29]

Burgess was particularly impressed with the merchants he had interviewed who frequented Times Square, particularly the famous New York Hippodrome theater. Opened in 1905, the Hippodrome spanned the full length of Sixth Avenue between Forty-third and Forty-fourth streets and became known as the theater for the city's masses. With a seating capacity of 5,200 the theater provided a range of middlebrow entertainment that mixed musical, dance, and vaudevillian performances with circus acts and visual spectacles to appeal to the modern urban consumer. The extravagant use of electricity to power the thousands of lights surrounding the theater's façade and interior, and the impressive hydraulic lifts to position the fantastic scenery and costumed performers onto the stages, further heightened visitors' overall sensory experience. More importantly, the tickets set at 25¢ to $1 made the Hippodrome an indulgence that was both financially and socially accessible to working- and middle-class New Yorkers alike.[30]

Burgess reported that the Chinese merchants in his study exclaimed their "fondness of the spectacular performances" and "everyone of them had attended the Hippodrome, some of them many times." While these men had attended other New York theaters, the Hippodrome remained a consistent favorite. A fifty-year-old Chinese grocery store owner, who had lived in the United States for over thirty years and frequently traveled for business to Chicago, Pittsburgh, and St. Louis, declared "that the Hippodrome had the finest performances he had seen in New York." In another interview a forty-year-old waiter at a Chinese restaurant also proclaimed his immense appreciation and marveled at the "way in which, women, in the form of birds, beautifully adorned, flew out over the audience."[31]

The extent to which Chinese New Yorkers' participated in these more mainstream commercial leisure activities generally escaped the attention of the city's social reformers and newspaper reporters. Instead, these agents focused mostly on Chinese participation in Chinatown's commercialized vices, particularly activities such as prostitution, opium smoking, and gambling. The broad circulation of these narratives of the Chinaman's peculiar moral deviances called into question the wisdom of allowing Chinese men free mobility throughout the city. By the late nineteenth century Chinese fraternal organizations known as tongs had helped to create a working-class masculine world of commercialized underground leisure, catering to the city's predominantly Chinese male laboring population. Contemporary social reformer and newspaper accounts often illustrated vividly Chinese immigrants' participation in these illicit activities, focusing on colorful individuals such as Tom Lee, the reputed Chinese mayor of Chinatown and head of the On Leong Tong, or Mock Duck, the leader of the rival Hip Sing Tong.[32] To the dismay of this era's Progressive reformers aiming to rid both commercial vice and municipal corruption, many of these activities were not so hidden from the public but seemed to run "wide-open" in the Chinatown area. Reformers were especially disturbed by their encounters with prostitutes, who solicited inside Chinatown clubs as well as publicly on the streets.[33] One social reformer interviewed a prostitute who claimed that local policemen regularly received "protection money" ranging from $12 to $20 per woman each night, and the amount "was generally paid to wardmen or somebody deputized by the Captain or wardman to collect."[34] A 1901 report, based on the testimony of a Chinese American informant, listed a number of gambling establishments in numerous buildings along Mott and Pell Streets featuring games of chance, including fantan and lottery or policy drawings.[35] The report further charged that the gambling houses also commonly paid $15 per month to the police for "protection" and Tom Lee was the intermediary.

Opportunities for Chinese laborers to engage in commercial vice were not confined to the Chinatown area, as some also sought out similar offerings in white-owned establishments in other parts of the city. An investigator for the Committee of Fourteen making his nightly rounds in 1913, for example, witnessed a prostitute's hearty greeting to two Chinese men when they entered Sharkey's, a nightclub on Fourteenth Street. The men appeared to be the prostitute's regular clients and were also well known among the club's wait staff and performers. The investigator noted that the Chinese patrons quickly threw themselves into the activities of the club by leaping onto the stage following an invitation by the piano player to join him in his performance.[36]

While investigators found ample evidence of similar vice activities patronized by other New Yorkers throughout the city, this awareness did not lead them to denaturalize the connection between Chinese immigrants and social deviance. Chinatown's status as a vice district, where activities such as opium smoking, prostitution, and gambling were often visible, informed the public's perception of Chinese immigrants as a distinct racial group marked by a peculiar set of social and moral deviances that stood them apart from other New Yorkers. A journalist writing in 1893, for example, pronounced that discussions of Chinatown opium joints were greatly exaggerated, but also affirmed that "[t]wo vices are characteristic of the Chinaman—opium and gambling."[37] Louis Beck, though acknowledging that by 1898 opium consumption could be found among numerous New Yorkers living throughout the city, argued that the practice in Chinatown had special significance: "Chinatown is responsible for the introduction of the awful practice into this community, and as it is more openly, and perhaps more systematically, carried on there, and particularly as it is a prominent feature of daily life in Chinatown, we naturally look there for its practical illustration."[38]

This constant linking of Chinese immigrants with the Chinatown vice district and its specific array of socially deviant activities meant that Chinese attempting to establish businesses outside of the Chinatown area were often not welcomed. Long before the Sigel murder the city's social reformers and policemen often suspected that "chop suey" restaurants providing inexpensive fare to predominantly non-Chinese customers were disorderly places that promoted prostitution or opium smoking. Social reformers' concerns with these sites were augmented by the added possibility for race mixing they believed these places and vice activities facilitated. Often staying open late into the night, such restaurants were part of a citywide commercial nightlife that had emerged by the end of the nineteenth century.[39] A 1901 report by Committee of Fifteen investigator W. C. Steele Jr. identified 568 Seventh Avenue as a "chop suey restaurant full of Negro and white prost[itutes] soliciting."[40] Steele claimed further that the rooms located above the restaurant were used by prostitutes. In 1905 a restaurant at 94 Third Avenue, owned and managed by Yon Hopp, also became the target of investigation. According to a report filed on the premises the establishment was a "typical Chinese restaurant" and did not sell liquor on the premises. However, the investigator charged that opium was available for purchase and warned that there was "[a]fter twelve not a decent person there."[41]

On occasion social reformers acted on information supplied by Chinese and non-Chinese informants. According to a 1901 report filed by Quan Yick Nam, who occasionally worked as a police interpreter, a cigar store located on Seventh Avenue between Thirty-second and Forty-first streets was operated by Li Quen Chong, who also went by the name of "Boston," the reputed "King of Opium Joints in New York."[42] In 1911 S. Robinson complained to the Committee of Fourteen of deplorable moral and social conditions in Harlem in the hopes of prompting an investigation. A "chop suey joint" situated on the corner of Eighth Avenue and 125th Street appeared among his list of "the most popular resort places after midnight" and "ha[d] small rooms and much disorderly conduct."[43]

The concern with Chinese establishments was not limited to places of commercial leisure such as "chop suey" restaurants. Police and social reformers routinely targeted many Chinese-owned businesses out of the same concerns that they harbored Chinatown vices such as opium dens or prostitution.[44] In 1901 J. H. Brown, an investigator for the Committee of Fifteen, examined several businesses owned by Chinese immigrants including one cigar store and several hand laundries in his search for prostitution in midtown Manhattan's west side. However, Brown did not report seeing any evidence of disorderly activities in the buildings he visited.[45] A 1912 Committee of Fourteen report on houses of prostitution, for

Figure 2.1 A typical "chop suey" joint found in New York City at the turn of the century. The lack of "Oriental" ornamentation in both the restaurant's interior decor and the Chinese workers' dress suggests that these more modest establishments did not necessarily aim to evoke the same exotic atmosphere as the more upscale Chinatown tourist restaurants. Instead they resembled similarly small-scale eateries found throughout the city. *Source*: William Brown Meloney, "Slumming in New York's Chinatown," *Munsey's Magazine* 41 (September 1909): 825. Courtesy of Yale University Library.

example, charged Li He Laundry at 200 West Twenty-eighth Street with selling opium.[46]

Even more common than "chop suey" restaurants, Chinese-operated hand laundries could be readily found throughout the city. Between 1880 and 1890 the number of Chinese-owned laundries had increased seven-fold to 819, and comprised nearly 70 percent of the city's total number of laundries.[47] In 1897 the *Trow Business Directory of New York City* listed roughly 1,000 Chinese-owned laundries throughout the city under the separate heading of "Chinese Laundry."[48] The method employed to categorize laundries in the city directory also suggests that the general public recognized Chinese-owned laundries as a separate institution marked by the racial distinctiveness of its owners and employees. Unlike the listing of a non-Chinese owned laundry, that displayed either the name of the business or proprietor along with the location, an entry under the "Chinese Laundry" category showed only the address, suggesting the sameness or interchangeability of all Chinese-owned laundries.

The wide geographical dispersion throughout New York's residential neighborhoods made the commonplace laundry even more of a concern than the fewer numbers of "chop suey" restaurants. Whereas the latter tended to be situated in commercial areas and were linked with an urban nightlife that courted a more rough, working-class clientele, laundries provided a practical service employed by many city residents, from working-class to middle-class to white-collar workers in the growing corporate sector.[49] Police and social reformers worried about the proximity of these businesses to the neighborhood's white residents out of the fear these neighborhood Chinese laundries also brought with them the immorality and vices associated with Chinatown. The proliferation of laundries throughout the city threatened to upset the neat urban moral geography of "darkness and daylight" that separated the city's poor and working-class tenement districts from the reputable residential areas of the middle and upper classes.

*↳ laundries as centers for - the spread
community + residencies + businesses = spread
of of chinese = vice*

A THREAT TO THE CITY'S WOMEN AND CHILDREN

Although laundry work along with most domestic labor was popularly viewed as "women's work," the Chinese hand laundry space was not necessarily seen as feminized or domesticated. Mostly inhabited and operated by single, Chinese male laborers, police and social reformers also viewed the Chinese hand laundry—similar to Chinatown—as a sexually deviant, bachelor, or masculine space. The Chinese laundry represented, in effect, a netherworld that was masculinized and feminized, and therefore must be defined and confined to prevent corrupting the inhabitants of the surrounding neighborhood. The seemingly chaotic mix of work and residential spaces that blurred the boundary between public and private went against both Victorian and Progressive middle-class standards of moral propriety and public hygiene and accentuated the lack of female domesticity and respectability. Social reformers feared that the Chinese hand laundry, inhabited by such a group of sexually repressed and ambiguously gendered workers, posed a serious danger to the general population, particularly the city's women and children. But as a domestic-related service, laundries were more likely to be frequented by women. Usually located on the street or at the basement level, laundries were also easily accessible to all passers-by, including children. As social reformers and law enforcement officials called attention to the need for regulating women and children's access to Chinese-owned businesses, the Chinese hand laundry as a public moral and sexual menace came to be a recognized racial and gendered trope as familiar as Chinatown in law, popular literature, and film.

gender + laundry

The New York Society for the Prevention of Cruelty to Children (NYSPCC), incorporated in 1875, paid close attention to the city's Chinese-owned businesses and warned the public against allowing children, especially young girls, to visit such establishments. The charge that Chinese men inveigled the city's children was familiar to turn-of-the-century New Yorkers. In the 1880s, accusations that Chinese used opium-laced candy to entice Irish and Italian immigrant children had already circulated in lower Manhattan.[50] As Chinese immigrants set up laundries throughout the city, such stories of inveiglement often followed them. The NYSPCC 1892 annual report charged "Nearly every Chinese laundry in our midst is a sink-hole of vice and depravity, it is not-safe to allow a child to enter one, even on a most simple errand. This conclusion is reached after an experience so vast and varied that there can be no doubt as to the diabolical measures taken by these wretches to ensnare and then ruin our beloved ones."[51] The NYSPCC took an active role in bringing cases involving Chinese laundry workers and teenage girls to the attention of the police and court. In 1886 a neighborhood resident notified the NYSPCC that a number of young girls regularly visited a laundry owned by Sam Lee at 146 Columbia Street. An NYSPCC officer was assigned to observe the laundry and ascertain the girls' names. The stakeout resulted in Lee's arrest and a prison sentence of ten months.[52]

In an 1892 case the NYSPCC suspected that William Sam, who worked in a laundry at 1614 First Avenue, had "induced three school children, named J—— B——, R—— N—— and R—— W——, aged twelve, fourteen and thirteen years respectively, to enter his rooms and there used them for immoral purposes." The NYSPCC presented enough evidence to secure a conviction against William Sam, but the case did not finish there. The girls, it appeared, had visited the laundry on more than one occasion. The report accused him of using "money, Chinese nuts, handkerchiefs, etc." to inveigle the children into the laundry. The court decided to also commit the children to reform institutions, "where better influences and more watchful eyes will guide them to discern right from wrong, and teach them to become good women." Not only was the Chinese laundry worker punished, the young female victims were also seen as equally in need of both protection and proper discipline to guard against the temptation such material goods offered.[53]

Even in situations where white witnesses supported the defendant's claim of innocence, it was difficult to overcome the well established image of laundries and Chinese workers as threats to the city's children. In 1898 fifty-one-year-old laundry owner, Sing Lee, faced charges of indecent exposure. According to the testimony of ten-year-old Hannah Gallagher and eight-year-old Mary Doyle, on September 9, 1897 Sing

Lee called them into his shop, located at 276 First Avenue, and exposed his private parts to them. The children, who came from Irish American working-class families from the neighborhood, recounted the story to their respective mothers. That evening the two girls returned with their older married sisters to the laundry to confront Sing Lee. By the time the neighborhood beat officer, Thomas J. Gleason, arrived on the scene, a large, menacing crowd had gathered in front of the laundry. After speaking with Mrs. Tennant, the sister of Hannah Gallagher, he arrested Sing Lee, whose limited English-speaking ability prevented him from defending the charges made against him.[54]

At the trial Sing Lee presented his side of the story through an interpreter, Reverend Jin Fuey Moy of the Morning Star Mission. Under questioning he denied doing anything improper and countered that the children "came often to the store to bother me for nuts, and I chased them out." Sing Lee also provided a lengthy description of the general layout of his store, which was located in the basement of the building at "four steps down from the street," making clear that all activity taking place in the store could be easily seen by anyone passing by on the sidewalk. Sing Lee, who had opened the First Avenue laundry only a few weeks before the incident, had operated another laundry on Seventeenth Street. As a result he was familiar to several people in the neighborhood, including the arresting officer. A few of his neighbors came to his defense at trial. Mary Joyce, the housekeeper for the building, corroborated his claim that the children had pestered him that day. "I was sitting right in front of the Chinaman's store on the stoop," Joyce testified, "and I could see the little girls in the place. I saw the little girls all the time while they were in the store and I swear positively that nothing improperly occurred." She added further that Sing Lee was well liked in the neighborhood, stating "his character has always been good." In addition to Joyce, Sing Lee also relied on other European immigrant laborers from the neighborhood as character witnesses: Myer E. Heller, an umbrella maker who also resided at 276 First Avenue, and Earnest Mugiani, a driver who worked for a Chinatown grocery store delivering goods to Chinese-owned businesses in the city. Heller not only testified that he had "never heard anything wrong about him," but added that he had seven children, including two girls, who "frequently go into the Chinaman's place." Even with the testimony of these witnesses the jury returned a guilty verdict, convicting Sing Lee of indecent exposure.

Despite the widespread concern that Chinese men were potentially immoral and presented physical threats to women and children, cases of rape and abduction brought to court did not automatically result in convictions. In 1898 Ling Ong, a laundry worker, was indicted for perpetrating acts of sodomy against two eleven-year-old-boys. The East Broadway laundry was located in a building adjacent to a store owned by the uncle

of one of the children. According to the boys' testimony, they were playing in front of the store when Ling Ong invited them into the laundry. He
then allegedly performed acts of sodomy and gave the boys ten cents each.
At the trial's conclusion, however, Ling Ong was acquitted of both
charges.[55] In 1905 NYSPCC agent Vincent Pisarra attempted to build a
case against Sam Sing, a thirty-two-year-old laundry worker.[56] At the time
of his arrest in May, Sing had resided at 493 Tenth Avenue for nineteen
months. Pisarra charged that Sing committed two separate crimes and alleged that in April he abducted and had sexual relations with a minor,
fourteen-year-old Dora Bagatell. Pisarra further claimed that the following
month Sing abducted another minor, fourteen-year-old Mamie Vogel, for
the purposes of committing sexual intercourse. The two girls, however,
failed to make affidavits. The only affidavit was filed by Pisarra, who
claimed that the two teenage girls had informed him of the crimes. The
charges were later dismissed because of the lack of witnesses. In 1907 a
Chinese man accidentally bumped into a girl on a crowded city street. Her
screams of "lynch him" alerted the crowd and resulted in the man's arrest
for disorderly conduct. He was later discharged by the magistrate.[57]

Acquittals, however, did little to alleviate the racialized fear of the lust-
ful Chinese laundry worker who ensnared small children throughout the
city. In a 1914 case, for example, Judge William Wadhams, upon sentenc-
ing a Chinese laundryman accused of raping a teenage girl, connected this
individual case to what he perceived to be a more widespread and growing problem. While announcing his decision to hand down the maximum
sentence of five to ten years imprisonment in a state prison, the judge
voiced his hope that the sentence would help to "save our girls."[58]

The notion that Chinese-owned laundries posed moral and sexual
threats to women and young children was also reinforced in popular
cultural depictions such as Mary Heaton Vorse's 1908 short story,
"Mrs. McClanahan, the Chinese Laundry, and Beller." The story's main
character, Mrs. McClanahan, is the owner of a small dressmaking shop situated in the working-class section of Greenwich Village who must confront
the moral threat posed by the loathsome Chinese laundry in the basement
of her building. Vorse makes clear that the laundry's location in her building threatens the hard-earned respectability of this proud Irish American
tradeswoman and the shop's other female workers. She writes that although Mrs. McClanahan becomes "kind o' sick to think o' all them
Chinymen all doped right under our feet," the proprietress does not want
to jeopardize her own respectability by becoming involved with the police
and consequently being publicly associated with an opium joint. On the
suggestion that Mrs. McClanahan report the laundry to the police, she exclaims, "It'd look nice in the papers, wouldn't it, that Mrs. McClanahan's
place was over a dope-joint? It'd be good for business to have the *po*-lice

and reporters running in, an' me testifying in court."[59] Mrs. McClanahan never comes into direct contact with the Chinese workers, but catches whiffs of opium being smoked and hears rumors from others in the neighborhood that the place basically serves as an "opium joint." Vorse injects additional rumors that "colored boys" also went to the laundry to suggest that the Chinese laundry facilitated even further questionable race mixing.

The story's turning point comes when Mrs. McClanahan's concern with the welfare of Beller, a precocious girl from the neighborhood, hardens her resolve to have the laundry removed from the building. Vorse portrays the shop's female workers as matronly moral guardians of the neighborhood who fear that Beller, a young girl fast-approaching thirteen, could be led morally astray by either Dave, "a big negro lad" in the neighborhood, or the Chinese laundrymen and their opium joint. After discovering that Beller had been secretly visiting the laundry to catch glimpses of the Chinese men "lyin' around all doped," Mrs. McClanahan hatches a scheme to remove the offending laundry without implicating herself. The story concludes with the laundry's successful eviction and its racialized moral threat against the vulnerable Beller safely averted.

The rise of the American film industry in the late nineteenth century provided additional visual narratives to reinforce the popular notion of Chinese laundries as a conduit for Chinatown vice and sexual impropriety. Films such as *In a Chinese Laundry*, released in 1897, and *New Chinese Laundry*, produced in 1903, played on the familiar image of the lecherous Chinese laundry worker plotting his sexual advances toward the young, white female customer.[60] The vulgar actions and manners of these "Chinamen," drawing upon Vaudeville conventions of racial performances with exaggerated accented speech and slapstick humor, more likely provoked laughter than fear. Other films, however, employed these same recognizable racial tropes to more dramatic effect.

Similar to Birth of a nation

Early silent productions such as *The Heathen Chinese and the Sunday School Teachers*, completed in 1904, drew upon this familiar image of the Chinese hand laundry to foreshadow the impending Chinese male sexual and moral threat to the film's white female characters. In the opening sequence a white working-class female customer enters to pick up her laundry. The Chinese laundrymen, portrayed by white actors in a typical "yellowface" performance, stop working to retrieve her bundles.[61] To pay for her laundry the woman needs to retrieve her emergency reserve of cash hidden in her stocking. She gestures to the "Chinese man" to look away and waits for him to do so before reaching for her money. The audience catches him sneaking a peak at the woman's leg when she hoists her skirt to reach for the money. Because the camera remains fixed upon this risqué image of the woman's stockinged leg, the audience is forced to be a fellow participant in this "Chinaman's" voyeuristic act.[62]

The hidden dangers of this seemingly typical Chinese hand laundry are revealed in the scene that takes place in a shabbily outfitted "opium den" concealed in the basement of the laundry. As the scene unfolds the audience sees a group of Chinese men lying in semiconscious state on makeshift platforms in the basement den. Meanwhile another Chinese man, sitting on a stool next to the door, acts as the sentry. Two missionary women from a previous scene enter with their two students, the laundry workers. The women quickly become curious and are soon unbuttoning their jackets and lying down on the platforms to smoke the pipe. The image fades and then reemerges to reveal the opium den a few hours later. The women, all white, appear to be disheveled and in a state of undress as they continue to puff on their pipes. The opium den scene ends with the police bursting through the door, rousing and dragging the Chinese men out. The missionaries, fully awake and sober, confront their temporary moral decline; they demonstrate their guilt and self-reproach by sobbing and shielding their unkempt faces with their hands. Only with the timely intervention of the police is the women's descent into immorality safely halted.

Such plots, where respectable white women are tricked into entering opium "joints" run by Chinese men, were fairly familiar to this period's filmgoers. The 1900 film *A Raid on a Chinese Opium Joint* depicts a "Chinaman" luring a white girl to an opium den and then convincing her to take up the habit. In a 1915 film, *Secret Sin,* the theme of female opium addiction is repeated with a white working-class victim. Grace, a young garment worker, inadvertently becomes an addict after trying to come to the aid of her financially strapped family. After a long day at the sewing machine, Grace accepts an addict's request that she go to a Chinese opium den to bring him more of the drug. The proprietor, who is played by the well-known Japanese actor Sessue Hayakawa, convinces her to take a hit from the pipe before leaving the premises. Curious, she takes a smoke and is hooked after her "first taste" and quickly descends into the life of an addict.[63] The specifically gendered narratives of these popular films, portraying the ease with which young, innocent white females could be lured into opium smoking, drew upon the same gendered constructions of Chinatown as a danger to white womanhood. Allowing places such as Chinese-owned laundries or restaurants—physical extensions of Chinatown—to proliferate unmonitored would destroy the moral health of the city.

For Chinese immigrants attempting to scratch out a living in turn-of-the-century New York, these gendered and racialized spatial and social boundaries were palpable. Although many "bachelor" laborers were able to set up laundries and restaurants outside of the Chinatown area, their non-Chinese neighbors, who were often more familiar with these cultural representations of Chinese men and Chinatowns as conduits of vice than real life Chinese workers, viewed their presence with suspicion. Seen as a potentially immoral force, police and neighbors vigilantly monitored the activities in these Chinese establishments. Yet male Chinese laundry workers living and working outside of Chinatown did not necessarily experience lives of social isolation; the Chinese hand laundry or chop suey restaurant was hardly separate and cutoff from the city's streets. These Chinese-owned businesses, as sites of cultural, social, and economic exchange, became an important part of urban neighborhood street life.[64] Even as residential neighborhoods marked by ethnicity, class, and race had emerged by the latter half of the nineteenth century, the cases appearing in the city's courts suggest that New York's streets continued to hold open possibilities for varying forms of social interaction among men, women, and children of different socioeconomic classes and ethnic and racial groups. As a result geographical, racial and gender boundaries could be renegotiated in these daily contacts between Chinese proprietors and workers and their non-Chinese neighbors. Often the city's writers, social reformers, police, and judicial system intervened in such encounters, formalizing what were once loosely configured spatial and social arrangements. Even more than any film or routine police raid, the real-life murder of Elsie Sigel reminded the public of the importance of scrutinizing closely Chinese-owned places of business and residence such as those located at the murder site at 782 Eighth Avenue.

Inside Leon Ling's Lair

Chinatown, Jacob Riis alleged, was not unlike a spider's web. Any of the Chinese-owned laundries, cigar stores, and restaurants, he claimed, could be "one of the hundred outposts of Chinatown that are scattered all over the city, as the outer threads of the spider's web that holds its prey fast."[65] Accounts of the Sigel murder readily drew upon and reaffirmed these cultural constructions of the workplaces and residences of Chinese immigrants as self-contained satellite settlements of Chinatown, and not part of the larger metropolis. Though located throughout the city, they were not seen as part of the people and cultures inhabiting those neighborhoods. The readiness of police and newspaper reporters to connect Sigel's murder to Chinatown points to the degree that this perception was held by the general public.

Journalists frequently reported that messages between Chinese in Chinatown and those residing throughout the Greater New York area, also including Long Island and northern New Jersey, were delivered with great rapidity through an unseen and mysterious communications network. Journalists reported to their readers that these messages sent outside of the proper post office channels contained secret correspondences conspiring against the city's police and residents, suggesting that these secret modes of travel and communication had allowed Leon Ling to successfully elude the police for so long. By implication these descriptions also suggested that the city's Chinese not only traveled within their own community undetected but that the entire city and country was also at their disposal. Such depictions drew and expanded upon the many contemporary rumors and popular depictions of secret networks of subterranean tunnels hidden beneath Chinatown that allowed Chinese residents to roam the city unseen and unobstructed.[66] These stories of secret tunnel networks helped to restore an urban moral geography, that had been disrupted by the growing presence of Chinese businesses in neighborhoods throughout the city, by reaffirming the division between the city's neighborhoods into areas of "darkness and daylight." Rather than suggesting Chinese hand laundries could become a part of the "daylight" neighborhoods of the white middle and upper classes, the insistence that the Chinese inhabited subterranean tunnels and their workplaces remained linked to the Chinatown vice district perpetually associated them with "darkness."

Descriptions of the crime scene at 782 Eighth Avenue severed the Chinese restaurant and apartments from the surrounding neighborhoods of Times Square and the Tenderloin district. Generally ignoring the building's non-Chinese tenants, including a bicycle store and storage facility, journalists described the furnishings of the suspect's apartment in the same racialized language used to describe Chinatown. The *World* described the rooms as "miserable and tawdry a picture of Mongolian life in an American city as could be imagined. Everywhere were the indications of the usual Chinatown den, but raised to the slightly higher place of an Eighth avenue tenement house top floor."[67] These descriptions transformed the Eighth Avenue flat into a physical extension of Chinatown itself, collapsing the distance between these two different parts of the city.

A *New York Herald* description of the rooms also showed its gendering as an overtly masculine space in the same manner as Chinatown. "All these rooms were decorated more or less gaudily in the Chinese fashion. They were hung with placards bearing Chinese inscriptions and the walls were covered with pictures, mostly photographs of white women. Some of these pictures had been cut from magazines, but the majority had undoubtedly been obtained from the owner."[68] Its absence of familiar markers of domesticity made clear that the room was specifically inhabited by that particularly feared and loathed class—the bachelor Chinese laborer. Not only did Leon Ling appear to have a peculiar fascination for white women, as shown by the collection of photographs, but the author suggested further that these women were victims ensnared in his web whose photographs he proudly displayed like trophies on a wall.

The descriptions of personal objects found in Leon Ling's room continued to fit this narrative of racial masquerade and seduction.

> Over on the window sill was a little box of rouge powder in a Chinese box with a little mirror over it. Contrasted with it the picture of the Virgin and Child hanging over the dresser in the room where the trunk was found told an equally legible story of cant and imposture. More characteristic of such a place, though not less eloquent of the occupants, were the numerous vases in hideous forms of devils and evil gods, and cheap, highly colored pictures of other Chinese fancies.[69]

The quote illustrates the dichotomy between truth and artifice in Leon Ling's character as reflected by his apartment's furnishings. Anything suggesting American acculturation or Christian conversion was immediately described as an object of masquerade—"cant and imposture"—used by Leon Ling or William Leon to fool good intentioned but gullible white middle-class Americans. The seemingly "Chinese" objects, however, were said to signify his real self as representing the "heathen Chinee."[70] Similar to the pictures of women hung on the wall, Elsie Sigel was another unfortunate who had been completely fooled by his disguise as a pious Christian convert. By going to Leon Ling's room she had crossed over clearly delineated spatial, racial, and gender boundaries and thus sealed her own fate.

These popular depictions of New York City's Chinatown and the Chinese American population at large fostered the image of Chinatowns and other Asian ethnic communities as impenetrable enclaves or colonies. The physical presence of these colonies, in the form of Chinatowns or similarly defined ethnic enclaves in the urban landscape, served as reminders to white New Yorkers that Chinese immigrants remained foreign in their habits. Simply put, as a group they had failed to assimilate. Although the building at 782 Eighth Avenue also housed non-Chinese owned businesses and tenants, police and reporters mostly focused on the "chop suey" restaurant and the rooms occupied by Sun Leung and the two Chinese suspects. While each Chinese person encountered in the vicinity of the restaurant was immediately under suspicion for knowing something about the murder—as shown by the quick arrests of the Chinese found in the restaurant and building—all non-Chinese were depicted as completely ignorant of the building's goings-on and completely hoodwinked by the Chinese residents. The restaurant, similar to Chinatown itself, was in New York but not of it.

CONTAINING THE MALE CHINESE SEXUAL MENACE IN URBAN AMERICA

One week following the discovery of the Sigel murder, police witnessed eighteen-year-old Florence Rhoades enter the side entrance of Ton Yoh's laundry at 518 Myrtle Avenue in Brooklyn. Heightened concerns with racial and sexual trespassing spurred police to apprehend the pair. News of the arrest quickly spread throughout the neighborhood and a crowd of onlookers gathered inside the court room for the arraignment. The magistrate placed Rhodes under the custody of Mrs. L. E. Taylor, a probationary officer, to be taken to a home until the court date. Ton Yoh, however, was held on $500 bail on the charge of disorderly conduct. When police led Ton Yoh away from the courthouse, he came face-to-face with an even larger unruly throng that had gathered along both sides of the street. He "evidently feared mob vengeance, for he ran as if for dear life as he passed from the court room to the van."[71]

With emotions running high Chinese elites acted swiftly to ensure that the attention from the Sigel murder would not provoke already angry whites to commit violence or justify further lobbying for increased Chinese immigration restrictions. Business owners also took extra precautions to ensure that the behavior of their employees would not be misconstrued to heighten racial tensions. In Washington, D.C., newspapers reported seeing signs in Chinese posted in laundries that warned workers to limit severely their interactions with white female customers, restricting conversations to "yea, yea, and nay" and for "business" purposes only.[72] Similarly worded posters were also reportedly seen in Chinese-owned laundries in Newark, New Jersey.[73] As the circulation of these notices makes clear the Sigel murder impacted all types of social interactions between Chinese men and white women.

Reporters argued that laundry owners posted these placards to curb improper behavior on the part of Chinese laundry workers toward white women, ignoring the more likely explanation that owners used them as part of a larger defensive strategy to protect themselves from backlash. The operation of a laundry facilitated the interaction between Chinese male workers and white female customers within the same space. Laundry owners most likely feared the misunderstanding and anger of whites as much as, if not more so, than any improper behavior on the part of their own workers. By regulating and restricting contact between Chinese male workers and white female customers laundry owners tried to protect their businesses as well as their workers from the hostile retaliation of local whites, who might attack Chinese-owned establishments in the name of protecting white womanhood. With the constant reporting of police raids on Chinese businesses and homes in efforts to locate the missing murder suspect, Leon Ling, Chinese owners were probably warranted in fearing that their businesses could become the targets of mob violence or heavy police surveillance.

Similar concerns surrounding "chop suey" restaurants were also voiced in other eastern cities with substantial Chinese immigrant populations. The need to maintain strict racial and gender boundaries in Chinese establishments again figured prominently in these complaints. In 1910, under the cry of maintaining "public order, decency and morality," the Massachusetts State Legislature attempted to introduce a bill that would prevent females under the age of twenty-one from entering a hotel or restaurant conducted by a Chinese proprietor.[74] During the Sigel murder investigation a year earlier a twenty-five-year-old Chinese man named Yee Kin Wah was arrested by Boston area police upon the mistaken belief that he was connected to the case. While investigating his alibi that he was in Manchester, New Hampshire at the time of the murder, police learned of the reason for his recent arrival in Massachusetts. According to newspaper accounts he had been working at his brother's restaurant in Manchester until he was arrested on the complaint that he had kissed a young white female customer twice while she was waiting for her order. Whether or not this was an actual case of assault remains unclear because he was shortly released and dismissed of all charges. As a precaution, however, Yee Kin Wah's brother advised him to leave town immediately, and he quickly made his way to the Boston area.[75]

Such rumors of Chinese male sexual assault coupled with the widespread publicity around the Sigel murder fueled local fears that these Chinese restaurants posed potential physical and sexual dangers to respectable white women. The following March the Massachusetts Legislature asked the opinion of the state Supreme Judicial Court whether or not it was "within the constitutional power of the Legislature" to enact a law that would inhibit the movement of young women into a hotel or restaurant owned by a person of Chinese descent. The court, citing the Fourteenth Amendment and its application in several cases, including *Powell v. Pennsylvania* and *Yick Wo v. Hopkins*, made clear in their opinion that such a law would be "a harmful discrimination of persons of the proscribed class, founded wholly upon their race and nationality" and thus would deprive them of equal legal protection under the law.[76] Casting further doubt on the ability of such a law to promote "public order, decency and morality," the court noted that the legislation was not aimed at the prevention of "real evils" or any actual offense and failed to take into account the actual conditions of an establishment. Following the logic of the legislation the court charged that "it forbids the entry of a young woman into the hotel or restaurant of a Chinese proprietor, even if it is a model of orderly and moral management, and it permits the entry of young women into a hotel or restaurant kept by an American, when it is known to be maintained in part for the promotion of immoral or criminal practices."[77] With such an unambiguous opinion, the Supreme Judicial Court of Massachusetts took the position that it would not uphold such a law if passed by the state legislature. If the maintenance of racial and gender boundaries in public areas, for example restaurants, could not be achieved through legislation, other types of policing such as periodic surveillance and raids needed to remain in operation.

The policing of social and sexual activities of Chinese immigrants in New York City as well as other Northeastern cities was certainly not limited to geographically bounded, identifiable sex/vice districts such as Chinatown but crossed into workplaces and private residences. Official and informal surveillance of sexual and leisure activities regarding the city's Chinese population ventured beyond the usual suspects of commercial leisure institutions, such as dance halls or Raines law hotels, and into private and commercial spaces such as the neighborhood Chinese hand laundry. The popular fear that these men and the places they inhabited were hidden conduits for social and moral deviance—such as opium addiction or interracial sex—followed Chinese men regardless of where they chose to live or work. The constant movement and settlement of Chinese workers throughout the city disrupted the city's racial geography by creating new sites of interracial contact that consistently vexed police and neighbors.

Such concerns can be discerned from Nelson Harding's cartoon, "Converted," published in the *Brooklyn Daily Eagle* a week after the Sigel murder.[78] The cartoon exposes the interior of the ubiquitous neighborhood Chinese laundry, normally hidden from public view. A white missionary woman has left behind a missionary tract on top of the counter for the worker to read, a fruitless and naïve endeavor as suggested by Harding's sketch. Lurking behind the laundry counter are the various objects that signify the vices associated with Chinatown; a curled piece of rope and bloody dagger conjure up tales of tong violence, while a box of raw opium and lit pipe evoke horrifying images of drug addiction. To complete the message Harding even includes cards and lottery tickets as reminders of the "Chinaman's" other moral weakness—gambling. The demonic grin of the "Chinaman" leering after the recently departed white female missionary suggests that she could very well turn up as his next victim.

Such cartoons also make clear that the problem with containing Chinese male mobility was not merely about policing the movements and actions of Chinese workers in the city. As seen in the case of the Massachusetts State Legislature's attempt to exclude women from Chinese establishments, the mobility of urban white female populations presented

CONVERTED !

Figure 2.2 This cartoon appearing after the Elsie Sigel murder questioned Chinese missionary work by warning of the hidden dangers lurking in the many Chinese hand laundries established throughout the city. *Source*: "Converted!" *Brooklyn Daily Eagle*, June 25, 1909.

an equally vexing problem. Even if Chinese male laborers could be limited to the Chinatown area or to the city's Chinese laundries and restaurants, the question of how to police the actions of the white female population who also ventured into these places remained unresolved. At the same time that the Massachusetts Legislature debated the merits of banning white women from Chinese establishments it was also considering other bills to curtail women's access to commercialized vices, by enacting an ordinance "to prohibit the sale of liquor to women in saloons."[79] Indeed, how to deal with these overlapping geographies of the city's Chinese male and white female populations became the central question arising from the Sigel murder.

The image of Elsie Sigel's body locked inside Leon Ling's trunk only further alerted New Yorkers to the dangerous consequences of unchecked female mobility that eschewed the need for masculine protection. New Yorkers became convinced that the city's white female population, whether as middle-class missionaries, working-class laborers, or urban consumers, were learning to traverse the city's racially and class distinct neighborhoods in ways that increasingly threatened their respectability and safety. If allowed to wander among the Chinese immigrant population, sooner or later these women would become ensnared by the tendrils of the Chinatown web. How to protect women from such immoral urban influences presented a serious challenge to the city's journalists, social reformers, and law enforcement officials. Many quickly realized that keeping the physical mobility of the female population in check also required containing the burgeoning consumer and sexual desires of this generation of urban women.

CHAPTER THREE

Policing Urban Girls' and Women's Mobility and Desires

THREE DAYS AFTER THE DISCOVERY of Elsie Sigel's body Brooklyn police took into custody three Chinese men and three young white women, ranging in age from seventeen to twenty-two, at a Chinese laundry at 146 Hoyt Street. The patrolmen, while making their tour of the neighborhood, noticed the three women visiting successively two Chinese laundries on Atlantic Avenue and then the one on Hoyt Street. As the prisoners were being led to the patrol wagon a rowdy neighborhood crowd formed, yelling "Chinks" and calling for harsh punishments to be exacted upon the Chinese men. Concerned that public agitation over the Sigel murder would foment trouble in the neighborhood the policemen decided to call for assistance in bringing the arrested men to the police station. The three Chinese men were discharged on the same day when they proved that they had committed no offense against the women.[1]

Meanwhile, two of the women were released into the custody of their mother, Caroline Bennett. Although the patrolmen arrested both the Chinese men and white women found at the laundry, the arresting officers clearly viewed the actions and motivations of these parties differently. The three women had approached these laundries seemingly of their own volition, but the Chinese men were still depicted by the police and newspaper reporters as the aggressors. The police's description of the women as fainting and weeping, while the Chinese prisoners "did not seem to worry and maintained the expressionless stolidity characteristic of their race," painted the women as victims rather than making them accountable for their decision to enter the Chinese laundries. Furthermore the police contrasted these three women with the white women residing in Chinatown, suggesting that their timely intervention may have prevented these women's fall beyond moral redemption. "Efforts will be made to find out something about the antecedents of the three girls, who were too much distressed to be able to tell much about themselves. The police believe that they belong to a class of misguided girls who associate with the Chinese, but they are young and rather better appearing than the 'white wives' of Doyers and Pell streets."[2]

Following the Sigel murder police not only monitored the behavior of the Chinese men who labored and lived in the city, they were equally concerned with the activities of white women and girls who entered Chinese-owned establishments. In both cases it was the physical mobility of white teenage girls and young women that particularly caught the attention of the city's policemen and prompted the raids on these Chinese-owned businesses. What was perhaps most troubling to police and the public at large about this and other similar cases was that these teenage girls and young women had entered the premises of their own free will. In effect their desire to enter these Chinese-owned establishments suggested that they could not be easily described as victims who had been lured by opium or tricked by sinister Chinese men. These stories appearing after the Sigel murder suggest a more complicated set of motives on the part of these girls and women to seek out Chinese men and a more complex history of Chinese-white sexual relations in New York City. The city's journalists, police, and social reformers at the turn-of-the-century were disturbed by these overt expressions of female desire and sexuality on the part of these young working-class girls and women, whom they deemed to be social and sexual delinquents. They quickly realized that the policing of Chinese men and the residential and work spaces they occupied, such as restaurants, laundries, and the Chinatown neighborhood, was inadequate. They also needed to contain simultaneously white working-class female sexuality by specifically restraining physical mobility in the city and curtailing any inappropriate sexual and consumer desires.

RACIAL PURITY AND NATIONAL STRUGGLE: EXAMINING THE RAPE/ABDUCTION NARRATIVE

Established narratives of Chinese and white sexual relations had circulated prior to the Sigel murder through various forms of nineteenth-century popular culture: penny press, dime novels, magazine and newspaper articles, plays, social reformers' reports, and tourist guidebooks to name just a few. These accounts typically were less concerned with trying to depict the real lives of these couples than to render exotic or sensational portrayals of life in Chinatown. For example the 1905 play *A Night in Chinatown*, by Walter Campbell, hardly representative of Chinese-white relationships, nonetheless provides a window into popular turn-of-the-century notions of Chinese male and white female morality and sexuality.

Mildred Claire, the heroine, appears to be a poor but generous young woman who is struggling to survive on her paltry earnings from her flower stand on Chinatown's Mott Street. Early in the play Antonio Gonzales, a Spaniard and one of the chief villains, learns that Mildred is actually an heiress whose parents had died when she was very young.

With the recent death of her grandfather, Mildred has become the sole heir of his estate. Gonzales, hoping to steal her wealth, decides to woo Mildred in the hopes of marrying her. When she refuses Gonzales resorts to underhanded tactics and orders his business partner, Moy Key, "a Chinese highbinder," to kidnap Mildred and bring her to his opium den. There, Gonzales plans to have Crazy Kate, a white "opium fiend," take away Mildred's street clothes and have Mildred adorned in a fine Chinese silk dress. Once ensconced in these sensuous "Oriental" surroundings Gonzales hopes that she will be seduced by these luxuries and succumb to opium consumption, losing all sense of self-control and rational judgment, and yield to his requests to be his wife. Moy Key agrees to carry out the plan but is secretly in love with Mildred and wants her for himself. Early in the play he demonstrates his love for Mildred by occasionally leaving anonymous envelopes of cash at her flower stand. Mildred, however, is in love with Jack Rivers, a sailor, and chooses to wait for his return from sea. Gonzales and Moy Key carry out the kidnapping but Jack Rivers returns to the city in the nick of time. With some help from Mamie, a Chinatown "tough girl" who is herself an opium addict, and Barney Brogan, a policeman of Irish ancestry, Rivers rescues Mildred from the clutches of Gonzales and Moy Key. At the play's end Barney Brogan proposes to Mamie, who agrees to give up her opium smoking and Chinatown life to marry him. Through her future marriage to Brogan, Mamie envisions her new self as a "real high toned loidy doin' me washin' Monday, me ironin' Tuesday, gettin' me husband's dinners— and rushin' de growler every evening, just like all de swell people do in Harlem."[3] The play also concludes happily for Mildred, who eventually learns of her inheritance and decides to marry Jack.

Though the story reads like many of the period's fantastic and highly improbable dime novels, a closer look at the play may help to explain the ways in which Chinese-white sexual relations were portrayed in turn-of-the-century popular culture. The play weaves together familiar elements of period dime novel narratives—such as the waif turned heiress, and the young innocent woman facing impending sexual peril because of the absence of family and by inference patriarchal protection. The sentimentalist tradition of Victorian social reformers and romance fiction writers often employed standard narratives of "seduction" and "betrayal" to explain and pardon female sexual transgression by portraying these girls and women as victims of male sexual aggression.[4] In his analysis of nineteenth-century serialized tales of factory girls, Michael Denning argues that the "seduction/rape plot" was more about class conflict than gender and showed "heroic working-class resistance to the unwanted advances of the wealthy and powerful."[5] Mildred embodies the characteristics of the working-class heroine. She shows great pride in her abilities to operate her flower stand and voices her displeasure at receiving those anonymous envelopes of cash, which she equates with charity. When Jack Rivers proposes marriage and suggests that they move out of the city, she asserts her independence by stating that she prefers the excitement of the city over the monotony of the countryside. As an orphan, Mildred is without any familial or male protection. When confronted with the advances of Moy Key and Gonzales, she fights them off and even threatens to kill herself if Moy Key dares to approach her, thereby keeping her virginity intact.

The play, however, is not just about class or gender conflict because the issue of racial conflict, more specifically miscegenation, is critical in driving the plot. The characterization of Moy Key draws upon similar nineteenth-century depictions of Chinese men as overly libidinous, innately attracted to young white women.[6] Though Moy Key and Gonzales clearly possess more wealth than Mildred, the poor flower girl, the issue of class conflict is not clear-cut. The two villains are not her employers so they hold neither economic nor social power over her, but can only threaten her through physical intimidation—forced abduction and later rape and possible opium addiction.

The central role of Antonio Gonzales as a villain adds another dimension to the racialized sexual threat posed to Mildred. Though stories of Chinese "highbinders" were common in the nineteenth-century popular press, Spaniards in Chinatown were not. How should one account for this seemingly odd appearance of a Spanish antagonist in a play situated in Chinatown? Mildred's description of Jack Rivers, the play's hero, helps to explain Gonzales's presence as well as to reveal one of the central themes: the role of race in the building of the American nation and empire. In pronouncing her admiration for Jack, Mildred declares "he's been fighting the Philliponos [sic], and the Spainiards [sic] and the Chinese Boxers wounded him, but he got well on the voyage."[7] Written in 1901, shortly after the 1898 annexation of the Philippines in the Spanish–American War and in the midst of the U.S.–Philippine War, Campbell's casting of Gonzales along with Moy Key as the play's dastardly villains makes sense.[8] By the same token, Jack Rivers, an American sailor who served under Admiral George Dewey in the Philippines, embodies the perfect all-American hero whose manly bravado vanquishes the country's chief foreign threats: Asia and Spain. In other words, the appearances of Moy Key, Gonzales, and Rivers transform this seemingly basic dime novel seduction/abduction/rape plot to an allegory of racial conflict, national struggle, and empire expansion. By defeating both Gonzales and Moy Key to rescue Mildred, Jack Rivers simultaneously protects both white womanhood and the American nation from defilement.

The play's suspense, drawing on the threat of rape and miscegenation, hinges on Mildred's ability to thwart the advances of Moy Key until

Rivers can come to the final rescue. When Mildred refuses his proposal of marriage, she exclaims, "Let go my hand and don't you ever dare to touch me again. If you can't understand how degraded a white girl must feel at the idea of marrying a Chinaman, you at least can understand me when I tell you that I love someone else, a good, honest, man of my own race and color and whom I intend to marry."[9] The dramatic tension then is a question of whether or not Mildred can maintain her virginity and racial purity and escape from the clutches of Moy Key so that she can safely marry her American sailor, Jack Rivers.[10] Through Rivers's timely intervention the threat of miscegenation is eliminated and social order is restored, with Mildred removed from her dangerous existence on city streets and safely contained within the bounds of white heterosexual romance and marriage.

The fact that the audience is made aware at the outset that Mildred is not really a flower girl but an heiress, also works to transform her from a working-class girl of perhaps questionable virtue to a lady of upper-class respectability and noble character. This plot device also clearly separates Mildred from the other working-class female characters in the play—Crazy Kate and Mamie—whom the audience has identified as the "opium fiend" and "tough girl" respectively. To what degree these women could be seen as virtuous or morally redeemable not only depends on their chastity but their relationships to the Chinese men in the play. Despite their shared class status, the audience is meant to draw different conclusions about the moral character of Crazy Kate and Mamie. As a tough-talking, opium-smoking, and hard-drinking street urchin, Mamie's virtue is unconvincing until her final assent to wed Barney Brogan. Her marriage to Brogan, an Irish American cop of working-class origins, securely brings her back within the bounds of respectability as the wife of a workingman. Crazy Kate, however, is clearly beyond social redemption, because of opium addiction brought on by her former unhappy liaison with Gonzales and particularly due to her subsequent role as Moy Key's concubine or prostitute. Instead the conclusion emphasizes her mentally and physically broken state. She remains the play's central tragic figure, a warning against female indulgence in "oriental luxuries" and interracial sex. ⟵ *About limits of respectability for women*

VICTIM OR PREDATOR: SOCIAL CONSTRUCTIONS OF WHITE FEMALE SEXUAL DEVIANCE

New York's journalists similarly classified the city's women, distinguishing the innocent and virtuous from the depraved. In 1892 the *World* published a lengthy story on the upcoming wedding of twenty-one-year-old Fannie Eustis to Charley Woo, the owner of a cigar factory at 96 Park

Street. Eustis, whom the reporter dubbed "Fickle Fannie," was said to be wavering in her decision to marry Woo. Though clearly fond of her Chinese American beau, Eustis was also considering other possibilities: leaving Chinatown altogether, or simply continuing her life as an opium addict and staying with her other white female friends who frequented the same "hangout" on Doyers Street. The reporter noted clearly that Eustis was unlike the typical lower-class women whom nineteenth-century readers had come to expect to cohabitate with Chinese men or hang around Chinatown. Raised within a respectable middle-class family, Eustis attended a public school in Portland, Maine and later St. Catherine's Hall, a young ladies' boarding school at Augustus. By her account she experienced a strict upbringing under the protective gaze of her parents and brothers and did not dare to keep company with young men. The family may have experienced a financial decline as she became a working woman following graduation. She joined her brother at the Western Union telegraph office at Portland where she acquired the proper skills to work in a telegraph office and was later hired as a stenographer in a reputable law firm in Boston.

By contrast Fannie Eustis's cousin, Grace Gordon, whom Eustis named as the one who introduced her to Chinatown and its vices, was described by the reporter as a thirty-year-old opium fiend and occasional prostitute. The article recounted a fantastic tale of Gordon's running away at the age of fourteen and ending up on a ship by masquerading as a cabin boy for several months until the ship's crew eventually learned of her true sex. After falling in love with a Chinese steward, whom she met during her voyage, she became a resident of Chinatown. The reporter described how Gordon, "a habitue of the Chinese quarter," had visited Fannie Eustis in Portland on several occasions and "with each visit incited the girl's passions and curiosity."[11] Through her intervention Eustis took a downward moral path that eventually led to her socioeconomic decline and residence in Chinatown. If it had not been for Gordon's role in introducing Eustis to opium and facilitating her acculturation to Chinatown life, the reporter suggested, Eustis may have remained a respectable young working woman, perhaps eventually marrying and settling down to a life of genteel domesticity.

These two different portrayals of Eustis and Gordon demonstrate the ambivalence in turn-of-the-century attitudes toward women who led what were deemed socially and sexually deviant lives. If these women were indeed opium addicts or the victims of white slavery, forcibly held in Chinatown against their will, they deserved to be pitied and helped. Thus, Eustis, seen as the unwitting victim of her morally reprehensible cousin, was portrayed in comparatively sympathetic tones. Gordon, however, exemplified the potential dangers of working-class women's unrestrained sexuality and breached gender boundaries. Her gender transgressions of cross-dressing and seeking independence and romance were described as directly leading to her opium addiction and sexual promiscuity with Chinese men. Not only a danger to herself Gordon posed a grave social menace by acting as the chief agent for the downfall of young innocent white women such as Fannie Eustis. The issue of agency, therefore, largely determined whether a woman could be considered a blameless victim or a destructive force responsible for her own predicament and therefore a social menace in need of proper physical restraint and disciplinary action.

An amoral agent as potentially dangerous as the bachelor Chinese laborer, Gordon was not pitied but scorned by the public at large. Through her ability to move outside of Chinatown she was also capable of bringing immoral Chinese ways into the larger social body and infecting others like her cousin Fannie Eustis. In effect women such as Gordon were feared as much as the syphilitic prostitute, a "'sinister polluter' of the social body," who could easily transmit immorality and disease to unsuspecting families, bringing death and disruption to the urban domestic order.[12] The possibility of bearing children adds another dimension; whether or not these women engaged in these relationships freely, the biracial children they bore pointed to their role in the moral pollution and mongrelization of the white race.

The reporter also suggested that regardless of how these women came to their drug addiction and association with Chinese men no viable path of return or social redemption was available. Eustis told the reporter that she was seriously considering leaving Chinatown and had tried with some success to reduce her opium consumption. "In a week I think I'll be cured," Eustis told the reporter, "and either go back to telegraphing or get into a law office as stenographer." The reporter, however, remained unconvinced and claimed that by the end of the interview Fannie was once again thinking of marrying Charley Woo. "Fannie's five months of peculiar indulgence have wedded her to the Chinese. She will quit smoking, but she will probably never leave these people."[13] Permanently tainted by her association with the Chinese the reporter suggested that an end to her addiction would not bring about moral or social redemption. Rather, the journalist concluded that the marriage to Charley Woo posed the only viable path out of her current state of addiction and wandering in Chinatown's opium dens. Charley Woo, depicted with an American-style haircut and suit and described as "a capitalist," may have been a man of economic means who could have helped her to overcome her opium addiction. Marriage to a Chinese man, however, would not serve as the means to a full social rehabilitation that would allow her to recapture her former respectable standing and be fully accepted back into the folds of her former society.

Journalists like William Norr saw a connection specifically between the delinquent behavior of teenage girls and young women entering *(margin note, handwritten): Women earn $ + can spend it in new ways*

Chinatown and industrialization's erosion of patriarchal authority in working-class families. In the introduction to *Stories of Chinatown*, his collection of so-called real life sketches of life in the neighborhood, Norr asked "how young and comely women can cast their lot with the repulsive Chinese." He answered his own question by suggesting that the problem rested not so much with the "repulsive Chinese" as with the larger society: "[I]t speaks ill for a civilized world when a little kindness will drive our women into the arms of heathens."[14] Norr, however, did not completely dismiss the established race- and class- inflected seduction narrative in explaining the genesis of interracial relationships, because some of his stories clearly followed this same formula. While he conceded to the possibility that the women somehow exercised their agency in beginning and remaining in these relationships, his emphasis on opium addiction and the women's poor, working-class background, suggested that these relationships were mostly based on physical and economic necessity rather than real mutual affection or companionship.

In "A Chinatown Tragedy," Norr narrated the story of the moral downfall of the once virtuous Cavanagh sisters, working girls seduced by Chinese men through the lure of opium and alcohol. Norr began by describing the precarious nature of the Cavanagh home life. He painted a stereotypical nineteenth-century portrait of an Irish American, working-class family teetering on the brink of economic disaster because of the father's employment failures and alcoholic problem. Forced to seek work as factory laborers, his three daughters replaced their father as the primary wage earners and barely managed to keep the family financially afloat. The father's drinking forced Mamie, the eldest, into the unnatural role of family head and provider and resulted in endangering his daughter's feminine virtue.

When the younger sister Kate similarly succumbed, Norr lamented, "Those who know the history of the two handsomest girls in the Chinese colony vaguely wonder whether Tim Cavanagh will contribute any more to the immoral colonization of Chinatown."[15] By attributing the two women's downfall to the father's original failure to protect his daughters, Norr returned to the subject of the Irish workingman's predilection to alcohol and suggested that intemperance eroded patriarchal authority, leading to a collapse of the working-class moral order. The high cost of this breakdown was the "immoral colonization of Chinatown." Thus, opium, alcohol, and Chinatown were threatening not only as symbols of white female degradation, but also because they ultimately endangered the white, working-class, patriarchal family.

Norr also faulted the excesses of working-class female consumption for the sisters' predicament. The sisters' entry into factory work also introduced them to the modern consumer habits of urban working girls. By using their wages to keep the family from starvation, however, the sisters could not partake in the working-class material culture enjoyed by other girls in the factory. The combined effects of the family's economic necessity and the working girl's individual consumer desires, Norr suggested, drove young virtuous factory girls such as Mamie Cavanagh to ignore the wrath of their families and live in disgrace in Chinatown with Chinese men who could better provide for their material wants. Norr took special care to emphasize the change in Mamie's dress and appearance when she finally returned home. "She had grown handsomer in the year, and was richly dressed, with a plentiful display of jewelry. Altogether an entirely different person from the poorly dressed working girl who had walked out of that room a year ago with her modest lunch in a brown-paper parcel."[16] By highlighting the economic exchange implied in her decision to live with a Chinese man in Chinatown, Norr made clear that she had descended into the life of a prostitute.

When the younger sister, Kate, ventured into Chinatown to find her sister Mamie, she also became ensnared. Norr's depiction of Kate's seduction by Chinese men in a Chinatown restaurant, however, suggested that Mamie's own reckless behavior is the cause of her younger sister's downfall. "She, herself, however, was emptying the tiny cups as fast as the Chinese sailor could fill, and pretty soon she threw her disengaged arm about him and he carried the liquor to her lips."[17] Despite Kate's pleas to leave the restaurant, Mamie's inebriation prevented the two from departing, allowing Kate to succumb to the men's seduction. Thus Norr's "A Chinatown Tragedy" warned of the social and moral consequences of an industrial order that allowed for working-class girls' and women's sexual and consumer independence without patriarchal surveillance and control. This disruption of the working-class patriarchal order made women vulnerable to Chinese male sexual aggression and facilitated the breaking down of racial borders.

CONTAINING FEMALE ADOLESCENT SEXUALITY

More disturbing to American readers and social reformers, than these stories of white women who chose to cohabitate with Chinese men, were the real-life cases of adolescent girls who ventured into Chinatown. Teenage girls such as sixteen-year-old Sarah Rosen, the daughter of Jacob Rosen, a grocer in Weehawken, New Jersey, became the concern of this period's police and social reformers. In 1901 Sarah ran away from home and traveled to neighboring Jersey City, where she lived on the streets for several months before being arrested for vagrancy. The court decided to return Sarah to her father's custody but she soon left home again, venturing into lower Manhattan. By November that year she was staying in Chinatown, but having "relations with [an] Italian bartender in Jersey City."[18] Her father began to search day and night for her in the Chinatown neighborhood and learned that she could be found at Calahan's saloon on Bowery near Division Street, slightly northeast of Chinatown. He spotted her upon his arrival at Calahan's, but she escaped when he left to fetch the police. Rosen eventually tracked her to 11 Mott Street where he went with police officers to retrieve her. When they arrived at the Chinatown apartment Rosen and the police discovered that she was hiding in the rooms of a white woman named Jennie Hall. The police then arrested Hall for harboring a minor for the purposes of prostitution. Chu Lem, the lessee of the apartment, was also taken into custody. The case against Hall and Chu Lem, however, was later dismissed by the grand jury in the Court of General Sessions. Her intent to run away and hide from her father and the police may have convinced the jury that Sarah was simply a wayward teenage girl and not the innocent victim of abduction.

Sarah Rosen was hardly alone in her nocturnal wanderings in the streets of lower Manhattan. Since the early nineteenth century, New York's poor and working-class populations had fashioned for themselves a distinctive social world with its own codes of ethics and morality that revolved around the city's seemingly rough and dangerous streets.[19] Street life was particularly important for this group because the relative lack of private residential space available in working-class districts meant that socializing and play typically occurred in the public spaces of neighborhoods: building stoops, sidewalks, alleyways, and streets. Working-class women and children, for example, reconfigured their neighborhood's heavily trafficked and congested thoroughfares into impromptu playgrounds and centers of gossip.[20] In addition to these familiar neighborhood locations, specific locales in the city such as the Bowery, Coney Island, and the Tenderloin district, that had long-established reputations as places brimming with popular cultural amusements, also became important centers of urban working-class subculture, attracting visitors throughout the greater metropolitan area.[21] The Chinatown neighborhood, abutting the Bowery and near the Lower East Side, was also part of this urban landscape of commercial amusements easily accessible to the city's working-class men, women, and children. The presence of young women and children participating in the street culture of these neighborhoods, particularly Chinatown, was met with alarm by the city's police, magistrates, and social reformers.

Fears of Chinatown as a moral threat to women and children occurred at a time when the city's reformers worked to define women and children as a distinct social class requiring special legal protection. As early as 1853,

Charles Loring Brace founded the Children's Aid Society (CAS) to address what he perceived to be the problem of masses of unruly, poor children populating Gotham's streets.[22] The New York Society for the Suppression of Vice, founded by Anthony Comstock in 1872, was one of a number of late-nineteenth-century institutions that specifically concentrated on protecting middle-class children from the immoral and delinquent influences in the city.[23] This concern with protecting urban poor and working-class children led to the establishment of 250 child welfare agencies nationwide by the end of the nineteenth century.[24] Attempts to protect the city's girls and women gave rise in the 1880s to the Young Women's Christian Association to provide wholesome amusements, affordable housing, and job training. The concern with redeeming and rehabilitating young girls and women also led to the organization of three large state reformatories to work with those teenage girls and women who, despite their transgressions, had not yet turned into inveterate "hardened" criminals.[25] In the midst of this growing social concern the city's police and courts worked to limit Chinatown's accessibility to women and minors. Adolescent working-class girls, because of their age, class, and gender, were seen as particularly vulnerable to the perceived immoralizing effects of urban streets and commercial amusements in neighborhoods such as Chinatown and their protection required active state intervention.

Working-class teenage girls, however, did not necessarily see themselves in need of special protection or restraint. Like their older sisters they eagerly participated in the many commercial amusements found throughout the greater New York metropolitan area and developed a distinct subculture that was marked by heterosocial romance, sexual experimentation, consumerism, and economic dependency on young men. Sixteen-year-old Emma Gatjen, for example, frequently visited Coney Island. During one visit she met another girl of similar age and the two later visited a concert hall together. On that particular occasion Emma stayed away from home for a week until her mother had her arrested.[26] Similarly, fifteen-year-old Catherine Kent ran away from home with a girlfriend. The pair stayed away for a week, during which time Catherine visited "a house that had a bad name." At her trial she admitted that "she had been wild and disobedient," but she did not seem remorseful. Operating within a working-class female subculture that allowed teenage girls to experiment with sex and alcohol, Catherine asserted that "she saw nothing wrong while she was there."[27]

These teenage girls' attempts to assert a more public, sexually expressive adolescence quickly ran up against state laws and institutions. By the late nineteenth century state agencies began to eclipse voluntary and religious groups by taking on a more invasive role in policing and criminalizing female adolescent sexual behavior, particularly among the poor and working class, and racial and ethnic minorities. Progressive Era reformers, unlike their Victorian counterparts, no longer saw these girls as the victims of unscrupulous male seducers. Instead, they acknowledged female sexuality and worked to contain and control its expressiveness in adolescent girls. While mid-1880s social reform efforts involved raising the age of consent laws to protect teenage girls and punish male seducers, Progressive reformers looked for social and economic conditions that contributed to female sexual delinquency. In response they lobbied for the creation of a range of state institutions, including "special police officers, juvenile courts, detention centers, and reformatories, to monitor and correct female sexual delinquency."[28] By socializing in more easily accessible and highly visible public spaces such as streets, amusement parks, and movie theaters, working-class girls were more easily targeted by police and social reformers than their middle-class counterparts who often had the luxury of more private spaces for socializing.[29] The city's courts increasingly criminalized a wide range of sexually expressive behavior, arresting and sending many teenage girls to state-operated reform institutions such as the New York House of Refuge.[30]

Working-class girls' independence from their families was fostered by their socialization and participation in a female work culture that revolved around discussions of material consumption, popular commercial amusements, and heterosexual romantic love. Whether on the factory floor or behind department store retail counters, young working women shared fashion and cosmetics advice along with vivid stories of their romantic encounters and liaisons with the opposite sex. Immigrant working-class parents grew clearly alarmed at their daughters' participation in this subculture and attempted to limit their daughters' increased economic and sexual independence. Ironically, the structure of the working-class family economy itself encouraged daughters to participate in the public sphere and fostered their self-reliance and independence. The labor of children, especially daughters, often played an important role in the working-class family economy. Whether helping their mothers with shopping, tending to boarders and younger siblings, or doing piecework, working-class daughters often labored in their tenement flats and neighborhoods.[31] Most working-class parents, however, could not afford to keep their daughters at home permanently and remove them from the immoral influences of the city's streets. Instead, many working-class girls engaged in wage work outside of the home before entering into marriage and motherhood. The court testimony of many working-class families suggests that social and economic pressures eroded the authority of many immigrant working-class parents, thwarting their attempts to enforce obedience within the home.

Struggling to maintain family order and discipline, working-class parents turned to resources available from the courts and other local and state institutions in their last attempt to control what they interpreted as the rebellious behavior of "out of control" and sexually active daughters. An examination of case histories from New York's House of Refuge, for example, shows that large numbers of teenage girls had been arrested on the charge of being "disorderly," which was often described as alcohol consumption or sexually expressive behavior. Often a parent initiated the girl's arrest and incarceration when parental discipline alone failed to control their teenage daughter's behavior. In 1891 Laura Carter personally brought her thirteen-year-old daughter, Rebecca, to the Brooklyn Police Court after she decided her daughter "had become disobedient, and got beyond her control."[32] She was also charged with being disorderly and sent to the House of Refuge, where she remained for three years. Gussie Stegman's father, a coal peddler, burdened with the task of single-handedly rearing his five children after the death of his wife, grew frustrated at Gussie, who he believed was "growing wild, and going out to [sic] much." At his wit's end, he suggested to the House of Refuge that she remain in their facility for at least two years.[33]

Probation officers and social workers further assisted the courts by making home visits to check on the moral rehabilitation of inmates following their release from correctional facilities. Upon finding evidence of further delinquent activity, social workers often pressured parents to intervene by committing their unruly daughters to state reformatories. Such decisions were often not based upon whether or not the teen had actually perpetrated a criminal act, but instead on her general behavior or demeanor as interpreted by the court and its agents. After losing her job at a dry goods store, one thirteen-year-old teenager drifted among her friends in the city until she entered a Chinese-operated laundry, where she was spotted and arrested by police. Her mere presence in a Chinese-owned laundry had been enough cause for the patrolman to investigate. Upon questioning she claimed that she was in the laundry only to try to hide from her mother. After eliciting a tearful confession and apology from the defendant, the court allowed her to return home under the supervision of her mother. Not satisfied with her subsequent behavior, however, the court later decided to intervene further to place her "out of harm's way" and had her committed to the New York Juvenile Asylum.[34]

Not all parents willingly complied with social workers' requests to confine their daughters. One social worker began an investigation of fourteen-year-old Yetta Fish, who resided at the edge of Chinatown at 55 Bayard Street. After receiving news that Yetta was "seen about the streets of Chinatown, asking the Chinamen for money to go to the moving picture shows," the social worker visited Yetta's mother, who refused to believe the accusations. Despite the mother's protestations, the social worker continued the investigation by checking on Yetta's attendance and work performance at the Girls' Technical High School, located at the corner of Grand and Lafayette streets in lower Manhattan, but found that "her attendance is pretty regular, and that her work is fairly well."[35]

In cases involving minors private child welfare agencies such as the NYSPCC worked in concert with the police and courts in controlling and modifying the behavior of female adolescents. In 1889 a number of city agencies responded shortly after learning of the marriage of Winifred Corman to K. Moto, a Japanese steward residing in the lower Manhattan waterfront district. Following the marriage service at the Five Points Mission, the couple settled in a section of Water Street, where other Chinese and Japanese men resided. The appearance of a young white woman in the midst of a predominantly Asian male laboring population soon caught the attention of other residents in the area, and the police and NYSPCC were called on to investigate. Upon examination the court determined that Corman was actually fourteen years old and not seventeen as she had informed Reverend O. R. Bouton of the Five Points Mission. Because she was under sixteen years old, the legal age of consent, and the marriage had taken place without the knowledge of Corman's parents, Moto was charged with abduction as defined by Section 282 of the penal code and faced "imprisonment for not more than five years or by a fine of not more than one thousand dollars, or both."[36]

Interestingly, the NYSPCC claimed that Corman was not ashamed of her actions until summoned to appear before the court. Moto had treated Corman with great affection and clearly took the marriage seriously. "He intended saving money enough to carry his wife to Tokyo, Japan, to show her to his people, and he was going to get a nice home for her as soon as possible. He would not have kept her long in Water Street. He did not like it himself. He was a ship's cook and steward and showed good references." The court, clearly impressed with Moto's intentions and character references, decided to dismiss the abduction charge made against him. Nonetheless the court did not go so far as to see their relationship as a legitimate marriage and moved to have it dissolved. Judge Hogan extended his leniency toward Winifred Corman after her contrition and assurances convinced him that she had no interest in continuing the marriage and was willing to accept the court's guidance. Because the marriage had not been consummated, Corman was seen as not having completely fallen, allowing for the possibility of her social rehabilitation. The court granted the NYSPCC custody of Corman until "a home was found for her with a family in a neighboring city, where she will have excellent opportunities for good."[37] This decision not only separated Corman from Moto but, by placing her with a different family in another city, also severed all of her connections with her former life. Such a drastic move was seen as necessary by the court to remove potentially harmful environmental influences that might hinder her moral reform.

While the court demonstrated leniency toward Moto and Corman, it was less forgiving toward the minister who had allowed the marriage to be performed in the first place. According to Section 376 of the penal code, a minister who knowingly performed a wedding where either party was under the age of consent was guilty of committing a misdemeanor. Reverend Bouton, however, argued that he did not know that Corman was under the age of consent since he had been informed by the couple that she was of age. The court chastised the Reverend for failing to make the proper inquiries to ascertain Corman's correct age and conducting the marriage between "a Heathen and Christian."[38] As an agent of both the church and state, ministers were charged with the dual task of upholding the law and public morality. In this case Reverend Bouton had clearly failed to carry out either duty and had to endure the wrath of the court.

Aside from following up citizens' and police complaints, the NYSPCC also participated in periodic raids into the Chinatown neighborhood. In December 1889 twelve NYSPCC agents and forty police officers executed a mass raid on Doyers and Pell streets. Divided into several groups, the NYSPCC and police officers simultaneously entered the businesses and homes located at 9, 11, and 19 Pell Street; and 9, 13, and 17 Doyers Street. In their *Annual Report* NYSPCC officers boasted of their efficiency in executing the raid. "Within five minutes the officers had passed through every house from cellar to garret, holding command of every door front and back and of every means of ingress and egress from floor to roof." The officers encountered several white women during the search but not the female minors that they had expected. Nonetheless the police did not look kindly upon the women they found, taking them into police custody despite the fact that they were not charged with any crime. They were eventually released but "with the caution never to be found in Chinatown again if they valued it."[39]

Clearly many of these teenagers resented social workers' intrusions into their lives and were hardly willing objects of reform. An examination of social workers' reports, for example, suggests the extent to which the girls understood how to manipulate social workers' assumptions of working-class girls' naivete and innocence to their own advantage. In 1910 a social worker questioned fourteen-year-old Henrietta Buckerman and fifteen-year-old Esther Gassman after she saw them being taken by a white man to 18 Mott Street, "an immoral house led by Chinamen." The two teens quickly proclaimed their innocence and explained that they had been looking for work when they met up with the man. The social worker confidently reported that she had successfully rescued the two girls who were "at present working and living at their homes." In follow-up home visits six months later, however, the social worker quickly discovered that the two may not have been as contrite and forthcoming as they had first appeared. At Esther's home at 54 East 107th Street the social worker learned from her mother that she had been disobedient and continued to engage in delinquent behavior. Out of frustration Esther's parents had her committed to a home. As for her companion, Henrietta, the address she had given to the social worker turned out to be false.[40] From using narratives of innocence and victimhood and feigning cooperation with social workers, police, and courts, to giving false biographical information, these teens learned from their peers to employ a range of strategies to avoid arrest and institutionalization.

Despite their acts of parental defiance, deception, and manipulation of social workers' expectations, not all of these teenagers and young women were ready for the serious challenges of living on their own and providing for themselves in the city. Many were, in fact, vulnerable to victimization by unscrupulous men and women who took advantage of their age, precarious financial situation, and severed familial contacts. Such cases also made their way into the city's courts. Sixteen-year-old Josephine Steiner, who enjoyed going out for candy and ice cream and attending the theater, became sexually active in her teenage years. She and her father frequently quarreled over her "being out late at night," "keeping company with young men," and failing to "attend to [her] house." Josephine eventually left home and found work as a domestic. Although domestic service held a low social status for working-class women, it remained a popular alternative for young, unskilled girls and women like Josephine who lacked the resources to secure a factory position. More importantly it allowed Josephine, who was clearly unhappy with her home life, to live apart from her family, which would not have been possible on typical factory wages.[41]

The watchful eye of her employer and the long workday, however, may have resulted in less freedom and opportunities to socialize than Josephine had anticipated.[42] She returned home after a month but quickly left again; this time with another young man, Joe Reid, and the two stayed away for three days. Reid along with his brother, Willie, then brought Josephine to an apartment at 11 Mott Street that was occupied by Lee Woh and his common-law wife, Lillie Miller. According to Josephine's police complaint she waited several days at the apartment for the Reid brothers to come back, but was instead made a prisoner in the apartment and forced to have sexual intercourse with three Chinese men who had arrived at the apartment after the Reid brothers had departed. When the police entered the apartment that evening, they found Josephine in a state of undress and quickly arrested the couple and the three Chinese men present in the apartment. Lee Woh and the other three Chinese men were eventually acquitted of the charges of rape and abduction and the case against Lillie Miller was also dismissed.[43]

On occasion Chinatown residents came to the assistance of these teenagers in need. Caroline Schmidt, an orphan who resided with her uncle in Philadelphia, received a card stating that a job was available for her in New York City. The address proved to be in Chinatown. When she realized where she had ended up, she became distraught. A Chinese man passing by attempted to inquire into her predicament, but "she could not answer him, for she could not speak English." "Crying bitterly," she eventually came to the attention of a social worker who, misinterpreting the scene, quickly "pushed the Chinaman aside" to question Schmidt. She then brought Schmidt to the home of another social worker, Maude Miner, who helped her to locate work.[44] Similarly, seventeen-year-old Louise Elbert of Rosemond, New Jersey came to Chinatown after receiving a letter from a friend who told her to go there for a job. While trying to locate the author of the letter Elbert was later found by Chinatown resident Elsie Lee, the white wife of a Chinese man. Elsie Lee then took Elbert to a restaurant on Doyers Street where she bought her supper and later placed her in the care of Rose Livingston, a Chinatown social worker. Livingston then brought her to the Waverly House at 163 West Tenth Street, a home for young girls maintained by the New York Probation Society.[45]

The presence of teenage runaways, prostitutes, domestic partners, and wives in the neighborhood greatly complicated efforts by the police, social reformers, and the general public to discern "respectable" wives from the women of "ill-repute" who also resided in the area. Nonetheless they often claimed to be adept in decoding manners of dress and speech and other superficial characteristics in determining whether an unknown woman appearing in public could be safely categorized as virtuous or depraved. They usually claimed that they did not need to see a suspected prostitute in the act of "hooking her victim" to become convinced that the woman was indeed soliciting. Through the interpretation of clothing styles and behavior, reformers, police, and other agents of the court attempted to determine whether or not a woman found in places like Chinatown was a prostitute. Too often, clothing, rather than being a clear marker of working-class women's respectability or immorality, actually worked to blur these distinctions for middle-class observers, as working-class women often appropriated aspects of the prostitute's style of dress and sexually aggressive behavior in defining a modern urban sexual persona.[46]

Even as styles of dress alone could not easily define a woman's character, reformers and police claimed that a woman's behavior nonetheless remained a good indicator of her virtue. The sight of an "unaccompanied"

woman in the rough, working-class male space of the saloon, for example, was enough to convince social reformers that prostitution existed in
an establishment. Vice investigators hired by the Committee of Fourteen,
for example, typically counted the numbers of unescorted women to determine the extent to which an establishment was disorderly. After visiting
an establishment at 12 Chatham Square, through an entrance on Doyers
Street, the vice investigator lastily noted four single women who were
"keeping time with music with their fingers" and engaging in a sexually
risqué dance of "moving their bodies on chair[s] in grizzly bear fashion."[47]

As historian Kathy Peiss asserts, working-class women often operated
within their own set of cultural values, sexual mores, and economic conditions, which differed from those of the middle-class social reformer.
Turn-of-the-century New York increasingly offered young working-class
women an array of "cheap amusements" in the form of dance halls,
amusement parks, and movie theaters. Located outside of the confines
of traditional ethnic working-class neighborhoods, these commercial
amusements provided the venues where "young women experimented
with new cultural forms that articulated gender in terms of sexual expressiveness and social interaction with men, linking heterosocial culture to a sense of modernity, individuality, and personal style."[48] Young
women's unmarried and wage-earning status made these opportunities
more available to them. As they increased their physical mobility throughout the city, their mothers remained limited to sexually segregated activities
within the neighborhood.[49] These working girls often rejected the notion
of female virtue as tied to chastity to forge their own definitions of respectability and employed "treating"—the exchanging of sexual favors for
dates, gifts, or male attention and protection—as part of their overall strategy for daily economic survival. Known as "charity girls," these women
saw themselves as different from prostitutes because they did not accept
money outright in their sexual relations with men. These nuanced definitions of working-class women's respectability, however, often resulted in
middle-class reformers' increasing difficulty in interpreting and understanding working-class women's sexuality.

While white working-class women who chose to cohabitate with
Chinese men operated within the same set of values and sexual mores,
their racial transgressions set them apart from other urban working-class
women in this period. Interracial sexual liaisons made their sexual deviance become permanent rather than transitory, lowering their social
position to levels that did not automatically improve upon marriage.
While marriage and motherhood could redeem socially many working-
class women who seemed to have fallen as a result of temporary sexual
transgressions, this was not the case for the women who had been involved with Chinese men.[50]

SOCIOLEGAL STATUS OF CHINATOWN'S INTERRACIAL COUPLES

Social reformers' and journalists' efforts to publicize these cases informed public opinion on the morality and legitimacy of Chinese-white relationships. These turn-of-the-century constructions of the sexuality and morality of white women residing in Chinatown went beyond the mere creation of stereotypical images to having serious material repercussions on their lives and relationships. Periodic sweeps of Chinatown and Chinese-owned businesses, resulting in the arrests and expulsion of women and teens from the area, constantly disrupted the lives of neighborhood residents. Captain Galvin's two month "crusade" in Chinatown in 1909, for example, removed all white women from the area who could not produce an official marriage certificate. Following the Elsie Sigel murder, police continued with such surprise raids throughout the Chinatown area. According to James Gleason, of the Second Inspection District, the police without prior provocation made routine sweeps of Chinatown to "go through all the buildings there for --- to see if there is any violation of law for any reason."[51]

To understand how such raids were legitimized and accepted despite the absence of anti-miscegenation laws, it is important to understand how the city's magistrates viewed these women and their relationships. An examination of this period's court cases involving white wives or companions of Chinese men who resided in Chinatown provides glimpses into the lives of these women. The trial transcripts suggest the extent to which these women's relationships, married or not, were not recognized as morally legitimate or equivalent to similar relationships with whites. These proceedings also reveal the extent to which the judiciary worked to legitimize the maintenance of racial and sexual borders among its citizens.

A 1906 murder trial involving a fatal shooting in Chinatown demonstrates the extent to which white women's marriage to Chinese men was deemed important by lawyers, judges, and jurors in determining their social standing and by implication their claims to being reliable witnesses. In this case the testimonies of the arresting police officers and the coroner were pitted against the word of Margaret Wing, a white woman residing at 11 Pell Street with her Chinese husband, Charles; and Hunter Durben, a black man who lived and worked as a janitor at 16 Pell Street. Wing was a witness to the shooting and stated that she did not see George Tow, the accused, fire any weapon. Instead Wing claimed that she saw George Tow "standing in front of No. 11, and, when the uproar of shots was fired, he [ran] down towards where the shooting had been going on, and an officer took him, and had him in his hands."[52] In essence she claimed that the police arrested the wrong man.

During cross-examination the assistant district attorney, James R. Ely, failed to ask Margaret Wing a single question regarding the shooting or what she witnessed in the street; instead he focused his questioning entirely on her marriage to her Chinese husband and her prior criminal record. Margaret Wing testified that she had been married to Charles Wing for two years and that they resided in a building in Chinatown where a number of white women also lived. Ely took great pains to solicit the names of these women and to impress upon the jury that they were most likely disreputable and not legally married to their Chinese companions, challenging Wing's own claims to be a married woman.[53] Ely also questioned Wing about her prior criminal arrest. Wing at first defiantly replied that she had never been convicted of any crime, but upon further questioning admitted that one of the lawyers of the defense, Daniel O'Reilly, had once served as her legal counsel on an earlier conviction. Ely, satisfied that he had shown Wing to be a questionable witness, did not ask any more questions regarding her conviction.[54]

In closing Ely spoke directly about Wing's character to convince the jury that she was an incompetent witness. Ely did not so much challenge Wing's testimony in terms of its factual accuracy as to simply paint Wing as an unreliable witness because she had a Chinese husband and resided in Chinatown. The lawyer for the defense, Lyman Spalding, attempting to salvage her testimony as crucial to the defense of his client, addressed her moral character: "Now, Margaret Wing. Of course she is married to a Chinaman, her position in life isn't very high."[55] Yet he added that he hoped the jurors would be able to ignore her marriage and character and believe that Wing was a reliable eyewitness to the shooting because the prosecution failed to contradict her testimony. Spalding in essence was equally as patronizing to Wing as Ely and agreed with Ely's assessment of his witness.

In the 1912 case *People vs. Jung Hing*, the testimonies of five white women who resided in Chinatown were crucial in the conviction of a Chinese man alleged to have been involved in a shooting. In an effort to malign these witnesses' credibility the defense inquired into these women's "reputation for chastity." During the course of the trial the women were asked to describe their family histories and give reasons for their living in Chinatown. One witness, Catherine Earl Powers, testified that she resided with Foong Pong for eight years at 9 Pell Street. During this time she would occasionally go on long visits to her mother's home in Boston. Ella Faund, the second witness, was a friend of Powers. She originally came from Philadelphia and settled in New York City's Chinatown in 1907 or 1908. For the past year she resided with Wong Ding in the same building as Powers. She stated to the court that she had not lived with any other Chinese men during her time in Chinatown. Lillie Hennie, the third witness, resided with Philip Jung for the last two years at 5 Chrystie Street, located a few blocks from Chinatown. The fourth witness, Lillian Bates, had lived with Charles Wah for the last five years but had also occupied an apartment on Division Street, a few blocks from Chinatown, for about eight years. Bates also knew Catherine Powers from Boston. The fifth and final witness, Gertrude Williams, cohabitated with the murder victim, Yee Toy, for the last five years. Before living with Yee Toy, at the age of sixteen she took up with a white American man with whom she had also dwelled in Chinatown.[56]

Because these women did not conform to middle-class definitions of respectability, the court clearly had difficulties in dealing with the women's testimonies. Powers, originally from Sherben, Massachusetts, was once sentenced to a penal institution for eight months on a drunkenness conviction; she later broke parole by committing larceny. She also revealed during her testimony that she had other prior convictions. Lillie Hennie, who was married at the age of nineteen, left her husband, a white man named Lawrence Hennie, after a year of marriage and then took up with Philip Jung. None of the couples was legally married, but as noted by Judge J. Rosalsky, "lived in meretricious relationship[s] with Chinamen."[57] To further complicate matters the Chinese partners of two of the women, Powers and Bates, belonged to one of Chinatown's most powerful fraternal societies, the Hip Sing Tong. The defense lawyers argued that the murder trial was related to ongoing tong wars, and they attempted to show that these women were being coerced by their Chinese partners and the Hip Sing Tong to testify against their client.

The prosecution realized early on that the jury's assessment of the moral character of women living in Chinatown might throw the case in jeopardy. In the opening statement of the People's counsel Nott tried to impress upon the jury the differences between "kept women " and "street walkers" or "Bowery 'floaters' that take men to hotels, or anything of that sort," and instead emphasized that they were "living with one Chinaman, not promiscuously."[58] While he did not go so far as to claim them to be "moral women," he urged jurors to believe that the women could still make reliable witnesses despite their questionable virtue. Taking no chances Nott also emphasized that these women's testimony was not crucial to the conviction of the defendant, reminding the jury that "if the testimony of these girls is to be believed, it simply rounds out and corroborates the officers' testimony."[59]

Despite Nott's statements the women's relationship with Chinese men, more so than their previous criminal trespasses, continued to be of paramount importance in determing the women's credibility. In the face of intense public scrutiny and disapproval the women, when questioned about their relationships, exhibited no signs of shame for their present lives and made no attempts to conceal the fact that they were not married to their Chinese partners. For all five women their current Chinese partners were the only Chinese men they had ever cohabitated with, and they further established that they did not see other men in the years that they lived together. Nonetheless the testimony of these women presented a clear enough challenge for the jury that Judge Rosalsky felt compelled to give special instructions on how to handle their testimony in light of what he perceived to be the women's flagrant immorality and appalling lack of remorse for their way of life. Emphasizing that it was the women's testimony rather than their character that needed to be weighed, Judge Rosalsky instructed the jury that "the law only requires corroboration of enough of the testimony of women of ill-repute to prove that their stories are circumstantially true."[60]

Even in cases where the couples were legally married and the wives lacked a criminal record, their legitimate marriages did not necessarily confer respectability to the white wives. Journalist Thomas Knox warned readers not to be fooled by the presence of a marriage certificate, claiming that "[w]hen arrested and brought into the police courts they claim to be the wives of Chinese, and either produce marriage certificates or bring their alleged husbands to swear to the matrimonial relation."[61] Police and courts similarly treated the white wives of Chinese laborers with great suspicion. In the 1913 case *People vs. Lee Dock, Eng Hing,* Maud Hop, a thirty-three-year-old white woman married to a Chinese man was called to testify for the defense. Her husband, Jung Hop, worked in a laundry on First Street in Hoboken, New Jersey. The couple had been together for fifteen years and had several children.[62] At least one child, Rosina, had been baptized at the Church of the Transfiguration at 29 Mott Street.[63] At the time of the trial Maud Hop was visibly pregnant. During summation the prosecution described her as "this slovenly woman who was brought in by the defense."[64] Neither the legal confirmation of an enduring marriage nor the presence of children sufficiently protected the white wives of Chinese men from public censure. In effect Maud Hop was not viewed any differently from the unmarried white women who chose to cohabitate with Chinese men. Even so, the existence of a marriage certificate was perhaps the only means by which Chinese-white couples such as the Hops could legally protect themselves from undue police harassment. Because New York State law did not forbid interracial marriage these relationships, despite being viewed as morally reprehensible, were nonetheless legally sanctioned.

SETTLEMENT HOUSE WORKERS AND THE REDEMPTION
OF FALLEN WHITE WOMEN IN CHINATOWN

In 1904 public concern over the plight of white teenage girls and women in the Chinatown neighborhood prompted the establishment of the Chinatown Rescue Settlement and Recreation Room at 63 Bayard Street.[65] During its first year the settlement expanded its Chinatown focus and relocated to 10 Mott Street, later changing its name to the Chinatown and Bowery Rescue Settlement for Girls (CBRSG). As both names suggest the institution's mission combined the goals of "rescue" and "social uplift," working to take women away from their lives in the neighborhood and provide them with alternative means for work and amusement. Though imbued with a strong sense of Christian duty and spiritual uplift in their work, the institution resembled other settlement houses of the period in its non-denominational status and attention to the women's social and material needs. The CBRSG was not as socially progressive as some of the more well-known settlement houses of the Progressive Era, such as Henry Street Settlement in the Lower East Side or Hull House in Chicago. Rather, its continuing emphasis on spiritual and moral uplift made it resemble the "second tier" of the social reform movement that comprised smaller religion-centered settlement houses in Midwest cities.[66]

Unlike the "rescue homes" established in West Coast Chinatowns, such as Cameron House in San Francisco, CBRSG did not work with Chinese girls and women but with predominantly white women—immigrant and native-born—of varying ages and socioeconomic backgrounds who either lived in or often visited the neighborhood. Ideologically, however, the two institutions were similar in their efforts to recreate models of Victorian womanhood and domesticity. Institutions like the CBRSG were by no means unique in New York City; such homes for "wayward girls" proliferated throughout America's cities as social reformers bemoaned young women's vulnerability to urban vices and the changes in sexual mores among the city's working-class youth.[67] Without adequate work and protection of home or family, reformers feared that these girls and women would too easily succumb to the socially disruptive forces of industrialization and urbanization.

The CBRSG workers, however, believed their work was much more difficult than similar city institutions because of its location in the tough working-class neighborhoods of Chinatown and the Bowery. Chinatown's popularity as a sightseeing spot and the proliferation of dance halls and saloons in the area meant that the neighborhood attracted large numbers of female visitors nightly. The CBRSG estimated that 500 girls were "living lives of sin within five minutes' walk of the Settlement" at 10 Mott Street: 200 resided within Chinatown and the remaining 300 inhabited "neighboring dives."[68] Furthermore the CBRSG workers, following the work of Progressive social reformers, focused on the dangerous tenement conditions of the area to draw attention to the detrimental environmental influences. "Many of the Chinatown girls also live in most unwholesome surroundings, in poorly ventilated rooms, with very little light or air, in some cases with no windows, the halls dark, and in one old-style tenement the stairs are steep and slanting and most difficult to climb."[69] Thus, settlement house workers claimed that this combination of substandard housing and the immoral vices of Chinatown produced an even more degraded female victim. "It is harder in this neighborhood than in any other part of the city to save the girls for the simple reason that here they have sunk to lower depths, are more addicted to drugs, more diseased and in every way more incapable of becoming self-supporting members of the community."[70] The institution's main goal consequently was to convince women to leave the Chinatown neighborhood. This was accomplished chiefly by two means: arranging for temporary stays at CBRSG or other rescue homes in the city, and reuniting women with their estranged families. During its first year of operation, the settlement house received approximately 1,469 visitors, but only thirty-three women became temporary residents while another eighteen to twenty were directed to other rescue homes in the city.[71]

Despite the constant coming and going of women from the neighborhood, the CBRSG did not wish for the settlement house to resemble a transient way station or a boarding house. Instead settlement workers took pains to recreate in the dormitory and recreation rooms a genteel, domestic atmosphere—distinct from the working-class Chinatown neighborhood—that would enable the women's return to mainstream society. The list of items donated to the CBRSG, mostly by its officers and board of managers, provides a glimpse into the organization's efforts to recreate this homelike atmosphere. George Bramwell, a member of the board, for example, donated "books, magazines, medicine closet, china and fruit, window curtains, stain for floor, chairs, china, silverware, games, etc." Caroline Bunker, another board member, provided most of the bedroom furniture including three beds, an assortment of linens, and some dressers and bureaus. Some of the white wives of Chinese men living in the neighborhood also made donations of small household items. Kitty Lee donated a "cup and saucer" and Florence Quong donated "six cups and saucers, plates, knives and forks." Fresh flowers provided by the Fruit and Flower Association further contributed to this illusion of an urban oasis by creating the appearance and feel of a country-like atmosphere.[72]

Figure 3.1. The CBRSG's first floor "recreation room" was furnished to resemble a middle-class Victorian parlor in its explicit function as a space for female sociability and edifying amusements. *Source: Fourth Annual Report of the Chinatown Settlement for Girls* (1908): 7. Courtesy of New York Public Library.

To provide alternative amusements to the dance halls and saloons that sat within steps of the settlement house, the CBRSG organized get-to-gethers that mirrored the parlor socials of the Victorian middle-class, staging lectures or "special musical evenings" that aimed to uplift as well as entertain.[73] The recreation room featured an upright piano. As typical decorative centerpieces of the Victorian parlor, pianos and organs were meant to be played and worked to reflect and produce the refined sensibilities expected of "the genteel Victorian lady."[74] In addition, workers organized evening cooking classes in the settlement house kitchen to impart the basic skills of domesticity.

Convinced that the physical environment played an important role in transforming the moral character of their wayward charges, workers took the added step of arranging visits to the country. This desire to remove women to a pastoral setting went another step in 1908, when CBRSG began to work with Bellevue Hospital to provide free clinical treatment for drug addiction. Medical care aside, the treatment allowed for women to escape their immediate physical environment and personal connections and reside temporarily at "a cottage in the country."[75] To drive home the importance of environmental influences in the recuperation process, the CBRSG included a photograph of "the cottage" and an artist's rendering of an opium den in Chinatown in its 1911 annual report. The picture, with the caption "Smoking Opium," showed a disheveled white woman lying in bed smoking an opium pipe held by a Chinese man. Another white woman was also pictured lying in a bunk above her. By contrast, the picture of the cottage showed a large Victorian house in a rural setting. Instead of the dirt and chaos shown in the earlier "opium den" image, the cottage appeared to be a model of order and tranquility with women dressed in crisp white dresses neatly assembled on the large porch of the house.[76]

To fulfill their mission settlement workers did not just wait for women to drop into the recreation room, but took a more proactive approach by calling on women at their homes. In the first year workers made 4,275 such visits.[77] During the second year workers estimated that the number of visitations increased by 8.5 percent to 5,000.[78] At first women who resided in the neighborhood did not readily receive the settlement workers into their homes. As one social worker lamented, "all missionaries were looked upon with suspicion." To gain access to the women's residences workers brought along food, medicine, doctors, and nurses in the hopes that such gifts and services would make their presence more welcomed. The use of these presents, especially flowers, also made these visits appear to be neighborly and friendly, rather than official, in character. By the same token the CBRSG's annual reports portrayed the settlement workers as sympathetic and loyal sisters, emphasizing the women's "unswerving perseverance, tact, wisdom and love" rather than their educational or professional qualifications to conduct such work.[79] Once allowed inside the workers aimed to befriend the women and bring them to the settlement house and out of the neighborhood and onto the path of moral redemption and physical rehabilitation.

The CBRSG also supported evangelical activities among the settlement house workers and encouraged the formation of the "Lifting-up Society," a club "in which each girl pledges herself to endeavor to help some other girl to a higher life."[80] Although settlement house workers believed that the way to social and moral redemption could be greatly facilitated through renewed religious faith and adherence to Christian teachings, religious conversions were clearly not considered the main focus of their work nor the best measure of institutional success. Instead the CBRSG chose to measure its achievements by statistics like the number of "girls sent to hospitals," "girls sent to rescue homes," "girls receiving employment," and "girls prevented from crime."[81]

The departure of teenage girls and women from Chinatown and their return to their families meant the most successful fulfillment of the institution's mission. The CBRSG's annual reports took great pains to narrate such "success stories" of moral and physical recovery. Each case closely followed a set narrative structure that worked to establish the woman as the helpless "fallen woman" in dire need of rescue and deliverance through the intervention and moral guidance of the middle-class CBRSG worker. These stories began with a description of the woman's moral dissipation, as a result of adolescent sexual activity or socially delinquent behavior, leading to her eventual drift into Chinatown. The account then shifted into a description of the pivotal role of the settlement house in removing her from Chinatown and putting her onto the path of redemption, usually accomplished through family reunification, marriage, motherhood, or employment. One woman who had "been sent home to her mother in Pennsylvania" later wrote the CBRSG to report that she was "working and doing well." A former cocaine user had "regained her health and obtained work." A seventeen-year-old was reunited with her husband, from whom she had run away, and was reported to be "happy in their own home and devoted to the baby just born to them."[82]

This is not to say that all of the CBRSG's cases ended happily or that the institution chose only to report on their successes. Tragic cases also occurred and their reporting also served a morally didactic purpose. The CBRSG used these cases, such as the death of "Diamond M.," "[o]nce living in luxury, now deserted by those who had supported her, dying of an incurable disease—this girl found her way to the Settlement one night, gasping for breath as she struggled up the stairs and begged for help."[83] She died shortly thereafter and the CBRSG held her funeral service at the settlement house, requiring the fifty or sixty girls who attended to donate 25–50¢ each to help cover the burial expenses.

Despite settlement house workers' confidence that they could properly guide their working-class female charges to reform their errant ways, visitors such as seventeen-year-old Lizzie Olivevie had other ideas and utilized the available resources at the CBRSG as they saw fit. Olivevie was befriended by a settlement house worker when she fell ill. After her recovery she began to frequent the settlement house reading room where she eventually met and became infatuated with a Chinese actor performing at the Chinese Theatre. Believing that the man "would do his utmost for her," the settlement house worker urged Lizzie to marry him. Lizzie, however, decided not to commit to marriage and lived with him out of wedlock. She later met and married a young white man who worked as a street car conductor and appeared to settle down into married life. However, she continued to make use of the settlement house to maintain her former social connections in the neighborhood, including her relationship with the Chinese actor. She eventually left her husband and returned to the actor. Only through an exhaustive three day search, on the

Figure 3.2. Journalists attempted to connect Elsie Sigel to the settlement house at 10 Mott Street in order to claim that she was a Chinatown missionary. This photograph was titled "Mission Where Elsie Sigel Met Her Slayer." *Source*: Library of Congress, Prints and Photographs Division, NYWT&S Collection.

part of her angry husband aided by a social worker and policeman, was Lizzie finally located and compelled to leave the Chinese actor.[84]

The publicity surrounding the Elsie Sigel murder mounted a serious challenge to the settlement house's authority. In particular, the linking of Elsie Sigel to the CBRSG led many to question the wisdom of allowing white middle-class women to undertake such work. Despite their class privilege many believed that white female settlement house workers were vulnerable to the immoral influences of the neighborhood and its predominantly Chinese male population.[85] As one writer for *Munsey's Magazine* pointed out, Sigel was "a girl of refinement and good education." Her breeding and moral virtue should have protected her, yet she succumbed to an infatuation with a Chinese man. More disturbing for this writer was the realization that Sigel was not alone in her attraction, as evidenced by the many letters written by other white female admirers seemingly of middle-class backgrounds found in Leon Ling's room. These were not women "of the class that springs from the gutter and has natural association with the loose-living Orientals of Mott Street and Pell Street and that neighborhood," yet "they had thrust themselves into the haunts of these low creatures." To explain their unsavory attraction he suggested that it was a woman's natural "passion for adornment," combined with "a strong love of the exotic" that facilitated "a willingness to overstep race lines."[86]

The Sigel murder case occurred amidst great urban social and cultural transformations. The dramatic increase of young girls and women working and socializing outside of their homes brought about the emergence of a new public culture and female geography centered around material consumption and heterosexual romance. State policies toward female sexual deviance further shifted the Victorian constructions of female passionlessness to new depictions of adolescent girls and women as consumers and sexual agents with definable desires. These desires could be tolerated as long as they supported a form of safely contained heterosexual socializing that would result in respectable marriage and domesticity. Otherwise these desires needed to be disciplined or subdued, if not by parents, then by a variety of newly established state agents and institutions supported by an urban polity concerned with the maintenance of public moral order and decency.

Even as the public struggled with accepting these new modes of female sexuality that widened the bounds of feminine respectability, expressions of mutual attraction and affection between Chinese and whites remained difficult to accept. Interracial sexual relations between white women and Chinese men continued to be defined in the earlier Victorian terms of masculine assaults on vulnerable white girls and women. Indeed the presence of this racialized sexual threat, in the form of Chinatown and Chinese male laborers at large in the metropolis, continued to make the white urban working girl as sexual victim a viable social and cultural construct even into the modern era.

Those young girls and women caught pursuing relationships with Chinese men could not so easily be described as the victims of Chinese masculine predation; yet, they were also not portrayed as their own sexual agents. Unlike the modern working girl or woman who engaged in sexual acts for the sake of heterosexual romance, the white female companion of a Chinese man was more often depicted as one who was driven or imprisoned by her own material addictions and excesses that led to the unintended consequences of interracial sex. The fear, however, was that not only were working-class women susceptible to the lure of the material luxuries promised by life with a Chinese man; even middle-class women from comfortable, respectable families could be easily enticed. As suggested by the murder of Elsie Sigel, the "girl missionary," no woman in New York was truly safe from the dangers posed by contact with the Chinese and their establishments.

CHAPTER FOUR

Playing the "Missionary Game"

As THE POLICE LAUNCHED their investigation into the mysterious death of Elsie Sigel, the city's newspapers engaged the public in a debate over the benefits of Chinese missionary activities in the metropolitan area. Many writers echoed the sentiments of an editorial published in the *Newark Star* that the murder revealed the folly of Chinese missions, stating "[t]here is certainly a moral in this awful case of crime that should be pondered on."[1] Captain Arthur Carey of the NYPD declared to the press that Leon Ling must have deceived the well-intentioned missionaries whom he encountered with his claims to be a Christian convert and dismissed his church-going as part of a "missionary game" to meet impressionable young white women.

> "This Chinaman," Capt. Carey said, "has been working the missionary game for years. There's no question about it. He was one of the swell kind too, and had the very best of the white women missionaries to choose as his teacher. That's the way the Chinamen settle these matters. The queueless ones and the members of Chinatown's '400' get the pick of everything from their Sunday school teacher to their first choice of places in the joss house.
>
> "If the high tone Chinaman sees ordinary 'Chink' butting in and getting an attractive woman missionary to accept him as a pupil, the influential one whispers a little advice into the ear of the low caste Chinaman and the missionary wonders what became of her pupil."[2]

Carey's account depicted the activities of Chinese missions in a manner similar to the flirtatious encounters between unchaperoned men and women found in the city's working-class dance halls or chop suey restaurants. In effect his description of the "missionary game" went beyond trying to recount a profile of the accused murderer, Leon Ling, to indict all Chinese men who attended these missions.

The captain's move to unmask the "missionary game" sparked a number of heated responses in the city's newspapers. An editorial in the *New York Times,* though it acknowledged that not all Chinese converts attended these schools under false pretenses, nonetheless argued that the sentimentality of the female teachers prevented them from protecting themselves from unscrupulous men like Leon Ling, who "has posed for years as a convert of extraordinary piety." To the writer, the Chinese Sunday schools

Figure 4.1. Following the Elsie Sigel murder numerous cartoons such as this one appeared, questioning white female participation in the Chinese missionary movement. *Source*: Hy. Mayer, "Just Supposing," *New York Times*, June 27, 1909, fifth section.

performed an important function as a major Christianizing and Americanizing influence on the Chinese population, acclimating them to life in American society. "They must have, on the whole, a beneficial influence, if not in making Christians of their pupils at least to teaching them the language and something of the manners of this country."[3] Yet, to use female missionaries was an unnecessary risk. Male missionaries, he argued, were not ruled by sentiment and were more capable of making judgments on the sincerity of the Chinese pupils under their charge. Another editorial in the *New York Tribune* thought the practice of allowing white women to teach men—especially Chinese men—to be "shocking and dangerous."[4]

Other press accounts further accused Chinese converts of not living up to the sinless lives expected of them. The city's Protestant leaders however, realizing that their life's work was under attack, suggested another explanation for Sigel's murder to deflect attention away from their Chinese male pupils and converts. The *World* reported that the general view among the male missionaries, American and Chinese, was that "she couldn't have been 'really saved herself before she began the great work for the Lord of saving others.'" Some women, too, made a similar claim, exclaiming their shock that Sigel seemed to have "so forgotten her Redeemer as to sin."[5] From a thorough examination of the city's editorials and letters to the editor printed in newspapers during the course of the murder investigation, however, few among the public supported this view.

The criticism that women should not be allowed to teach Chinese men or that young women needed to be chaperoned had serious implications for the future of missionary work and the possibilities for professional women in the workforce. By arguing that women put themselves at great risk, when venturing into Chinatown or working in Chinese missions located throughout the greater metropolitan area, these writers essentially called for a reassessment of women's shifting gender roles at a particular historical moment when white middle-class women were increasingly entering the public sphere. These young, urban "New Women" as they were known in the popular press, increasingly made their way into the professional ranks, eschewing the traditional path of early marriage and lifelong domesticity.[6] Particularly troubling for these writers was the broadening of middle-class women's work roles that took them out of the protection of the home, allowing for frequent encounters with the opposite sex. Even more disturbing were those opportunities for middle-class women to interact with non-white men, that critics saw as harboring the potential for interracial sexual relations. These authors suggested that professional women should be either more carefully monitored or restricted in their actions and movements in their work and travels through the city. Such a criticism greatly alarmed missionaries, as well as working and professional women who saw themselves under attack for pursuing a livelihood or calling outside of the home.

In an effort to defend the city's Chinese Sunday schools and missions, Sanford Culver Hearn, a clergyman from Yonkers, submitted letters to both the *New York Times* and the *World*. Writing to set the record straight about Elsie Sigel and Chinese missions in the city, Hearn boldly charged that Sigel was not a missionary as the city's newspapers had alleged. The press's incorrect characterization of Sigel, Hearn argued, had done terrible harm to the reputations of the city's religious institutions. Chinese Christians also echoed Hearn's sentiments and quickly mobilized to dispute the popular opinion that Leon Ling was a Christian convert. Reverend Huie Kin of the Presbyterian Chinese Mission at 223 E. Thirty-first Street asserted to the press that "Leon was not a member of any mission. I know every mission school in Chinatown, and my workers and

THE INFERNAL QUESTION.

Figure 4.2. *Source*: Robert Carter, "The Infernal Question," *The World*, June 24, 1909.

CHRISTIANIZED?

Figure 4.3. These two cartoons further lampooned the efforts of female missionaries by suggesting that, despite the changes in the Chinaman's outward appearance, it by no means guaranteed a similar inward transformation had occurred. *Source*: "Christianized?" *The World*, June 23, 1909.

I have made inquiry and we have yet to find a regular Sunday school that he attended. The same is true of Miss Sigel. She is not known in any Christian mission, and as far as I know, she never taught in any mission."[7]

Despite these religious leaders' claims that Sigel was not a missionary to the Chinese and that Leon Ling was not a Christian, these statements came too late. The image of Elsie Sigel as the young, innocent missionary and Leon Ling as her insincere pupil was deeply impressed upon the vast majority of the nation's newspaper readers, and the press and public continued to describe her as the murdered Chinatown missionary. Overnight her grisly murder confirmed what many New Yorkers had already suspected: the domestic Chinese missionary enterprise was a failure, placing young white women in jeopardy and yielding few true converts among the city's Chinese laborers. Similar to Chinatown and Chinese-owned businesses, the Chinese mission became another racialized and gendered space that required the reassertion of white masculine authority to contain the activities of white women and Chinese men.

AMERICAN FEMALE MISSIONARIES ABROAD

At the time of the Sigel murder, the country had already witnessed nearly a century of American-sponsored foreign missionary activities. Although the U.S. foreign mission movement began in 1810 with the establishment of the American Board of Commissioners for Foreign Missions, the movement did not fully develop until the post–Civil War period.[8] By the 1880s American women increasingly came to play a dominant role in the movement. From 1880 to 1920 American Christian women participated in missionary work in unprecedented numbers, forming the majority of members and workers in both the domestic and foreign missions.[9]

Missionary work created new opportunities for young middle-class women interested in pursuing professional careers, and female missionaries quickly established a unique role for women in the movement. Their duty to work toward the salvation of native women set them apart from the work of male missionaries who, because of the rigid gender stratification in many of these societies, were usually barred from interacting with local girls and women.[10] In the eyes of female missionaries this gender-specific strategy created a special place for female workers, making them critical to the success of the missionary enterprise. Missionaries, identifying native women as the chief socializing agent in the home, reasoned that conversion of wives and mothers would eventually lead to the conversion of husbands and children. This belief did not just grow out of missionaries' observations of native societies but also from their own experiences with religious revivals back in the Unnited States, where women often took on leadership roles in bringing family members into the church.[11] Coupled with nineteenth-century domestic ideology that constructed women's home and family responsibilities as the means to maintain a moral and Christian society, female missionaries saw their role as the key to establishing Christianity in foreign lands.

In China single women filled the professional positions that specifically ministered to women—evangelists, teachers, doctors, and more. The presence of female missionaries in China and other parts of the non-Western world at times provoked controversy among missionary boards. Married women, accompanying their clergy husbands, posed no real problem to foreign missionary boards. The couple constituted a legitimate family and the wife was seen as an invaluable helpmate to her husband as well as an important source of unpaid labor for the missionary movement. Rather, it was the presence of single women that threatened to destabilize gender roles and the missionary social hierarchy as these female career missionaries often competed with their male counterparts for recognition and leadership positions among the local populations and sponsoring missionary boards. Missionary work also carried with it the same fears attached to other professional work, as potentially defeminizing in granting women leadership responsibilities.[12]

Nonetheless boards could not keep women out of the foreign field because their work, often in the form of cheap or unpaid labor, was vital to the movement. By the late nineteenth century a decline in prestige attached to missionary service, and increasing business and managerial opportunities available to college-educated males, meant that fewer men were willing to dedicate themselves to lower-paying missionary work.[13] The departure of white middle-class, native-born men from the missionary movement also paralleled a general decline in this group's involvement in the various Protestant churches. Although single women's work became crucial with this decline in male participation, their socioeconomic position in the missionary movement remained low in comparison to male clergy members. By the 1880s calls for a more virile "muscular Christianity" eventually led to movements to restore male participation and authority.[14]

The roles of women in Chinese foreign missions also differed from their domestic counterparts because of the radically different gender composition of their constituencies. With some notable exceptions such as the Chinese Mission Home, also known as Cameron House, in San Francisco, that specifically worked with Chinese women, most domestic missions worked predominantly with Chinese men.[15] Owing to the relatively small numbers of Chinese women in the United States, the gender specific proselytizing strategy used by foreign missions could not be fully adapted to the domestic context. The late-nineteenth-century decline in American men's interest in missionary work, coupled with the increasing numbers of female missionaries, meant that the labor of American women as missionary workers was needed to reach the communities of Chinese male workers in American cities. Unlike their sisters laboring abroad whose work with native women limited their contact with Chinese men, many missionary women working in Chinese American communities taught an overwhelmingly male student population. Although missionary boards had accepted the presence of female missionaries in domestic and foreign service since the end of the Civil War, the scope of their role in Chinese missions in the United States remained contested.

THE RISE OF DOMESTIC CHINESE MISSIONS

By the last quarter of the nineteenth century, missions and Sunday schools for Chinese operated in cities and small towns across North America. The Five Points House of Industry (FPHI) founded in 1850 became the first in New York City to establish special services for the Chinese population. Among the house visits made to neighborhood residents in 1865 were ten to Chinese Amercian families.[16] The increasing number of Chinese seamen arriving on merchant trading vessels in lower Manhattan's seaport district caught the attention of one FPHI worker, Sara Goodrich, who began a Chinese night school that focused primarily on English instruction. By 1872 Goodrich reported some success with the school, stating that three former students had gone on to study at Howard University. It was Goodrich's hope that two of the students, who had become Christians, would return to China as missionaries.[17]

By 1879 the New York Ladies' Home Missionary Society, through the Five Points Mission, had also begun planning for a Chinese school and mission at 14 Mott Street.[18] A year later the society's annual report proudly reported that "a promising young Chinaman, Moy-Jin-Fuey was baptized by us on the 7th of March."[19] An anonymous donor had heard about Moy and agreed to subsidize his education at the Pennington Seminary in New Jersey, preparing his way to become a missionary.

The New York Bible Society, an auxiliary branch of the American Bible Society (ABS), supplied Bibles and New Testament tracts to the city's Chinese missions and Sunday schools. In 1878 the organization provided ten New Testament tracts for the students in Goodrich's class and another fifty Bibles to the Methodist Episcopal Mission at 14 Mott Street.[20] In the next six years the ABS's distribution broadened through the establishment of eight more Chinese Sunday schools and missions of all Protestant denominations throughout the city.[21]

New York City churches' increasing interest in conducting missionary work in the Chinese community slowly yielded results. The Fifth Avenue

Presbyterian Church, for example, was particularly successful in attracting converts, listing nearly forty Chinese names as "Admitted on Profession" between 1888 and 1908. Almost all of the new Chinese members had the last name of "Chu," suggesting that family or kinship networks were important in bringing Chinese immigrants to this church.[22] As these missions began to attract a small number of loyal followers among Chinese immigrants, a few churches began to groom some of its Chinese members to take on more important leadership roles in the missionary movement. In 1888 the Methodist Episcopal Church of the City of New York established a Chinese mission at Seventh Avenue and Twenty-third Street. E. Reinhart and Mary A. Lathbury served as the mission's superintendents while Chu Bok, a Christianized Chinese, worked as the resident missionary.

Huie Kin, one of the city's better known Chinese Christian leaders, arrived in New York in 1885 after having attended Lane Theological Seminary in Cincinnati, Ohio. He became acquainted with New York's Chinese community and met Reverend George Alexander of University Place Presbyterian Church, who helped him establish a Chinese mission at 15 University Place.[23] One year later, with his papers from the Presbytery of Cincinnati, he was received as a candidate to the New York Presbytery.[24] Impressed with his religious education and his Chinese language abilities, the New York Presbytery groomed Huie Kin to take over their Chinese missionary work in the city.

In 1886 Huie Kin met his future wife, Louise Van Arnam, the daughter of a Troy, New York manufacturer, John T. Van Arnam. The two met when Louise attended a New Year celebration at Huie Kin's mission while she was a student at Bethany Institute of New York, a missionary training school in Manhattan. Interestingly, the New York Presbytery did not appear to have interfered in the couple's relationship and seemed to have supported their decision to marry once sufficiently convinced that the two were sincere in their affections. Perhaps in an attempt to avoid public controversy, the couple was married on April 1889 by Dr. Alexander in a quiet ceremony.[25]

Huie Kin remained in the New York Presbytery's good favor. Throughout the late 1880s he received praise for his work as the primary Chinese missionary at the Chinese Sunday school affiliated with the Presbyterian Church at University Place.[26] Under his direction an average of forty to fifty students attended regularly. In 1894, when Huie Kin underwent the examination for licensure, his test differed from the other candidates because he was "for special reasons excused from the delivery of a trial sermon."[27] No doubt the New York Presbytery's desire to pursue mission work among the Chinese helped to push his candidacy along by allowing him to forgo this part of the exam. On June 30, 1895, nearly ten years after his arrival in New York City, Huie Kin became ordained in a ceremony presided by his old friend Reverend Alexander at the University Place Church.[28]

In 1892 the Chinese Sabbath School Association of New York (CSSA) published a national directory of Protestant Chinese missions, listing 291 such institutions from 11 different denominations in 36 states, territories, and provinces across the United States and Canada. The majority of these institutions were located in major cities, serving considerable numbers of Chinese laborers in the restaurant and laundry businesses. A great many missions, Sunday schools, and churches could also be found in smaller towns and cities in the Midwest and South, including Omaha, Nebraska; Erie, Pennsylvania; Shreveport, Louisiana; and many others. Yet even with the proliferation of religious institutions that opened their doors to the Chinese community, the CSSA estimated that the "[w]hole number of Chinese male and female, children and adults, reached regularly or occasionally with Christian instruction to be 7,324."[29] Even with low conversion rates Protestant missionary boards continued to expand and support the work of Chinese missions. By 1904 the Woman's American Baptist Home Mission Society proudly proclaimed the proliferation of Chinese missions in cities throughout the East Coast.[30]

Domestic Chinese missions were unlike their counterparts working with European immigrant populations that aimed to hasten the social and cultural assimilation of their charges into American society. Although laboring in the United States, domestic Chinese missions remained ideologically and institutionally connected to the China missionary field as indicated by the structural organization and operating philosophy of the missions. Since the establishment of the first Chinese missions in the United States, missionaries hoped that their Chinese converts would one day return to China to become the movement's foot soldiers, spreading the gospel in their native tongue. In describing the goals of their Chinese mission at West Fifty-ninth Street, the Fifth Avenue Presbyterian Church discussed the important role domestic work played in promoting the success of the larger foreign missionary enterprise: "The scholars return to China from time to time, and it is our aim that they shall go back with a knowledge of the Truth, and a willingness to aid the Missionaries of Christ in the land in the Master's Work. We have reason to believe from reports received that our Christian converts who returned to China stand firm in their new faith."[31] Similar hopes were expressed by Mrs. A. L. Buell, superintendent of the Chinese Sunday school on Atlantic Avenue in Brooklyn, when she nurtured the religious education of Fong Bor, who also went by the name of Richard Fong Bowe. The success of Chinese students like Bowe, in attaining a religious education and committing to missionary work in China, justified the establishment and financial support of Chinese Sunday schools.[32]

Not only were missionaries impressed with the sincerity and religious fervor of some of their pupils, they also believed that Chinese students were better suited to carry out the work in the China field. Reverend Henry B. Hudson, pastor of Trinity Baptist Church, pointed to the case of a former student, Chang Kum Sing, who "came to our Sunday-school in the times when Christian children used to stone our pupils so that some had to be taken to a hospital."[33] His commitment led him to engage in proselytizing activities in Brooklyn and New Jersey.[34] He not only returned to China as a missionary but became more successful than his American counterparts. He counted sixty converts in one year, whereas the other forty-eight Baptist missionaries combined totaled only sixty-one. In addition Hudson charged that the hiring of Chinese missionaries would prove more economical in the long run. Chang Kum Sing required only a yearly stipend of $120, whereas the American missionary needed ten times the amount. Hudson's description of Chang Kum Sing's efficiency and frugality as a missionary likened him to the familiar image of the Chinese coolie laborer who posed unfair labor competition to white workers.[35] Better than his American counterpart, who required expensive, time-consuming language training and higher salary, Chinese missionaries like Chang Kum Sing could produce more and at a lower cost to his employer. Such "success stories" helped to promote the work of domestic Chinese missions as invaluable to the broader foreign missionary movement. Yet, as a setting that facilitated contact between Chinese men and white middle-class women, the domestic Chinese mission remained a suspect space that was vulnerable to public scrutiny and condemnation. Ultimately the controversy over Chinese missions and their employment of white women as teachers focused on how to define or confine their role.

Chinese Immigrant Participation in the City's Missions

Although domestic Chinese missions and Sunday schools operated to promote the foreign missionary movement, Chinese students and converts saw their potential for promoting their struggle for social, cultural, and political recognition in this country. Religious conversion and church involvement were often intertwined with Chinese immigrants' demands for social inclusion and legal citizenship, as many also recognized the advantages of such a social and religious affiliation. Most important was the opportunity to learn English through the Bible study that the mission classes provided. For Chinese working long hours in the city's restaurants and laundries, the missions' evening and Sunday school classes provided a readily accessible and inexpensive means to acquire English language instruction. Missions and Sunday schools also became important social centers for the small numbers of Chinese who attended. Students often looked forward to participating in the weekly suppers, excursions, and special holiday celebrations such as Christmas that occurred throughout the year. Annual boating trips with students and teachers from different Chinese missions in the city were always well attended.[36]

While teachers hoped that students would become more Christianized or Americanized in their outlook through their contact with the missions, students still maintained their ethnic identity in a variety of ways. Students of the Chinese Sunday school of De Witt Memorial Church at 280 Rivington Street, for example, not only raised their own funds for the school but also managed to send $15 to aid flood victims in China.[37] The Calvary Baptist Church also assisted in an anniversary celebration and fund-raiser for the Chinese Hospital located at 45 Hicks Street in Brooklyn; a combination of speeches by New York church leaders and Chinese Christians comprised the program for the celebration.[38] Aside from the celebration of Christmas or American civic holidays, schools often hosted Chinese New Year festivities. Though generally supportive of these types of Chinese community activities, missions were less encouraging when ethnic cultural practices conflicted with the missions' proselytizing goals. The holding of Sunday performances at the Chinese Theatre in Chinatown, for example, had not escaped the attention of missions in the area. Like the area's merchants, missionaries also awaited the large crowds of Chinese on Sundays to conduct their work. "[Sunday] is the field day, therefore, for the Morning Star Mission, and we take advantage of this floating multitude to thoroughly permeate it with Gospel Literature."[39] Not only did these performances violate the city's established Sunday laws supported by the city's missions but the theater drew crowds larger than the city's Sunday schools. Not surprisingly, missionaries down the street at 17 Doyers Street complained on several occasions "of the great annoyance caused by the discordant music in the theatre,"[40] requesting that the theater not be allowed to hold performances on Sunday. In this manner the missions and their schools played not only a religious but also a significant social role in the lives of the students.

As these examples suggest, this small group of Chinese Christians did not distance themselves from the Chinese community. Despite their adoption of Christianity, many remained keenly aware of their precarious social and legal status under the Chinese Exclusion Acts. Instead they used their church affiliation to create bridges to the wider New York society and establish an alternate base of sociopolitical power apart from the Chinese Consolidated Benevolent Association and the various family and village associations and tongs in Chinatown. Chinese Christians often turned to their churches and pastors for legal assistance and political support in times of need. When Huie Kin encountered problems with immigration officials while traveling with his sons through the port of San Francisco, he wrote to Reverend Frank Ellinwood, Secretary of Board of Foreign Missions, and Reverend Alexander for assistance.[41] In 1892 Sam Lung, who owned a laundry at 109 Eighth Avenue, turned to Reverend E. Tipple, pastor of St. Luke's Church, for assistance when he was continually harassed by boys in the neighborhood. Tipple promptly filed a complaint with the Sixteenth Precinct. When Tipple saw no immediate aid forthcoming, he then wrote to Mayor Hugh Grant to report that Sam Lung was "nightly stoned by boys" and that "repeated complaints have been made to police officers and to the captain of the precinct, but no relief has been afforded."[42] The mayor then referred the matter to Police Superintendent William Murray. Two weeks later, Captain Donald Grant of the Sixteenth Precinct replied to the superintendent that he had dispatched "officers in citizens dress" to watch over the laundry and that he had also directed officers to give that area "special attention."[43] In 1902 Wah Sing, following his arrest for allegedly assaulting Vernon E. King, a machinist, asked his Sunday school to intervene. E. J. Taylor, a missionary, wrote on his behalf stating that "being one of our Sunday School scholars we would like to see to it that counsel is engaged to defend him as we believe that what ever was done was done in self defense. If you will kindly give this your personal attention we will be very thankful to you."[44]

Following the passage of the Chinese Exclusion Act, increasing numbers of Chinese converts throughout the metropolitan region hoped to use their hard-earned membership with a Protestant church to establish their case for citizenship or permanent residence in the United States. In 1887 Ip-ki-Tsak, a laundryman residing in nearby New Haven, Connecticut, turned to the teachers at his Sunday school to ask for help with negotiating the legal obstacles preventing him from bringing his wife and six-year-old son into the country. Moses White, who wrote Daniel Manning, Secretary of the Treasury, on Ip-ki-Tsak's behalf, stated in his letter that community residents believed that "it would greatly improve the moral and social status of the Chinese residents if the Chinese who have wives could and would bring them here."[45] White further hoped that because his wife and son were by no means "laborers," they would not be denied entry into this country. White attached a petition, specifically stating that Ip-ki-Tsak was a student of the Sabbath school in New Haven and had proven to be a man of "honesty, sobriety, and faithfulness."[46] The petition was supported by two pages of signatures that included Yale dignitaries such as President Timothy Dwight, Dean Frances Wayland of the Law School, and other deans, professors, local clergymen, and residents. Despite the endorsement of such illustrious men of arts and letters, the Secretary of the Treasury declined the request, perfunctorily stating that "in view of the existing decision of this department and the U.S. Circuit Court of California to the effect that the wife of a Chinese laborer is a person whose original entry into this country is prohibited by said act, the Department has no power, under the law, to grant your request."[47]

Even with such refusals Chinese Christians, along with their teachers, continued to submit their requests for citizenship or exemption from the exclusion acts. In 1888 Mrs. L. S. Davis wrote on behalf of one Chinese laundry owner, a student at her Sunday school in New York City, to inquire into the procedure for allowing Chinese immigrants to exit and return to the United States. Emphasizing that "my scholar is a Christian man," Davis hoped that the man's religious status would convince treasury officials that he should not be treated as a common laundry worker.[48] In 1891 Lee Num, a Philadelphia resident, wrote to Secretary James Blaine requesting that he be allowed to return after visiting his elderly parents in China. Stating proudly that he had "lived in this country for nine years and [had] attended the Tabernacle Baptist Church and the Chinese American Mission for 3 years and was baptized at the Tabernacle Church December 21st 1890," Lee Num hoped that Blaine would grant his wish.[49] To further plead his cause Lee Num enlisted the aid of George E. Rees of the Sunday school to write a letter to the Secretary of the Treasury on his behalf. In the letter's closing Rees wrote, "Pardon my intrusion in writing you on this matter that may seem a small one, *but I like this Chinaman* and am anxious to help him if I can."[50] Although Sunday school teachers and church leaders saw their Christianizing work as critical in laying the necessary moral foundation for good citizenship, the immigration exclusion acts were simply based on the criteria of racial ancestry and economic class. Reply letters remained brief and to the point and did not even acknowledge the writers' religious affiliations. Like their non-Christian brethren, as long as the petitioner was a Chinese laborer it would not be possible to bring one's family members or return to the United States.[51] The demands of Chinese Christians for social and legal inclusion nonetheless challenged the institutional structure and goals of domestic Chinese missions as subordinate to the larger cause of the foreign missionary movement. By pushing for citizenship rights they demanded that the Protestant missionary movement fulfill the egalitarian vision of Christian fellowship and brotherhood promised to converts.

CLAIMING CITIZENSHIP: ST. BARTHOLOMEW'S CHINESE GUILD (*Bao Niang Hui*)

The St. Bartholomew's Chinese Guild or *Bao Niang Hui*, under the leadership of Chinese Christians, demonstrates the extent to which Chinese immigrant participation affected institutional change within the city's missionary movement. In 1889 the St. Bartholomew's Protestant Episcopal Church established the Guild at 23 St. Mark's Place under the direction of the rector, Reverend D. H. Greer, with John Thorne as the superintendent and Guy Maine as the interpreter.[52] While the Guild's founding reflects a partnership between Chinese and white Christians, Guy Maine and Jin Fuey Moy quickly emerged as key leaders in the organization. The following year Maine became the Guild's manager and took on the role of overseeing the Guild's daily operations. In 1894 Jin Fuey Moy took over the position of superintendent, and in 1900, Guy Maine replaced him as the president and superintendent.

Devoted Christians, Maine and Moy were nonetheless dissatisfied with the traditional Protestant missionary emphasis on religious conversion and salvation without equal interest in ameliorating the difficult lives of Chinese immigrants living under the shadow of social, legal, and political exclusion. Throughout their tenure with the Guild they would continually balance the secular and religious aspects of the organization's mission while pushing white missionaries and supporters at St. Bartholomew's to join them in the much needed work of legal advocacy and social work among the city's Chinese laborers.

From the outset the Guild placed less emphasis on religious conversion and instruction. As Guy Maine noted in his 1890 report, the Guild "was a long-felt want, for it fills the niche in the evangelization of this people that no Sunday-school or mission could have filled." Rather than placing religious conversion as its primary goal, the Guild aimed to address Chinese immigrants' material needs by giving "assistance whenever its members are in persecution, distress, sickness, or in whatsoever trouble, but religion and the elevation of this people are the solid basis of this work." In this manner, the Guild retained a clearly Protestant orientation, but with an emphasis on the material needs of the city's Chinese population. Indeed, the majority of the Guild's work was clearly not religious, but involved providing legal advocacy and welfare services: "interviewing landlords and agents, interpreting in courts, engaging stores, drawing up leases, settling disputes, writing letters, health department cases, corporation cases, visiting the sick, looking up scholars for teachers, translating, procuring police protection, and many other minor matters."[53]

The Chinese Guild, in many respects, combined characteristics associated with the Young Men's Christian Association (YMCA) and ethnic societies of the late nineteenth century in its emphasis on "social intercourse and good fellowship." With its public visiting rooms and library full of Chinese and English books and periodicals and a large gymnasium, the Guild was a rare institution for the city's Chinese, offering a place for physical and intellectual stimulation. Maine and other Christian members were also particularly active in promoting Bible study in the group. In one of the Guild's first reports published in 1889, Superintendent John Thorne explained that religious services would not be held regularly at the Guild because its leaders felt that it was important for members to regard the Guild as "a home for them all."[54] Moreover, many felt the need for religious instruction was already filled by the numerous Sunday schools and missions in the city. Nonetheless the Guild's Christian Chinese did hold several informal Bible classes for interested members that included readings, discussions, and singing.

The Guild's pedagogical approach to religious instruction differed greatly from the other missions and Sunday school classes sponsored by established city churches. As Maine reported, "the memorizing of Scriptural passages, repeating them in parrot-like fashion at the close of the session, is not in practice, nor do we observe the general rule that the Bible must be used on the Sabbath."[55] To allay the fears of the Guild's Christian benefactors, Maine then added that "Christianity is the keystone of our work" but first one had to replace the men's traditional Chinese worldview. "We try to eradicate old prejudices, superstitions and wrong ideas by free discussions of events of the past and of the present, great inventions, new discoveries, anything and everything that would help to build up a strong healthful mind that can think and act for itself without relying like a sightless man upon others."[56] Maine placed less emphasis on the individual's conversion experience as one of faith or spirituality; rather, his emphasis on "free discussions" and technology mirrored contemporary Chinese revolutionaries' attempts to modernize Chinese society through the introduction of Western liberal political traditions and science.[57] In addition Maine, unlike American missionaries, stressed the inculcation of social values over religious conversion. To Maine the Christian was not necessarily superior to a non-Christian if both men exhibited the same values of honesty, sobriety, frugality, and industry.[58]

The eclectic decorations and mix of books in the Guild's library also reflected the white leadership's attempts to promote Christian literature and worship while maintaining its orientalist outlook, even as the Chinese leadership attracted members by appealing to their shared ethnic identity and offering much needed social services. Thorne's private collection of "some rubbings of the great Nestorian Stone, showing evidences of Christianity in China at a very early period after the Christians were dispersed from Jerusalem" adorned the walls of the library along with Chinese pearl-inlaid furniture and silk scrolls purchased by funds raised by the Chinese members themselves.[59] The Chinese members, however, placed their own demands on the facility. Many laborers, for example, asked that the gymnasium be changed to facilitate "some light amusement" as many remarked wryly, "there is plenty of physical exercise in our place of business."[60] Members also hoped to have "a smoking or club room" as well as a parlor for group relaxation and entertainment.[61] In his 1900 report on the Guild, Maine wrote that "the members of the Guild and School have taken great pride in trying to fit up the room in the Parish House in the most unique Oriental fashion. The cost of the furniture and silk trappings will amount to about 600 Mexican dollars."[62]

Though many of the Guild's members were Christians active in missions and Sunday schools throughout the city, its primary objective to serve the medical, social, and legal interests of Chinese led them to gain a broader Chinese membership base than any of the city's religious institutions. About two hundred Chinese guests attended the Guild's official opening; weekly visitors numbered around thirty and Sunday visitors amounted to fifty-five.[63] By its second year Maine reported 612 dues-paying members and the need to limit the number of members.[64] By contrast, most of the city's missions and Sunday schools reported Sunday attendance figures of lower than twenty each.

After paying the Guild's $2 initiation fee and $1 annual dues, its members received a certificate confirming their membership, making them eligible for legal aid and translation assistance in court matters. In addition, disagreements between guild members could be subject to arbitration and judgment by the Guild's membership. The Chinese Guild also expanded its duties to provide rudimentary health insurance to its members. As early as 1890 Maine sought to convert rooms at the Guild to house sick members in need of medical care. Because of Chinese immigrants' suspicion of the city's hospitals, most did not go "except as a last resort, and go there to die."[65] Members who became ill or injured could contact the Guild for medical assistance from either a Chinese or American doctor. Patients were expected to pay all medical expenses, but in the case that such financial resources were unavailable the Guild would pick up the costs after satisfactory proof of the member's indigence. In addition the Guild would allow recovering members to convalesce in one of its rented rooms without charge.[66]

Although St. Bartholomew did not oversee the Guild's daily operations, the Guild relied upon the church's support in financial and sociolegal matters. The Guild leaders and members clearly welcomed their support and professional assistance. Within the first year of operation, Guy Maine was called to work on twenty-six cases. In reporting the progress of the Guild to the members of its sponsoring parish, Superintendent Thorne spoke of the demand for volunteer physicians and a good lawyer "who understands Chinamen or can get to know the Chinese mode of thought and action, so as to help them through the many law cases."[67] Demands for legal assistance increased alongside the climb in membership and changes in the Chinese Exclusion laws. Guild leaders and members helped to mount a Constitutional challenge to the 1892 Geary Act by participating in a test case "having one or three Chinamen in this country since 1880 arrested under it, and then to take out a 'habeus corpus.'"[68] The case, eventually known as *Fong Yue Ting vs. U.S.*, challenged the Geary Act's proposed system of requiring all Chinese immigrants to apply and carry certificates of residence or face deportation or imprisonment. In addition the case also tested the provision disqualifying people of "the Chinese race" from being witnesses to help petitioner's establish their residency in the United States, instead requiring the testimony of at least "one credible white witness."[69] Guy Maine, who had signed on as the interpreter for the case, tested this stipulation by offering himself as the sole witness for one of the three men in the case.[70] The court, however, upheld the Constitutionality of the Geary Act, and the Guild's work expanded to help its members navigate the new provisions of the law. By 1895 Superintendent Jin Fuey Moy claimed that the Guild worked on nearly five thousand cases ranging from vandalism to robbery and assault to immigration violations.[71]

In response to the ongoing problems of assault and vandalism, the Guild hired a private detective to investigate cases "of malicious boys throwing stones to break the windows of Chinese laundries" and offered rewards for the capture and conviction of such offenders.[72] The continuing harassment of Chinese-owned businesses led Guy Maine in 1901 to campaign for the Guild's incorporation. "As a private institution," Maine pointed out, "the Chinese Guild has no legal standing in any court, except as its superintendent may act as an interpreter in the case." Rather, he argued that incorporation would grant the Guild the "legal right in the courts to protect our members."[73] In 1909 Maine relocated the Guild's offices to a Chinatown location at 20 Chatham Street to better accommodate its Chinese members. A group of Chinese Christians rented the floor above the Guild to serve "as a home for the unemployed and the unfortunate sick."[74] Upon completing twenty years of service to the Chinese American community, the Guild proudly proclaimed that "over twenty-three thousand matters have been attended to; on an average of four in each working day." By contrast to the impressive number of requests for sociolegal advice and assistance, the Guild's religious work produced only a total of eighty-two baptisms.[75]

As these activities suggest, the Guild, with its focus on securing sociolegal protections, operated differently from the foreign mission imperative of the white American Protestant missionary movement. Instead, the Chinese Guild aimed to provide its members with a wide range of services to meet the everyday challenges of working and living under the restrictions imposed by the Chinese Exclusion Acts. As long as such issues did not wholly detract from the important work of religious conversion as envisioned by its original white missionary sponsors, such activities were not only tolerated but often warmly supported as evidenced by the range of non-religious services St. Bartholomew's church members and missionaries agreed to perform on behalf of their Chinese constituents. Indeed, many willingly came to the aid of their Chinese American students or colleagues in the name of Christian charity or fellowship. Yet this is not to suggest that questions of citizenship and social equality between whites and Chinese were well addressed. Rising controversy around the questions of inter-marriage and white female missionaries' roles in the movement suggests the degree to which these issues remained largely unresolved in the late nineteenth and early twentieth centuries.

THE QUESTION OF WOMEN MISSIONARIES IN CHINESE MISSIONS AND SUNDAY SCHOOLS

Though single women clearly made up a significant portion of mission-ary personnel by the late nineteenth century, the public remained uneasy with their presence in non-white or working-class immigrant communi-ties such as Chinatown. The issue of interracial marriage had already been used to undermine the validity of social movements that involved white and non-white participants. In the early nineteenth century north-ern abolitionists were often accused of dismantling important social and racial distinctions between whites and blacks because of their campaign to end not only slavery but "black laws." Though most abolitionists, with the exception of William Lloyd Garrison and his supporters from Massachusetts, did not attempt to remove laws prohibiting interracial marriage and sexual relations, their opponents nonetheless often ac-cused them of doing so.[76] In the infamous 1864 miscegenation hoax aimed to discredit the Republican Party, two northern Democratic Party members posed as Republicans to distribute copies of a pamphlet advo-cating sex and marriage between whites and African Americans.[77] In the late nineteenth century the issue of interracial marriage was no less volatile in northern cities such as New York.

Unlike their foreign missionary sisters, who were mostly shielded from such controversy because of their clearly defined role as ministering to na-tive women only, domestic missionaries remained vulnerable to such at-tacks because of their work with a primarily Chinese male constituency. In 1890 several of New York City's newspapers reported without critical commentary the marriage between a teacher and her student. Yoong Sing, a forty-year-old cigar maker who resided at 15 Forsyth Street, married Elizabeth H. Roundey, a forty-five-year-old teacher at the Chinese Sunday school of the Baptist Mariner's Temple at Oliver and James Streets, in lower Manhattan. Sing, who was baptized a year earlier, had been a regu-lar attendee of the school during his two-year residence in the city. Reverend Dr. MacArthur of the Calvary Baptist Church, at Sixth Avenue and Fifty-seventh Street, married the couple, who made their new home in Brooklyn.[78] Not only was she not censored for her marriage but she appeared to have remained in favor with the church. In his book on the history of the Calvary Baptist Church, Reverend MacArthur singled out Roundey and another female missionary, Mary S. Christopher, for praise in their missionary efforts that resulted in several Chinese joining the church. "The progress they have made under the tuition of these teachers is remarkable. A refinement of manner, as well as a knowledge of English and a familiarity with the Word of God, is a characteristic of the instruction they receive."[79] Perhaps Miss Roundey's older age and her established record of success as a Chinese missionary helped to deflect any attacks upon her reputation. Such protection, however, was by no means guaranteed, especially in the case of younger female missionaries.

Several controversies regarding the presence of female missionaries in domestic Chinese missions in the greater New York area erupted in 1891. Trinity Baptist Church Society, located on Fifty-fifth Street near Lexington Avenue, had organized a Chinese Sunday school serving an average number of thirty to forty students from New York City, Brooklyn, and Jersey City. Several of the city's newspapers reported a rumor that for the first time in the school's fourteen year history a white female teacher was soon to wed her Chinese pupil. The *World* reporter suggested that such a development was not surprising given that "[e]ach Chinaman has a teacher, and the prettiest and liveliest girls of the flock are the most successful in the work."[80] The *New York Times* named Lizzie A. Field of 160 Fifty-fifth Street and Wing Lee, a laundry owner in Brooklyn, as the mystery couple.[81] In her defense of the school and its female teachers, Augusta Carto, the founder of the Chinese school, denied those allegations vehemently, stating quite bluntly that the teachers were not young women but "with two exceptions, the teachers in my school are either widows or old maids. It isn't a nice remark to make, but it is the truth, nevertheless."[82]

Critics of the school also pointed to the suppers and luncheons served to Chinese students prepared by their teachers. According to the *World*, the church trustees deemed these social gatherings inappropriate and outside of the realm of missionary work and ordered them stopped. In defiance of the church's male leadership, Carto relocated the luncheons to her home located within the church's vicinity.[83] Similar to the general public criticism heaped upon the Sigel family for allowing Chinese men to visit their home, this blurring of social and spatial boundaries— private and public, missionary and friend, home and church—was similarly met with disapproval by late nineteenth century, middle-class New Yorkers. As a woman whose duty was to guard the home hearth with care, Carto was doubly faulted for violating proper missionary decorum as well as failing to perform her proper gender role as a wife.

Carto must have been taken aback by this seemingly sudden change in the church leadership's support of her missionary work. For over ten years her leadership remained unquestioned by the sponsoring New York City Baptist Mission Society (NYCBMS). In 1884 the annual report of the NYCBMS praised her work, proclaiming the school "a place to go when faith grows weak and interest lags in Christian work."[84] Regarding the practice of organizing social gatherings for teachers and students, the NYCBMS was also in full support. Far from condemning these types of activities as inappropriate and potentially dangerous, the NYCBMS published a favorable account of such a home visit of "lonesome Chinese boys with Mrs. Carto and the teachers, at which a motherly interest is shown in all their personal needs."[85] Indeed, the NYCBMS praised these gatherings as necessary for giving soothing "motherly care" and comfort to their homesick and persecuted Chinese pupils. Another report praised Mrs. Carto's "strong, womanly sympathy, coupled with clear judgment and marvelous courage and devotion" in making her the perfect missionary worker among the city's Chinese residents.[86]

Similar to other missionaries and reform workers of Carto's generation, this image of the woman missionary as a maternal figure and their Chinese male adult charges as small children in need of protection and nurturing drew upon Victorian notions of women's particular moral authority as derived from their feminine virtue.[87] Because the role of missionary as matron was so deeply rooted in Victorian notions of true womanhood, their work was not deemed socially threatening. Ten years later, public exposure of budding romances between young female teachers and their Chinese students subverted this earlier construction of the missionary-pupil relationship as one between mother and child. Rather than the mission taking on the attributes of a protected domestic space headed by matronly missionaries, the Chinese mission became a vehicle for miscegenation where young missionary women were in danger of losing their virtue. In effect, the Chinese mission space became as racially and sexually threatening as Chinatown itself.

By December of 1891 trouble also spread to the Sunday schools in Brooklyn. In a letter to the editor of the *Brooklyn Daily Eagle*, Reverend Valentine A. Lewis of 1091 Bushwick Avenue wrote to voice his disapproval over the state of Chinese Sunday schools. While Lewis agreed that religious work among the Chinese in the city was an important task to pursue, he proposed several critical changes to the work as it had been undertaken. First, he sought to replace one-on-one teaching with "graded classes of three or four." Second, he wanted Chinese with facility in the English language to assist in the instruction of their fellow countrymen as well as to support further those Americans who were fluent in Chinese. Third, he emphasized the importance of religious as opposed to English-language instruction in the schools. Fourth, he wanted to abolish the practice of gift giving by students to their teachers. Most importantly, he sought to end the practice of allowing "young women" to serve as teachers.[88]

Although Lewis listed these four items to address, the letter mainly elaborated upon his last point—the use of "young women" as missionaries. Lewis argued that the "thousands of unemployed Christian men and middle aged Christian women in our churches" comprised a ready pool of teachers; the men especially were "expert workers," unlike the young women currently employed. More importantly, he feared that these women were exposed to grave physical and moral danger as a result of their interactions with Chinese men. Lewis emphasized that such opportunities served to foster intermarriage, which should be seen as unnatural and a great horror. Pointing to a recent announcement of marriage between Foy Lee, a Chinese student, to Martha A. Comstock, his teacher, in Chelsea, Massachusetts, Lewis wrote: "Such a notice is an unanswerable argument in favor of a change of teachers."[89] Perhaps equally offensive to Lewis was that the marriage was printed as a notice in the paper, signaling social acceptance rather than public censure.

Lewis urged the employment of male or older female teachers to eliminate those disingenuous Chinese pupils who attended the schools only to seek the friendship of pretty young white women rather than religious instruction. Critics of women's entry into missionary work often argued that the process of religious conversion, with its appeal to the emotions, put female teachers into a highly passionate state, making them vulnerable to the amorous advances of their Chinese pupils. Young women, who were seen as particularly given to sentimental and emotional excess, were especially susceptible and needed even greater protection rather than exposure to Chinese heathens who were, for the most part, popularly portrayed as insincere converts harboring lecherous feelings toward their white female teachers.

The notion that women were ill-suited to the task of proselytizing the city's Chinese residents contradicted the day-to-day realities of the city's Chinese missions and Sunday schools because women often took the initiative in establishing these institutions. In relating the story of the beginning of the Trinity Baptist Church Sunday school, Augusta Carto described how she took charge of canvassing Chinese-operated laundries in her neighborhood to drum up students. "Impressed with the value of the opportunity, I began to call from laundry to laundry, two years ago, loaning or giving papers and tracts in Chinese, thus introducing myself as a teacher from San Francisco, believing I might quietly sow the good seed of the kingdom."[90] Far from feeling restricted by Victorian conventions of propriety, missionary women such as Carto visited Chinese laundries and restaurants without male escorts to carry out their work.

When the *Eagle* reporter asked H. B. Jarvis, the son of the founder of the Chinese school at the Sixth Avenue Baptist School, about the lack of male teachers, he explained that it was because of the lack of interest on the part of Christian men to become teachers. Furthermore, Jarvis pointed to the consistently good attendance of a class taught by K. P. Lee, a male Chinese member of the congregation. "They have not only a male teacher, but one of their own race. If they were to have any objection it would seem to be to that. Yet he has a good class every Sunday." When asked about the recent marriages between teachers and pupils, Jarvis laid the blame at the feet of the female teachers. "I say freely that my belief is that where any talk has arisen in connection with these schools it has been first the fault of the teacher. There have been a few cases of marriage, and I am satisfied that the proposition has come from the women and they have not been young women either." Jarvis added that the female teachers of his school behaved with great propriety and that they had been most "fortunate." "For while most of the other schools have been commented on for some reason or other, ours has been free from any cause for public comment."[91]

Lewis's attack against Chinese Sunday schools was not taken lightly by Chinese and non-Chinese supporters of these institutions. Dr. J. C. Thoms, the Chinese superintendent of the Chinese Hospital and a teacher at the Sunday school operated by the Washington Avenue Baptist Church in Brooklyn, sent a letter to the *Eagle* to dispute Lewis's accusations. Thoms adamantly protested Lewis's claim that Chinese attended Sunday schools simply to become acquainted with young white women rather than to seek religious instruction. Moreover, Thoms threatened to take the matter to a court of law.[92] Some of the *Eagle*'s readers also wrote the editor to protest Lewis's remarks.[93]

Not satisfied with the use of the *Eagle* as a forum to air out these differences, a group of the city's most respected Chinese Christians quickly banded together to place an announcement in the newspaper calling for Lewis to appear publicly to support his damaging claims. The committee carefully planned to use the upcoming debate to garner publicity and wider support for their cause. Chief among their goals was to ensure that the city's missionary agencies be allowed to continue their work with Chinese immigrants. The committee also dispatched invitations to many of the city's clergymen and Chinese missionary supporters and workers. When asked by reporters if he would appear, Lewis stated that he had not yet received word of this challenge and would in any event decline since he found Thoms's remarks to be "abusive and irresponsible." Even so Lewis clearly wanted to be heard in a public forum, though without facing his Chinese critics. He announced to reporters he had plans to "hire a hall and present my views, charging a small admission fee, the proceeds to go to some deserving charity."[94]

On December 29 the committee held their meeting. Approximately fifty Chinese and whites gathered at the Atlantic Avenue Chinese Sunday school to hear Dr. Thoms counter the charges made by Reverend Lewis; as expected, Lewis did not show up to defend his accusations. Dr. S. L. Baldwin, secretary of the Methodist Episcopal Mission Society and a former missionary in China, presided at the meeting.[95] Thoms attempted to dissuade the audience from believing in Lewis's accusations and create a sense of common purpose and camaraderie within this small, but racially mixed audience. By focusing his attack on Lewis as an outside agitator "from the West," Thoms managed to accomplish both of these goals. He then embarked on a lengthy rebuke of Lewis for failing to attend the open meeting, which concluded with his calling Lewis "a contemptible coward!" With this denunciation, the crowd broke into applause to express their support of Thoms. More importantly, Thoms saw Lewis's attack as part of the larger anti-Chinese movement that denied Chinese any legal protection in the United States and made them "persecuted and misrepresented even for going to Sunday school." Thoms did not just depict Chinese immigrants as a victimized group willing to endure in silence. Instead, he warned that "[t]he Chinese are getting to be strong through what they have learned," and would fight future injustices.[96]

Besides Thoms, a number of clergymen and Sunday school teachers also took to the platform. These speakers did not make the connection between Lewis's attacks and the broader anti-Chinese movement and upcoming renewal of the Chinese Exclusion Act. Rather, the clergymen and teachers mainly addressed Lewis's attacks on the presence of female teachers in the city's Chinese missions and Sunday schools. The main concern of these speakers was clearly the reputation of their own respective religious institutions and the missionary movement, which they saw as hinging upon the public's perception of the relationships between Chinese male students and their white female teachers. Most were ready to defend their own institutions against Lewis's allegations and denounce interracial romance as an obstacle to mission work. The treatment of Chinese in the United States and the legitimacy of interracial marriages were clearly secondary to these concerns.

One unmarried Sunday school teacher, Helen Clark, spoke in support of the missions and similarly stressed that the majority of teachers were men or older women like herself who were "on the other side of 30." At the same time, she also emphasized that the schools were run efficiently by "men, businessmen, who are practical and know what they are doing." Directly addressing the issue of one-on-one teaching, Clark argued that while classes were the ideal, this was not always possible because of the limited English spoken and understood by their Chinese students. In closing she added that she had made a list of the Sunday

← Lewis

schools in the city and could say with satisfaction that most of the teachers were "elderly women." The young women who had been allowed to work, she felt, were "picked out of a select class. Should she flirt, she would summarily be discharged from further duties by the superintendent if he learned of it. And the superintendents are on the watch for anything of this kind." But she quickly reassured the audience that such incidents were rare and the current agitation in the press may actually be beneficial to the movement. "If it succeeds in weeding out a few unworthy teachers who have been foolish so much the better."[97]

As a woman, Clark felt the urgency to stress further the respectability of Chinese Sunday schools and the good character of its students and teachers. By emphasizing the presence of older women as teachers and men in church leadership positions, she sought to protect herself and her fellow female teachers from further criticism for their choice to engage in Chinese missionary work. In addition, her suggestion that stricter surveillance of teachers also stressed her personal integrity and respectability by making it clear that she was also against too friendly interactions and willing to uphold racial boundaries within her institution. Yet this position clearly put established female missionaries like Clark in a bind. They could no longer count on gendered claims of female virtue and piety alone to establish themselves as respectable and competent missionaries. Instead, they found themselves caught in a growing controversy where the public demanded that they give up their independence and submit to scrutiny and management by the male clergy.

Interestingly Lewis could not be easily labeled as an anti-Chinese agitator, as he countered such charges by pointing to his record of service to California's Chinese immigrant communities.[98] Although the press neither confirmed nor denied Lewis's claims to be a protector of Chinese laborers, one need not necessarily doubt his sincerity simply because of his criticism of Chinese Sunday schools. Nor should one readily dismiss Lewis's views as idiosyncratic for the Chinese missionary field. Indeed, as the comments of Clark and others suggest, few missionaries would have vocally supported the fostering of romantic interests between teachers and pupils. While missionaries held out to their Chinese constituents the possibility of cultural acceptance and social assimilation following religious conversion, they stopped short of publicly articulating such a radical vision of social equality that included interracial marriage.

Lewis was also not alone in expressing the fear that the presence of young, unmarried white female missionaries threatened to destabilize the social and moral order of the mission. This was a commonly shared view that persistently cast a shadow over women's missionary work at home and abroad. Furthermore it is important to keep in mind that the Lewis controversy occurred at a time when the numbers of female missionaries—domestic and foreign—rose to exceed the number of men in the field. This entry of young women, Lewis and many other clergymen believed, forced young male and older female missionaries out of work. He argued that the exit of these young women and return of men to the missionary field would be beneficial to the movement as he believed that "more enduring results would appear from the *manly* discharge of the duty of the church to the Chinese in our midst"[99] (italics added).

Despite Lewis's hopes for a return of men to the field, during the late nineteenth century Christian men were slow to answer the call to foreign and domestic missionary service. In his explanation of why women tended to be the teachers at his school, Reverend Dr. R. B. Hull of Greenwood Baptist Church argued that it was simply impossible to find enough men to fill the need for teachers. "In my experience of 12 years in Chinese work, however, I have never known a single instance where the Chinamen coming to the school has asked for a lady teacher or expressed a preference for any teacher except a patient one. It is well-known that women are much more patient teachers than men. Indeed it is hard to get men to do mission work on Sunday."[100] Others also supported this view.[101] Hull's explanation also suggests the slowness of the male clergy to relinquish Victorian gender roles in the missionary movement.

On January 5 Lewis hired a hall in Brooklyn to air his views publicly. Approximately sixty attended the lecture along with five Chinese, a dozen reporters, and two policemen. The five Chinese men, representing several of Brooklyn and New York City's Chinese Sunday schools, included Dr. J. C. Thoms, Guy Maine, Huie Kin, J. M. Singleton,[102] and P. San Gow. The men tried to ask Lewis to agree to an open debate or, at the very least, let the men speak in defense of his allegations of immorality. Lewis firmly refused and the men left in protest. The issue continued to be debated. On the evening of February 1, 1892, the Brooklyn Presbytery held their regularly scheduled meeting at the Mount Olivet Presbyterian Church on Evergreen Avenue and Troutman Street. Lewis, who was also present at the meeting, was asked to defend his decision to be absent from the public debate organized by the Chinese missions. To which, he replied, "four of them had married white women and that lent a tint of bitterness to the dispute." In other words Lewis did not believe that these Chinese Christian leaders were able to engage in a rational debate for the good of the city's religious institutions, but were only capable of seeing Lewis's comments as personal attacks on their own marital relationships. Reiterating his past experience with the rescue missions in California, Lewis repeated his earlier allegations that Chinese were immoral and treated girls and women as slaves. Therefore he could not in good conscience support the idea of intermarriage, and thereby the presence of young white women in Chinese missions.[103]

In May 1892, a few months following the Lewis incident, the elope-ment of Edward W. Lee, an ex-laundry owner, and twenty-year-old Grace French of 8 Auburn Place in Brooklyn, added fuel to the Chinese mission controversy. Newspaper accounts alleged at first that Miss French was a Sunday school teacher at both Greenwood Baptist Church and First Baptist Church of Brooklyn, but reporters were later unable to confirm that she was an instructor at either location. Probably fearful of further controversy so soon after the Lewis incident, both churches moved quickly to disassociate themselves from the rumors by refuting the claim that Grace French taught at their schools.[104] Reverend Hull, pastor of Greenwood Baptist, also claimed that Edward Lee was not a member of his church but belonged to the Chinese Young Men's Christian Association, which he explained was not a church-sponsored organization but only used their premises for meetings, classes, and suppers. He added that he was most opposed to the idea of intermarriage between Chinese and whites especially in regard to missionaries and their students: "There is nothing that will kill off the Chinese work quicker than just that thing."[105]

A *New York Times* article described Lee as a con artist, and not a pious convert. "He [Lee] used to own a laundry in DeKalb Avenue, but a short time ago sold it out, discarded his Chinese clothing, and has been wearing silk hats and diamond scarf pins."[106] Clearly turning la-borers into dandies was not the sort of Americanizing influence mission-aries hoped to have on their Chinese pupils. To question Lee's character even further, the article also claimed that Lee had a wife and children in China. Thus, Lee was not only guilty of being an insincere convert, but a bigamist. In short, he was still a heathen at heart.

In describing Grace French's father's attitude toward the elopement, the journalist quoted him: "He must have drugged her. He met her at the bridge last Wednesday night told her I had received a letter about her and himself and was going to kill her. She was afraid to come home and went off with him."[107] Men like Lee who claimed to be Christian converts were more threatening than the so-called heathens of Chinatown, be-cause good-hearted whites, particularly naive female missionaries, could not see that his heathenish Chinese ways were still hidden behind his new persona. Lee moved easily outside of Chinatown and, by passing himself off as an Americanized, Christianized Chinese man, lured away young gullible women like Grace French.

Though opposed to the union at first, French's mother resigned herself to her daughter's marriage and visited the couple in their new home. "I think he is a good young man," she told an *Eagle* reporter, "but the ter-rible prejudice against the Chinese is what makes me revolt at the idea of my daughter marrying a Chinese man. It is an unwise marriage. She cuts herself off from the world by it and makes her friends unhappy. She seems satisfied, though. The marriage was her deliberate choice." French's mother also put to rest rumors begun by her husband that their daughter had been drugged, claiming that "there is not a shadow of foundation for it."[108]

About a week following the report of the elopement, Grace French, now Lee, allowed herself to be interviewed by the *Eagle*. The meeting took place at the home of Lee Wing, her downstairs neighbor at 983 Gates Avenue. Recounting the story of their courtship, Grace Lee told the reporter that they had met through church activities about a year earlier. Contradicting Reverend Hull, Grace Lee stated that she had indeed taught at Greenwood Baptist Church on Sundays. The couple had gotten engaged three months earlier but, fearing disapproval from her family, did not tell anyone. They were married by Reverend Huggins of Gates Avenue.

Lee Wing's mother-in-law, an English woman, was also present and "superintended matters." The mother-in-law told the reporter that she distrusted journalists and did not understand their interest in the couple's affairs. "Why do they invade the sanctity of a home?" the older woman challenged; "Why do they make more fuss about an American girl marrying a Chinaman then if she married a Turk, a German or a French count?" Despite the two women's attempts to defend intermarriage as socially and morally legitimate, the reporter made the older woman appear as a comical character and Grace Lee as a young innocent, easily misled by her Chinese dandy husband. "She is not quite 20 years of age and though intelligent is innocent and girlish enough to be only 14—a mere child." The reporter closed the story by writing sarcastically, "There is an empty flat on the second floor of 983 Gates Avenue, awaiting the next lucky Chinaman and his white bride."[109]

Occurring one month after the Lee-French scandal, the annual picnic organized by the area's Chinese Sunday schools and missions became of great interest to the press. The sub-headline of one *Eagle* article that proclaimed "Over one Thousand Pupils and Their Young American Women Teachers Take a Trip on the Grand Republic—Twenty Chinamen With White Wives on Board," suggested that the gathering was neither innocent nor socially appropriate.[110] To demonstrate the missionary community's attitudes toward mixed marriages, the reporter interviewed Mrs. A. M. Barnes, "a prominent worker among the Chinese and a teacher at the Atlantic Avenue Sunday school," who "did not approve of these marriages of Chinamen to their young American teachers. Among those she referred to were Dr. and Mrs. Thoms, Attorney Singleton, formerly Sing, who was wedded to Miss Hill, and J. Lee Wing, who recently married his teacher."[111] By naming the more recognized and respected names of Chinese American men married to white American women, the reporter suggested that no intermarriages, regardless of the Chinese husband's socioeconomic background, were condoned by Mrs. Barnes. If the reporter hoped to capture a seduction scene in progress, he was deeply disappointed. At the day's end the picnic turned out to be a "quiet, orderly and successful" occasion.[112]

The press's uproar over the elopements of Brooklyn's Sunday school teachers with their Chinese pupils also spawned several spurious rumors that the practice was rampant. One story involved Homer Wing Lee (or Lee Hum), brother of Edward Lee, and Mrs. Wenzel of 63 Cranberry Street. Lee operated a laundry on the same street and was a student of Mrs. Wenzel's at the First Baptist Sunday School at Pierrepont Street for two years. Both Lee and the Wenzel family firmly denied allegations that they were engaged to be married. Wenzel had actually stopped teaching a few months earlier because she had grown too busy and, ironically, alarmed at the newspapers' attack of the city's Chinese Sunday schools.[113] On July 20, 1892, the *Eagle* reported that another unnamed New York newspaper mistakenly reported that a Chinese laundryman named Charlie Lee Wud had married Mathilda Dreshler in Pearsalls, Long Island. In his attempts to follow up the story, the *Eagle* reporter not only failed to locate the alleged groom but also came to the conclusion that no Chinese laundry ever existed at the said location.[114]

The rising tide of negative publicity surrounding Chinese Sunday schools in the New York area adversely affected the attendance of students and teachers. At the 1892 meeting of the Chinese Sunday School Association, representatives of thirteen of the city's schools acknowledged that recent newspaper articles had caused a fall in attendance.[115] The following year the new Chinese Consul General, concerned with the recent negative publicity around the missions and the loss of the court challenge to the Geary Act, asked the city's Chinese Christian leaders to abandon the idea of holding their annual excursion for fear that "too much mingling with American women, might easily lead to trouble."[116] In 1894 the De Witt Memorial Church at 280 Rivington Street worked to change the structure of their school, namely by replacing their female teachers.[117] Despite the church's efforts women continued to teach at the Sunday school. Wary of the fragility of the reputation of the church and its Sunday school, superintendents and pastors maintained a watchful eye over the relationships that developed between instructors and students. In 1896 Superintendent Henry W. Wilson intervened in a relationship to break up "the sentimentalism of one teacher, one scholar."[118]

The crisis over the employment of female instructors revealed to female missionaries such as Helen Clark the limits of employing domestic ideology to fashion a specifically gender-based role in the domestic Chinese missionary movement. By the end of the nineteenth century these female missionaries increasingly attempted to break from essentialist Victorian notions of female piety to create a degendered role of the expert for themselves. Rather than emphasizing their "feminine" attributes of patience, nurturing, and the like, missionaries like Clark refashioned themselves as workers possessing specialized knowledge, through their years of extensive missionary experience, to claim equal status with male clergy. Within two years of the Lewis controversy, Clark approached the editor of *Century* magazine to write an article titled, "The Chinese of New York Contrasted with their Foreign Neighbors." Stating up front that she was the superintendent of the Morning Star Mission in Chinatown, Clark proceeded to list her professional qualifications to write such an article. "My work constantly takes me into every Chinese dwelling in Chinatown, and I am possessed of facts concerning these people which are not known to any other American in New York. Previous to my inauguration of this work among the Chinese I have done missionary work among the foreign classes on the east side of Chatham Square, and I believe I am therefore able to draw this contrast."[119] Through these claims Clark managed to deemphasize her gender and recast herself as a Chinatown expert and career missionary.

Not willing to jeopardize her position as the superintendent of the Morning Star Mission, Helen Clark also steadfastly refused to hire women to teach Chinese men. Her sponsors, the American Baptist Home Mission Society (ABHMS), clearly favored such an approach and praised her employment of "men teachers for men,—women teachers for women."[120] She continued this policy up to the time of the Elsie Sigel murder.[121] Interviewed about the case Clark reiterated her objections to the instructional system in the Chinese missions stating that she was not so much against the policy of allowing women to teach the Chinese, because such a criticism would undermine her own authority in both the Chinese American community and missionary circles. Rather, she objected to the "pernicious system" of one-on-one tutorials and the employment of young women to teach Chinese men. This arrangement, Clark asserted, "was directly responsible for the death of Elsie Sigel."[122] Clark saved her harshest comments for these young female teachers and the superintendents who allowed them to teach in the first place. Quick to praise the work of her generation of female missionaries, whom she viewed as well-trained and seasoned, she was equally swift to condemn the younger generation of female teachers as "foolish, frivolous girls, girls who had not yet found their bearings in life, girls who, for their own sake, as well as for the sake of the Chinese should never have been allowed to enter a Chinese Sunday school."[123] Clark further denounced her younger peers as weak willed and prone to temptation. Thus, for Clark the female teachers and their questionable behavior were of more concern than the Chinese male students who would have behaved nobly if not for their "frivolous" teachers. The hiring of women was possible as long as they were clearly experienced and well-trained experts like herself. As long as this new generation of female teachers was composed of young, frivolous girls, they could not be expected to assume the masculine role of authority.

Not only did Clark take care to hire male teachers, from the institution's establishment in 1892 she promoted the hiring of Chinese preachers to work with the Chinese community's predominantly male population, preserving the racial divide. By inviting a Chinese preacher, Je Hawk, to deliver the first sermon in Chinese, the mission attracted four hundred listeners to the mission's first meeting.[124] In 1893 the mission hired a young Chinese preacher, Fung Y. Mow, who had come to California at the age of seventeen, to work at the mission. Fung Y. Mow studied English and became a Christian convert while attending a Chinese mission and was appointed by the ABHMS to be a missionary on the Pacific Coast for two years. Before coming to New York City he returned to China and married Lee Fun Chun, the daughter of a deacon of the Chinese Baptist Church of Canton.[125] Lee Fun Chun later joined her husband at the Morning Star Mission. Impressed with her religious training, the mission asked her to teach Chinese women. In a letter to the ABHMS, she explained the challenges to reaching the women in the community: "I have difficulty in getting our women to go out of doors. Some of them do not go outside the house for months, so that I have to go to call on them by the high stairway. More of the women stay at home to do sewing to earn money for their husbands." The issue of gaining access to the women in the community led her to believe that a Chinese Christian woman like herself, "who understands the language and customs which are so different from the American," was uniquely suited for missionary work.[126] In this manner, the young couple recreated the foreign missionary model in its separation of work roles along gendered lines. Similar to other missionary husbands, Fung Y. Mow took on the leadership position but saw his wife as an essential helpmate in his work. Her ability to gain entry into the women's homes made her indispensable in the Christianizing of Chinatown's families. By employing a Chinese Christian couple the mission was able to split the teaching along racial and gender lines, protecting the institution from the type of slander that plagued other Chinese Sunday schools and missions in the city.

Despite these efforts to mollify the public's outrage over the employment of young, single white women in the city's Chinese missions, popular images of Chinese missions as potential breeding grounds for miscegenation and Chinese male students as tricksters and insincere converts persisted. Early silent films such as *The Heathen Chinese and the Sunday School Teachers*, produced in 1904, depicted Chinese laundry workers as lascivious by nature and white middle-class female missionaries as well-intentioned but naïve and impressionable. The Chinese mission and Chinese laundry became interchangeable as equally dangerous spaces breeding Chinatown's vices and interracial sex.[127] The extent to which these images of female missionaries and Chinese missions continued to saturate early-twentieth-century popular culture suggests that public anxiety over their work remained unresolved throughout this period. Not surprisingly these debates quickly resurfaced following Elsie Sigel's murder, as many asked the same question put forth by an editorial appearing in the *Brooklyn Daily Eagle* on June 21, 1909: "The people of this city are to-day asking a question which the churches concerned in mission work among the expatriated Cantonese of New York would do well to answer: Why is it that young girls are considered essential to the Christianizing of these shirt-washing heathens?"[128]

With such longstanding popular images of young female workers in the city's Chinese missions, it is not surprising that newspaper reports slipped into portraying Sigel and Leon Ling as Sunday school teacher and pupil, when evidence suggests that no such relationship actually existed between the two. Regardless of the actual cause of Sigel's murder or the extent of their real involvement in the city's Chinese missions, her death symbolized to both the New York public as well as the missionary movement the potential for racial and sexual transgressions in the domestic Chinese mission and the high cost of allowing women to engage in missionary work with Chinese men.

By blaming Sigel's murder on her work as a missionary to Chinese, such a narrative easily explained how she met and became romantically involved with Leon Ling. It allowed for these institutions—Chinese Sunday schools and missions—to be the culprit, leaving Sigel's own actions and motivations less scrutinized. Similar to the other missionary women who had appeared in the press before her, Sigel could remain the simple, naive, young missionary worker, who was ultimately victimized by her own good intentions. Unexplored and unacknowledged were questions regarding these women's own agency and desires in forming close relationships with Chinese men that went beyond the accepted bounds of "Christian charity."

CHAPTER FIVE

Chinese American Interracial Couples and Families in New York City

THE NEW YORK CITY POLICE investigation into the Elsie Sigel murder focused an unprecedented amount of publicity on the city's Chinese mixed-race couples. To better understand why a respectable white woman would choose to marry a Chinese man, one *New York Times* reporter interviewed Mrs. Young, a white woman living in Brooklyn with her Chinese husband L. Young, who was employed by the Russo-Chinese Bank in Manhattan. Clearly indignant at the reporter's intrusion into the private lives of couples such as herself, Mrs. Young voiced her anger over how the press's racially biased coverage of the Sigel murder challenged the legitimacy of her own marriage. "People should mind their own business," she said. "There would not have been so much stir if Elsie Sigel had been murdered by a white man. It happened that a Chinaman did it, and all at once everybody turns against the Chinese. They are as good as anybody else."[1] Undeterred, the reporter probed further into the couple's religious background, assuming that Mrs. Young was a Sunday school teacher. Mrs. Young flatly replied that though her husband was a Baptist she herself was not in any way connected to a Chinese mission, dispelling the popular belief that middle-class white women only met their Chinese husbands under such circumstances.

Kress Koyama, a Japanese man from Providence, Rhode Island, and his twenty-two-year old fiancée, Mary Louise Bollback, experienced similary unwanted attention when they attempted to locate someone willing to perform their wedding. Though Koyama was not Chinese, but Japanese, his distinctly Asian physical features led him to face the same racial antipathy directed at Chinese men involved with white women. According to a *New York Herald* article, the two had called on many ministers but they "declined when they caught sight of Mr. Koyama."[2] Faced with limited options the couple was forced to go to Reverend Henry Marsh Warren, who was associated with the chapel of the Frank E. Campbell Undertaking Company.

The public's awareness of Chinese-white couples began with the numerous press accounts of police encounters with mixed-race couples during the course of the murder investigation. One of the first witnesses questioned by the police was Mrs. Yim Kee, the white wife of a Chinese waiter who

worked at the restaurant located beneath Leon Ling's rooms on Eighth
Avenue. Mrs. Kee informed the police that she thought Elsie Sigel had been
murdered out of jealousy. She also added that Leon Ling and Sigel used to
visit a Chinese laundry in the neighborhood, located at 309 West Forty-
second Street, where Sigel became friends with another white woman who
was similarly married to a Chinese man. Such news stories increasingly
alerted New Yorkers to the surprising numbers of Chinese-white couples
living in their midst.[3]

The news that the police had discovered a series of "love letters" written
by Sigel to Leon Ling added another dimension to the public's understanding of their relationship. Descriptions of their contents implied that the
victim not only reciprocated the attentions of a Chinese man but actively
pursued a relationship with him. The general public, however, clearly had
difficulty accepting the idea of a mutually consenting relationship between
a respectable, middle-class white woman and a Chinese man. In an interview with the *World*, Dan Slattery, secretary to Police Commissioner
Bingham, voiced his opinion of their correspondences. "They were all what
I would call clean love letters but the endearing terms she called the Chinamen were revolting to me. . . . Every one read just as if the Chinaman had
been a white man and decently engaged to the Sigel girl." For Slattery and
others, Sigel had behaved inappropriately. By crossing over racial boundaries to engage in a romantic relationship with Leon Ling she disrupted
that period's established racial hierarchies, by placing Chinese and white
men on the same social plane. Reading like "the ingenuous love notes of a
girl madly in love with a man she respected and evidently considered her
equal in every way," the letters demonstrated to the public that Sigel felt
neither hesitation nor shame in forming her attachment to Leon Ling.[4]

A closer examination of interracial couples and families in New York
City needs to be undertaken to understand the larger context in which
Elsie Sigel and Leon Ling began their association. Contemporary mainstream accounts, mostly written by social reformers and journalists, often
deemed these relationships to be morally flawed because they failed
to follow established white middle-class norms of respectable family life.
Contrary to these assertions Lee Chew, a Chinese merchant interviewed
by *The Independent* in 1905, claimed that despite the checkered backgrounds of some of the wives in Chinatown, there were "many excellent
and faithful wives and mothers."[5] Alternate sources such as census surveys, marriage and baptism records, and immigration files support
Lee Chew's remarks and offer a different view of the daily lives of
Chinatown's interracial couples and families and their place in turn-of-
the-century New York. As the experiences of these families suggest,
many of these relationships were long-term commitments founded upon
mutual respect and affection, qualities that contemporary critics had

largely assumed to be absent in interracial marriages and family life. Whether they engaged in conventional marriages or alternative forms of companionate relationships, the lives created by these couples indicate the range of responses undertaken in the face of legal constraints imposed by this period's anti-Chinese immigration legislation.[6]

TURN-OF-THE-CENTURY POPULAR VIEWS ON CHINESE-WHITE COUPLES AND CHILDREN

In *How the Other Half Lives,* Jacob Riis described his fear that the "ages of senseless idolatry" of the Chinese would frustrate any attempts at social and moral reform. After describing the numerous vices he witnessed in Chinatown, Riis ended his account with an alternative solution to rid this quarter of its moral decadence:

> Granted, that the Chinese are in no sense a desirable element of the population, that they serve no useful purpose here, whatever they may have done elsewhere in other days, yet to this is a sufficient answer that they are here, and that, having let them in, we must make the best of it. This is a time for very plain speaking on this subject. Rather than banish the Chinaman, I would have the door opened wider—for his wife; make it a condition of his coming or staying that he bring his wife with him. Then, at least, he might not be what he now is and remains, a homeless stranger among us.[7]

With this appeal Riis ran counter to the popular current of anti-Chinese immigration sentiment of the day, that had supported the passage and renewals of the Chinese Exclusion Act. Rather than arguing for the elimination of Chinese labor, he suggested that it could be properly regulated and quite literally domesticated. Following the dictates of nineteenth-century domestic ideology, that placed women and her influence in the home at the basis of a moral society, Riis asserted that the absence of Chinese women and stable families fostered prostitution, gambling, and opium smoking.

While Riis accurately reported that the majority of New York City Chinatown's population was male, a reexamination of this period's census surveys shows that married couples and families did exist, though they were overwhelmingly interracial. From Riis's perspective these interracial households were not formed through respectable marriages capable of creating moral and social stability, but were questionable and temporary alliances. White women who were poor or addicted to opium and, "worshipping nothing save the pipe that has enslaved them body and soul," had no choice but to marry Chinese men to support their habit.[8] As "fallen women" these wives did not provide the domestic feminine virtues needed to counter Chinatown's unchecked masculine vices. Hence Riis prescribed precisely the entry of Chinese women rather than encouraged the ongoing practice of interracial marriage.

Riis's seemingly positive evaluation of Chinese womanhood, while appearing to depart from popular West Coast depictions of Chinese women as prostitutes, needs to be examined more closely. The visible presence of white prostitutes in New York's Chinatown, and the relative absence of Chinese women in this community, greatly affected the depictions of the latter. Whereas in San Francisco portrayals of Chinese prostitutes circulated widely, in the New York context these images were mostly replaced by the image of the prosperous and morally upright Chinese merchant wife.[9] Female sexual deviance in New York City's Chinatown, by contrast, was embodied by white working-class women and teenage girls who either resided in or visited the area. As a New York City journalist wrote, "the Class of Chinese women that have given the police of San Francisco a great deal of trouble is unknown in New York, their places being taken by white women. These last are not easy to discover in evil ways, for the reason that they have no relations with white men, but associate exclusively with Mongolians."[10] Thus these portrayals of Chinese women as morally upright were inextricably linked to narratives of white female sexual deviance in Chinatown.

Louis Beck provided readers with a more detailed account of the social and cultural life of the Chinese in New York. While Beck treated the residents of Chinatown more as exotic cultural curiosities than pitiable or incorrigible objects of reform, he shared many of Riis's views on interracial marriage between Chinese men and white women. For Beck the virtue of the white wives, along with the interracial couple's socioeconomic class and cultural and religious background, determined their respectability and social status. Conjuring a three-tiered hierarchy of mixed-race couples, Beck placed at the top what he termed "chiefly Christian families," married in accordance with American sociolegal customs. For Beck and other nineteenth-century writers, conversion to Christianity from heathenism connoted the first step to embracing American culture and becoming westernized. Thus, these couples received Beck's stamp of approval. Below this top tier were women deemed to be "former prostitutes," married by Chinese custom to their husbands. The women's sexual histories aside, Beck and other white American writers and officials often emphasized the Chinese lack of "material ceremony" versus American adherence to "legal formality" in creating a social and legal hierarchy for marriage whereby marriages performed according to U.S. laws and religious customs ranked above those that followed traditional Chinese practices. In the last rung were women who were described as "common prostitutes living with some particular man as his common law wife."[11] Despite these allegations, couples not married according to American religious or civil procedures should not be dismissed or delegitimized as temporary sexual liaisons as many contemporary writers have done, because even Beck admitted that many of these couples had children and lived as though they were husband and wife, implying a committed and long-lasting relationship.[12]

Doubts cast on the wife's character spoke immediately to her fitness to be a mother. Nineteenth-century domestic ideology and child-rearing practices demanded that mothers take on the main role of nurturing and protecting their children from harmful influences outside of the home.[13] If women were seen as the chief instrument for their children's socialization, then it would logically follow that dissolute women were incapable of proper child rearing. The depiction of interracial relationships, and these white wives as morally deviant, thus supported the popular belief that proper home life where children were nurtured would be nonexistent. Not surprisingly, an absence of representations of children becomes readily apparent upon examining contemporary discussions of interracial marriages.

During the first half of the nineteenth century, popular and theological beliefs regarding the nature of children also changed dramatically. Believed to be born in a state of grace, children were no longer seen as bearing the taint of original sin.[14] These views of childhood innocence, however, were not extended to include Chinatown's mixed-race children, the physical evidence of the parents' sinful relationship. For contemporary writers, the presence of children in these families did not necessarily connote the stability or permanence expected of either white middle-class or all Chinese families. A reporter for an 1890 *Harper's Weekly* article on Chinatown remarked, "it is only about twelve or fifteen years since these marriages began, so that the children are all yet young. What kind of people the hybrids will prove to be is yet an unsolved problem."[15]

Writers often dismissed interracial families in favor of the Chinese merchant family when representing children and family life in Chinatown. Beck provided a sketch of a Chinese mother and father holding their infant seated in their living room to illustrate "a domestic scene" in Chinatown. Beck noted that a number of interracial couples had children, and according to his estimates a total of forty-seven children of mixed-race parentage resided in the community: twenty-eight boys and nineteen girls. He argued that the care and treatment of the children could be differentiated and placed into the same categories he had established for distinguishing among the white wives of these mixed marriages—respectable Christians, reformed prostitutes, and practicing prostitutes. In other words Beck decided that the women's background alone predetermined their ability to be good mothers. The children belonging to couples of the first category were "treated with equal fairness and affection, whether male or female." In regards to the second and third categories, Beck claimed that these children

Figure 5.1. This drawing of a young Chinese-white family standing on the street corner in New York's Chinatown accompanied an article commenting on the uncertainty of the future of the neighborhood's mixed-race children.
Source: W. A. Rogers, "A Wedding in the Chinese Quarter, Mott Street, New York," *Harper's Weekly* 34 (November 22, 1890): 909–910. Courtesy of Yale University Library.

were poorly treated by their mothers, whom he described as "mainly ignorant and depraved women who treat their female children very much as do their husbands."[16]

Beck certainly took great liberties with the truth to paint elaborate stories of depraved mothers such as in the case of Mrs. Annie Lee, a white woman whom Beck accused of selling her five-year-old daughter for $44 to a Chinese man, who was later arrested for assaulting the child. Mrs. Lee had been formerly married to a white man named Glackner and the child was said to be from this earlier marriage. In her defense Mrs. Lee maintained that she had only allowed the Chinese man to care for her daughter temporarily. According to Beck, a child protection agency became involved in the case and turned the child over to St. Ann's House. Beck not only failed to inform readers of the outcome of the case but charged that this was perhaps not the first time that such a case involving the sale or assault of a child had occurred in Chinatown. He concluded his account by stating that Mrs. Lee and her Chinese husband had another daughter, Katie, who was also "alleged to have been sold to a Chinaman as his wife" several years earlier.[17]

In terms of the accusation regarding Katie, the details of this particular case found in the NYSPCC annual report for 1895 indicate that Beck was mistaken. Beck failed to inform his reader that a trial held in the city's Court of General Sessions in 1895 had prompted a full NYSPCC inquiry into Katie Lee's situation. The NYSPCC found that Katie was, as Beck had claimed, not residing with her biological parents. However, Katie had neither been turned into a slave nor a child bride, rather, she was living at 43 Mott Street with Chu Yen Ying and his wife, Ah May. The NYSPCC report suggested that the Lee family, because of their state of indigence, allowed for this arrangement to take place and absolved Annie Lee from any wrongdoing. The investigation "proved not only that the parents of the child had verbally consented to her adoption by Ying, but that there had been no 'sale,' as alleged, and that Chu Yen Ying was respectable, possessed of considerable means and seemed anxious to give the child proper care and training as a Christian."[18] Recorder Goff, the presiding judge at the trial, also agreed that the adoption was in the best interest of young Katie and granted permanent custody to Chu Yen Ying and his wife, dismissing the charges that the Lees had "sold" their daughter. Beck's more sinister portrayal of Annie Lee, however, suggested that she had morally declined to the level of typical Chinese heathen parents who willingly sold their daughters. By failing to mention that Katie's new Chinese parents were wealthy and respectable Christians, he also misled readers into believing that Chu Yen Ying was another stereotypical heathen Chinese who mistreated girls by engaging in child slavery or worse.

Accusations of the selling of daughters in Chinatown were by no means unique to mixed-race couples, but were commonly leveled at all non-Christian Chinese families. The plight of the young, helpless Chinese girl who because of her sex was doomed to a permanently inferior social position was a common topic among this century's social reformers and missionaries working with Chinese at home and abroad.[19] These stories often centered on the practices of arranged marriage, foot binding, child slavery, and prostitution. In 1885 Revered Otis Gibson, a former China missionary working in San Francisco's Chinatown, testified before the city's Special Committee of the Board of Supervisors that Chinese prostitution in the city could be linked to the buying and stealing of Chinese women in China.[20] An 1894 pamphlet describing Chinese missionary activities in the United States described a young American missionary's encounter with families who sold their daughters. Given the sums Chinese girls fetched in the open market and the purposes for which they were sold, the author asserted: "It is a well-established fact that young Chinese girls—even girls in their infancy—are bought and sold among the Chinese of San Francisco; and so remote are these people from American customs and influences that it is practically impossible for the laws to prevent this practice, or to rescue its victims, unless proof of specific acts of cruelty can be procured."[21] Writers employed these gendered narratives of female oppression to form the key tenets that distinguished an enlightened and egalitarian Euro-American civilization from a morally corrupt and despotic Chinese society. Social reformers and missionaries also used these stories to garner financial support and public sympathy for their Chinese missionary activities.

In a 1902 article, titled "Children of Chinatown," author Harry B. Wilson similarly focused his discussion of proper family life in Chinatown on the children of Chinese fathers and mothers. Wilson, however, concluded with a brief acknowledgement of the children of Chinese-white couples, but identified them as "a problem for which there is no solution." Though Wilson described two examples of such families where the children seemed to be happy and well cared for by their parents, he quickly added that such cases were rare. He claimed that the presence of these "half-caste" children did not connote a stable family life, since he believed that most of these American mothers and their children were sooner or later abandoned by their Chinese husbands. With such instability in these interracial families, Wilson believed these children posed a great social burden on the city's welfare services: "For such little waifs that are left in Chinatown there is only one hope—that they may be caught in the dragnet set out by one of the missions, where a new life is opened to them, where they are taught that crime is unnatural, and where they receive strength and encouragement in the up-hill struggle that confronts them."[22]

Figure 5.2 This photograph of a Chinese merchant family featured in the King's guidebook was accompanied by the caption "CHINESE FAMILY; prosperous merchant with his wife and children in their native attire in their home at 34 Mott St." The guidebook also noted that the white wives of Chinese men far outnumbered Chinese wives, but did not offer a more detailed description or corresponding family photograph. By choosing to use the above portrait of a Chinese father and mother as the representative image of the proper "Chinese family," the guidebook implied that this was the dominant—and clearly more acceptable socially—marriage and family pattern, when the opposite was true. *Source: New York's Chinatown: Ancient Pekin Seen at "Old Bowery" Gate* (New York: King's Booklets, 1908), 21. Courtesy of the Museum of Chinese in the Americas.

In response to Wilson's charge that Chinese fathers often deserted their American wives and families to return to China, examples of interracial families traveling to China can be found in the Chinese immigration files of this period.[23] By 1908 the number of American white wives traveling with their husbands to China so alarmed the U.S. Consul, Amos P. Wilder, that he chose to file a lengthy confidential report on the "sorry lot of American women who marry Chinese and come with them to China to live."[24] The consul painted a grave picture of the oppressed existence of these wives and was convinced that they were so miserable that "the advice of these women would be an unqualified 'Don't.'" Wilder was particularly appalled by what he viewed as these women's automatic assimilation into the Chinese husband's culture and society, that led them to accept non-Western practices such as foot binding or arranged marriages and the lowering of their social status and autonomy as women. Wilder's views were clearly informed by his own understanding of proper gender roles. Indeed, in a 1908 case involving a Norwegian laborer petitioning to immigrate to the United States with his Chinese wife and their biracial children, Wilder made a personal effort to meet the man's request. Despite the man's lower-class status, he viewed this relationship as more palatable simply because the reverse gender pairing of a European man with a Chinese woman seemed to suggest that the family would follow the authority of the Norwegian father.[25] Similar to the general concerns over white female missionaries working with Chinese male students, the marriages of white women to Chinese men not only failed to further the Christianizing and modernizing of China, but brought about the reverse by converting American white women to Chinese heathenism. Dire warnings such as these alerted the public to the potential social consequences of allowing mixed-race families to exist but, as other evidence suggests, these accounts offer only skewed and incomplete representations of the lives of these families.

THE RISE OF CHINATOWN'S WORKING-CLASS MIXED-RACE COMMUNITY

The desire to surmount the financial and legal obstacles to establishing marriages and families in the United States can be seen through the actions of many Chinese following passage of the 1875 Page Law and 1882 Chinese Exclusion Act. Aimed specifically to prevent the importation of women for the purposes of prostitution, the Page Law granted American consulate officials more latitude in scrutinizing and rejecting potential Chinese female immigrants before their departure for the United States, which severely restricted the numbers of Chinese women entering the country and reduced the pool of marriageable Chinese women. The 1882 Chinese Exclusion Act specifically barred the entry of Chinese laborers into the United States, and later court cases also determined that the immigration status of a Chinese wife was derived from her husband's status. Thus, the wives of laborers were also excluded from entering the United States. For the exempted classes—diplomats, merchants, clergy, and scholars—there still remained the thin possibility of marrying and bringing back wives from China, an option not available for the majority of Chinatown's population who were classified as laborers.[26]

The desire of New York City's Chinese residents to bring their families to this country can be gleaned from correspondences between Chinese husbands and fathers and the U.S. Treasury Department.[27] As long as the Chinese husband/petitioner belonged to one of the exempted classes, the application to bring family members into the United States would be fully considered. In 1886 merchants Lai Moon, of 91 Chatham Street, and Kwong Long Yuen, of 22 Mott Street, wrote the Treasury Department inquiring into the possibility of bringing their wives to New York City via San Francisco. Both men planned to visit China briefly for the usual reasons—to conduct business and visit relatives—but also hoped to return with their families. In both cases the department was sufficiently satisfied with the two men's claims to being merchants belonging to the exempted class, and granted their petitions.[28] For Chinese outside of the exempted classes, whose applications were routinely denied, they sought other alternatives.

In 1901 Sue Chung Chew, an interpreter, aroused the curiosity of New Yorkers when he began legal proceedings to adopt a five-week-old American baby boy, Thomas Lee. A forty-six-year-old widower who had resided and worked in the United States for over thirty years, Chew had proven himself to be a model applicant. Despite being ineligible for citizenship under the Chinese Exclusion Act, he made an application to become a U.S. citizen in 1898. At the child custody hearing he had the support of prominent white New Yorkers, including William C. Beecher, son of Henry Ward Beecher, who filed affidavits vouching for Chew's moral character. Most importantly, the parents of the baby boy had given their consent to the adoption. Chew desired to raise the child as his own son, changing his name from Thomas Lee to William B. Chew.[29]

Such adoption cases were rare, however. A more common option available to Chinese men was the practice of interracial marriage since New York, similarly to other states in the Northeast and Midwest, did not have any anti-miscegenation laws.[30] As documented by John Kuo Wei Tchen, even before the enactment of the Page Law or the Chinese Exclusion Acts, interracial marriage had by the mid-nineteenth century become the dominant marriage pattern for New York's Chinese population.[31] During the exclusion era interracial marriage continued to provide an alternative for Chinese men who still wished to marry and establish families in this country. In an 1888 article on the newly forming Chinatown neighborhood, Wong Ching Foo argued that Chinese-white marriages could form stable and distinctly "American" families in their adoption of the English language and "American ways and dress." He further claimed that Chinese men often made "better husbands than men of their own nation," and argued that these matches were often a step up for these "poor working girls, who through necessity married well-to-do Chinamen."[32] In contrast to Wong Ching Foo's assertion that interracial marriages were between "poor working girls" and "well-to-do Chinamen," a reexamination of census records actually reveals that Chinese laborers, much more than merchants, engaged in the practice.

For the predominantly working-class male inhabitants of Chinatown, marriage or cohabitation with non-Chinese women probably provided the most available opportunity for establishing families in this country during the early decades of the exclusion era. Despite allegations of immorality or impermanence, I argue that these interracial couples represented the beginnings of a working-class family life for the city's Chinese immigrant community. In 1870 census takers recorded approximately thirty-five Chinese men residing in the Sixth Ward.[33] Some of these men may have migrated from lower Manhattan's multiethnic seaport district, since a number of seamen were listed as residing in the area—such as John Acoo who, along with his English wife Susan, ran a boarding house for fifteen Chinese seamen.[34] Most of the Chinese men residing in the Sixth Ward, however, worked as cigar makers. No Chinese women were listed as residing in the ward, but a significant number of Chinese had clearly married white women and begun to establish families in the area. Aside from the Acoo family, another ten mixed-race couples and families resided in the ward. In effect over one-fourth of the Chinese men residing in the Sixth Ward were married to non-Chinese women.

By 1880 the federal census takers' house-by-house surveys for the area in the Sixth Ward—beginning to be identified as "Chinatown"—show the Chinese community to have nearly tripled in size, with a Chinese male population numbering less than 150.[35] The mixed-race families noted in the 1870 census, however, no longer appeared. Eight different Chinese-white couples and families were listed as residing in the Sixth Ward, with seven living on Mott Street. The other remaining couple lived at 106 Park Street. As with the 1870 census there were no Chinese-Chinese couples listed as residing in the ward, and interracial marriage remained the dominant if not the only marriage pattern for Chinese immigrant men residing in New York City. Even though these families seemed to have clustered on one street, they were similar to the rest of the ward's predominantly European immigrant and working-class inhabitants in terms of their socioeconomic background. With two exceptions all of the husbands worked as cigar makers; John Lee was a tea merchant while Ging Sak, who resided with his family at 43 Mott Street, worked at a candy factory. Most of the wives were of either Irish or English ancestry, but John Lee's wife, Mammie, was born in New York of German parents.

Similar to the composition of other immigrant and working-class households in lower Manhattan during this period, Chinatown's households were not necessarily composed of nuclear families. Yet several of the families had extended kin residing as well as took in boarders—Chinese and white. The existence of these complex mixed-race households suggests the extent to which Chinese-white socializing, outside of mixed-race marriages, also occurred in this area. Charles Penn, a Chinese cigar maker, boarded with John Aging and his English wife Annie, at their home at 106 Park Street. Bridget Murphy, a young widow working as a laundress, and her five-year-old daughter Maggie, boarded with Ging Sak and his family. Census takers also recorded two households with mainly Chinese occupants where white women worked as servants. At 49 Mott Street twenty-two-year-old Mary Lyon worked as a cook for two Chinese boarders, Ah Fong and Ah Gee. Ah Fong worked in the cigar trade while Ah Gee labored in a laundry. At 101 Park Street, thirty-four-year-old Mary Long worked as a cook for two Chinese men and a young boy.

The lack of Chinese-Chinese marriages in the 1880 census records could have resulted from census takers' undercount. Language differences and residents' wariness of American government officials may have affected census takers' abilities in carrying out their work.[36] Surveys of writings on Chinatown during this period suggest an undercount was as likely to have happened with interracial marriages. An 1885 *New York Tribune* article claimed that the first baby born to a Chinese father and mother finally occurred in Chinatown.[37] Five years later a *New York Times* article described the first Chinese-Chinese weddings to take place in the community.[38] Chew Gin, a grocer in Chinatown, married Shang Fong, and Chew Jim, a laundry worker, married Ling Fong. The couples had actually met in Victoria, British Columbia, where they were married according to Chinese custom. Out of concern that immigration officials would not recognize their marriage, the husbands decided to undergo an American wedding ceremony.[39] Interestingly the couples were aided by the Irish wife of a Chinese grocer living at 17 Mott Street, who directed them to Reverend Bouton of the nearby Five Points Mission at 63 Park Place, and they became the first Chinese bride and groom to be recorded in the mission's registry.[40]

A look at the marriage and baptism records of the Five Points Mission from 1880 to 1890 suggests that the numbers of interracial couples continued to grow during this period. A total of ten interracial marriages and eleven baptisms of mixed-race children were performed at both the Five Points Mission and its Chinese Mission located at 14 Mott Street.[41] Many of these mixed marriages involved working-class Chinese men: five of the grooms were listed as cigar makers or laundrymen while the other five had no occupation listed. Some of the couples seem to have been well acquainted with one another. In 1890 twenty-five-year-old Ong Que married twenty-one-year-old Lena Smith, a native-born New Yorker. Two days later the groom served as the witness to Ah Wah's marriage to Kittie Williams, a Brooklyn native.[42]

By 1900 census records indicate a total of 133 marriages in Chinatown with fifty-one Chinese men married to Chinese women, but eighty-two Chinese men married to non-Chinese women.[43] The surveys also show that approximately 40 percent of the mixed-race couples had children. This enormous leap in the number of marriages in Chinatown from 1880 to 1900 and the rise in the Chinese population, suggest that Chinatown during this twenty-year period continued to attract new residents and interracial marriage remained the main marriage option. The ethnic and racial diversity of women living in Chinatown increased as a result of these marriages. Eighty of the mixed marriages were between Chinese men and European immigrant or white native-born American women, and the remaining two marriages were of black women to Chinese men. Unlike earlier census listings, the women noted as "white" in the 1900 census were not necessarily of Irish ancestry. Rather the surveys show that forty-three of the women and their parents were native-born whites, with forty listing New York as both generations' birthplace.[44] Another, twelve women were clearly of Irish descent; nine were of English ancestry, and another nine were of German descent. The remaining eight wives were distributed evenly in the following ethnic categories: Scottish, Canadian, French, and Spanish.

During this period marriages between Chinese men and African American women remained extremely low, as only a small number of such families were found in marriage and baptism registries or the federal census. During the 1880s, John and Barbara Archung asked Reverend Bouton to baptize three of their children.[45] On the baptism record of L. Archung, the Reverend remarked "Father Chinese Mother Negro." The 1900 census recorded only two Chinese-black couples residing in the Chinatown area. Forty-two-year-old Hon Chu, an actor, and his twenty-one-year-old Cuban wife Laura, had been married for six years and resided at 9 Pell Street with four of Hon Chu's cousins. At 30 Pell Street sixty-year-old Lok Chin lived with his twenty-five-year old wife of ten years, Ellen, and his son from a previous marriage to a Chinese woman. Lok Chin was a Chinese doctor and his son, Charlie, worked as a truck driver.

By looking at the occupations of Chinese men residing with their wives in New York City, class differences between the men with Chinese and non-Chinese spouses can be seen. Thirty-six or nearly 70 percent of the Chinese men married to Chinese women were listed as merchants, as opposed to only fourteen or less than 18 percent who were married to non-Chinese women. The chief occupations among those men married to non-Chinese women were laundry and restaurant work; thirty-nine or 48 percent were listed as "laundryman" and eleven or 13 percent had occupation designations as "restaurant," "cook," or "waiter." In contrast only one Chinese man married to a Chinese woman was noted as a restaurant worker and three others were laundrymen.

The class difference is hardly surprising; judicial interpretations of the Chinese Exclusion Acts only allowed women married to men of the exempted classes to immigrate. For the majority of this period's Chinatown residents who were not of the exempted classes, but wished to marry and establish families in the United States, intermarriage was very likely the most available option. The census records suggest that many of the Chinese-Chinese marriages originated in China, for the length of these marriages either matched or exceeded the period of time the wives had resided in the United States. Thus, Chinese women entered not as single women but as married women dependent on their husband's immigration status.[46]

As a transatlantic seaport, it is hardly surprising that New York City received a number of interracial couples from Great Britain or the Caribbean. In 1917 Harry Fang sold his grocery store, Kwong Chong Lang & Co. in Liverpool, and came with his wife, Amelia, and their two young daughters, Daisy and Doris, to New York. Amelia Smith was born in Manchester and the couple was married in Liverpool in 1906. Before departing England Fang made arrangements with the owners of Tuck High & Co. at 19 Mott Street to begin work after his arrival.[47] In 1921 twenty-four-year-old Olga Claudine Chin traveled with her young daughter, Carlton Chin, from her native country, Trinidad, to join her Chinese husband in New York City. Unlike Amelia Smith Olga Chin was, according to H. D. Baker, the American Consul in Trinidad, "only partly Chinese, being mostly of colored race."[48] Her part-Chinese racial classification, however, subjected her to the Chinese exclusion laws, making her immigration status dependent on her husband's. Because of his established identity as the proprietor of a Chinese restaurant valued at over $20,000, she was entitled to a Section 6 certificate, and thereby allowed to land.

By the time Elsie Sigel and Leon Ling became acquainted with one another, interracial marriages outnumbered or equaled those of Chinese men to Chinese women. In 1900 60 percent of all marriages in New York City's Chinatown were between Chinese men and white women. Although by 1910 the number of interracial marriages declined by almost 25 percent, they still made up approximately half of all marriages in the neighborhood.[49] These census figures suggest the extent to which Chinatown's working-class male population turned to intermarriage to establish families in the United States, challenging the social isolation imposed by anti-Chinese immigration legislation. As a result New York City's Chinatown was not a community wholly without women. Marriage to non-Chinese women could more than double the number of women in the community. Though small in numbers these marriages still made Chinatown a more racially and ethnically mixed community than what has been commonly perceived. However, popular attitudes and fears about miscegenation worked to limit the number of interracial marriages. Categories of sexual and moral deviance worked to check Chinese men's and non-Chinese women's social and physical mobility. Nonetheless, as census figures show, non-Chinese women did enter into long-term marriages with Chinese men. Census figures alone, however, can only provide a broad look at marriage patterns in the community. Combining census data with other institutional records, such as marriage and baptism certificates, reveals another dimension to interracial marriage, sexual relations, and family life in Chinatown.

MIXED-RACE FAMILY AND COMMUNITY PORTRAITS

From as early as the 1860s the names of children born to Chinese fathers and non-Chinese mothers, such as John Aloo and Mary Ellen Ahong, began to appear in the baptism records of the Church of the Transfiguration, a Roman Catholic church located in the heart of Chinatown.[50] Begun as a "basement congregation" in 1825 by a Cuban priest, Felix Varela, the church moved to several locations in lower Manhattan before permanently settling at 29 Mott Street in 1853. At the time the church served the growing Irish immigrant Catholic populations residing in lower Manhattan. By the 1890s, however, Italian immigrants began to replace the once largely Irish congregation.[51] As the area around Transfiguration became known as Chinatown during the 1880s and 1890s, Irish American and Italian immigrant parishioners continued to traverse the shifting neighborhood boundaries to attend weekly masses, weddings, baptisms, and funerals at the church. Unlike the Protestant denominations, the Catholic Church was slow to respond to the rising Chinese immigrant population in the city. Subsequently, Transfiguration did not attract many Chinese converts. A Chinese mission, located around the corner from Transfiguration, was not established until 1909 and it was four years later that Father Hilarius Montanar succeeded in baptizing thirty Chinese men—all of whom were already married with families remaining in China.[52]

Such low conversion rates and the Church's opposition to mixed-faith marriages resulted in less than ten cases of interracial marriage recorded in the Transfiguration marriage registry for the period between 1870 and 1910.[53] The Catholic wives of Chinese men, despite not having their marriages performed by the Church, still attempted to hold onto elements of their faith. From 1860 to 1911, in contrast to the low numbers of interracial weddings at Transfiguration, approximately eighty-five baptisms of children born to Chinese fathers and non-Chinese mothers were performed.[54] These Catholic mothers held onto one of the most basic religious and cultural practices with which they had been raised and attempted to confer their ethnic identity and religious faith to their children.

The case of Teresa Ferrara demonstrates the tenacity of one Italian American woman in maintaining her ethnic and religious affiliations following her marriage to Lee Young, a Chinese man. In 1904 twenty-one-year-old "Tessie," a New York City native with Italian immigrant parents, married forty-six-year-old Lee Young at Transfiguration. Lee Young, who immigrated to the United States in 1880, worked as a self-employed carpenter.[55] Tessie's family appears to have accepted her marriage to Lee Young and continued to play a role in the couple's lives. Five years later Teresa gave birth to a daughter, whom the couple named Edna Anna Filomena. The decision to give her daughter an Italian name and have her baptized at Transfiguration suggests that Teresa wished to affirm her daughter's Italian ancestry. By selecting Angelo Ferrara and Maria Donotero to be Edna's godparents, Teresa cemented her daughter's bonds to her own family and the Italian American community. The family also chose to reside at 49 Mott Street, an area simultaneously bordering both the Chinese and Italian immigrant neighborhoods.[56] The Youngs' residence in a building consisting entirely of working-class Italian American households, further suggests that Teresa's marriage to Lee Young was likely accepted by their Italian American neighbors.

For Italian American wives, in particular, the decision to marry outside of their ethnic community and to a Chinese man at that, could not have been made easily. All segments of the Italian American community participated in the policing of heterosexual socializing among unmarried Italian American youth, and marriage was intended to maintain the security and continuity of the family.[57] As late as 1920, 971 out of 1,000 Italian American mothers in New York were married to Italian men.[58] Because "outmarriages," especially one between an Italian American woman and a Chinese man, were rare in the Italian immigrant community, their occurrence, as in the case of the Youngs, provides an interesting case of community acceptance. These examples also counter contemporary claims that women who married Chinese men automatically assimilated completely into Chinese culture and experienced social ostracism by their own ethnic communities. Some couples appear to have received the support and blessing of non-Chinese relatives and friends, who also agreed to serve as witnesses at their weddings or as godparents to their children.

The baptism records of three different families with the surname of Chin Tin, found in both the Five Points Mission and Transfiguration baptism registries, further capture the complexities of this emerging social network of interracial families in the Chinatown area. In the early 1880s two of the Chin Tin families baptized their children at the Methodist Five Points Mission. John and Elizabeth Chin Tin baptized their infant son, Philip Henry, on February 25, 1883; Charles Chin Tin and his wife Elizabeth baptized their baby daughter, Elizabeth, on January 11, 1885.[59] Both families then stopped attending the Five Points Mission. A year later Charles and Elizabeth Chin Tin began to take their family to the Church of the Transfiguration. On October 24, 1886 Charles and Elizabeth Chin Tin baptized two daughters, Annie and Henrietta. The parents asked Bridget Fitzpatrick and Martha McGowan to be the godmothers of their two girls.[60] A year later another daughter, eight-year-old Mary Jane, was baptized on August 7, 1887. A fourth daughter, Theresa, was born and christened one year later. John Fitzpatrick and Martha George were Mary Jane's godparents, while Jacques Hanlon and Hattie Elmersdorf were Theresa's. During this period a third Chin Tin family also began to attend the Church of the Transfiguration. On May 13, 1887 James Chin Tin and his wife Elizabeth Holden baptized both of their sons, twelve-year-old Charles Henry and ten-year-old William George, at the Church of the Transfiguration. Owen Fallon and Bridget Fitzpatrick were the godparents of Charles Henry, while William Hacket and Delia Fitzpatrick were the godparents of William George.[61]

Although the records do not actually state that these three Chin Tin families were related, the information provided in each child's baptism record strongly suggests that John, Charles, and James Chin Tin were possibly brothers or cousins.[62] These families also shared a lasting friendship with the Fitzpatrick family, as Bridget, Delia, and Daniel Fitzpatrick were called upon to become the godparents of the children of two different Chin Tin families. Bridget Fitzpatrick seems to have been a favorite, as she was twice made the godmother of children in these two families. This reciprocity—between New York's interracial couples and families and their Chinese and non-Chinese relatives, friends, and neighbors made possible by the rituals of baptism and marriage—fostered and maintained communal and family ties that cut across racial boundaries.

An examination of this period's census records suggests that these social bonds expressed in baptism records could have been formed as a result of interactions among the multiracial population residing in the Chinatown area. By 1900 Chinatown's families—interracial and not—had clearly begun to cluster in several of the larger tenement buildings in the neighborhood, carving out a separate residential space for themselves among Chinatown's predominantly "bachelor" laborer population. Over 60 percent of Chinatown's Chinese-Chinese families were concentrated in four buildings along Mott Street. Similarly, more than 60 percent of Chinatown's interracial families lived in seven buildings that had at least four mixed-race families each.[63] Unlike Chinatown's Chinese-Chinese families which tended to cluster in several buildings on Mott Street in particular, 50 percent of the community's interracial couples and families were dispersed over the entire Chinatown area, with many of the remaining 50 percent of the families residing on Pell Street. The residential patterns of these two groups did overlap at times as mixed-race families also resided in the four buildings inhabited predominantly by all Chinese families. Several buildings had equal numbers of all Chinese and mixed-race families living on the premises. 13 Mott Street, for example, was home to four Chinese-Chinese and four mixed-race families; 28 Mott Street had two Chinese-Chinese and two mixed-race families.

In 1900, 43 Mott Street was the home to twelve Chinese-Chinese and four interracial families.[64] Nearly all of the Chinese husbands residing in the building worked as merchants or cigar makers. One mixed-race, two-generation household, composed of the Mon Ki and Lum families, formed particularly close friendships with two of the other interracial families residing in the building, the Toys and the Bocks. In 1864 twenty-four-year-old John Lum married sixteen-year-old Sarah Duncan, who was of African American ancestry, in South Carolina. Shortly after their marriage the young couple moved to New York City and settled in lower Manhattan where John, like the majority of Chinese laborers in the city, found work as a cigar maker. In 1868 Sarah gave birth to their first child, George. By 1870 the family settled onto Baxter Street and took in forty-two-year-old Thomas Aloon, a fellow countryman and cigar maker.[65] Sarah gave birth to six children in all but only three survived into adulthood.

Being of partial African American ancestry did not seem to dampen the marriage prospects of their only daughter, Cynthia, who married a Chinese immigrant with the surname of Mon Ki. In 1890 at the age of eighteen she gave birth to their first child, a daughter, whom she named Sarah after her mother. The couple had two more children: Kung Poi, a son, and Ellen, a second daughter. Unfortunately Cynthia's husband died shortly after Ellen's birth in 1897, leaving her a young widow in her mid-twenties. During this period Cynthia remained close to her family as she and her children continued to live with her parents and her brother, John, at 43 Mott Street, where the family also kept a dry goods store.

The Lums and Mon Kis formed close relationships with the Toys and the Bocks. Charles Toy was a merchant who had immigrated in 1880. In 1890 he married seventeen-year-old Josephine, who was born in New York City to a Chinese father and Cuban mother. A year later Josephine gave birth to their first child, Edward. Raised in the Catholic faith,[66] Josephine also wanted her son to be baptized and asked Cynthia Mon Ki to become his godmother.[67] Nine days after the boy's birth family and friends gathered to celebrate Edward's baptism at the Church of the Transfiguration. Around this time Joseph Bock, a laundryman, also moved into the building with his family. In 1882 Joseph met and married Sarah while he was working in Kentucky and the couple had a daughter, Josephine. After their arrival in New York Sarah gave birth to a son, Lawrence, in 1893, and the Bock family also called upon Cynthia Mon Ki to be the godmother of their son. These baptisms formalized the bonds that had formed among these three neighbors. The commonalities shared among these families went beyond their mixed-race composition. Cynthia Mon Ki and Josephine Toy were only one year apart, and Sarah Bock was approximately six years older than the two women. Each of the three families also had children ranging in similar ages.[68]

Shared residence, though helpful, was not necessary for creating close friendships among the area's interracial families. Charles Wing and his wife Mary Bernheimer asked the white wife of his Chinese friend, Valentine Tang, to become the godmother of their only son, Henry, who was born at Baxter Street in 1881 and later baptized at the Church of the Transfiguration. Henry's godfather was Dong Fook, a cigar maker.[69] All three men knew each other from living and working in the Chinatown neighborhood. Valentine Tang and Dong Fook were cigar makers while the Wings kept a fruit stand at the corner of Pell and Doyers streets.[70] When Henry Wing reached the age of thirty-five he married nineteen-year-old Annie Young Hoy, the daughter of another one of Chinatown's interracial couples, Charles Young Hoy and Margaret Romer.[71]

Even during the period of the Elsie Sigel murder, when police and social reformers attempted to reinscribe Chinatown's racial and gendered borders, mixed-race households composed of married couples, boarders, and extended kin continued to persist in the neighborhood. According to the 1910 census surveys, three multiracial households occupied apartments at 19 Pell Street. Thirty-four-year-old Ping Wong, a merchant, lived with his twenty-three-year-old wife of three years, Nellie, in one apartment. The couple also had boarders, including Nellie's younger sister, Katherine Roberts, and several Chinese and white boarders: Frank and Pauline Artist, Frances Wilson, Biu Lee, and Bock Look. Frank Artist was a newspaper printer, Biu Lee worked as a cook, and Bock Look was a waiter.[72] In another flat thirty-six-year-old Suey Chu lived with his twenty-eight-year-old wife, Anna. To supplement Suey Chu's income as a store salesman the couple took in five boarders, including another interracial couple, Charlie and Emma Chu, two Chinese men, Kee Bow and Sing Bow, and one white woman, Anna Armstrong. In the third residence, Alice Chu and her Chinese husband also shared their apartment with his two cousins, Yet Chu and Gow Leong, and a white lodger, John Mayers.

The existence of these social networks—composed of Chinese and non-Chinese relatives, friends, neighbors, and work or business associates—did not mean that Chinatown's interracial families were easily maintained or resistant to the same socioeconomic problems that threatened to undermine the stability of other immigrant working-class families in the city. Many of these relationships were fragile because of these couple's precarious financial positions and the Chinese husband's laborer status under the Chinese Exclusion Acts. Ing Ine How left the United States to go to China in the late 1910s, but failed to apply and receive the critical return certificate and became separated from his wife,

Julia, and their two children, Arthur and Mabel.[73] Forced to remain in Lam Dun village in Hok San district, Guangdong Province, his wife in 1923 attempted to petition the Department of State and the Bureau of Immigration to allow her husband's return to the United States. Both departments, however, denied her request. By 1924, nearly six years after Ing Ine How had left the United States, Julia decided to send Arthur to China as it was the only way for father and son to be reunited. In effect the exclusion acts, by refusing to grant legal immigration status to Chinese laborers such as Ing Ine How, worked to turn these interracial families into a similar form of split transnational households endured by many of the city's Chinese "bachelor" laborers, who were forced to leave behind their Chinese wives in their home villages.[74]

Social ties among the Chinese immigrant community became all the more necessary for sustaining these mixed-race households in moments of great personal and family crisis and were particularly invaluable in the caring and rearing of children in such situations. Wing Kwong Lang, or Felton as he was known by his classmates, was born in his home at 12 Pell Street, on December 25, 1896. His father, Ng Lang Suey or "Charlie," was a Chinese laborer who had worked as a laundryman as well as a janitor in a Chinatown store. Nellie Johnson, his mother, was fourteen years younger than his father, and worked as a dressmaker.[75] Unfortunately for Wing Kwong Lang and his sister Rose, their parents died while they were both still minors. Following their death Wing Kwong Lang, then a teenager, was able to take advantage of an extensive Chinese immigrant support network that helped him to obtain work at Mee Woh Low, a Chinese restaurant located in Lynn, Massachusetts. In 1912, Wing Kwong Lang, then sixteen years old, went to China to stay with relatives at his father's home village.[76] Similar to other American-born Chinese boys who had returned to China, Wing Kwong Lang's relatives arranged for his marriage to a Chinese woman, Jew She, with whom he had two sons before returning to New York City in 1915.[77]

These social networks may have chiefly operated along gendered lines. His only surviving sister Rose did not find similar support within the Chinese community. Unlike her brother, who was taken care of by their father's friends and family, she was adopted by an American minister and moved to Pennsylvania. Unfortunately, no explanation was provided for this difference in treatment. Yet, looking at other immigration cases, sending girls back to China occurred infrequently since the privilege of Chinese schooling was usually reserved for sons. Chinatown's social networks, arising from a predominantly male laboring population, perhaps, could not accommodate the care of girls. Lastly, given the popular image of Chinese slave girls, the courts may have decided adoption by an American minister, rather than by a male Chinese relative or friend, was in the girl's best interest.

Carrie Wah, a German immigrant woman who married William Wah in 1911, took over the care of their godson, Joe Fook, after his parents, Harry and Bertha Joe, separated. Joe was born in 1926 when the family resided at 41 Mott Street. After learning that Bertha had a serious drinking problem, Harry removed Joe from the home and placed him in a hospital. The couple separated shortly after the move, leaving Joe in his father's custody. After starting work as a seaman Harry then turned to Carrie Wah to help provide a more stable and permanent home for his son. She agreed and the Wahs continued to care for Joe even after moving to Long Beach, Long Island, where they enrolled him in the local public school. When Joe reached the age of nine his father wished for him to be educated in China. The Wahs had clearly become devoted guardians as Carrie Wah informed immigration officials that she was going to China for at least one year to help her godson adjust.[78]

When family and community support was lacking or inadequate, families turned to available social service agencies for assistance. In 1912 when Thomas Ring took sick, his wife Sarah turned to her friend Mabel Tie for help. Not able to offer any financial assistance Mabel then wrote Chinatown missionary Rose Livingston, whom she had known for many years, to request help in finding a job for her friend. Livingston responded by sending Sarah $6 and some clothes for the upcoming Christmas holidays.[79] When Thomas Kirk died in 1924 he left behind his young twenty-two-year-old widow, Gurli Dohn Kirk, and their one-year-old son, Elliot. Gurli, a Danish immigrant, had difficulty finding work while simultaneously caring for their young son. After a year Gurli decided to place two-year-old Elliot at the Hopewell Society of Brooklyn. Gurli Dohn Kirk later remarried and began a family with her new husband. In 1930 she arranged with the Hopewell Society to have Elliot go to Hong Kong to live with his paternal grandparents. Following a satisfactory investigation by China Child Welfare, Inc., which showed that the grandparents could provide satisfactory living arrangements, the Travelers Bureau of the Salvation Army agreed to support the boy's travel expenses to China.[80]

In certain situations, however, the dim view on interracial marriage held by social workers and government officials could mean that state intervention would just as likely exacerbate, rather than ameliorate, the plight of these families. In 1918 Margaret Hanratty, an Irish immigrant, became the common-law wife of Lee Hang and resided at Third Avenue around 125th Street near the restaurant where Lee Hang was employed. On February 10, 1919, Margaret gave birth to their son Tom. Although not legally married Lee Hang's Chinese acquaintances nonetheless accepted the new family, visiting them after their return from the hospital. Despite Lee Hang's promise to wed Margaret the couple never married and went their separate ways two years later. Lee Hang left New York altogether while Margaret found work as a governess for a family on West 114th Street.[81]

In 1923 Lee Lin Yeck, who had boarded at Margaret's house, offered to adopt Tom and take him to his village to be raised and educated by his family. Lee Lin Yeck knew Lee Hang well since both came from the same village and worked in New York's restaurant industry. Margaret agreed to let Lee Lin Yeck adopt Tom, but the decision appears to have been difficult and she remained ambivalent regarding her feelings toward her son. She was obviously concerned for his welfare, stating to immigration officials that she only consented to the adoption because he would be under the care of Lee Lin Yeck, a close family friend. "Were I not fully satisfied that the boy is to be taken care of, educated and maintained by Lee Lin Yeck, I would not be here to-day to assist in having him secure a Return Certificate to the United States." Yet she also added that she wished "the boy will never return to the United States," despite the fact that she was testifying to help him to secure a citizen's return certificate. In her closing comment to the immigration official, she seemed to change her mind again, stating that "I do wish he will be allowed to come into the U.S. in the years to come."[82]

Immigration Inspector P. A. Donahue was hardly sympathetic to the situation, summarizing the case as one of "a mother trying to rid herself of an illegitimate child by a Chinese father."[83] Although immigration officials were convinced that Tom Lee was a native-born American citizen and thereby eligible for a return certificate, they chose not to issue one and went outside of the department to intervene further by challenging the adoption. After a court hearing Justice Levy of the Children's Court deemed that "no proper guardianship" could be established for the child, since the adoption had not been formalized through a court, and decided to grant the NYSPCC temporary custody of Tom Lee pending a full investigation into the matter.[84] At the time of the hearing Tom Lee had already begun living with Lee Lin Yeck, but since his adoption was never formalized by a court of law, Lee Lin Yeck's claim of guardianship was not recognized. These support networks, informal by nature, could be easily destabilized through the intervention of state officials and social agencies.

As the above cases suggest, interracial couples and families often socialized together but were also well integrated into the larger Chinatown community. Their established social networks, comprised Chinese relatives, co-workers, and friends in China and the United States, and broadened to include their non-Chinese relatives and friends. In essence the relationships sustained by these families over time and space suggest that Chinatown's interracial families were not as isolated as contemporary popular press accounts or immigration officials alleged. These relationships, critical in times of financial and legal crisis or familial distress, formed the backbone of working-class Chinese American family life in turn-of-the-century New York.

PORTRAITS OF CHINATOWN'S INTERRACIAL MERCHANT FAMILIES

Though much smaller in numbers, some members of the exempted classes also participated in the practice of intermarriage. As seen in the case of Chinese Christian leaders such as Guy Maine or Huie Kin, their higher social or economic class standing meant these religious, business, and community leaders often wielded considerable influence within and beyond the Chinese immigrant community. Class privileges, however, did not necessarily protect these mixed-race families. As the extended family histories of merchants Charles Sing and Chung Hong suggest, such socioeconomic benefits could be transient and racial discrimination remained an obstacle for people of Chinese descent during the exclusion era.

Charles Sing, also known as Chung Ding Shing, did not enter the United States as a merchant. Rather he arrived in San Francisco in 1861 at the age of thirteen, twenty-one years before the enactment of the Chinese Exclusion Act.[85] He stayed in Weaverville, California until the age of eighteen and then found work in Virginia City, Nevada and San Francisco. At the age of twenty-two he helped to secure the historic 1870 contract between the North Adams, Massachusetts shoe manufacturer, C. T. Sampson, and San Francisco labor contractors, Ah Young and Ah Yan, to bring seventy-five Chinese men across the country to work in Sampson's shoe factory for a three-year period.[86]

Despite tensions between the Chinese and white workers at the factory, Sing and his fellow Chinese workers were not socially isolated from the rest of North Adams. A section of North Adams's middle-class residents clearly saw the presence of Chinese laborers in their town as an excellent opportunity for conducting missionary work.[87] In certain cases the zeal to teach the Chinese workers was reciprocated by their enthusiasm for English classes and curiosity about Christianity.[88] The Chinese workers also opened some of their social activities and cultural celebrations to the town's residents. The local newspaper, *The Adams Transcript*, often described at length the Lunar New Year celebrations held in town and at the shoe factory where Chinese and American participants gathered.[89] The extent that the workers may have viewed their stay in North Adams to be long can also be seen in the Chinese community's purchase of a burial lot in the village cemetery rather than shipping the bodies of the dead back to San Francisco or China.[90]

For several enterprising Chinese with a bit of capital, North Adams presented potential economic opportunities.[91] Sing's financial success through his position of business agent, for example, allowed him to emerge quickly as one of the town's recognizable Chinese leaders and local businessmen.[92] His rising socioeconomic status was not without some controversy in the Chinese community, however. The application of differing pay scales for Chinese laborers and contractors had on more than one occasion aroused the ire of the Chinese workers at the factory.[93] Yet his economic position, combined with his membership at a local church and ability to speak fluent English, made him a popular and recognizable figure in the larger North Adams community. The local newspaper often reported on the activities of Sing as well as some of the other prominent local Chinese residents.[94] The extent that he seemed to embrace life in the United States can be seen in his application for American citizenship in 1874.[95] Following his examination by Chief Justice Gray in 1876, Sing was granted full American citizenship. From local reports it appears that Sing took his new citizenship status seriously and duly exercised his voting privileges.[96]

That same year, Sing opened on Main Street his own wholesale and retail store specializing in Chinese curios, teas, and groceries. An announcement in the *Adams Transcript* described the store as a "miniature museum—an exhibition of curiosities that is well worth coming miles to see."[97] A month after the store's opening Sing made a bold business decision. Not satisfied with just being a "miniature museum," selling mainly Chinese curios, Sing expanded his store's merchandise to carry bulk grocery items including flour, syrups, molasses, and other staples. This move made the store more attractive to the general North Adams populace and placed his establishment in direct competition with the white-owned dry goods stores in the town. To advertise his store's new identity as a general goods store rather than an Oriental curio shop, Sing placed a new advertisement in *The Adams Transcript*. Unlike the earlier announcement that aimed to evoke an Oriental, exotic mystique, the new advertisement presented the new store in the American no-nonsense business terms of economy and quality and stated that "Chas. Sing's motto in business is, 'Pay for what you get, and be sure and get what you pay for. . . . Sing wants the house-wives of this village to examine his line of spices. They are purer, and are selling at lower prices, than at any other place in town.'"[98] In other words, any mention of Chinese goods or curios was removed from this new ad in his efforts to remake the store's image.

His entrepreneurial activities eventually allowed him to accumulate enough capital to purchase a gold mine in Morrisville, Virginia. In 1878 he met Ida V. Wilburn of Pine View, Virginia, while visiting his investment, and the two were married on July 23, 1878. The couple returned to North Adams and on May 15, 1879, Ida V. Sing gave birth to their first child, Herbert. Similar to other proud new parents in the community, the couple placed a birth announcement of their son in the *Adams Transcript*.[99] The birth of the Sings' baby boy seemed to be of great importance to the entire North Adams Chinese community as they joined the Sings in an important Cantonese practice of celebrating the one month anniversary of the birth.[100]

Shortly thereafter Charles Sing sold his store in 1881 to A. Wilburn & Co.[101] Sing was one of the last Chinese from the original group hired to work at Sampson's factory to leave North Adams.[102] The Sing family then settled in Yonkers where they rented a house on the corner of Kellenger and School streets, located across from their landlord, Marvin R. Oakley.[103] On May 30, 1883 Ida gave birth to another son, George. Ida Sing eventually gave birth to seven children but two died while in their childhood.[104] Though they lived in Yonkers for only two years the family became friendly and remained in contact with their landlord and the Johnsons, their neighbors across the street.

Once in Yonkers, Sing again seized opportunities to move beyond his own ethnic community and the lowly socioeconomic niche they occupied as Chinese laborers/strikebreakers. Sing's measured successes before the onset of Chinese exclusion suggest the possibility of socioeconomic mobility for some Chinese, particularly those who through their position as labor contractors or business agents were ranked above the common laborer. This freedom to live and work outside of the Chinese community, however, proved difficult by the 1880s after the family's move to Manhattan and the passage of the Chinese Exclusion Act. There he encountered the more strictly enforced racial and geographic boundaries separating the Chinatown area from the rest of lower Manhattan. Putting his past retail experience to work he became a merchant in the Chinese firm of Sun Hung Lo at 196 Park Row, located on the outskirts of Chinatown. Unlike his North Adams dry goods store, that dared to compete with local white-owned businesses, Sun Hung Lo catered to Chinese residents and the curious.

Despite Charles Sing's own lack of interest in returning to live in China and his interest in acquiring American citizenship, he was ultimately not so different from other middle-class Chinese immigrants in New York City. Similar to other Chinese merchant families, Charles Sing sent his son George to China to receive a Chinese education. Many Chinese merchants believed both American and Chinese schooling to be important in order for their sons to maintain their businesses in the Chinese immigrant community. Chinese schooling also served as additional insurance against the possibility that the United States would one day decide to close its borders to all classes of Chinese immigrants.[105] The death of Ida Sing in 1897 may have also influenced Charles Sing's decision to send fourteen-year-old George to China, where he could be looked after by relatives in his home village. Before his departure, however, Charles Sing had to make certain that his son would be allowed to return to the United States and applied for the necessary return certificate, form 430, designated for native-born American citizens of Chinese descent.[106] In order to establish that George was a native-born American, Charles Sing required affidavits of two white witnesses to provide evidence of his son's birth in Yonkers. Marvin Oakley and Sylvester Johnson came to his assistance and declared in their statements that they knew the family well and that Ida V. Sing was "an American lady of good standing, well known and respected."[107] George received his citizen's return certificate and departed for China to attend school in his father's natal village, Gow Low How village in Hoiping district, Guangdong Province.[108] Typically the stay also meant an opportunity for marriage for merchant sons who were sent to study in China. After two years of living in the village, George, at the age of sixteen, married Wong She of Woo How Bin village, a seventeen-year-old with bound feet. George did not return to the United States until February 1902. Charles Sing passed away a year later at the age of fifty-five and was buried in Los Angeles.

Although George was an American citizen by birthright, he decided not to exercise his citizenship privileges to bring his young family to the United States. It is unlikely that George was able to follow in his father's merchant footsteps. By the 1920s he was working as a waiter at the Gee Shu Restaurant at 108th Street and Third Avenue. His waiter's salary may have prevented him from bringing his family to the United States; instead, his family became yet another split transnational household. All three sons—Fook Wing, Fook Dong, and Fook Lin—were raised by their mother in Gow Low How Village, and later married and became farmers. In effect, George Sing's separation from his family made his experience not unlike the other Chinese laborers whose class status excluded their wives and children from joining them in the United States. George Sing remained in the United States for the next twenty-one years, not making a return trip until April 1923. Later that year his eldest son Chung Fook Wing, who was twenty-five years old, became the first son to journey from China to the United States.

The local and transnational business and social networks of Chinatown's merchants could also be called upon to aid these interracial families in times of crisis. In 1894 Chung Hung, a partner at an import/export store located at 22 Mott Street, married Ellen or "Nellie" McGuiness. On March 10, 1894 Nellie gave birth to a son, Arnold Irving, at their home at 30 Bayard Street. He was baptized a month later at the Church of the Transfiguration.[109] The parents chose Chung Suen, who was likely one of Chung Hung's business partners, and Sadie Fofty to be the godparents. Nellie clearly wished to raise Arnold as a Catholic as she chose not to enroll him in the neighborhood public school, preferring to place him at Transfiguration's grammar school. Nellie gave birth to five children in all but only Arnold survived into adulthood.[110] She, also, did not live long and died at the age of thirty.

After his mother's death Arnold, who was then six, stopped attending school and for the next three years lived with his father at the store, where the other partners and workers helped with his care. In 1902 Chung Hung, similar to other merchants with financial means, decided to send nine-year-old Arnold to China for his schooling. Jung Chung, an accountant at Chung Hung's firm, was asked to accompany Arnold to China and bring him to his uncle, Chong Jow, to live with the family at Dung Hing Village in Hock San District, Guangdong Province.[111] During his son's absence, Chung Hung continued to manage the Mott Street firm and also invested in two stores in Philadelphia's Chinatown and another one in Mexico. A few years after Arnold's departure Chung Hung at the age of forty-seven unexpectedly took sick and died at a hospital in Philadelphia. He left Arnold his interests in both the Mexican firm and a Philadelphia store, Chong Wo and Company, located at 909 Race Street.

Following his death Chung Hong's business partners in the United States and relatives in China became the informal guardians to the now orphaned Arnold. In the United States his father's former business partners ensured that Arnold would receive dividends from the businesses, sending periodic remittances to China. Meanwhile relatives in China continued to oversee Arnold's education and secure a suitable match to a Chinese girl, Fong Shee.[112] When Arnold returned to the United States in 1912, he had to provide witnesses to establish that he was a native-born U.S. citizen. Several of his father's former Chinatown business associates testified on his behalf.[113] In addition Emma Wing, a kindergarten helper at a school for Chinatown's children at 10 Mott Street, also testified to immigration officials that she knew the Chong family. With the support of his father's former business partners, Arnold hoped to be employed in the Philadelphia firm, Chung Wo and Company, as an accountant. He also planned to send for his young Chinese wife who remained in China. Through the support provided by this tight network of family, friends, and business associates that spanned two continents, Chung Hong was able to ensure that his son would reap the benefits of his investments and inherit a place in one of his enterprises.

These examples also demonstrate that entry into an interracial marriage did not necessarily mean that Chinese merchant husbands could easily safeguard their social and economic position in America. Keenly aware of the ongoing limitations imposed on people of Chinese descent during the exclusion era, these fathers strove to maintain their ties with Chinese relatives and business associates in the United States and abroad, integrating their families into Chinatown's social, cultural, and economic life. They did not see their children as inherently less Chinese, needing to be raised in a manner different from other Chinatown children with two Chinese parents. The fact that many of these fathers purposely sent their sons to China to achieve a Chinese education suggests that they acted like other merchant fathers who hoped to pass on their hard-earned socioeconomic status in the Chinatown community to their sons by grooming them for positions in their firms. The arranging of their sons' marriages to Chinese women indicates that for the merchant class interracial marriages did not threaten to replace Chinese-Chinese marriages altogether. Chinese education and Chinese brides for their American-born sons remained important markers of their higher socioeconomic status.

THE LEE/LEM FAMILY: A MULTIGENERATIONAL PORTRAIT

The anecdotal evidence provided in the immigration case files indicates a high rate of geographical mobility for Chinese in the United States. Indeed, like their "bachelor" counterparts, Chinese American interracial families did not necessarily remain within the Chinatown neighborhood. To understand the extent to which these families often struggled simultaneously to maintain their socioeconomic position and claim physical space in New York City, this section examines the history of the Lee/Lem family over three generations. Elizabeth, nee Reynolds, an English woman by birth, married Lee Fee and gave birth to Emma while they were still residing in Sydney, Australia. In the 1870s the young family journeyed from Australia to San Francisco and New York City. Following their arrival in the United States Elizabeth also gave birth to four boys: Steven, Elijah, Joe, and Elisha.[114]

On May 12, 1894 Emma, who was then seventeen, married thirty-six-year-old Henry Lem, a Chinese laborer, who had also come to the United States during the 1870s. Despite the age difference Emma's parents appeared to have approved of their marriage. Lee Fee and Elizabeth Lee served as witnesses for the wedding at the Five Points Mission. The newlyweds moved to Spring Valley, New York where Emma gave birth to a daughter, Elizabeth, a year later. By 1900 the couple had returned to Chinatown and settled at 15 Mott Street. Over the next ten years the Lem family lived in various addresses in the neighborhood. To accommodate the growing family the Lems moved to 34 Mott Street, a large apartment building where many of Chinatown's families resided.[115]

Like other Chinatown families the Lems called upon the assistance of a popular local midwife, Teresia Russo, to help deliver their children who, with the exception of Elizabeth, were all born while the family resided in Chinatown. During these years Emma gave birth to Rose, Ida, Emma, Henry, and Henrietta. When Henry Jr. was born on December 11, 1905 at 24 Mott Street, the parents were overjoyed. After giving birth to four girls, Emma finally had a son. To show their appreciation the Lems bestowed gifts upon Teresia's daughter, Annie, who had come to assist her mother with the delivery. Henry Sr. gave Annie $10 while Emma gave her a silk shawl.[116] Like other children in Chinatown the Lem children attended the neighborhood public schools. Henry Jr. entered the first grade at P.S. 108 located at 60 Mott Street and later transferred to P.S. 23 located on the corner of Bayard and Mulberry streets. Though the children had Chinese names they mostly identified themselves by their English names in their interactions with the outside world.[117] Chinese was most likely not spoken in the Lem home as Emma's Chinese vocabulary was probably limited.[118]

Upon their return to New York, Henry Lem went to work as a butcher and eventually established his own successful wholesale meat and vegetable supply business specifically catering to Chinese restaurants. He bought and cut meat obtained from the Figge-Hutwalker Company, located at West Fortieth Street in the midtown meat packing district, and stored vegetables and supplies at his storefront at 56 Mott Street. By 1920 Henry had accumulated enough money for the family to purchase their first house at 94 Washington Avenue in Grantwood, New Jersey. A few years earlier the Lems had moved out of Chinatown, briefly residing in several towns in New Jersey—Palisades and Cliffside Park.[119]

By 1926 three of the Lem daughters who had survived into adulthood—Elizabeth, Rose, and Ivy—had married Chinese men. Similar to Emma's experience, the three daughters had no difficulty finding Chinese husbands given the severe gender imbalance among the Chinese immigrant population during the exclusion era. The eldest, Elizabeth May Lem, married F. C. Lang and the couple later settled in Cliffside Park, New Jersey. Rose, the second oldest, however, moved back with her family after leaving her Chinese husband when she unexpectedly discovered that he was already married with a wife and two children living in China. Ivy married Chan Joseph Dick and the couple settled in Brooklyn.[120] The youngest daughter, Emma, remained single, continuing to live at the family home in Grantwood until her early death in 1928.[121]

In 1926 Henry Jr. started to work for his father after acquiring the necessary skills for the trade. That same year Henry Sr. made plans with Henry Jr. to visit China for the first time since his departure as a young man nearly fifty years earlier. Both father and son went through the rigors of obtaining citizens' return certificates in preparation for their trip, but never made the journey. Henry Jr. died shortly after at the age of twenty-one.[122]

The youngest surviving son Harvard, born at 34 Mott Street in 1914, followed quite a different path from his older brother Henry. Unlike the older Lem children, who attended the local public schools in the Chinatown area, Harvard first attended Cliffside Public School No. 4 in Grantwood, New Jersey. At the age of fifteen he decided to learn an industrial trade and took classes for several months at the New York Electrical School in Manhattan. By 1930, with the onset of the Great Depression, the family began to fall on difficult financial times and moved out of their home on Washington Avenue into another home on Grant Avenue in Grantwood. Harvard, then sixteen years old, left school to work for Charles Kelbel, a plasterer in West New York, New Jersey, and continued with his studies by taking evening classes at George Washington High School in New York City. Work remained steady for three years but by 1933 Harvard was only able to obtain a series of temporary jobs as a day laborer. In 1935 Harvard, along with many American youths his age, applied and was accepted into the Civilian Conservation Corps (CCC), a New Deal work program begun in 1933 that specifically employed youth from low income and limited educational backgrounds.[123] In 1936 he left the CCC and managed to find work again with Charles Kelbel where he remained for one year. By 1937 Harvard decided to become a seaman and three years later he joined the war by registering for the United States Maritime Training Service. In 1943, just months before the repeal of the Chinese Exclusion Acts, Harvard applied for a citizen's return certificate to travel to Havana, Cuba where he planned to get married.[124] Harvard was not the only one in the family to be swept up in the war. His sister Rose, who never remarried after leaving her bigamist husband, continued to live with her parents in Grantwood. Rose joined the war effort and found work as a drill press operator in the Bendix Aviation Corporation in New Jersey.[125] As it had for large numbers of women and racial minorities, the Great Depression and World War II brought new opportunities in industrial work for the younger Lem children.[126]

Charting the history of one particular interracial family over three generations provides an interesting glimpse into why Chinatown's interracial families might have disappeared from census records as their numbers began to decline after their peak in 1900. While it is possible that some of these relationships ended, it is also likely that these families had simply relocated. The Lems, who appeared in the 1900 census survey for New York City only, experienced great geographical mobility often related to their family's particular economic situation. Anecdotal evidence provided in the immigration files of individual family members shows that their marriages and family ties were long lasting despite their constant uprooting. While it would be a mistake to use one family to represent Chinatown's interracial families, the Lee/Lem family history offers a critical response to the often pitiably doomed portraits of Chinatown's interracial families represented by contemporary writers, social reformers and state officials.

Although little reliable information regarding Leon Ling and Elsie Sigel's relationship has survived, it is clear that the choice to engage in an interracial relationship was hardly unique or original by the early twentieth century. Indeed their travels throughout the city easily led them to become acquainted with working-class and middle-class Chinese-white couples. While interracial marriage provided an option for Chinese laborers to form lasting companionate relationships and establish families in the United States, it was clearly not without difficulty. Even with the absence of anti-miscegenation laws in New York State, these alliances were often publicly attacked as immoral or simply dismissed as temporary or illegitimate. Within this hostile climate Chinatown's interracial couples attempted to construct lives and support networks for themselves that involved both Chinese and non-Chinese relatives, friends, neighbors, and coworkers here and abroad. Faced with economic challenges and problems posed by their precarious immigration status, these Chinese men and their non-Chinese wives and companions nonetheless dared to contest religious, racial, and gender boundaries and build new lives for themselves.

CHAPTER SIX

"The Most Remarkable Get-away in Police History"

IN THE MIDST of the heated murder investigation, Elsie Sigel was quietly laid to rest on the afternoon of June 21 at Woodlawn Cemetery in the Bronx. Only her father along with her two brothers and an uncle accompanied her body to the cemetery. Her family wished to dispense with further publicity and declined to hold services before her interment.[1] With the murder suspect still at large and nagging questions regarding his relationship with Sigel unanswered, the police continued with their local, national, and international manhunt for Leon Ling and his roommate Chong Sing. Police Commissioner Theodore A. Bingham targeted specifically the country's many Chinese American neighborhoods, homes, religious institutions, and places of business. No segment of the Chinese American population was exempt from police scrutiny. Inspector James McCafferty, head of the New York City detective bureau, boasted that the "coast to coast" manhunt was one of the largest ever instituted by the city's police department. "If Leon escapes finally, it will be the most remarkable get-away in police history. So well are the police of all cities working together that the entire country may well be likened to an enormous rat trap, with Leon in hiding somewhere within the circle. Every possible avenue of escape is watched day and night, and eventually when he tries to make a break from his hiding place it is almost certain he will be caught."[2] With such a sweeping search underway police and lay citizens across the country firmly believed that Leon Ling would be apprehended quickly.

The police's earliest descriptions of the two Chinese suspects issued on June 19 emphasized their American dress and haircuts, making Chinese men fitting that description more vulnerable to harassment by police officers and local vigilantes. Another circular released four days later added that Leon Ling "may now be wearing Chinese costume and have on a false queue."[3] With any number of disguises at his disposal, the suspect could appear as either an "Americanized" or un-Americanized Chinese man. The police's belief in Leon Ling's protean qualities provided justification for stopping and questioning any Chinese man encountered. At the New York Central Railroad station in Schenectady, New York, a Chinese man wearing a long quilted silk cloak was quickly

detained when he appeared at that location. Believing the man to be
Leon Ling in disguise, police searched his suitcase but determined that
he was not the murder suspect.[4]

Leon Ling's chameleon-like powers dovetailed into popular racialized
views of the Chinese as physically homogenous and undistinguishable to
whites, conditioning the public's acceptance of mass arrests of Chinese
men as necessary for their capture. The mass publication of the two suspects' photographs and descriptions allowed, if not encouraged, ordinary citizens to take part in the manhunt; and throughout the country
police officials and lay citizens alike responded vigorously to Commissioner Bingham's call to inspect all Chinese. No Chinese person was
above suspicion: laundry workers, restaurant staff, diplomats, students,
and house servants were all detained. As the manhunt unfolded, Chinese
Americans were not the only ones to be caught in the dragnet. With
police and civilians doubling their efforts to scrutinize every Chinese
person in the country, these encounters demonstrated the problems derived from executing a search for a man that ultimately depended on the
illusion of racial differences and classifications for success.

THE HUNT FOR LEON LING

Particularly within the greater New York metropolitan area, the murder
profoundly impacted upon the daily lives of Chinese residents. In
Chinatown Captain Michael Galvin of the Elizabeth Street Police Station
made a thorough search of the "dark dens and crannies of Chinatown"
for Leon Ling, but concluded from talking with his informers that Leon
Ling was not hiding there.[5] For Captain Galvin the Sigel murder could
not have come at a better time. A month earlier Galvin had embarked on
his campaign to "cleanse" Chinatown by closing gambling halls and removing all white women in the neighborhood. Sigel's death fueled strong
support for Galvin's campaign. By the first week of July Galvin could
boast to reporters that he had closed down thirty-six gambling halls and
driven out 110 "disorderly women" from the Chinatown area.[6] The
thorough combing of Chinatown for Leon Ling and Chong Sing closely
resembled those earlier house-by-house searches for illegal gambling and
"disorderly women" that comprised Galvin's anti-vice campaign.

On June 19, in the hopes of garnering additional aid from police and
ordinary citizens throughout the country, the NYPD authorized the circulation of lengthy descriptions of the missing suspects. Aside from noting age, height, and weight, these police circulars described the men as
Americanized in appearance because of their closely cropped haircuts
and western style of dress. Yet Leon Ling was clearly portrayed as the

*MAN SOUGHT FOR DEATH OF ELSIE SIGEL, HIS ROOM-MATE,
AND FACSIMILE OF PORTION OF GIRL'S LAST LETTER.*

Figure 6.1. Photographs of the missing suspects, Chong Sing and Leon Ling circulated in newspapers throughout New York City and across the nation. *Source: World*, June 20, 1909.

more "Americanized" and refined of the two men. Not only was he described as one who "talks good English," but the lengthy physical description—including patent leather shoes, "tight fitting" trousers, and a prized "gold hunting case watch with the initials W. L. L."—also highlighted Leon Ling's efforts to shed his Chinese appearance. Indeed the adoption of the American name, William Leon, suggests the degree to which he may have attempted to erase his "Chineseness" to create an ambiguous racial and ethnic persona. The police description of Chong Sing was brief in comparison, stating only that he had a "smooth face, short hair, American style. Dresses like an American."[7]

Once the police circular became public the press proved instrumental in circulating and reinforcing to its readers this description of Leon Ling as a Chinese man of polished and attractive "Americanized" physical features and personal character. Leon Ling, or William Leon, was unlike the typical period depictions of the "Chinaman" laborer with his long braid and traditional Chinese dress. Instead Leon Ling with his flashy clothes, jewelry, and sexual desirability to women, appeared to more accurately fall in between two nineteenth-century American urban social types—the "dandy" and the "sport."[8] Indeed, one newspaper went so far as to allege that Leon Ling was a "Chinese sport" who worked as "a steerer for Chinese confidence men. He would dig up the men for the other Chinamen to rob, and the other fellows would divide the money with Leon."[9]

Both the "sporting male" and "dandy" were marked by their celebrations of "self-indulgence and sexual promiscuity." While the "sport" was more affiliated with displays of physical prowess and connected to the working-class male subculture of the Bowery, the dandy was seen as having more elite social aspirations. Either type was defined by their ability to move freely through different social worlds and city neighborhoods in their search for sexual fulfillment and adventure. Leon Ling's facility with the English language and sociability around Chinatown and the Bowery, as well as among middle-class New Yorkers such as the Sigels, granted him a form of social mobility not associated with this period's Chinese immigrants who appeared hopelessly attached to their fellow countrymen and ensconced in their urban Chinatown neighborhoods. This depiction of Leon Ling simultaneously emphasized his American-ness, along with his masculinity and attractiveness to the opposite sex, in a manner that complicated and challenged contemporary popular portrayals of the "Chinaman" as sexually repulsive and ambiguously gendered. Early depictions of the Chinese laborer, such as in Hinton R. Helper's classic *Land of Gold*, positioned them as the opposite of white working-class masculinity exhibited on California's gold mining frontier. The "pig-tail" of the Chinaman, Helper declared, worked to make him appear to be a young girl, and the similarities between the clothing of Chinese men and women, consisting of flowing blouses and loose-fitting pants, created difficulties for differentiating between the sexes.[10] The exclusion of Chinese workers from industrial work, which impelled their entry into domestic labor and laundry work—tasks associated with the female domestic sphere—only furthered his emasculation.[11] Not surprisingly, nineteenth and early-twentieth-century narratives of interracial sex between Chinese and whites insisted such relationships occurred chiefly as a result of the white women's dire physical or economic needs and not the Chinese partners' masculinity or sexual desirability.[12]

Whiteness and masculinity were deeply intertwined at the turn of the century. As the chief proponent of the "strenuous life," Theodore Roosevelt believed that a virile, superb masculine physique was critical for exercising democratic citizenship as well as demonstrating white racial superiority. Yet, even for the robust Roosevelt the manly physique he presented to the world as an adult was not formed at birth, but carefully sculpted. Through rigorous physical exercise Roosevelt transformed himself from a boy, of delicate disposition with a weak physical frame, to a burly man of strict martial discipline. Roosevelt as well as other American leaders concerned themselves with safeguarding the state of American manhood at the turn of the century.[13] The rise of corporate power and consumer excesses had undermined the independence and work ethic expected of the white working man, sapping his physical and moral strength. Roosevelt and others exhorted the country's youth to follow his example of self-strengthening and discipline—to undergo a similar transformation to protect the nation and white manhood by forming a muscular democracy. As cultural historian John Kasson has argued, a new popular interest around the physical display and consumption of the white male body emerged shortly following Roosevelt's era. It focused on the possibilities for physical metamorphosis to dramatize "the transformation from weakness to supreme strength, from vulnerability to triumph, from anonymity to heroism, from the confinement of modern life to the recovery of freedom."[14] Young men in the early-twentieth century aimed to vanquish these social and bureaucratic challenges to their manhood and make their body over into such inspirational models of masculine virility as exemplified by the strong man Eugene Sandow or escape artist Harry Houdini.

If manliness was not guaranteed by whiteness alone but had to be fastidiously cultivated, then could not Chinese men such as Leon Ling through similar disciplining and manipulation of their body and behavior undergo an equally impressive metamorphosis in their physique and identity? Harry Houdini's transformation, for example, was not simply about conditioning his body to endure the physical rigors of his escape routines but also involved shedding external markers of his Jewishness, such as changing his name from Ehrich Weiss to craft a white masculine identity.[15] For Chinese men such a transformation could also include acquiring an American name and shedding physical markers, such as their ethnic clothing and queue as well as gaining full mastery of the English language. Written descriptions and photographs of Leon Ling published in newspapers demonstrated to readers the extent to which his ongoing efforts at cultivating a modern, cosmopolitan outlook and appearance may have eclipsed his Chineseness and established an undeniably Americanized, possibly white masculine persona. For example, the *World* published a striking portrait of the suspect with a western haircut and wearing a fashionable suit and chose to identify him by his American alias "William L. Leon."[16] With the discovery of the many love letters received by Leon Ling from Elsie Sigel as well as other white women, the press dubbed him a "Chinese Don Juan" who "seemed to have broken hearts with the utmost facility."[17] Far from being the androgynous and sexually repulsive Chinaman, Leon Ling, the Americanized Chinese man, was portrayed as socially polished and undeniably handsome and irresistible to the opposite sex.

This focus on Leon Ling's masculine and sexual persona modified the public's perceptions of his socioeconomic status as well as his Chinese ethnic and racial characteristics. Despite the fact that the newspapers and police noted Leon Ling's past experience as a restaurant cook or waiter, the suggestion that he was somehow more cosmopolitan than the typical Chinaman led many to assume he belonged to a higher socioeconomic class than laborer. George Anderson, a yard master for the West Shore Railroad Company, went by these assumptions when he reported to the police that he recalled seeing the missing Chinese men on the evening of Wednesday, June 9. He identified them because the men were in American clothing. More importantly, he noted that "one was a very good-looking Chinaman, with the Chinese characteristic not very strongly, stamped. This man was well dressed. His companion was of a more decided Chinese cast and was more shabby in appearance."[18] Anderson was hardly alone in thinking that Leon Ling was somehow more urbane and less Chinese in his overall appearance. This popularly shared assumption would quickly lead to growing public confusion and anxiety over how to proceed with making a proper racial identification in their attempts to locate the missing suspect.

As the manhunt swiftly grew from a local search to a national and international one, police and ordinary citizens relied upon these descriptions accentuating the Americanized features of the Chinese fugitives to guide them in their search. Throughout New York State sightings of the suspects resulted in sweeping searches, often producing false arrests.[19] In Schenectady, when Police Chief Rynex received copies of the wanted circulars transmitted by Commissioner Bingham, he immediately dispatched two police detectives to search every Chinese-owned establishment in the city. While searching the back room of a Chinese restaurant located at 22 Center Street, Detectives Van Dusen and Rooney came upon a Chinese man in American clothing lying in the back room who they believed bore

THE CHINESE JEKYLL AND HYDE

Figure 6.2. Although descriptions of Leon Ling emphasized his cosmopolitan ways and attractiveness to the opposite sex, such cartoons lampooned the notion of a genuinely "Americanized" Chinaman. *Source*: Nelson Harding, "The Chinese Jekyll and Hyde," *Brooklyn Daily Eagle*, June 27, 1909, News Special.

a clear resemblance to the murder suspect and quickly concluded that the Chinese workers were conspiring to hide him. The man, however, protested the accusation, explaining instead that he was taking a break from his duties as the restaurant's cook.[20] The detectives nonetheless took the man into custody and telegrammed New York City police that they had the missing fugitive. Reginald Sigel, Elsie Sigel's brother, upon receiving the news hurried to that town to identify the suspect, but upon his arrival he realized the police had arrested the wrong man.[21] An editorial appearing in a Utica newspaper nevertheless applauded the quick action of the Schenectady police. The writer stated that not only did the wrongfully accused man, Chu Hop, physically resemble the suspect in stature, hair, and clothes, but he was also "a Christianized Mongolian." The police's aggressive stance and ready response should be looked upon as demonstrative of the town's civic pride. The Schenectady police had shown by "their zeal" that their town "is not the place of refuge for Leon Ling, William H. Leon or any other suspected Chinaman."[22]

Aside from notifying police throughout the state, Commissioner Bingham specifically alerted local police departments in parts of the country where Chinese communities were present. In Boston Deputy Superintendent William D. Watts responded by assigning Inspectors Daniel Hart and Edward Conway to the case. The two detectives searched Boston's Chinatown until the early morning but found no evidence of Leon Ling having been in their city.[23] Nonetheless the police continued a strict watch over Boston's Chinatown residents, and in nearby Worcester police questioned several Chinese men regarding the Sigel murder.[24] On July 1 police arrested Yee Kin Wah, a twenty-five-year-old Chinese laundryman from Manchester, New Hampshire, because he was identified as a stranger to Boston's Chinatown.[25]

New York police quickly alerted the Washington, D.C. authorities after learning that a few days following her disappearance on June 9 the Sigel family had received a telegram signed "Elsie" that was sent from that city telling them that she would return home the following day.[26] Local police and reporters' attempts to track down information regarding the mysterious telegram led them to the National Hotel located at Sixth Street and Pennsylvania Avenue, where hotel workers and local drivers claimed to have seen Leon Ling accompanied by Sigel. Yet it remains unclear whether or not employees actually saw these two or another mixed-race couple, since many simply recalled "a pretty girl was walking with a Chinaman" and that the man had "a large bank roll and dressed like a millionaire."[27] Although police believed that the June 12 telegram had been sent from the hotel they were unable to obtain any information regarding the suspect's whereabouts.[28] Police in Washington, D.C. and Baltimore similarly conducted thorough searches among their small Chinese American populations.[29] As in other cities, arrests quickly followed. Lem Park, a New York resident who arrived in Washington, D.C. on June 24, was picked up at Union Station when bystanders and a policeman noticed a "dapper little Celestial, wearing a blue suit and panama hat."[30] Lem Park was discharged when his Washington Chinese friends testified that he was not Leon Ling. The Eighth Precinct police also arrested C. J. Kong because the man was said to be "Americanized" and resembled Leon Ling. Kong was only recently released from the workhouse where he had served thirty days for a charge of vagrancy. He was "loitering" in a local freight yard waiting to "hop" a freighter going westward when police spotted him.[31]

On June 23 a similarly large-scale search commenced in San Francisco, home of the largest urban Chinese immigrant population in the country. Acting Captain of Detectives Fitzgerald assigned two detectives of the "Chinatown squad" to search the entire Chinese community.[32] San Francisco police also kept a careful watch of the port district, paying particularly close attention to the Pacific Mail docks where the *Manchuria* awaited its scheduled departure at one o'clock the following afternoon. Police stood guard "at every approach to the wharves and at each entrance to the big steamer."[33] Pacific Mail company workers and city policemen checked each passenger as they embarked, and extra guards accompanied all Chinese passengers leaving the immigration detention sheds to board the steamer. By sail time, however, the extra precautions had not managed to produce the missing murder suspect. Not taking a chance, police continued to take similar precautions with all vessels bound for Asia.[34]

The smaller population of Chinese immigrants residing across the bay was no less affected. Upon receiving information from New York City police that claimed Leon Ling was the head of New York's Hip Sing Tong, Oakland's Acting Chief of Police Peterson ordered a raid on the headquarters of a local tong.[35] Peterson also carried out New York's instructions to investigate Leon Ling's friends and relatives living in the Oakland area.[36] Neither action yielded any information regarding the missing suspect however. On June 26 Oakland police visited nearby Hayward to investigate a young Chinese stranger dressed in western clothes and speaking fluent English who was seen reading an American newspaper.[37] Police also searched in nearby farming towns in case Leon Ling was attempting to pose as a Japanese or Korean laborer.[38]

The hunt also spread to other parts of the country with smaller populations of Chinese residents. On the evening of June 22 in Johnstown, Pennsylvania, two Chinese American men, Lee and Wah Sing, saw "an Americanized Chinaman" whom they thought might have been Leon Ling. The two Chinese men later informed reporters that the Chinese stranger may have boarded an electric car for Windber, approximately nine miles from Johnstown, where several Chinese resided.[39] Police officers in that town later arrested Wee King Song, who had arrived from Altoona, Pennsylvania. In their excitement the police publicly announced that they had not only apprehended Leon Ling but had obtained his confession to the murder before realizing their mistake and releasing the prisoner.[40] In Jackson, Tennessee police arrested a man whom they believed to have matched the description of Leon Ling.[41] On June 27 police in Chandler, Oklahoma believed they had arrested Leon Ling when they picked up a Chinese man whom witnesses saw leaving a freight train. The man denied he was Leon Ling and claimed to have come from St. Louis.[42]

And in the South, Leon Ling sightings were no less uncommon. New York police asked authorities in Galveston, Texas and New Orleans, Louisiana to search all areas inhabited by Chinese for the missing murder suspect.[43] In Gulfport, Mississippi a Chinese man said to look like Leon Ling was arrested on the morning of June 27, when he attempted to board a train for New Orleans. He was held until his landlord could travel from Mobile, Alabama to identify him.[44] Reports of Leon Ling's capture continued to appear throughout the country's newspapers for some time. Even three months after the beginning of the murder investigation, police in places such as Dallas, Texas continued to make claims that they had arrested the long missing fugitive.[45]

As these descriptions of mistaken arrests of innocent Chinese men suggest, ordinary citizens played an instrumental role by keeping careful watch over the activities of the Chinese American population in their locale. While New York's police department communicated with law enforcement agencies throughout the country, newspapers took on the role of disseminating information about the missing suspects and murder investigation to the general public, mobilizing lay citizens to hunt for a handsome and refined Americanized Chinese man. In Chicago several residents contacted police after reading about the murder and the description of the Chinese suspects in their local newspapers. J. Conley, an employee of the Parmalee Company, claimed that on June 18 he had seen two Chinese men stopping in Chicago on their way to Vancouver, B.C. Not until Conley read about the Sigel murder a few days later did he alert the police.[46] Dora Levin also became suspicious when a Chinese man, seemingly educated and fluent in English, stopped into her hotel at 137 Canal Street and inquired about a room. She immediately notified the Chicago police and six detectives were promptly dispatched to the address.[47] In Philadelphia two customers and two workers at a restaurant claimed to have seen Leon Ling and Chong Sing dining there on June 15. May McDermott, who had waited on the two Chinese men, claimed to remember Leon Ling because he matched the newspaper descriptions as a "good-looking Chinaman" who was "well dressed and intellectual looking." The owner of the restaurant, Marvin Reed, also made similar comments on the dress and attitude of the man he believed was Leon Ling, stating that he thought the man acted like a diplomat and was "so well dressed and put on such a front."[48] These reported sightings of Leon Ling corresponded to other reports made throughout the country. The newspaper coverage of the Sigel murder and the changing descriptions of Leon Ling led many Americans to participate in the implicit and explicit policing of Chinese residents, as every Chinese person recently encountered was closely examined to determine if he was indeed the murder suspect.

The city's newspapers seemed to be aware of their own importance in fueling the massive manhunt. *The New York Tribune*, for example, claimed that its own investigative journalism provided police with vital new leads to the murder case.[49] *The New York Times* meanwhile boasted to its readers that their coverage of the murder made them an indispensable ally to the nation's law enforcement agencies. The mass printing and distribution of newspapers "peppers the land with such a volume of pictorial and verbal information as no police department in itself could ever hope to equal," with the resulting effect that "Leon and Chong Sing are as well known to the eyes of San Franciscans as they are to New Yorkers."[50] By informing ordinary citizens of the search's progress and providing up-to-date descriptions of the missing suspects, newspapers enabled the nation's readers to receive the information needed to assist local police in their hunt.

The line between surveillance and vigilantism often blurred as a result of the public's zeal to participate in the dragnet. Chicago police arrested George Moy after he was spotted at West Madison Street wearing American clothes and carrying a suitcase. A large crowd of onlookers quickly assembled on the street and proceeded to follow Moy and the arresting officer all the way to the police station.[51] In Newark, New Jersey three Chinese men were chased by a mob when one of the men in American dress was mistaken for Leon Ling. The men were attending an open-air vaudeville show in Electric Park when someone in the crowd shouted "Leon Ling, the murderer of Elsie Sigel, is here!"[52] On July 6 in nearby Paterson, New Jersey, a riot almost ensued when residents became convinced they had captured Leon Ling. Wah Lee, a laundry worker at 75 Ellison Street, went to visit his cousin William Sing, at 332 Grand Street. A number of people thought they saw an unidentified Chinese man resembling Leon Ling accompany Wah Lee to Sing's laundry and immediately notified the police. When Reserve Officer Cooke later arrived at the laundry, he had difficulty getting inside because of the excited throng that had quickly gathered outside the building.[53] As the number of rumors claiming that the missing Chinese fugitives were hiding somewhere in the country continued to escalate with each report of mistaken arrest, ordinary citizens longed to participate in the capture and bring an end to this police drama. One *New York Times* reporter commented dryly, "The hallucination of 'seeing' the missing Leon continued yesterday all over the United States, with the result that many innocent Chinamen unfortunate enough to wear American dress underwent embarrassing inquisitions without any new clue to the fugitive being obtained."[54]

The hunt for Leon Ling was not simply a national drama, as the search quickly expanded beyond the nation's borders. On June 21 in Revelstoke, British Columbia, approximately 380 miles east of Vancouver, local police detained a Chinese man riding westbound on a Canadian Pacific train. A newspaper description of the arrested man matched the others circulating within the United States: "The man talks good English, is well dressed, and gives an unsatisfactory explanation of his business."[55] Along the U.S. southern border several reports of Leon Ling's arrest also emerged in the Mexican towns of Ciudad Juarez, El Cajon, and Juarez.[56]

The NYPD took an active role in instigating the international manhunt by contacting police in foreign cities for assistance. Although Inspector McCafferty believed that Leon Ling was still in the country, his men took the precaution of researching the departure schedules of steamers bound for China, and discovered that there was only one vessel the suspect could have boarded. Because that vessel was due to dock in Yokohama on July 3, the inspector notified the authorities to have the steamer examined immediately upon landing. Japanese authorities readily complied and boarded and searched every vessel coming from the United States.[57] In Tokyo all passengers on board the *Minnesota*, including the fifty-three Chinese riding in steerage, were also carefully examined. The two first-class and two second-class Chinese passengers searched on board turned out to be students.[58] Working from another tip that Leon Ling may have sailed from Philadelphia to Itosaki, Japan on board the steamer *Helene Rickmers*, New York police cabled several cities along the Mediterranean, Suez Canal, and Indian Ocean to conduct similar searches.[59]

abroad

Equally invasive searches also took place in foreign lands. In early July police in Budapest began to sweep the Chinese residential area after an anonymous source stated that Leon Ling was hiding in the home of a local Chinese family.[60] Almost a week later in London, a visiting American reported to Scotland Yard that he had seen Leon Ling outside of a jeweler's shop near the Royal Exchange. The American attempted to convince a nearby policeman to make the arrest but the officer hesitated, allowing the suspect to flee. Though the patrolman did not believe the American's claim, Scotland Yard still took the precaution of sending photographs of Leon Ling to all London police stations.[61] Similar to cities in the United States, London police announced that thorough searches of that city's Chinese immigrant population would occur: "As the number of Chinamen in England is small compared to the number in America, it will be easier over here to examine all the Chinese residents and discover any strangers."[62]

The NYPD in their haste to capture Leon Ling did not necessarily wait for the U.S. State Department's assistance in contacting foreign governments for assistance. On July 7 New York police sent a direct telegram to the Captain Superintendent of Police in Hong Kong when they suspected that Leon Ling had managed to flee to that colony. By communicating directly with the Hong Kong authorities, the New York City police department broke established diplomatic protocols that required requests for extradition to be relayed through the office of the American Consul General. Writing in protest to the U.S. State Department, American Vice Consul General Stuart J. Fuller stated that his office only learned of the request that morning from the *South China Post*, an English-language publication. The newspaper had printed an article stating that the Captain Superintendent of Police in Hong Kong had received a telegram from the NYPD requesting arrest and extradition of "Li On Tong." To Fuller's annoyance his office had "received no communication either from the New York Police or from any other source in regard to the matter."[63] At first Hong Kong police believed the telegram to be a fake because it had contained little information about the murder case and did not come through the proper diplomatic channels.[64] But they eventually responded to the call, dispatching a telegram asking for further details of the missing murder suspect. In reply to Fuller's complaint, Wilbur J. Carr on behalf of the Secretary of State replied that the police had sent such communications in other cases when they had deduced that the missing suspects had fled the country. Nonetheless Carr assured Fuller that the New York telegram should be seen only as a request to arrest and not for extradition. If extradition was needed his office would be duly notified.[65]

The belief that Leon Ling could be hiding abroad led New York District Attorney William Travers Jerome to send an urgent telegram on July 15 to New York Governor Charles Evans Hughes, asking to proceed with extradition requests from "any country with which we have treaty."[66] The governor, in turn, had his secretary relay Jerome's request to the U.S. State Department. American ambassadors throughout Europe had begun sending telegrams to the U.S. State Department seeking instructions in the event that Leon Ling should be apprehended in the country where they were stationed. On July 14 Naples chief of police contacted U.S. Ambassador Leishman to inquire if the consulate should begin extradition proceedings if local police managed to apprehend Leon Ling.[67] U.S. Ambassador Reid in London and U.S. Ambassador Hill in Berlin sent similar correspondences to the State Department.[68]

Although newspapers in major cities abroad such as London and Paris had reported on the Sigel murder shortly after the discovery of her body, it was the NYPD's aggressive pursuit that impelled foreign police departments into action. As the manhunt continued to escalate, Chinese traveling or living abroad also found themselves under suspicion and their overseas communities under tight surveillance by their local governments. In an outcome similar to the NYPD's domestic requests, these calls for assistance did not produce the elusive Leon Ling as much as worked to reinforce already existing racial and national boundaries by singling out Chinese immigrants from the local population for scrutiny.

The Imprecision of Racial and Ethnic Markers

The constant reporting of mistaken arrests suggests the degree to which police and laymen's attempts to identify the suspects through race had been ineffective. These mass arrests reconfirmed earlier notions that the Chinese were simply physically indistinguishable to whites, as depicted in a 1905 *New York Times* cartoon with a befuddled policeman attempting to "find the guilty one" in a sea of identical looking Chinamen.[69] The extent to which these notions of racial homogeneity continued to shape white perceptions of, and interactions with, Chinese can be seen in the police's attempt to follow Leon Ling's trail to Newark, New Jersey. Working on a rumor that Leon Ling had made his way to that city on the night of the murder to dispose of the trunk at a chop suey restaurant at 64 Market Street, police attempted to locate both Li Sing, the restaurant owner, and James Halstead, the cab driver, for questioning. Upon interrogation, Li Sing insisted that he had refused to accept the trunk and that Leon Ling hired Halstead to take the trunk back to the Eighth Avenue apartment. Yet when police caught up with Halstead and showed him a photograph of the fugitive, he hesitated: "Well, it does look like him, but then, I'm not much on identifying Chinamen. They all look alike to me, more or less." Instead, Halstead had much more faith in his ability to identify the trunk and confidently claimed that "I would know that trunk the moment I saw it."[70]

The popular belief that the racial homogeneity of the Chinese made them impossible to tell apart did not just affect the Chinese population in the United States. Throughout the country a large number of Japanese Americans were likewise detained or arrested on the belief that they were the murder suspect. Police in Washington, D.C. raided a house when they received news that Chong Sing and Leon Ling were hiding with a white woman at that location. The police later discovered that the residents were Japanese.[71] In New Jersey police arrested several Japanese domestic servants on their way to meet their employers, including a man working for the Governor.[72] In Birmingham, Alabama on June 24 Deputy Sheriff Ed Wilson received a tip that a man resembling Leon Ling's description was seen at a restaurant on Second Avenue. After rushing to the location

Figure 6.3. Cartoons such as this one illustrate the popular attitude that Chinese faces were not only inscrutable but completely indistinguishable by whites. These views helped to support the logic of mass arrests chiefly based on racial identification. *Source*: Hy. Mayer, "A Raid in Chinatown Puzzle Find the Guilty One," *New York Times*, April 30, 1905.

the Deputy Sheriff discovered that the man was Japanese and recently hired as a cook at the restaurant. Undeterred by their mistake, the Birmingham police maintained a careful watch over Chinese-owned laundries in the city.[73]

New York City's Japanese immigrant and American-born population of roughly 1,000 quickly became the next set of victims to be caught up in the clumsy attempts to identify Leon Ling based on popular definitions of racial differences.[74] When a pedestrian noticed Kosuke Rannato, a cook at 338 West Fifty-seventh Street, walking up Second Avenue, he immediately informed a nearby patrolman that he believed the man to be Leon Ling. Rannato was later released after being detained at the Queensboro Bridge station.[75] Despite his vociferous protests Marshal Kopayashi, a lecturer residing at 832 Vyse Avenue, the Bronx, was picked up at 177th Street and Boston Road.[76] On the evening of June 25 Policeman Higgins of the West 125th Street Police Station arrested Ken Ki Chi, a clerk, at 573 Eighth Avenue, because he thought the clerk resembled Leon Ling. A throng of onlookers quickly gathered around the two and additional policemen were needed to control the crowd and prevent injury to the arrested man. Once at the police station the suspect sufficiently proved that he was indeed Japanese and not Leon Ling.[77]

Not willing to accept ongoing police harassment of their persons and community, some Japanese men such as W. K. Igawa attempted to resist these seemingly arbitrary arrests of Asian men. Disturbed by his mistaken arrest in Massachusetts, Igawa, on his return to New York City in September, visited police headquarters in the hope of obtaining a signed certificate issued by the police stating that he was not Leon Ling.[78] At first the officer who listened to Igawa's request seemed to agree to issue the certificate, but explained that a detailed physical description of Igawa would need to appear on the certificate so that he would not be able to transfer the certificate to another individual. Igawa readily agreed and the officer took a number of measurements of his body required by the turn-of-the-century Bertillon system of identification and proceeded to issue the certificate.[79] Problems arose, however, when the policeman approached Inspector McCafferty to sign the document. Although McCafferty stated that he believed Igawa's request was "for a proper purpose" he refused to sign the certificate, stating his fear of "the possibilities that might occur if such a document with my signature on it should fall into any one else's hands."[80] Not wanting to venture back onto the New York streets without some form of identification distinguishing him from Leon Ling, Igawa "twice begged to obtain the memorandum without the Inspector's signature." The police officer refused, claiming that it had been destroyed.

Feeling that he was "improperly treated at the Headquarters," the following morning Igawa chose to approach both the Japanese consulate and the New York City mayor's office for redress. At the Japanese consulate he planned to obtain a letter of introduction to Mayor George McClellan, to whom he wished to send a letter of complaint. After listening to Igawa's story, the consulate declined to issue an introductory letter but advised him to carry his Japanese passport at all times. In the unfortunate event that Igawa would be arrested again, he would at least be able to prove readily that he was a Japanese subject. Igawa, still unsatisfied, proceeded with his decision to write a formal complaint letter to Mayor McClellan describing his ill treatment by Inspector McCafferty and demanding a proper response to his initial inquiry for an acceptable identification document. A few days later Igawa received a brief note from the mayor's office quoting Inspector McCafferty's report of their interaction and his statement that "Mr. Igawa was treated with the same courtesy that is shown to everybody else."[81] Taking the letter as a personal affront, Igawa wrote a second letter of complaint to the mayor's office refuting McCafferty's description of the day's events. Igawa concluded his six-page letter by making his frustration clear and calling McCafferty's character into question: "I shall not appeal to you, sir, again, and it is unnecessary to fight with any one who is not manly and who makes a false statement."

Igawa, upset by his experience with the NYPD, was especially perplexed by McCafferty's explanation for his refusal to sign the certificate. The two men clearly differed in their understanding of racial and ethnic markers that distinguished between Chinese and Japanese men. As a Japanese man, Igawa had no difficulty seeing himself and other Japanese men as wholly different from Chinese men. Indeed, the nation's Japanese American population found it astonishing that the police could not detect the obvious differences between Chinese and Japanese peoples in terms of bodily physique, language, and culture. As A. M. Kashiwa, a Japanese American restaurant owner put it, "if Ling was posing as a Japanese, I would have found it out pretty quick. We Japanese always speak with one another in our own language, and it's hardly probable that Ling would have been able to talk Japanese."[82] Not surprisingly, Igawa accepted that the written physical descriptions and measurements were sufficient to establish his national and individual identity.

McCafferty, however, after witnessing more than two months of embarrassing arrests of Chinese and Japanese men who were mistaken for Leon Ling, probably believed that neither he nor his officers were capable of distinguishing among people of Asian descent. At best they were only able to identify Chinese and Japanese people as racially distinct from whites. If police officers were incapable of telling Leon Ling apart from another Chinese or Japanese man, then was it not also possible for them to make the mistake of believing that the holder of Igawa's certificate was Igawa when he was really another person? In actuality, McCafferty's discomfort with the use of identifying certificates was hardly particular to the Leon Ling manhunt. Since the 1880s, custom house officials were frustrated with the difficult task of screening out Chinese laborers attempting to circumvent the Chinese Exclusion Acts to enter the country. Officials soon discovered that Chinese laborers were illegally crossing the border through the illegal transfer of laborers' return certificates issued to Chinese laborers returning to China who had arrived in the United States prior to the enactment of the Exclusion Act. The transfer of these return certificates was made possible because identification was based on written physical descriptions alone.[83] As with immigration officials, McCafferty feared that the physical measurements and descriptions on the document were insufficient to prevent its use by another Asian man, such as Leon Ling himself. Viewed by whites as racially similar to Chinese, Japanese men like Igawa had no other recourse than to carry their Japanese passports as proof of their national and individual identity.

These mass arrests of Japanese men is perhaps not surprising given that the descriptions of Leon Ling emphasized his American dress and haircut or more precisely, how much he did not resemble the "typical" Chinese man in either appearance or mannerisms. Thus police could not as easily apply the popularly recognized racial and ethnic markers used to identify Chinese men—such as the queue or ethnic clothing—in their search for Leon Ling. Because Japanese immigrants had quickly adopted Western dress and haircuts, Americans had often distinguished Chinese and Japanese immigrants on the basis of these superficial features. During this period, the majority of the small numbers of Japanese in New York consisted mostly of students, merchants, and professionals who comprised the better educated *himin* class.[84] With the police paying special attention to Chinese men with cropped hair and Western dress, it is not surprising that they also arrested large numbers of Japanese men. Yet these arrests of Japanese men also suggest the degree to which such subtle shifts in racial identification could easily blur boundaries between different Asian ethnic groups, leading to their reclassification into a singular shared category. Indeed, the attempts by lay citizens and police to identify Leon Ling suggest the degree to which the language of racial identification remained fluid despite popular turn-of-the-century beliefs in the unbridgeable separation and hierarchical ordering of the races.

Japanese Americans were not the only unintended victims of the police dragnet. The extent to which the hunt for Leon Ling disrupted established ethnic and racial categories can be seen in the cases where non-Asians were similarly mistakenly arrested. On June 29 in the southern port city of New Orleans, what at first appeared to be another mistaken arrest almost turned into an international incident when police arrested Lieutenant Colonel J. Alexander Pasos y R. of the Nicaraguan Army, who was traveling by train to New Orleans for a surgical operation. Described as "a rather handsome young man, with a smooth face and swarthy skin, with jet black hair and eyes, and dresses very neatly," his physical appearance and distinctive accent apparently caught the attention of the train conductor, who was convinced that he was a Chinese man matching the description of Leon Ling.[85] The conductor then asked John Dooling, a special officer for the Louisville and Nashville Railroad, to walk through the car to take a closer look. Not certain if the man was indeed Leon Ling, Dooling chose not to act. Upon arriving in New Orleans Dooling, "still satisfied that the man was a Chinaman," immediately alerted the New Orleans police to the stranger's presence in the city. Several detectives quickly appeared on the scene and despite Pasos's vociferous protests, he was taken to police headquarters. Once at the station, he had little difficulty establishing his identity and was quickly released with numerous apologies. Pasos was nonetheless upset by his mistreatment at the hands of the New Orleans police, and threatened to report the matter to the Nicaraguan minister in Washington, D.C.[86]

This incredible mistake is easier to comprehend when one realizes that Spanish-speaking Chinese were a familiar sight in turn-of-the-century New Orleans, an important port city for Chinese traveling between Hong Kong, California, and Cuba.[87] Since the Reconstruction era, sugar planters imported Chinese contract laborers to discipline and compete with newly freed African American slaves.[88] Many of these Chinese workers came from Cuba, where a great number had learned to speak Spanish and adopted Spanish surnames through their baptism by the Roman Catholic Church.[89] Rumors circulating that Leon Ling was in New Orleans to attempt an escape to Central or South America may have also convinced the public that the murder suspect was proficient in Spanish.[90] While Chinese Latinos may not have been a strange sight in New Orleans, mistaking a Nicaraguan army official for Leon Ling suggests the extent to which racial markers were not clearly established and universally recognized at this time.

Race was similarly illegible in the case of W. M. Lynch's reported sighting of the suspect at his home in Annandale, Virginia, on the afternoon of June 19. Lynch informed Alexandria police that a stranger "with short hair and wearing a black sack suit, a white shirt, and a flat brim white straw hat applied at his house for food, and in excellent English stated that he wanted to find the nearest point where he could board a Chesapeake and Ohio train for the West."[91] The man's Americanized appearance and mannerisms confused Lynch, because "at first glance he did not realize that the man was a Chinaman, but upon closer scrutiny he became convinced that he was of that nationality." Racial identification, equally dependent upon speech, dress, etiquette, and mannerisms, could be easily thwarted by the person's ability to render a passing cultural performance. If the mystery man was indeed a Chinaman, it would appear that his physically based racial markers were temporarily effaced by his American dress and ability to speak fluent English and affect an American persona.

In contemporary dramas involving racial "passing," only characters whose biracial or multiracial ancestry had endowed them with white racial characteristics that erased or hid their non-white physical markers could surreptitiously slip across the color line.[92] In the cases described above, however, it is the disruption of the boundaries between Chinese and white, alien and citizen, and masculine and feminine that seemed to allow Americanized Chinese men the slightest opportunity to traverse the racial divide. Such disruptions to the color line were by no means unheard of in this period, which also witnessed several formal court challenges regarding the racial eligibility of immigrants from the Middle East to obtain U.S. citizenship. The same year as the Elsie Sigel murder, the U.S. Bureau of Immigration questioned whether Syrians who had previously been classified as whites should be identified as Asiatics, thus rendering them ineligible to citizenship. On December 24, 1909, the Circuit Court of Massachusetts decided that Armenians should be classified as white, but the nation's courts continued to debate the racial classification of Syrians until the 1920s.[93] The examples of these racial reclassifications, whether formally through the legal system or informally through ordinary daily encounters, demonstrate the instability and elasticity of whiteness as a socially and culturally constructed category.

With the blurring of racial categories that supposedly separated Chinese men from white men, not only did Chinese men seem to be able to "pass" as white men but white men could also find themselves mistaken for Chinese men. Such was the case of John W. Basil, a white man who was traveling from St. Louis. When Basil arrived in Shipman, Illinois a police constable believed him to "resemble an Oriental," and immediately arrested the man and telegraphed New York police with the news that they had captured the elusive fugitive. Only after intense physical scrutiny did police confirm that the person they were holding was definitely a white man. On July 16 Shipman's mayor issued the embarrassing statement that the police were not holding Leon Ling as claimed.[94]

Taken together, these and other cases of mistaken identity involving Asians, Latinos, and whites suggest that the language of racial identification and definitions of racial difference were by no means uniformly recognized among the mainstream population. Even as social scientists were beginning to divide the world's population into assigned racial categories, in vernacular culture the deployment of racial classifications remained highly irregular. In the case of Leon Ling the physical descriptions circulated by the police and popular press stressed his Westernized or Americanized appearance over his Chinese foreignness. In other words the construction of racial categories went beyond the simple identification of physical or biological differences between Chinese and non-Chinese. Popular images of Chinese men as wearing queues and dressing in traditional Chinese clothing were just as important in defining racial difference. The description of Leon Ling as an Americanized Chinese man, however, forced newspapers, police, and ordinary citizens to expand the racial category of Chinese to include so-called Western cultural traits, confusing what had been popularly accepted distinctions between Chinese and American, or Chinese and white. Greater chances of mistaken arrests of non-Chinese men occurred as these unfixed socially constructed categories of race became even less defined.

The public's racial views of the Chinese as physically indistinguishable initially condoned, if not applauded, the massive police dragnet, but as the police investigation continued to drag into August some New Yorkers questioned the police's motivations and abilities. With a longstanding reputation for corruption and ineptitude, the city's police department became an easy target for the public's frustrations with the lack of progress in capturing Leon Ling. One *New York Times* editorial simply accused the police of spinning fantastic tales about the Chinese as an excuse for their lack of progress in the case. "That all sorts of strange yarns about secret societies of Mongolians in this town, banded together to commit crimes and baffle the police should gain color through such a display of inefficiency is not surprising."[95]

Not only did the nation's police departments detain large numbers of Chinese men on the mistaken belief that they were the missing murder suspect, but did so also on the popular assumption that Chinese communities in their jurisdictions were conspiring to hide Leon Ling. If the man arrested turned out not to be Leon Ling himself, the police then reasoned that the man in custody would be able to impart information regarding his whereabouts. Earlier commentators such as Jacob Riis had long claimed that the failure to track down Chinese criminals could not be wholly "ascribed to the familiar fact that to Caucasian eyes 'all Chinamen look alike,' but rather to their acting 'alike,' in a body, to defeat discovery at any cost."[96] As discussed in chapters 2 and 3, the belief that Chinatowns were "terra incognita" full of secret tunnels that allowed the city's clannish Chinese American residents to move clandestinely throughout the city was already well-established and popularized through popular tales of Chinatown. Police drew upon these notions of secret Chinese mobility and ethnic solidarity to explain Leon Ling's disappearance and garner public support for heightening surveillance of Chinese communities. Following a tip that Leon Ling was hiding in New Jersey with a Chinese friend, Deputy Commissioner Woods and Inspector McCafferty, dispatched ten detectives to Paterson, Passaic, Hackensack, and other towns in northern New Jersey to continue the search for Leon Ling.[97] When Pittsburgh police suspected that Leon Ling had kin in that city, they immediately went to the house of the Lee family to search for the fugitive. Yin Lee, however, refused to allow police to enter. When one police detective threatened to "kick in the door," Lee "came out with a knife, but was knocked senseless with a revolver butt."[98] Only a few days into the murder investigation Chicago police had already detained and questioned about a dozen Chinese men.[99] Police paid special attention to the over two hundred Chinese-owned laundries located outside of Chinatown, particularly targeting the community's most recent arrivals.[100]

Although a *New York Times* editorial asked readers not to condemn all Chinese for the Sigel murder, the author nevertheless suggested that Leon Ling was able to elude capture by the police because he had continuously received aid from his fellow countrymen. While all Chinese may not be capable of committing murder, they were nonetheless still "guilty" and deserving of harsh treatment because of their perceived clannishness and blatant disregard of American law.[101] Clearly it was easier for police, journalists, and the general populace to accept that Leon Ling had vanished through an ongoing conspiracy perpetrated by his fellow Chinese immigrants than to suggest that he might have somehow "passed" unnoticed into the general American population, a feat deemed impossible given the public's belief in the obvious racial differences between Chinese and whites. Yet the descriptions of Leon Ling generated by the nation's police and newspapers, by corrupting the boundary between white and Chinese, made the stereotypical physical and cultural markers used for the purposes of racial or ethnic identification unusable. The level of ethnic and racial misidentification exposed during the course of the manhunt suggests that Leon Ling may have successfully pulled off his "remarkable getaway" precisely because of the indeterminacy of race. Even as Leon Ling's escape undermined notions of racial difference and suggested the possibilities for Chinese integration into American life, the reactions of the police and public by continuing to employ racial markers to detain large numbers of Chinese men nonetheless worked to reify racial classifications as socially viable categories.

The story of Leon Ling's successful elusion of law enforcement officials across the nation should be seen as a subversive narrative countering this period's racial ideologies, particularly in its assumptions of space and mobility for non-whites. If popular cultural representations portrayed Chinese immigrants as clannish and enclosed within distinct urban spaces such as Chinatowns, laundries, and restaurants, then Leon Ling's ability to maneuver within and without these spaces clearly disrupted these neat narratives of racial containment. Nonetheless Leon Ling's racial and gender subversions hardly made him a heroic figure. Certainly, if he was guilty of the murder of nineteen-year-old Elsie Sigel, his escape from the law provides an unsettling end to this heinous crime. Yet neither Leon Ling nor his guilt is the main issue here since most onlookers, regardless of race, were readily convinced of his guilt. Indeed the public's shock and horror came from the startling discovery of her body and subsequent revelations of her romantic attachments to Chinese men, and not from the idea that her death was wrought by the hands of a jealous Chinese lover. The public had little difficulty accepting Leon Ling's guilt, given the popular belief that Chinese immigrants as a race were morally unfit for U.S. citizenship. With the manhunt rapidly escalating and all efforts at locating the Chinese fugitive coming to naught, the public faced the disturbing conclusion that a Chinese man could somehow circulate freely among them undetected. It was not the fear of a murder suspect at large as much as what his mobility as a Chinese man represented that became the focus of the press and its mainstream audiences. As stories of the numerous arrests of Americanized Chinese men from all parts of the country made its way into the nation's newspapers, the public was forced to acknowledge that ongoing attempts to maintain social, physical, and legal separation between whites and Chinese through their legal classification as perpetual aliens, had not fully prevented Chinese immigrants from entering and merging into the nation's public and private spaces and acquiring the markers of whiteness allowing them to become one of them.

The notion that Leon Ling or any Chinese man, Americanized or not, could simply vanish into the general American population seemed too unbelievable. Such a feat would rival even the most death defying escapes flawlessly executed by his contemporary, the great Harry Houdini. Nearly a year after the discovery of Sigel's body, the *New York Times* published one last fanciful sighting of Leon Ling that simultaneously endeavored to restore these breached racial boundaries and provide a fitting conclusion to the global manhunt. Leon Ling, the brief article claimed, had hurriedly escaped to Canada immediately after the murder and before the discovery of Sigel's body. From Canada, he was secretly smuggled by a fellow countryman to China. And there he remained, working on a farm.[102]

CHAPTER SEVEN

"Disgrace on the Whole Body of Our People"

WHILE LEON LING MANAGED TO ELUDE the long arm of the law, the nation's Chinese American population was not so fortunate. For months the ongoing search for the missing murder suspect led police, reporters, and ordinary citizens to invade the homes, workplaces, and neighborhoods of Chinese Americans throughout the country. The relentless public scrutiny of their racially marked bodies meant that simple everyday acts such as taking a walk or riding a streetcar could lead to a maelstrom of unwanted attention. Chinese Americans, already constituted as a suspect class through the state-sponsored policies of Chinese exclusion, found themselves struggling even harder to maintain their livelihoods and composure. Acutely aware of their lack of social and legal recognition as perpetual aliens barred from U.S. citizenship, Chinese throughout the country nonetheless developed a myriad of individual and collective responses against the unyielding publicity and police activity. From personal complaints to organized protests to American and Chinese officials, the country's Chinese population not only demanded proper protections to safeguard their persons and property, but also used the occasion to expand their social and physical place in the nation.

The Chinese men linked to either the murder victim or suspect no doubt bore the heaviest brunt of this public examination. Chu Gain, rumored to be Elsie Sigel's other secret Chinese paramour, was quickly taken into custody when police learned that the deceased had frequently visited the well-known Port Arthur restaurant he managed on Mott Street in Chinatown.[1] The police's subsequent discovery of letters in Chu Gain's apartment, written by Sigel and "filled with terms of endearment," confirmed their suspicions that he had played a role in her death.[2] Chu Gain quickly became the center of the investigation as the city's police and journalists attempted to establish an acceptable murder motive and narrative. Police and newspapers argued that Chu Gain's growing relationship with Sigel had enraged Leon Ling to the point of murder. With jealousy as the suspected cause, numerous unsubstantiated rumors suggesting that Chu Gain and Sigel were engaged in a clandestine love affair appeared in the press. The World, for example, claimed that she had adroitly manipulated the affections of both men until Leon Ling discovered her deceit. Citing letters she had written to both men just before her disappearance, the article claimed that they were "couched in endearing terms, but while Leon is assured of her love Chu is told in a way that he could not misunderstand that he held the chief place in her affection."[3] The article also claimed that Leon Ling had appeared at Sigel's doorstep in a drunken rage the night before she vanished and that Chu Gain had been present on the scene.

To what degree Chu Gain and Sigel were actually romantically connected, as the press and police alleged, is difficult to determine. The proof of secret correspondences between the two certainly supported this speculation. The *New York Times* printed the contents of her last letter to him on June 8, the evening before her disappearance, when she had attempted to mollify him after a recent visit from Leon Ling to her house. She dismissed the incident as an unwanted social obligation and assured Chu Gain by saying, "I love you and you only and always."[4] By his own admission to the police, Chu Gain was undoubtedly on fond and familiar terms with the victim and her family and often paid them weekly visits that lasted upwards to an hour.[5] Upon learning that she was missing he also acted alone in placing a notice in the *New York Herald*, hoping the missive would bring her home. It read, "E. J. S.—Mother very ill. Come home dear one."[6] But as rumors of the interracial love triangle escalated in the press, Chu Gain found himself in the position of defending his and the murder victim's reputations by challenging the press's numerous allegations regarding their relationship.

The public's fascination with Chu Gain extended beyond his position as the critical link to the widely accepted love triangle theory. In the absence of Leon Ling, he also became the best living example of the cosmopolitan, Americanized Chinaman the public longed to behold. The press paid careful attention to Chu Gain's religious conversion to Christianity, allegedly through the intervention of the Sigels, and provided detailed descriptions of his overall physical appearance and demeanor as the debonair manager of the Port Arthur restaurant. Taken together, such portrayals worked to make Chu Gain appear as Leon Ling's safer alter ego. In one instance the *New York Times* went as far as to offer the theory that Sigel had wanted to marry Leon Ling, but that her mother had preferred her to marry Chu Gain, a "thrifty Chinaman" with "quite a snug fortune."[7] Yet the public was hardly so willing to condone this interracial romance even when the Chinese partner was of a more acceptable socioeconomic class, preferring instead to condemn Sigel's daring to engage in such familiar relations with Chinese men.

For several days the police continued to hold, for ongoing interrogation in the Tombs, Chu Gain along with the other Chinese men arrested at the Eighth Avenue crime scene following the discovery of Sigel's body. Chu Gain remained cooperative throughout his incarceration and pledged not to run away if released. The coroner, Julius Harburger, apparently impressed with Chu Gain's general demeanor and socioeconomic status, agreed to lower his bail from $1,000 to $100, allowing for his release from confinement and return to Chinatown. The coroner also lowered the bails of the men from the Eighth Avenue chop suey restaurant: Sun Leung, Yee Kim, and Chin Song. All three men were able to raise bail and leave the Tombs.[8] Chu Gain quickly realized that his every move continued to be closely monitored, however, when he attempted to take a short trip to Atlantic City to escape the constant police and press attention. Upon reaching the Twenty-third Street ferry a police detective who had been assigned to follow Chu Gain, prevented his boarding and escorted him to the office of Assistant District Attorney Ward, who denied him permission to leave the city out of fear that he would later not appear when called as a witness. Determined to leave the New York area for a respite, Chu Gain offered to put up a $1,000 bond to insure his return. Ward steadfastly refused and Chu Gain was forced to endure additional scrutiny.[9] As the police and press's attention on the Chinese restaurateur established jealousy as the prime motive, the remarkably speedy capture of the roommate Chong Sing further fueled the public's hopes for a quick end to the murder mystery and manhunt.

THE ARREST OF CHONG SING

The June 21, 1909 *Amsterdam Evening Recorder and Daily Democrat* hailed the arrest of Chong Sing by their police as "one of the most notable in the history of the local police department, for the solving of the mystery connected with the crime which has horrified the entire country."[10] The article, with its unmistakable local booster flourishes, proudly declared that the town of Amsterdam, New York had accomplished what the entire NYPD and the rest of the country's police had been unable to do— bring about the capture of one of the two Chinese fugitives. Similar to other police departments throughout the country, after receiving the circular detailing the appearances of Leon Ling and Chong Sing, Amsterdam Chief of Police Packwood had his men search the town for Chinese matching the descriptions. Upon receiving information that a Chinese man from New York City had recently arrived at nearby West Galway, to take on the position of cook at the summer home of Harvey Kennedy, the police decided to investigate further. After arriving at the Kennedy home to interview the Chinese stranger, they immediately decided that the cook was the "dead image" of Chong Sing and took him into custody. Chong Sing did not put up a struggle but readily admitted his identity and went willingly. He was brought to the Amsterdam police station to await the arrival of police officers from New York City.

News quickly spread throughout Amsterdam that Chong Sing was being held at the local police station, and residents rushed to catch a glimpse of the suspect. Similar to a Coney Island sideshow oddity, the police obligingly placed Chong Sing on display: "Sing sat in a chair in the chief's private office and the crowd was allowed to file past him, going in one door and out the other. No one was allowed to linger and everyone was given the opportunity to view the much wanted Celestial. Not only men, but hundreds of women were included in the throng and it is estimated that during the day, while the Chinaman was kept at headquarters, several thousand pairs of eyes looked curiously at him."[11] The combination of the arrested man's racial otherness with his alleged criminality turned him into the perfect racial spectacle for the town's curious residents. The rumors of Leon Ling's Americanized good looks and charm had clearly left their imprint on the minds of the townspeople, as many came with the hopes of catching a glimpse of such an uncharacteristic Chinaman. They were quickly disappointed by Chong Sing's lack of resemblance to the "Chinese Don Juan," as many female onlookers uttered, "well, who could care for him," and "aint he the awful looking thing."[12] Chong Sing meanwhile tried to ignore the gawking crowd and quietly smoked a cigar.

In Chong Sing's interview with a reporter from the local Amsterdam newspaper, he offered a few biographical details about his life. He was thirty-five years old and married, but his wife remained in China. Having arrived in the United States about ten years earlier, he had mostly worked as a cook. In the last four or five months he had held this position in a chop suey restaurant at 482 Twenty-ninth Street in New York City. Chong Sing downplayed his relationship to Leon Ling stating, that although the two of them lived on the same floor they only saw each other about once every two weeks. Similar to other Chinese laborers, Chong Sing often slept in his place of work rather than making the trip to his apartment. The arrested man also admitted to knowing the Sigel family and that he had visited them at their home. Although he confirmed that a close relationship existed between Leon Ling and Sigel, he asserted that he had never seen her visit Leon Ling at his apartment.[13]

Chief Packwood refused to grant Chong Sing permission to send a telegram to friends or relatives notifying them of his arrest. The next day New York City police officers took Chong Sing back to the city for questioning.[14] The Coroner fixed Chong Sing's bail at $10,000 and had him held at the House of Detention. During thirty hours of continuous questioning by the police, Chong Sing eventually broke down and confessed to having seen Leon Ling murder Sigel on the afternoon of Wednesday, June 9, the last day that the Sigel family had seen Elsie alive. Though he maintained that he did not take part in the murder, his questioners doubted his avowal of innocence and pressed him further about

Figure 7.1. Chong Sing surrounded by police and reporters upon his arrival in New York City after his arrest in Amsterdam, New York (June 22, 1909). Courtesy of Library of Congress, Prints and Photographs Division, NYWT&S Collection.

the day's events. To explain how he knew Leon Ling was the murderer, Chong Sing claimed to have witnessed a quarrel and struggle between the two by looking through the keyhole and transom of the door that adjoined their rooms.[15] After another day of questioning, however, Chong Sing recanted his story. Police revisited the murder scene and discovered that no such transom existed and the view from Chong Sing's keyhole could not have provided him with a good view of Leon Ling's room. Confronted with this information, he gave a new statement. This time he told police that he was sleeping in his room when Leon Ling called him into the room and directed him to assist in putting Sigel's already lifeless body into the trunk.[16]

Not convinced that Chong Sing was telling the truth, police prevailed upon the assistance of Quan Yick Nam, whom one New York Times writer described as being "regarded by the police as a shrewd Chinaman and the wicked ones of Chinatown feel that Nam is not a man to be fooled." Quan Yick Nam had made a reputation for himself among New York City's court and police officials by working as a court interpreter in cases involving the city's Chinese residents.[17] In addition he had in the past aided some of the city's Progressive reformers in their attempts to uncover evidence of municipal corruption.[18] For Quan Yick Nam and other Americanized Chinese, who were at pains to distance themselves from

Leon Ling, providing assistance to the murder investigation was critical for ameliorating their much tarnished public image. Adept with the English language, Chong Sing did not require the assistance of an interpreter. The police hoped that Quan Yick Nam would be more effective in convincing Chong Sing to tell the truth. They were, however, disappointed because Chong Sing continued to deny that he had helped Leon Ling kill Sigel.

On June 25 detectives took Chong Sing back to the scene of the murder in an effort to elicit more information.[19] After returning to his prison cell he acknowledged to Captain Carey that he had overheard an argument between Sigel and Leon Ling.[20] After a few more days of intense questioning, the police and press voiced their frustration with Chong Sing's shifting responses. "Chong has contradicted himself so often and told so many versions of his movements the morning of June 9," one reporter lamented, "that the police have been able to credit only such bits of information as conform to known facts in the case."[21]

Chong Sing's integrity as a witness proved to be a great problem for reasons beyond his changing testimony. The police and District Attorney's office frequently stated to the press that they did not believe that he was telling the truth in stating his innocence. As a "Chinaman" Chong Sing simply could not be trusted. As the days of strenuous cross-examination continued, Chong Sing did indeed change his story in ways that more closely reflected the confession that the police and District Attorney's office had envisioned. Yet the District Attorney's office's past experiences with Chinese witnesses in other cases had already convinced them that they did not make good witnesses. In discussing another case where the testimony of Chinese witnesses was crucial to the trial, for example, Acting District Attorney Nathan A. Smyth noted that "our experience with Chinese witnesses has been that they are entirely unreliable, and we find that juries are unwilling to believe their testimony except when corroborated by very strong evidence."[22]

Readers and the press also questioned what they perceived to be the strong-arm tactics of a desperate police department trying to wring a false confession from an exhausted Chong Sing. William T. Smith wrote the *New York Times* to express his indignation over the treatment of the prisoner by the police and the District Attorney's office in extracting a declaration of guilt by putting the suspect through a tortuous session of "the third degree." Under these conditions, Smith argued, how could anyone accept such a confession. Despite these harsh words, such letters of protest also reveal the extent to which New Yorkers subscribed to popular notions of American cultural superiority and Chinese cultural inferiority in shaping their views on Chong Sing's character. "[I]t is a disgrace to our police and to our civilization, and this cruel harrying of an alien of low intelligence and morals is worthless for results," Smith charged.[23] Writing from his own observations on Chinese prisoners, journalist Thomas Millard discussed the futility of such tactics on Chinese suspects by describing the "stoicism" of Chinese prisoners under torture or physical punishment. Though Millard wrote in the article that he did not believe the Chinese to be "more indifferent to physical pain and to death than Westerners are," the article nonetheless suggested that "the stoicism of the Oriental is undoubtedly one of the greatest obstacles between the New York police and the solution of the Sigel mystery."[24]

With Leon Ling still at large, police continued to hold Chong Sing at the House of Detention. After more than a month of incarceration his counsel filed a writ of habeas corpus, asking for his release on $1,000 bail. Reluctant to release their only witness in the case, Assistant District Attorney Mayper responded to the petition by applying to the Supreme Court to keep bail at $10,000.[25] On September 9 Judge Malone in the Court of General Sessions reduced Chong Sing's bail to $500. A bond for the amount was quickly posted by Michael Morris, whose office was located right next to Chinatown at 79 Bayard Street, and Chong Sing was finally released from his nearly three month confinement at the House of Detention. He returned to a cousin's home in the Chinatown neighborhood. Still unwilling to accept Chong Sing's claims of innocence, the District Attorney's office proceeded to obtain a warrant from the Court of General Sessions to charge Chong Sing with murder in the first degree. The warrant was not served however.[26] On September 24 the Coroner's court formally charged Leon Ling with Elsie Sigel's murder. Although one juror requested that Chong Sing also be held, Coroner Harburger refused and ordered his release.[27] Police did not bother Chong Sing again.

THE MANHUNT TAKES ITS TOLL

On June 29 police arrested Gee Yim, an American-eduated nineteen-year-old Chinese American, in Roxbury, Massachusetts, when his strange behavior caught the attention of fellow streetcar passengers. The young man had disappeared from his place of work, a laundry in Marlboro, a few days earlier. The laundry owner contacted the president and secretary of the local branch of the On Leong Tong in Boston to request their help in finding the young man. The On Leong leaders and Gee Yim's father, Gee Kee, a wealthy Boston merchant, proceeded to the police station when they heard of the boy's arrest. The laundry owner stated that the boy had complained of headaches and began raving about the Sigel murder. The *Boston Globe* explained that "the disgrace cast upon his race by the recent murder in New York [had] preyed upon his mind."[28]

Aside from mental and physical stress, the increased police activity also made the Chinese immigrant community an easy target for New York City's thieves and con men. John Brown and Joseph Bennett used the disorder and panic in the Chinese immigrant community, created by the murder investigation and sensationalized newspaper coverage, to intimidate and swindle a number of Chinese restaurant workers and owners. Masquerading as police officers, these men visited Chinese-owned *crime* establishments to extort money. The men showed their counterfeit police badges to the Chinese owners, threatening to arrest the owners and their staff on the fictitious charge of having allowed white women to visit their establishments. These bogus policemen then offered to let their victims off for a sum of money. With the city's real police conducting sweeps of Chinese-owned businesses and rounding up Chinese men, many Chinese saw no reason to doubt the pair were genuine. Indeed, the pair's claim to police white female mobility was all too plausible given the public's intensified hostility against race mixing. In only a week's time over fifteen Chinese businesses claimed to have been harassed and cheated by these two.[29]

Police finally apprehended the pair on June 26 when John Brown, alias Patrick O'Hara, and Joe Bennett attempted to rob George Ching at his restaurant at 456 Seventh Avenue. Brown grabbed the thirty-eight-year-old Ching at the neck and informed him that he was a police officer. With his partner Brown began a search through the premises and took a small sum of money from Ching's pants, along with a ring from one of Ching's vests hung in the rear room of the restaurant. Immediately after the two dashed out the door Ching blew a police whistle and caught the attention of Police Officer Archibald Wood, who immediately gave chase. Within ten minutes Wood brought Brown back to the restaurant where Ching positively identified him and his stolen ring. Brown later pleaded guilty to grand larceny in the second degree. Bennett, who had escaped at the time of Brown's arrest, was caught by the police a few weeks later.[30]

Within one week of the beginning of the murder investigation, the *New York Herald* observed that the police searches of Chinatown were beginning to affect adversely the lives of the area's merchants, restaurateurs, and residents. New York police announced to reporters that nearly half of Chinatown's Chinese American population had departed for Boston, Baltimore, Chicago, New Orleans, San Francisco, and China, as well as smaller towns throughout the country. Yet neither the police nor the press attributed the community's decline to be a result of the continuous police harassment or heightened public hostilities toward Chinese New Yorkers following the murder, but instead pointed to potential tong violence within the Chinatown community as the culprit. "Rather than face death or arrest in consequence of these possible outbreaks," the article explained, "it is thought by those well acquainted with them that many of the better class of Chinamen decided to give up their business here and start again elsewhere."[31] In depicting the police's role in hastening the departure of Chinese from the city, the article merely stated that Captain Galvin's anti-vice efforts in closing down gambling dens "also caused many of the idlers to move on to more open pastures." Police power, portrayed as civically minded anti-vice campaigns, became reinterpreted as a positive community influence and benefit in helping to rid the city of its lower-class Chinese residents. The issue of the police's abuse of power, through the random arrests, illegal searches, and seizures directed at the city's entire Chinese American population, became obscured in this sanguine narrative of anti-vice policing.

Aside from the constant harassment and arrests endured by the Chinese community during the Sigel murder investigation, Chinese Americans also realized the increasing damage to their community's public image wrought by the media's portrayals of the murder suspect and the city's Chinese community. At first, the sensational newspaper coverage of the Sigel murder drew large numbers of thrill seekers and sightseers to Chinatown, temporarily boosting tourist-related businesses.[32] The constant police surveillance of the neighborhood, and campaigns to deter white females from entering the area, eventually began to discourage visitors. These activities, however, also kept many more Chinese from visiting the neighborhood because they feared being stopped and arrested on suspicion of being connected to the Sigel murder.

As business activities slumped, Chinatown's merchants began to voice their concerns. Tom Lee, also popularly known as the "Mayor" of Chinatown, explained the community's growing economic hardships to the *New York Times*. "Owing to the frequent raids and the constant turmoil in Chinatown our business has fallen off within the last two weeks at least 70 percent. Some of the stores are doing no business at all. Sightseers seem afraid to come to Chinatown any more, or the few who do come here hesitate to go into the stores. The Chinese merchants cannot stand this much longer."[33] Lee along with other merchants in the area hoped that relief would be forthcoming from the Chinese minister. On July 2, Chinatown merchants gathered to select a small delegation to travel to Washington, D.C. to appeal to the Chinese Legation for assistance and protection. Chinatown leaders chose three representatives— Charles Fon Poo of 13 Mott Street, Fong Ging Ton of 9 Mott Street, and Chu Sik Chee of the Chinese Six Companies—to meet with the Chinese minister. In assessing the Chinatown delegates' trip to Washington, the *New York Times* concluded that it was highly unlikely that the State Department would be able to do anything. "The general belief is that the

Government will permit the local authorities to pursue their investigations unhampered as the affair scarcely can be interpreted as coming within the range of diplomacy."[34]

The coming of the Fourth of July also worried many Chinese leaders, who feared that the traditionally raucous holiday celebrations would lead to mob attacks on Chinese residents in the city. On July 2, not trusting the police to provide adequate protection for the city's Chinese residents, the CCBA decided to issue handbills warning residents of possible violence during the coming Fourth of July. "Because Leon Ling has not yet been captured," the notice warned, "the business of this one man has caused Chinese of all communities to suffer deeply."[35] The handbill also pointed to the June 30 murder of Wu Xue Ming,[36] a Chinese laundry worker at 124 Stanton Street in lower Manhattan, as an example of vigilante violence following the Sigel murder. The leaflet then strongly urged all Chinese to take extra safety precautions for the upcoming holiday and not to venture outside or go to work, but instead to take a day of rest.

In response to the New York City Chinatown delegates' pleas for assistance, on July 3 the Chinese Legation sent a memorandum to the U.S. State Department to request that additional protection be provided for the city's Chinese community. The Legation pointed to the recent murders of two New York Chinese, "a laundryman, by name Wu Yao,[37] living at 124 Stanton Street. . . . [and] a keeper of a restaurant at 583 Fulton Street, Brooklyn," as evidence of anti-Chinese agitation resulting from the murder. "In view of the approach of the Fourth of July celebration, when a large number of the lower classes of this country will be idle," the Legation warned, "It is feared that they may on that occasion make a general attack on our people, resulting in serious outbreaks."[38]

In hindsight the New York Chinese community's and Chinese Legation's fears of a Fourth of July attack by the city's "lower classes" against New York's Chinese community were perhaps unnecessary, but by no means difficult to understand. Throughout the nineteenth and early-twentieth centuries, white middle-class New Yorkers expressed their distaste and fears of Fourth of July festivities that frequently led to deaths and destruction of property. Seeing such celebrations as excessive and symptomatic of working-class hooliganism, middle-class New Yorkers aimed to curb Fourth of July activities by passing ordinances and promoting "safe and sane" celebrations. At the same time, race riots against blacks in the city, such as the infamous 1863 draft riots, had occurred periodically throughout the nineteenth century.[39] Given the preestablished fears around working-class unrest on the Fourth of July, and the long-standing history of anti-black riots in the city, the Chinese Legation and the CCBA had ample reason to fear for the safety of the city's Chinese immigrants.[40]

In response to the Legation's request, on the evening of July 3 Huntington Wilson, the Acting Secretary of State, sent a confidential telegram to Charles Evans Hughes, Governor of New York, notifying him of the appeal for extra protection of Chinese in New York and Brooklyn.[41] Having left Albany for Saranac Lake, Hughes did not receive the telegram until the following morning, but then quickly sent confidential telegrams to the mayor and the police commissioner directing them to prepare for a possible violent outbreak against the Chinese in these two boroughs.[42] The State Department issued a memo to the Chinese Legation announcing that New York State and New York City officials had been made aware of their request.[43]

Allaying the governor's fears of social unrest, Acting New York City Mayor Patrick F. McGowan replied that the mayor's office had already begun working with the police commissioner and local precinct captains to prevent any acts of violence. First, the police commissioner ordered any "locality mainly occupied by Chinese in this city completely covered with policemen both in uniform and in plain clothes and he furthermore had all the captains of the different precincts warned that they would be held responsible for any attacks on Chinese in their districts."[44] Despite the examples of hostilities toward Chinese laborers reported in the city's newspapers and presented by the Legation and Chinese immigrant leaders, McGowan downplayed the potential for violence against the city's Chinese residents. Echoing the press reports of violence within the community being more likely, McGowan concluded his report by stating that "[t]he main difficulty in the future will be to keep the rival Chinese societies separate, rather than abuse of Chinese by white citizens. Investigation fails to show any sentiment against the Chinese tending to foment an outbreak of any kind." Satisfied with McGowan's report, the Governor forwarded the letter to the Secretary of State.[45]

Aside from stationing policemen and plainclothes detectives in the Chinatown area, the police commissioner also directed patrolmen to visit with Chinatown's merchants to enlist their cooperation. As the *New York Herald* reported, "detectives went in and out of the Chinese houses constantly yesterday, and from most of the occupants such weapons as they had were taken. The Chinese were not permitted to stand in groups while lounging about and were kept on the move at all times. At night an extra detail of police was sent into the district, while the reserves were kept in readiness in the Elizabeth street station."[46] The day after the Fourth of July, the *New York Times* repeated the assertion that the police kept a tight watch over Chinatown during the holiday because of possible tong retaliation—a result of "the death penalty having been meted out to five members of the Hip Sing Tong by Judge Brown in Boston on Saturday, for shooting up Boston's Chinatown on Aug. 2, 1907."[47] The article added that the extra police presence in the

Figure 7.2. Police detectives in Chinatown during the Fourth of July holiday (July 6, 1909). Courtesy of Library of Congress, Prints and Photographs Division, George Grantham Bain Collection, LC-USZ62-69697.

area was necessary, not because of unruly white working-class celebrations of the holiday, but because the Chinese were known for their "elaborate celebration on the Fourth. Sometimes, of course, they become careless, and then we have to have a cop near to keep them within bounds." The *New York Tribune* also stated that tong hostilities had increased because "the Hip Sings have been trying to fasten the murder of Elsie Sigel on the On Leongs. They say that Leon was an On Leong and that the On Leongs are sheltering him."[48] But another article appearing in the *World* reported the opposite to be true, stating that the On Leong Tong took advantage of the police investigation into the Elsie Sigel murder to bring trouble and harassment on the Hip Sing Tong.[49]

Regardless of the accuracy of these claims, city officials purposely ignored the warnings issued by the Chinese Legation and the State Department that the city's Chinese population was in imminent danger from increased racial antipathy. Rather they publicly declared that violence or disorder, if there were any, would be internecine as a result of feuding tongs. The request for police protection, then, did not necessarily result in making an already anxious Chinese American population more secure. Instead, the appeal had the unintended result of legitimizing further state surveillance of the Chinese immigrant community under the dubious claim of protecting the Chinese from themselves.

The constant harassment of Chinese persons and their communities prompted many into action. In addition, numerous American newspaper editorials urged the Chinese immigrant community to prove their inno-cence by aiding the police in their investigation, arguing that such self-policing would prevent further persecution of their people. This way, one editorial reasoned, they would change the public's negative opinion "and all wild denunciation of the Chinese as Chinese."[50] As Chinese leaders throughout the country weathered the press's negative portrayals of their communities, many sought ways to counter their increasingly tarnished public image through public acts that demonstrated their willingness to cooperate with the police to bring about Leon Ling's capture.

Posting rewards for example met both of these goals, simultaneously spurring on the investigation while garnering good publicity for Chinese American community leaders. In New York City, the Oriental Club of 5 Mott Street met on June 21 and resolved to post a $500 reward for the capture of the murderer of Elsie Sigel.[51] Reverend Fung Y. Mow, of the Morning Star Mission, offered a $1,000 reward for the apprehen-sion of the murderer.[52] In Chicago, the Chinese Freemasons and the Hong Xun Tong combined to put up an additional $500.[53] Nearly a month into the murder investigation, the CCBA branch of San Francisco also added another $200 to the already sizable pot. Information regard-ing this last award was publicized in the Chinese community by a large red poster hanging in Geary Street. The poster was apparently torn down soon after its posting. In its report on the incident, the *Chinese Daily Paper* hinted that a local tong possibly allied with Leon Ling may have been responsible.[54]

The posting of so many rewards, however, may have ultimately worked to the disadvantage of both the Chinese community and investigators. The promise of reward money encouraged the flow of useless leads as well as augmented police and ordinary citizens' incentives to scrutinize and detain every Chinese person encountered. Mary Ellen Stewart of Philadelphia, for example, admitted that she hoped to collect on the re-wards when she notified police that Leon Ling had a white American wife residing in Philadelphia.[55] One reporter suggested wryly that policemen across the country, after indiscriminately arresting Chinese men, would send "a telegram (collect) to the New York Police Department: Have arrested Leon, (or Chong Sing as the case may be.) How much reward is offered and where do I get it? Send some one after prisoner."[56]

Aware of the popular accusation that Chinese Americans were collec-tively scheming to hide Leon Ling from the police, Ou Shou Tchun, the chargé d'affaires of the Chinese Legation in the absence of Minister Wu Ting Fang, issued a directive to all Chinese communities throughout the country to assist in the capture of the missing murder suspect. Aside from giving a description of the murder case, the proclamation also stated that the crime had clearly thrown "disgrace on the whole body of our people in this country."[57] The shame of the crime, Ou Shou Tchun declared, had to be borne by himself as well as the rest of the Chinese community. Thus, he urged his countrymen to assist the police in any way to bring about the capture of the fugitives. "In this way," the Chinese chargé d'affaires assured, "you will help to remove any stigma that may be attached to our people on account of this case." The same edict was then issued to other Chinese Legation representatives stationed in major cities throughout the country and quickly disseminated to the general public. In San Francisco, for example, the entire proclamation was published in full by a Chinese language daily.[58] The consulate also posted the letter on walls lining Chinatown's streets. In Washington, D.C., the *Washington Post* declared that the Chinese merchants and business owners responded to the Legation's order, assuring "the police that they are willing and eager to offer all assistance possible to bring Ling to justice."[59] Not satisfied, however, a number of Montreal's Chinese Christians gathered to jointly petition Minister Wu Ting Fang to issue personally a proclamation to all Chinese in the United States to assist in the capture of Leon Ling.[60]

Throughout the country, local Chinese leaders echoed the Chinese Legation officials' appeals for police cooperation by urging Chinese residents to assist law enforcement agents in capturing Leon Ling. Chicago Chinese community leader, Louie Sing of 343 Clark Street, explained to American reporters that aiding the police was important "because the American people are inclined to think the Chinamen shields his countrymen in crime."[61] Huang San De, the head of the Chinese Freemasons, similarly addressed the Chinese in that city. Arguing that because the hunt for Leon Ling had negatively affected the reputations of the Chinese community and all tong organizations, he stated that all Chinese must assist in the apprehension of the missing suspect.[62]

In New York the news of the Chinese Legation's proclamation was greeted warmly by the American press, as one journalist expressed his hope that the message would push the murder investigation forward.[63] The extent that Chinese throughout the country responded to the Sigel murder could be seen in the response of Robert L. Park, managing editor of the *Chinese World*, published in San Francisco. On July 1, the *New York Times* printed a story claiming that the city's police department and district attorney's office were displeased with the Chinese translation services available to them. To remedy the situation District Attorney Jerome wrote to Professor John Endicott Gardner, of the Department of Oriental Languages at the University of the Pacific in San Francisco, to request his assistance in the translation of letters and papers amassed throughout the murder investigation. The article also disputed the statement made by Chinese residents of Chinatown that they were fully cooperating with the police in the arrest of Leon Ling.[64] The next day, Robert L. Park wrote to District Attorney Jerome to offer his translation services. The District Attorney, however, thanked Park for his offer but declined, stating that "the statement published in the newspapers that this Office is in need of an interpreter for this case is quite incorrect."[65]

Realizing that the city's English-language newspapers acted as a forum for shaping the public opinion of American readers, numerous Chinese American leaders penned letters for publication. T. G. Hom, President of the Chinese Y.M.C.A., wrote a letter to the *New York Times* emphasizing that criminal behavior was neither unique to nor widespread among the Chinese American community as alleged by the press. Similar to writings by black middle-class leaders in this period who labored to improve the status of their "race" and their community's public image, Hom wrote to defend the reputation of the Chinese community in America. "As a race we are no less law-abiding" than are other nationalities, and never before have we known or heard of a crime of this character having been committed by a Chinese."[66] In addition, he stressed that the Chinatown community was appalled by the murder and in response made numerous efforts to aid the police in their investigation. Not content simply to defend the community against racist attacks, Hom went on the offensive and suggested to readers that Leon Ling may have actually acquired the idea for the murder by reading about similar acts of violence in the sensationalistic American press.

The Chinese Freemasons, or the Lone Gee Tong, also wrote the *New York Times* to dispel the rumor that Leon Ling was a member of their society. The authors stated further that membership would not have induced other society members to shield him from the law. Like the letters of Chinese Christians that emphasized the similarities between Chinese and Western/Christian morality, the authors employed a similar strategy to portray their organization, stating that "the order is organized on lines similar to that great and honorable fraternity, the Grand Lodge of Free and Accepted Masons in the State of New York and of the world. The Lone Gee Tong teaches and inculcates friendship, morality, and brotherly love, and teaches and practices charity, relief, truth, honor, and virtue, regardless of race or creed."[67] Even with these letters and proclamations from the Chinese Legation, the press held fast to the belief that the Chinese community operated in mysterious, "Oriental" ways and that they continued to shelter Leon Ling.[68]

The shared experience of police arrests and harassment during the Sigel murder investigation worked to break down temporarily the social boundaries separating different socioeconomic segments of the overseas Chinese population: laborers, merchants, diplomats, and students. These latter two groups shared little socially or culturally with the larger Chinese laboring and merchant populations. Diplomats came into contact with Chinese laborers and merchants while executing their administrative duties, whereas students' lives revolved more around their respective universities. But as police broadened their search for Leon Ling, students also found themselves the targets of the hunt. With the description of the suspect as "Hair cut American. Dresses like an American. Talks good English," Chinese students, especially, found that they had become obvious targets for the police.[69] Their Western dress and mastery of the English language made them more vulnerable to arrests and detention than their working-class brethren, who were often much less "Americanized" in appearance with their traditional Chinese clothing and less than fluent English. The students quickly used their facility with the English language to their advantage by waging a battle for public opinion through writing. By submitting letters to the editors of the city's newspapers for publication, students urged readers to consider the profound impact the Sigel murder investigation had on the Chinese American population at large. More importantly, the students used this public forum to protest against police harassment of their fellow students and the broader Chinese population in the city.

Po Heng Lum, a student at Columbia University, submitted a letter to the *New York Times* editor, describing his grievances over the police investigation and press accounts of the Sigel murder. Similar to the writings of other Chinatown leaders, Po Heng Lum emphasized the community's willingness to assist the police, urging readers to believe that the city's Chinese population was sincere in its efforts to capture Leon Ling. But Po Heng Lum went further, suggesting that the police's failure to apprehend Leon Ling was due to his receiving assistance from someone outside of the Chinese community. "We must not forget that Leon, the suspected murderer, has loved other American girls, as alleged by the police some time ago. It is more than probable that Leon is under the protection of some one who loves him more than justice. So if there is a chance for the Chinese, there will be equally a chance for the American."[70] In closing, the letter denounced the sensationalism of yellow journalism that "ha[s] aroused ill-feeling of the American toward the Chinese, hurt the Chinese market, and put Chinese dignity in danger when a Chinese walks in the streets."

Student protests became more organized through the efforts of V. K. Wellington Koo, a twenty-one-year-old law student at Columbia University.[71] Before entering Columbia University in 1905, Koo had graduated from the Episcopal Church of America founded St. John's College in Shanghai and also studied at Cook Academy in New York. Editor of both *The Spectator*, Columbia University's daily newspaper, and the *Chinese Students' Monthly* (CSM), the English-language publication of the Chinese Students' Alliance of Eastern States, Koo had already gained vast experience in conveying his social, political, and economic views to both Chinese and mainstream American audiences. In his letter to the *New York Tribune* editor, Koo began by asking, "Will not the thinking Americans—the liberty loving and justice seeking people—lend a willing ear to the plea of a Chinese student for fair play and a square deal?"[72] The letter then specifically called attention to the overly aggressive tactics of the police in their mass arrests of Chinese men and concluded with an appeal to "the thinking part of the public to do something in order that such deplorable abuse of the police power may be put to an end, and that the thousands of innocent, peace loving Chinese in this country, known to be the freest on the earth, may receive from the police and the detectives a just and decent regard for their inviolate personal rights and liberties."

The use of particular phrases in Koo's letter suggests that he directed his appeal to a particular segment of the New York public—the city's Progressives. By strategically employing the notions of "fair play" and "square deal," stock political phrases made famous by Theodore Roosevelt and his generation of Progressive political reformers, Koo made himself appear to be an all-American college man and fellow civic-minded reformer working to check municipal corruption.[73] With police abuse of power a longstanding topic of reform in New York City, Koo touched on an issue that was all too familiar to *Tribune* readers, adroitly shifting focus away from questions of race to the issue of police authority.[74] Although Koo abhorred the "ruthless exploitations of 'yellow' journalism," he realized that the effects of the sensational news coverage would not be nearly so devastating if it were not for the tacit support of the state and police. Thus, he appealed directly to the city's Progressives to rein in police abuses and end the persecution of Chinese in the city.

The Sigel murder and subsequent manhunt deeply impacted the lives of Chinese students in America. In subsequent writings published in the *CSM*, students continued to refer to the murder investigation and newspaper reportage as examples of sensational newspaper coverage and harassment of Chinese in the country.[75] For men such as Koo and Lum, poised to become China's future political and intellectual leaders, demanding justice for the Chinese immigrant community was clearly a matter of Chinese national pride. Yet for laborers and merchants, keenly aware of their precarious social and legal status under the provisions of Chinese exclusion, mounting an organized protest against their ongoing harassment by the press and police meant directly challenging their social and political marginalization.

SAN FRANCISCO'S CHINESE COMMUNITY MOVES TO ACTION:
THE FOUNDING OF THE SHEN GONG LI HUI

In San Francisco, the formation of the Shen Gong Li Hui (SGLH)[76] led to
the rise of a grassroots movement against the negative portrayals of
Chinese by mainstream newspapers following the murder. The SGLH
began as a joint effort by that city's three Chinese daily newspapers:
Chinese Daily Paper or *Chung Sai Yat Pao (Zhong Xi Ri Bao)*, *Chinese
World (She Jie Ri Bao)*, and *Da Tong Ri Bao*. In their first official statement
to the Chinese community, printed in the July 15, 1909 issue of the *Chinese
Daily Paper*, the SGLH described its functions to the Chinese community:
"to protect the reputation, lives and property of the overseas Chinese community."[77] In response to this major crisis the SGLH proposed to mount a
popular campaign, consisting of Chinese and sympathetic non-Chinese
against the country's newspapers' biased and unsubstantiated coverage on
the Elsie Sigel case. The group also stated that it would seek legal redress
when appropriate, such as in cases involving the loss of life or property.
The group also sent a formal letter to Minister Wu Ting Fang, as notifica-
tion of the group's creation, and urged the minister to petition officially the
American government to protect the overseas Chinese community.[78]

In this campaign, the SGLH members chiefly turned to writing letters
for publication in the English and Chinese press as their main protest
strategy. In the event that their letters would not be printed, the group
also proposed to publish their own writings in the form of pamphlets
for popular distribution in both languages. Despite their ineligibility for
citizenship, organizers were clearly aware of American political and
legal culture. An editorial written by a SGLH organizer pointed out, "In
a country with a Constitution where freedom of speech is a right,
whether one is a prince, general, minister, trouble maker or criminal
everyone is entitled to the same right. This right is also given to newspapers. Thus I cannot prevent anyone from speaking, yet no one can prevent me from debating."[79] The organization also fostered democratic
principles, emphasizing open debate and requiring all actions taken by
the group to be sanctioned through a vote by the group's membership.[80]

Through the power of the pen they hoped to intervene by publishing
their own letters that countered the press's negative portrayals. As evidence of the SGLH's immediate impact in the battle over public opinion,
the group recounted to the Chinese community the number of letters that
had been written and published in the few days since the group had
formed. One report stated that a Portland minister and merchant had
each written letters that had been published. In addition Ng Poon Chew,

editor of the *Chinese Daily Paper*, had already composed and published three letters in mainstream newspapers, the longest in the *San Francisco Examiner*. Editorials constantly urged readers to notify the group if they were to come across a negative article regarding the Chinese community or to take action themselves by penning a letter to the offending newspaper that would counter the charges through an appeal to "law, reason or the facts."[81] The group also approached sympathetic white Americans to write letters to major mainstream American newspapers on their behalf and distribute them to newspapers in major cities such as Chicago, Philadelphia, Washington, D.C., New York City, Boston, and Baltimore, as well as a number of smaller cities such as Portland, Maine; Buffalo, New York; and New Haven, Connecticut.[82]

The primary strategy of letter writing may have privileged those members of the Chinese community with English and Chinese writing skills, namely those belonging to higher socioeconomic backgrounds. Yet the group made a concerted effort to attract all members of the overseas Chinese population to their cause. The organization did not require membership dues, and its July 17 open invitation to its regular evening meetings held at the Newspaper Reading Society's rooms specifically stated that Chinese of like and different classes were welcome to attend.[83] An examination of the list of donations published in the *Chinese Daily Paper* suggests that the SGLH garnered widespread local and national support in the Chinese American community.[84] Donations from individuals and Chinese-owned businesses ranging from 50¢ to several dollars were regularly listed. Supporters were welcomed to send their donations to any of the three Chinese dailies in San Francisco.[85] In New York City, Chinese gathered at the CCBA on July 24 to raise $56 for the organization.[86] By August 10, the organization proudly announced that they had received over $1,000 in donations from all over the country.[87]

The group also attempted to cross political and cultural divisions within the Chinese immigrant community to promote ethnic solidarity. Article six of the organization's by-laws specifically stated that for the purpose of maintaining group unity, organization divisions based on political factions or tong membership would not be tolerated.[88] The co-operation of San Francisco's three Chinese language dailies with their different constituencies also made the organization appear to be a vast grassroots social movement rather than the outgrowth of any one particular political group's agenda. The SGLH's rallying cry of "protecting the reputation of our overseas Chinese brethren, protecting our lives, and protecting our property" was one that all Chinese in the United States could easily identify and understand. Because the organization did not challenge Chinatown's established power structure, it managed to receive support from a wide range of different political and social organizations in the Chinese community. By directing its organizing efforts against outside white American institutions—overzealous police, biased court officials, unresponsive government agents irresponsible newspapers, and criminal vigilantes—the SGLH focused attention away from Chinatown's own political leaders and institutions. As a result, the SGLH rarely brought up the shortcomings of the Chinese community leaders or organizations during the Sigel murder investigation.

A July 19 advertisement for the group ended with an appeal to readers to send letters on their experiences with, and views on, the Sigel case investigation and provided the address of Wong Wing Tuck, the Superintendent, at 777 1/2 Sacramento Street, for all future correspondences.[89] Readers who responded often had their letters published in one of the Chinese newspapers. On August 4, for example, the group received a letter written by Zhang Wen Huan and published the entire contents in two installments in the *Chinese Daily Paper*. Zhang Wen Huan, who signed the letter as *xiang di* or "humble fellow villager," began by expressing his excitement in reading in the Chinese newspaper about the establishment of the organization for the sake of all overseas Chinese. He then added his opinions on several points in the history of Sigel's missionary work with the Chinese community in New York, casting doubt on her character. Although he believed that Sigel's mother had indeed engaged in sincere missionary work for several years, he accused Elsie Sigel of behaving improperly, suggesting that her association with the Chinatown Settlement's work with white prostitutes in the area may have affected her morality.[90]

On several occasions, SGLH members identified negative editorials published in the mainstream press to translate into Chinese for publication in a Chinese newspaper.[91] The group also printed in the local Chinese dailies full translations of letters in American newspapers that challenged the press's negative depictions of the Chinese community.[92] In late August the group ran in two installments a report of what they had determined to be the facts regarding the Sigel murder case.[93] A few more articles regarding the activities of the SGLH continued to appear sporadically for the rest of the year. With the release of Chong Sing and the New York coroner's inquest verdict in September, the public's attention to the case appeared finally to diminish. The sudden appearance of a play about the Sigel murder a year later, however, brought the organization and Chinese communities throughout the country to mount once again an organized protest.

"The Chinatown Trunk Mystery"

As the cultural capital of the nation, it was not long before New York-based commercial leisure entrepreneurs recognized the lucrative potential in catering to the public's prurient interests in the murder. After all, news-papers in the city and across the country had certainly profited from their continuous sensational coverage of the unfolding details of the manhunt and police investigation. Converting this public spectacle, of murder and in-terracial sex already made familiar by the city's newspapers, into yet an-other product for mass consumption would not prove to be difficult. Across the river in Bayonne, New Jersey, one such entrepreneur repackaged the murder as an "exhibition of moving pictures" in just three weeks following the discovery of Sigel's death. The exhibition immediately proved to be very popular and played to several crowded audiences on opening night before attracting the attention of Bayonne's mayor, Pierre Garven. Concerned that "such pictures would have a bad effect on the morals of children," Mayor Garven quickly put an end to the showings.[94]

By August the following year news of either the manhunt or murder investigation had finally dissipated. The city's Chinese immigrant popu-lation had weathered what they hoped to be the last of the media bar-rage when a play about the murder, titled the *The Chinatown Trunk Mystery*, appeared at the Lipein Theatre on the Bowery. News of the play quickly reached New York's Chinese community, and local elites hastily organized to halt all future performances. The CCBA dispatched a report to Minister Yang Yu Wing of the Chinese Legation with the hopes that the Minister would prevail upon city officials to close down the production. The Minister, however, decided the matter did not fall within his jurisdiction and did not intervene. Instead, local leaders took it upon themselves to publicize the matter to Chinese communities across the country, and requested that letters demanding the ban of fu-ture performances be sent directly to New York City officials.[95]

On August 4 eight Chinese students from Columbia University, includ-ing V. K. Wellington Koo, signed and submitted to Mayor William Jay Gaynor a petition against the showing of the *The Chinatown Trunk Mys-tery* at the Lipein Theatre. The petition declared that the play's attempt to portray the Sigel murder created a "common nuisance, inasmuch as both the malicious laying of the plot of the show and the inflammatory language used . . . is calculated to stir up racial animosity between the Chinese and the American people and thereby create occasion to disturb the peace and good order of the city."[96] A day after Mayor Gaynor received the petition he responded by sending a letter to Acting Police Commissioner F. H. Burger, to investigate, requesting that a "competent person" be sent to "see if there be anything indecent or immoral in it, upon which we can stop it."[97] Succumbing to mounting pressure from the Chinese American community, Minister Yang visited Mayor Gaynor on August 8 to request that he personally intercede to stop the play. The mayor, however, doubted that he could take any action to terminate the play's run, but assured the minister that he would provide adequate protection for all Chinese in the city. When the CCBA learned of the unsatisfactory outcome of Minister Yang's meeting, the organization decided to appeal to Minister Chang in Washington, D.C. to contact the U.S. State Department to intervene.[98] Seattle's Chinese community also responded with a similar petition to Minister Chang.[99] Despite these collective protests, the play was allowed to continue uninterrupted.[100]

Meanwhile a new rumor that a film was also in the works led the SGLH to engage a lawyer to petition the New York City District Attorney's office to halt its production.[101] The District Attorney's office promptly investigated the charge, but on August 16 sent a report of their inquiry and stated that no such film production existed. The report acknowledged that a play titled _The Chinatown Trunk Mystery_ had recently been performed at a Bowery theater, but claimed that the matter had already been dealt with by the police.[102]

As it had been with the previous year's manhunt for Leon Ling, the matter quickly became an issue of national concern for the country's Chinese immigrants. After its run in New York City, the play was subsequently staged in a number of theaters throughout the country. As the play made its way to other cities that winter and the following year, Chinese communities mobilized to organize similar campaigns against the production.[103] On January 8, 1911 the "Weekly Dramatic Calendar" of the special Sunday entertainment section of the _Oregon Journal_ announced the play's one week performance at the Bungalow Theater in Portland.[104] Upon receiving this news, Chinese Legation representatives and Portland Chinese leaders immediately contacted the mayor to stop the performances.[105] Having followed reports of mounting protests against the play by Chinese across the nation, the Chinese immigrant communities of Seattle and San Francisco were prepared to launch similar actions when _The Chinatown Trunk Mystery_ appeared in their cities.[106] In towns where smaller numbers of Chinese resided, local Chinese residents contacted larger nearby Chinese communities for assistance. In late January 1911, when _The Chinatown Trunk Mystery_ reached a small town in California, Huang Yi Shun wrote to the _Chinese Daily Paper_ to report the play's arrival in his town. Huang also requested the aid of CCBA leaders in San Francisco, who responded by engaging a lawyer to bring a complaint to the governor.[107] The town's merchants also on their own initiative banded together to petition Chinese Legation officials stationed in neighboring cities as well as the governor of California to ban the production.[108] As in New York City and elsewhere, the performances proceeded despite the vigorous protests from local Chinese residents.

What exactly made _The Chinatown Trunk Mystery_ so attractive for mainstream theater audiences? Unlike a true theatrical whodunit, audiences were familiar with the ending even before stepping inside the theater. The play was hardly a critical success in breaking new dramatic ground or presenting an accurate account of the events leading up to the murder. Even though notices advertised, "a play taken from real life," the play's producers were far from faithful to the characters or facts of the case as revealed during the months of police investigation.[109] With an all-white cast, yellowface performances were used to portray Chinese characters.[110] Indeed, the play did little to impart any nuanced or objective insights into Leon Ling and Sigel's relationship and the racially and ethnically diverse world they inhabited. As the *Daily News Portland* reported, the play featured not only "an exact likeness of 'The Mission School,'" but also an "Opium Den of the Oriental Restaurant."[111] The use of such settings suggests the level to which the play's producers drew upon the more recognizable sensational newspaper accounts, as well as utilized familiar staging conventions of "Chineseness," in their attempt to reanimate the murder for theatrical consumption. Despite the fact that the police investigation did not reveal that Sigel had ever visited an opium den and had called her missionary status into question, audiences and critics did not seem to mind the play's distortions of the case. Instead audiences flocked to see what was billed "the most sensational melodrama on the boards today."[112]

What may have made *The Chinatown Trunk Mystery* so compelling a year after the murder was the use of the theatrical genre of the melodrama to contain and correct the various racial, gender, and sexual transgressions exposed in the course of the Sigel murder investigation. The play utilized familiar racial and sexual spectacles such as white womanhood under assault by lascivious Chinamen, Chinatown opium dens, and missions to call into question the possibilities for Chinese integration, lending further support to Chinese exclusion. At the same time the play worked to impart the necessary moral lessons against the very real public concern over racial mixing. In a period when urban, white working-class and middle-class women were exercising their consumer desires and exploring the urban world at large, such popular narratives of racial and sexual danger helped to keep their mobility in check and maintain racialized and gendered urban geographies. As a theatrical notice in Portland, Oregon advertised, "It is the desire of 'The Chinatown Trunk Mystery' to convince our public intelligently of the pitfalls which confront our women who consider it their duty to enter Chinatown and teach a people who are loath to give up their traditions."[113] In effect the play continued the earlier efforts of the police and press to repair the breached racial and gender borders in the aftermath of the murder.

The production of *The Chinatown Trunk Mystery* provides a fitting last chapter to this unresolved case. The play came to replace the long sought after missing courtroom resolution by allowing audiences to act the part of the jury in this mock recreation. The translation of the Sigel murder into a theatrical melodrama also mirrors its initial chronicling in the front pages of New York City newspapers. The play, as with the sensationalized press accounts, amused theatergoers with its presentation of familiar racial spectacles while allowing them to experience the shock and horror of this tale of murder and miscegenation. Unlike the real life murder case that remained unsolved and unpunished, the play as "a story of villainy, greed, virtue and right . . . with sufficient comedy interwoven to relieve," provided the missing narrative closure and catharsis as it entertained its audiences.[114] But for Chinese immigrants the murder case, with its anti-miscegenation and anti-integration legacy, further restricted socioeconomic mobility, reaffirming and extending the social and spatial limits of Chinese exclusion.

Epilogue

WITH THE POLICE'S FAILURE to capture Leon Ling and mount a courtroom trial, many questions concerning the murder and Leon Ling's relationship with Elsie Sigel remained unanswered. News coverage of the murder slowed to a trickle by September 1909, though references to the case continued to surface from time to time over the next several decades. In 1913 San Francisco police arrested Lee Dor on the charge of trafficking in opium. While searching through his apartment, police came upon a large collection of press clippings about the Sigel murder. Though police hoped the discovery would provide the much hoped for break needed to capture the missing fugitive, no such resolution unfolded.[1]

In 1935 the gruesome murder of a white Chicago resident, Ervin Lang, once again placed the Sigel murder into the public spotlight. Police suspected that Lang's mother-in-law, Blanche Dunkel, had hired a Chinese-white couple, Evelyn Smith and Harry Jung, to commit the murder. Lang's body was found partially dismembered and stuffed inside a trunk. Among the couple's belongings the police found a "detective magazine containing an account of the murder of Miss Sigel."[2] The pages of the article had been marked, leading police to speculate that the story had given the couple the idea of placing Lang's body inside a trunk. In yet another similarity to the Sigel murder, Harry Jung, described as an Americanized Chinese man, disappeared. Police efforts to locate Jung resulted in several raids in Chinese American communities and the detention of at least sixteen men for questioning. Aside from the number of Chinese men arrested, a Chinese-white couple were also picked up in nearby Rockford, Illinois but later released. The police did manage to arrest Evelyn Smith and Blanche Dunkel, who were eventually tried and convicted for the murder. Both were given long prison sentences with no chance at parole until sixty years had been served. But Jung, like Leon Ling, was never found.[3]

Aside from these spectacular cases, the rare mentions of the Sigel murder were generally brief and often linked to the exotic and seamy underside of New York City's Chinatown, as it had been in the initial reporting. Whereas the press's original racialized descriptions of the crime scene turned the Eighth Avenue flat into a physical extension of Chinatown and collapsed the distance between these two different parts of the city, some later versions simply transposed the murder's discovery to Chinatown itself. For example contemporary New York food critics Michael and Ariane Batterberry, in their discussion of popular dining establishments in

Chinatown at the turn of the century, describe the neighborhood streets as lined with tough, working-class dance halls and saloons alongside tongs engaged in opium and white slave trades. To describe the neighborhood's transformation from a vice to tourist district, the authors make the claim that "the area was 'cleaned up' in 1910 following the discovery of the dismembered body of Elsie Sigel in a trunk on Doyers Street."[4] Considering that the public's initial reactions to the Sigel murder largely involved concerns with policing and containing the Chinatown neighborhood and Chinese male immigrants in the city, the authors' misreporting of the location of the body's discovery in this later retelling seems fitting.

Despite these occasional mentions of the case and plays based on the murder events, the death of Elsie Sigel eventually faded into obscurity, largely forgotten by New Yorkers and Americans alike.[5] Other sensational crimes eventually supplanted the Sigel murder in the public's imagination. Also lapsing from public memory along with the murder were the social, cultural, and legal processes whereby this multiracial and multiethnic lower Manhattan neighborhood became known only as "Chinatown," a vice district containing the city's predominantly Chinese male immigrant enclave. This spatial and discursive formation worked also to limit the mobility of Chinese American men and white working-class and middle-class women in and out of this part of the city. As increasingly rigid racialized and gendered boundaries emerged around the Chinatown area during the first decades of the twentieth century, this district came to be ever more identified as an area only occupied by Chinese with mainly "bachelor" laborers and a small number of "pure" Chinese merchant families. The many interracial couples and families and other non-Chinese that participated in the daily life of the neighborhood, as well as the majority of the city's Chinese immigrants whose everyday lives took place outside of the confines of Chinatown, gradually slipped from public memory.

Increasingly the popular notion of Chinatowns as insular, bachelor Chinese communities gained more legitimacy and prominence because of its acceptance and perpetuation in both the popular media and the emerging academic field of sociology. By the mid-1920s, with the country's national borders closed to all Asian groups with the exception of Filipinos, social thinkers turned their attention to studying how American society could best absorb and assimilate, or at the very least, render harmless those who remained.[6] The rise of social science, especially the field of sociology, was contemporaneous with this public anxiety over the assimilation and containment of Asian immigrants and their children, the American-born second generation of Asian Americans who were U.S. citizens by birthright.[7] What became increasingly accepted and unquestioned was the idea that ethnic communities were organized along shared cultural and linguistic commonalities that promoted ethnic solidarity and prevented them from assimilating into the wider American society. The presence of distinctly Asian American communities, then, was interpreted as the physical manifestation of these groups' ethnic cultural retention and nonassimilation. How the geographic formation of these ethnoracial communities may have also been shaped by the deeper history and continuing effects of legally based processes of racial exclusion, that did not end until the post–World War II era, easily became obscured.

This conception of Asian American urban communities such as Chinatowns, as structured along the lines of racial and ethnic solidarity and homogeneity, did not end with these early social science inquiries but continued to dominate the field of Asian American studies that began to emerge in the late 1960s and early 1970s.[8] Although more nuanced in their approaches to understanding the social and cultural organization of life in Chinatowns throughout urban America, these later scholars, particularly those engaged in community studies, continued to apply this definition of Asian ethnic communities as both geographically bounded and racially and ethnically homogeneous. As a result the study of Chinese American urban life became equated with the study of Chinatown communities, ignoring the wider geographic and social mobility of earlier groups of urban Chinese immigrants and the racial and ethnic diversity of urban neighborhoods. These scholars did not fully interrogate the historic geographic formation of racialized territories such as Chinatowns and their continued presence in the late twentieth century. Instead they often posed the same familiar questions: To what extent are America's Chinatowns culturally, socially, economically, and politically separate from the American mainstream? Are they communities built and sustained by Chinese immigrants on the basis of ethnic solidarity? Or should they be understood as the product of the Orientalist discourse and anti-Asian hostility of a particular period and locale?

This ready acceptance of Asian ethnic communities' borders as socially and geographically fixed and impenetrable has meant the failure of most scholars to investigate fully the role of racial discourses in the formation of spatial relationships in Asian American communities. In turn, this myopia has obscured an understanding of how these spatial arrangements, once formed, work to stabilize and reproduce the unequal social and economic relations that had erected this physical landscape.[9] Such an ahistorical and nonspatial understanding of Asian American community formation has yet to explain satisfactorily how the making of an urban territory such as New York City's Chinatown in lower Manhattan specifically in the late nineteenth and early twentieth century was formed and sustained out of the racial and sexual politics of Chinese exclusion.

The singular emphasis on race and ethnicity has also obscured the historical importance of gender and sexual politics in the making of Chinatown. Indeed, to understand the making of Chinatown as a social, cultural, and geographical formation, historians must ask when and why gendered as well as racialized borders began to appear in lower Manhattan, creating a physical entity popularly known as "Chinatown." By doing so I do not approach this study of turn-of-the-century New York with the assumption that a geographically distinct Chinese immigrant neighborhood formed and persisted primarily as a result of the residents' need to maintain their ethnic identity and solidarity. Instead I explore how social, political, cultural, and economic conflicts among diverse groups over the regulation of space have shaped the physical and discursive formation of New York City's streets and neighborhoods. That is, Chinatown was not simply a physical space in lower Manhattan. To nineteenth-century New Yorkers and Americans at large, the word "Chinatown" not only referred to the place where Chinese immigrants resided, but also implied deeper social and cultural meanings of urban racial and sexual dangers. In much the same way as scholars have studied popular, commercial cultural sites in New York City, such as Coney Island or Times Square, I have whittled away at these popular cultural representations of Chinatown to uncover the daily realities confronted by the historical actors who populated this space—police and residents, Chinese and non-Chinese, male and female, laborers and merchants, "bachelors" and families.[10]

It would be tempting to dismiss these popular cultural representations of Chinatown as an immoral, dangerous space as the product of New Yorkers' racist assumptions or the fanciful imaginings of authors of a particular literary genre such as the dime novel and argue that there is an authentic Chinatown buried underneath these sensational narratives. As a result, one would simply unearth the lived experiences of Chinese in New York to reconstruct an accurate social history of this population. Rather, I argue along with other Asian American studies scholars that these imagined, fictive narratives, no matter how "false," still played an integral role in shaping the lives and place of Chinese Americans in this period. Such an approach means locating and deconstructing popular cultural representations of the "Orient," and Asian immigrants and their communities, to unmask the power relations and political ideologies that allow the circulation of these images to remain in operation.[11] In terms of Chinatown's historical formation as a racialized and gendered space in lower Manhattan, the everyday realities of Chinatown life depended on the uninterrupted flow of such popular cultural images. As popular cultural narratives around the Elsie Sigel murder make clear, the speculations of police, social reformers, and journalists on the topics of interracial sex and Chinese moral and social deviance had serious material repercussions, profoundly shaping the range of acceptable physical movements and social interactions among the general public and the city's Chinese male residents.

An examination of the Sigel murder also contributes to an understanding of how familiar academic and popular Chinatown narratives, by emphasizing racial and ethnic borders, lead to the erasure of those members of the Chinatown community who are of mixed-race parentage or not of Chinese descent from these chronicles. This emphasis on Chinese exclusion era Chinatowns as bachelor, laborer communities also results in the privileging of male, working-class history in Asian American historiography, an imbalance that is currently being readdressed.[12] For New York City's Chinatown, this meant particularly the disappearance of non-Chinese women and their families from the community's historical record and the absence of gender analysis in Asian American community studies.

The 1909 Elsie Sigel murder offers present day readers an opportunity to rethink Chinatown as both the symbolic articulation and physical manifestation of race, class, and gender relations in urban space. It is particularly the intersections of the unstable, socially constructed categories of race, gender, and sexuality that help to explain the establishment of the Chinatown neighborhood in late nineteenth and early-twentieth-century New York. The creation of both racialized and gendered identities and urban territories required the constant surveillance and regulatory efforts of the police, courts, social reformers, and journalists. The creation and maintenance of racialized boundaries were clearly dependent on the circulation of sexual narratives of urban danger and the entrenchment of gendered boundaries to contain the physical and social mobility of Chinese men and white women of different socioeconomic classes. Public concerns over the place of Chinese immigrants in the city and nation at large echoed this period's worries and criticisms of women's unencumbered mobility that disrupted New York City's carefully laid out gendered and racial geogphies and racial hierarchies. Debates over Chinese men's and white working-class and middle-class women's proper place in the urban polity ranged from their participation in social reform and missionary movements to their material consumption and participation in modern commercial amusements. By bringing these insights into reexamination through the Elsie Sigel case, we can see once again the ways in which these Chinese and non-Chinese urban actors negotiated contemporary racial and gender politics and attempted to carve out meaningful lives in and out of Chinatown, thereby broadening the definition of a Chinese immigrant community.

Notes

INTRODUCTION
"FIND MISS SIGEL DEAD IN TRUNK"

1. "Arrest Friend of Miss Sigel," *NYT*, June 20, 1909.
2. "Girl Missionary Strangled, Body Packed in Trunk; The Victim Was a Granddaughter of General Sigel," *NYH*, June 19, 1909.
3. Ibid.
4. "Find Miss Sigel Dead in Trunk," *NYT*, June 19, 1909.
5. "Arrest Friend of Miss Sigel."
6. The term "heathen Chinee" was made popular by the line in a Bret Harte piece: "That for ways that are dark/And for tricks that are vain/The heathen Chinee is peculiar." See "Plain Language from Truthful James," *Overland Monthly*, September, 1870, 287–288.
7. For some fine examples of "mystery" histories, see Natalie Zemon Davis, *The Return of Martin Guerre* (Cambridge: Harvard University Press, 1984); Amy Srebnick, *The Mysterious Death of Mary Rogers: Sex and Death in Nineteenth Century New York* (Oxford: Oxford University Press, 1995); Patricia Cline Cohen, *The Murder of Helen Jewett* (New York: Vintage Books, 1998).
8. "Dies Mysteriously with His Bride," *NYH*, June 19, 1909.
9. "112 Unsolved Murders in Manhattan and Bronx Alone Since Jan. 1, 1906," *World*, July 4, 1909.
10. Sucheng Chan, "Asian American Historiography," *Pacific Historical Review* 65 (August 1996): 363–399; Gary Y. Okihiro, *The Columbia Guide to Asian American History* (New York: Columbia University Press, 2001), 193–241. Two important studies examining the discursive and material construction of North American Chinatowns include Kay Anderson, *Vancouver's Chinatown: Racial Discourse in Canada, 1875–1980* (London: McGill-Queen's University Press, 1991); and Nayan Shah, *Contagious Divides: Epidemics and Race in San Francisco's Chinatown* (Berkeley: University of California Press, 2001). Both Anderson and Shah demonstrate the importance of seeing Chinatown as a cultural and spatial construct that is both a product and a reproducer of social, political, and economic relations. See also K. Scott Wong, "Chinatown: Conflicting Images, Contested Terrain," *Melus* 20 (Spring 1995).
11. Judith Walkowitz, *The City of Dreadful Delight: Narratives of Sexual Danger in Late-Victorian London* (Chicago: University of Chicago Press, 1992), 11.
12. A German immigrant who arrived after the Revolution of 1848, Franz Sigel joined the Union army during the Civil War. *The National Cyclopaedia*, s.v. "Sigel, Franz"; Stephen D. Engle, *Yankee Dutchman: The Life of Franz Sigel* (Fayetteville: The University of Arkansas Press, 1993), 2, 100–119.
13. Engle, 228.

14. "General Franz Sigel a Power in Politics," *NYH*, June 19, 1909.

15. "The Sigels in Chinatown," *NYT*, June 20, 1909.

16. "Arrest Friend of Miss Sigel"; "Won't Admit Identity," *NY Tribune*, June 20, 1909.

17. "Arrest Friend of Miss Sigel."

18. "Girl Missionary Strangled."

19. "Won't Admit Identity."

20. "Arrest Friend of Miss Sigel."

21. "The Sigels in Chinatown."

22. "Police Find 35 Love Letters from 'Elsie' in Suspect's Trunk," *World*, June 20, 1909.

23. "Arrest Friend of Miss Sigel."

24. "Father Now Identifies Girl," *NYT*, June 21, 1909.

25. "Arrest Friend of Miss Sigel."

26. "Chinese Merchants Ask for Protection," *NYT*, July 4, 1909.

27. "Blue Days for Chop Suey Town and Fantan Land," *World*, July 11, 1909, third section.

28. There are a few historical studies that deal with interracial marriage and sexual relations between Chinese men and non-Chinese women during this period. John Kuo Wei Tchen's work on Chinese-Irish marriages in mid-century New York City, was one of the first promising historical studies of Chinese-white intermarriage in a northern city. John Kuo Wei Tchen, *New York before Chinatown: Orientalism and the Shaping of American Culture, 1776–1882* (Baltimore: Johns Hopkins University, 1999), 76–79, 159–162, 225–232. Two studies that focus on Chinese in the South argue that the small size of the Chinese population and its geographical dispersal rather than its concentration in urban Chinatowns helped to loosen ethnic ties and solidarity among the Chinese to allow for intermarriage. In other words, these studies do not challenge existing notions of Chinatowns as racially and ethnically homogeneous. Rather, they see these southern mixed-race communities as distinct from northern urban Chinatowns. See Lucy Cohen, *Chinese in the Post–Civil War South: A People without a History* (Baton Rouge: Louisiana State University Press, 1984); and James Loewen, *The Mississippi Chinese: Between Black and White* (Cambridge: Harvard University Press, 1971).

29. George Peffer, *If They Don't Bring Their Women Here: Chinese Female Immigration before Exclusion* (Chicago: University of Illinois Press, 1999); and Sucheng Chan, "The Exclusion of Chinese Women," in *Entry Denied: Exclusion and the Chinese Community in America, 1882–1943*, ed. Sucheng Chan (Philadelphia: Temple University Press, 1991), 94–146.

30. See for example, Madeline Y. Hsu, *Dreaming of Gold, Dreaming of Home: Transnationalism and Migration between the United States and South China, 1882–1943* (Stanford: Stanford University Press, 2000).

31. Judy Yung, *Unbound Feet: A Social History of Chinese Women in San Francisco* (Berkeley: University of California Press, 1995).

32. Works ranging from Mary Roberts Coolidge's *Chinese Immigration* (published in 1909) to Gunther Barth's *Bitter Strength* and Victor Nee and Brett deBary Nee's *Longtime Californ'* are prime examples of the pervasiveness

of this view of Chinatown. While these studies specifically focus on the history of San Francisco's Chinatown, this view of Chinatown communities as intrinsically bounded by clearly defined ethnic or racial borders has been applied to other Chinatowns throughout the country. The extent that this ahistorical assumption has been adopted can be seen in Min Zhou's discussion of Chinese immigration history in her 1992 study of New York City Chinatown, *Chinatown: The Socioeconomic Potential of an Urban Enclave*. Mary Roberts Coolidge, *Chinese Immigration* (New York: Henry Holt and Company, 1909); Gunther Barth, *Bitter Strength: A History of the Chinese in the United States, 1850–1870* (Cambridge: Harvard University Press, 1964); Victor Nee and Brett de Bary Nee, *Longtime Californ': A Documentary Study of an American Chinatown* (New York: Pantheon Books, 1972); and Min Zhou, *Chinatown: The Socioeconomic Potential of an Urban Enclave* (Philadelphia: Temple University Press, 1992), 39.

33. Several articles on the Elsie Sigel murder appeared in these newspapers. See for example "Claims that Chinese Murderer Passed through Binghamton Last Evening," *Binghamton Press and Leader*, June 21, 1909, evening edition; "Leon Not in Boston," *Boston Globe*, June 20, 1909, morning edition; and "Was Strangled by her Chinese Lover," *San Francisco Chronicle*, June 19, 1909.

34. Timothy Gilfoyle, *City of Eros: New York City, Prostitution, and the Commercialization of Sex, 1790–1920* (New York: W. W. Norton & Company, 1992), 92–116.

35. "Think These the Suspects," *NYT*, June 21, 1909; "Many Chinamen Arrested," *NYT*, June 22, 1909.

36. "Clew Given Here in Sigel Murder," *Chicago Daily Tribune*, June 21, 1909.

37. "There Are No Elsie Sigels in Chicago's Chinese Missions," *Chicago Daily Tribune*, Sunday edition, Metropolitan Section, June 27, 1909.

38. "Police Close Up Chinese Mission," *Chicago Daily Tribune*, June 28, 1909.

39. "Arrest Teacher and Chinese Pupil," *NY Tribune*, July 4, 1909.

40. "Chinese Driven Out," *Washington Post*, July 4, 1909.

41. Ibid.

CHAPTER ONE
"TERRA INCOGNITA"

1. "Scenes and Persons in the Chinatown Mystery," *New York Evening Journal*, June 21, 1909.

2. Petition to William Jay Gaynor, August 4, 1910. Box GWJ-100, Mayors' Papers, NYCMA.

3. The term "terra incognita" was used earlier by Alan Forman in describing Chinatown. See Alan Forman, "Celestial Gotham," *Arena* (April 1893): 620.

4. Charles Somerville, "The Yellow Pariahs," *Cosmopolitan* 47 (September 1909): 467.

5. Ibid., 467–468.

6. William Brown Meloney, "Slumming in New York's Chinatown," *Munsey's Magazine* 41 (September 1909): 818.

7. Numerous works have addressed the urban/rural dichotomy in nineteenth-century writings. For example, see Paul Boyer, *Urban Masses and Moral Order in America, 1820–1920* (Cambridge: Harvard University Press, 1978); Warren Susman, *Culture as History: The Transformation of American Society in the Twentieth Century* (New York: Pantheon Books, 1973), 237–251.

8. Meloney, "Slumming in New York's Chinatown," 823.

9. Ibid.

10. Ibid., 829.

11. Boyer, 132–142.

12. *Appleton's Dictionary of New York and Vicinity* (New York: D. Appleton & Company, 1879), 54. D. Appleton & Company used nearly the same description of Chinatown in the subsequent editions of their guidebook.

13. Elizabeth Blackmar, *Manhattan for Rent, 1785–1850* (Ithaca: Cornell University Press, 1989), 172–182.

14. The epidemic was rumored to have started in a cellar on Baxter Street. Richard Plunz, *A History of Housing in New York City: Dwelling Type and Social Change in the American Metropolis* (New York: Columbia University Press, 1990), 50. For a broader discussion of the Five Points area in the 1832 and 1849 cholera epidemics, see also Charles Rosenberg, *The Cholera Years: The United States in 1832, 1849 and 1866* (Chicago: University of Chicago Press, 1962), 1–39, 101–120.

15. Charles Dickens, *American Notes* (Middlesex, England: Penguin Books, 1972), 136–139. Dickens originally published *American Notes* in 1842.

16. James McCabe, Jr., *Lights and Shadows of New York Life* (New York: Farrar, Straus and Giroux, 1970), original publication date 1872, 398–421.

17. These gangs have been immortalized in the following: Herbert Asbury, *Gangs of New York: An Infernal History of the Underworld* (New York: Blue Ribbon Books, 1939), 21–45; and Luc Sante, *Low Life* (New York: Vintage Books, 1991), 197–235.

18. *Five Points Monthly Record* 15 (November 1871): 100.

19. Mona Domosh, *Invented Cities: The Creation of Landscape in Nineteenth-Century New York and Boston* (New Haven: Yale University Press, 1996), 15–25.

20. David Ward, *Cities and Immigrants: A Geography of Change in Nineteenth-Century America* (New York: Oxford University Press, 1971), 106–109.

21. Kenneth Scherzer, *The Unbounded Community: Neighborhood Life and Social Structure in New York City, 1830–1875* (Durham: Duke University Press, 1992), 49–96.

22. Domosh, 64.

23. For more on the importance of the skyscraper as a cultural symbol of modernity, corporate power and capitalism, see Gail Fenske and Deryck Holdsworth, "Corporate Identity and the New York Office Building: 1895–1915," in *The Landscape of Modernity: Essays on New York City, 1900–1940,*

eds. David Ward and Olivier Zunz (New York: Russell Sage Foundation, 1992), 129–159; Thomas Bender and William R. Taylor, "Culture and Architecture: Some Aesthetic Tensions in the Shaping of Modern New York City," in *Visions of the Modern City: Essays in History, Art, and Literature*, eds. William Sharpe and Leonard Wallock (Baltimore: Johns Hopkins University Press, 1987), 189–219.

24. Domosh, 65–76.

25. "A Glimpse of New York's Chinatown," *Seen by the Spectator: Being a Selection of Rambling Papers First Printed in The Outlook* (New York: The Outlook Company, 1902), 206. This premodern image continued to be reinforced in later guidebooks. For example, one 1926 guidebook referred to the Chinese residents in the neighborhood as "living in an atmosphere hardly altered from that along the Yellow River." Clement Wood, *The Truth about New York's Chinatown* (Girard, Kansas: Haldeman-Julius Company, 1926), 7.

26. John Kuo Wei Tchen, *New York before Chinatown: Orientalism and the Shaping of American Culture* (Baltimore: Johns Hopkins University Press, 1999), 96–130.

27. John Kasson, *Amusing the Million: Coney Island at the Turn of the Century* (New York: Hill and Wang, 1978), 69.

28. Hutchins Hapgood, *Types from City Streets* (New York: Funk & Wagnalls Company, 1910), 95–112.

29. William Norr, *Stories of Chinatown: Sketches from Life in the Chinese Colony* (New York: 1892), 3.

30. Louis J. Beck, *New York's Chinatown: An Historical Presentation of Its People and Places* (New York: 1898), 1–2.

31. Similar descriptions can also be seen in numerous journalistic writings on Chinatown. See, for example, "A Glimpse of New York's Chinatown," 193–206; Arthur Trumble, *The "Heathen Chinee" at Home and Abroad* (New York: 1882), 71–83.

32. Beck, 11. Park Street has since been renamed Mosco Street.

33. John Kuo Wei Tchen, "Quimbo Appo's Fear of Fenians: Anglo-Irish-Chinese Relations in New York City," in *New York Irish, 1625–1990*, eds. Ronald H. Bayor and Timothy Meagher (Baltimore: Johns Hopkins University Press, 1995), 11.

34. Tchen, *New York before Chinatown*, 233.

35. In antebellum New York, Irish Americans had struggled to heighten their social and political standing in the city by gaining influence in the Roman Catholic Church and pushing for acceptance in the Democratic Party; ibid., 167–224. See also David Roediger, *The Wages of Whiteness: Race and the Making of the American Working Class* (New York: Verso, 1991), 140–144.

36. During the 1870s, Chinese laborers were contracted to work in a shoe factory in North Adams, Massachusetts; a steam laundry in Belleville, New Jersey; and a cutlery company in Beaver Falls, Pennsylvania. Tchen, *New York before Chinatown*, 168–184. Edward J. M. Rhoads, "Asian Pioneers in the Eastern United States: Chinese Cutlery Workers in Beaver Falls, Pennsylvania in the 1870s," *Journal of Asian American Studies* 2 (June 1999): 119–155.

37. Emmanuel Tobier, "Manhattan's Business District in the Industrial Age," in *Power, Culture, and Place*, ed. John Mollenkopf (New York: Russell Sage Foundation, 1988), 77–105.

38. Henry Tom, "Colonia Incognita: The Formation of Chinatown, New York City, 1850–1890" (master's thesis, University of Maryland, 1975), 61, 63.

39. Beck, 24.

40. For views on ventilation and disease control in tenement housing reform see Roy Lubove, *The Progressives and the Slums: Tenement House Reform in New York City, 1890–1917* (Pittsburgh: University of Pittsburgh Press, 1962).

41. A. E. Costello, *Our Police Protectors: History of the New York Police from the Earliest Period to the Present Time* (New York: 1884), 523, 524.

42. Frank Yeager, "New York City—The Opium Dens in Pell and Mott Streets—How the Opium Habit Is Developed," *Frank Leslie's Illustrated Newspaper*, May 19, 1883, 204.

43. Jacob Riis, *How the Other Half Lives* (1890; reprint, New York: Penguin Books, 1997), 76. For more on Riis's discussion of interracial sex in Chinatown, see chapter 3.

44. Commissioner & Mrs. Ballington Booth, *New York's Inferno Explored* (New York: The Salvation Army, 1891), 31. See also Allen S. Williams, *The Demon of the Orient, and His Satellite Fiends of the Joints: Our Opium Smokers as They Are in Tartar Hells and American Paradises* (New York, 1883); Hamilton Wright, "Report on the International Opium Commission and on the Opium Problem as Seen within the United States and Its Possessions," *Opium Problem*, 61st Congress, 2nd Session, February 21, 1910, 45.

45. The 1878 California U.S. Circuit Court decision, *In Re Ah Yup*, barred foreign-born Chinese the right to naturalization. Although small numbers of Chinese were naturalized prior to this date, their numbers were hardly large enough to pose any political challenge. See Sucheng Chan, *Asian Americans: An Interpretive History* (Boston: Twayne Publishers, 1991), 47.

46. David Musto, *The American Disease: Origins of Narcotic Control* (New Haven: Yale University Press, 1973), 1–4, 31–34, 43.

47. Nineteenth-century fears of narcotic addiction were firmly linked to larger anxieties over the social and political status of foreign or racial minorities in the United States. Similar to urban whites' overblown fears that Chinese and opium smoking posed a threat to American civilization, southern whites in the early twentieth century feared that cocaine use by blacks resulted in a similar danger. This fear was greatly exaggerated and coincided with the rise of lynchings and Jim Crow laws; ibid., 6–8, 97–102. Reformers even linked together narcotic consumption of blacks and Chinese. In preparation for the 1909 meeting of the Shanghai Commission on the international opium trade, Dr. Hamilton Wright, one of the U.S. commissioners at this conference, issued a report on opium smoking in the United States specifically stating that the practice was introduced by Chinese migrants, but was not contained within the Chinese population and quickly spread to whites and blacks. Wright, "Report on the International Opium Commission," 45.

48. William Wirt Mills, *New York's Chinatown: Ancient Pekin Seen at "Old Bowery" Gate* (New York: King's Booklets, 1904), 22.

49. This view of Chinatown was also endorsed by other contemporary writers. For example, see *The Real New York* (New York: The Smart Set Publishing Company, 1904), 147–166; Helen F. Campbell, *Darkness and Daylight or Lights and Shadows of New York Life* (Hartford, CT: 1895), 549–573. Stewart Culin, a late-nineteenth-century anthropologist, presented several articles of this nature, including "China in America: A Study in the Social Life of the Chinese in the Eastern Cities of the United States"; paper presented before the Section of Anthropology, American Association for the Advancement of Science, New York, 1887; "A Curious People: Sketch of the Chinese Colony in Philadelphia," *Philadelphia Public Ledger*, September 22, 1888.

50. In the introduction to part I of this article, which focuses on the assimilation of European immigrants, Simon wrote: "It seems best to treat of the Chinese as a class apart from the rest of the immigrants, owing to the peculiar conditions surrounding their life in America." Sarah E. Simons, "Social Assimilation," part II, *The American Journal of Sociology* 7 (January 1902): 539. See also Sarah E. Simons, "Social Assimilation," Part I, *The American Journal of Sociology* 7 (November 1901): 386.

51. Carol Groneman and David M. Reimers, "Immigration," *The Encyclopedia of New York City*, ed. Kenneth T. Jackson (New Haven: Yale University Press, 1995), 582–583.

52. The following household information comes from the 1910 Federal Census, New York City, Supervisor's District 1, Enumeration District 45.

53. Beck, 69–70.

54. George F. Miller to Abraham Hewitt, October 26, 1877, Box HAS-30, Mayors' Papers.

55. John McCullagh to Alex S. Williams, November 7, 1887, Box HAS-30, Mayors' Papers.

56. Application of A. F. Kerr for license to give Vocal and Instrumental Concerts, December 19, 1893; Alexander S. Ward to Superintendent Byrnes, December 22, 1893. Box GTF-15, Mayors' Papers.

57. Chu Fong to William L. Strong, April 5, 1895; Chief clerk of the Police Department of the City of New York to John Jeroloman, July 29, 1896, Box SWL-46, Mayors' Papers.

58. Beck, 92.

59. Chief clerk of the Police Department of the City of New York to John Jeroloman, July 29, 1896, Box SWL-46, Mayors' Papers.

60. Ibid.

61. Letter to Abraham Hewitt, July 25, 1887, Box HAS-31, Mayors' Papers.

62. John McCullagh to William Murray, August 3, 1887, Box HAS-31, Mayors' Papers.

63. Huie Kin, *Reminiscences* (Beijing: San Yu Press, 1932), 50–53.

64. Letter to Abraham Hewitt, June 1, 1887, Box HAS-29, Mayors' Papers.

65. John McCullagh to William Murray, June 13, 1887, Box HAS-29, Mayors' Papers.

66. McCullagh cites the date May 29, because several of the building's residents had been arrested prior to that date. However, it remains unclear if the occupants were actually guilty of the charges filed against them since the arrests seem to have

resulted from a domestic dispute between neighbors, Ah Yen and his common-law wife Emma Lewis and Wah Lee, at 11 Pell Street. Emma Lewis had lived with Wah Lee prior to moving in with Ah Yen. John McCullagh to William Murray, June 30, 1887, Box HAS-30, Mayors' Papers.

67. James O'Leary, Edward O'Toole, Joseph Wright, Michael O'Rourke, and Jere. O'Connor to Abraham Hewitt, September 1, 1888, Box HAS-32, Mayors' Papers.

68. John McCullagh to William Murray, September 19, 1888, Box HAS-32, Mayors' Papers.

69. Beck wrote that there were "[t]hirty white boys, fifteen Negroes and five Chinese are so employed regularly." Beck, 118.

70. At this time, the Lower East Side had more dance halls than any other area in the city. A 1901 survey conducted by the University Settlement Society of New York counted thirty-one dance halls in the area between Houston and Grand Streets, east of the Bowery. Kathy Peiss, *Cheap Amusements: Working Women and Leisure in Turn-of-the-Century New York* (Philadelphia: Temple University Press, 1986), 89.

71. Investigators for the Committee of Fourteen, for example, named a number of such establishments. See "Information. Arranged According to Streets," 36–37; Report submitted to G. W. Hooke by Stockdale, August, 12, 1910, Box 28, Committee of Fourteen Papers, NYPL.

72. "Information. Arranged According to Streets," 37. Committee of Fourteen Papers.

73. Report by A. E. Wilson, no date, Box 4, Committee of Fifteen Papers, NYPL.

74. The Port Arthur was located on Mott Street. The Oriental, Savoy, Tuxedo, and Chinese Delmonico were on Pell Street. *Seeing Chinatown* (New York: Bignew Publishing Company, 1906), 25.

75. Michael and Ariane Batterberry, *On the Town in New York* (New York: Routledge, 1999), 71–75, 85–86, 162–165. The association with the Delmonico appears to have worked. One guidebook described the Chinese Delmonico as a "typical high-class Chinese restaurant, one of the best in America," Mills, 9.

76. Reports submitted by Chas. S. Briggs, January 29, 1914, April 25, 1914, and May 9, 1914; Box 28, Committee of Fourteen Papers.

77. Mills, 3.

78. Chuck Connors's real name was George Washington Connors. Alvin F. Harlow, *Old Bowery Days: The Chronicles of a Famous Street* (New York: D. Appleton and Company, 1931), 428–435. Wirt Howe, *New York at the Turn of the Century, 1899–1916* (Toronto: privately printed, 1946), 25–26. Hapgood, 31–42.

79. Mills, 11. *Scene in a Chinese Restaurant*, American Mutoscope & Biograph, 1903. Chuck Connors, *Bowery Life* (New York: Richard K. Fox, 1904), 2–3. "Claws of the Dragon Losing Grip on New York's Famous Chinatown," *Sun*, June 15, 1913, section 4.

80. Elliot J. Gorn, *The Manly Art: Bare-Knuckle Prize Fighting in America* (Ithaca: Cornell University Press, 1986), 137–142, 185–193; Gail Bederman, *Manliness and Civilization: A Cultural History of Gender and Race in the*

United States, 1880–1917 (Chicago: University of Chicago Press, 1995); Jackson Lears, *No Place of Grace: Antimodernism and the Transformation of American Culture, 1880–1920* (New York: Pantheon Books, 1981), 103–107.

81. Roberta J. Park, "Biological Thought, Athletics and the Formation of a 'Man of Character,'" in *Manliness and Morality: Middle-class Masculinity in Britain and America, 1800–1940*, eds. J. A. Mangan and James Walvin, (New York: St. Martin's Press, 1987), 7–34.

82. "The Conversion of the Spider," *Daily Picayune*, July 1, 1909.

83. Marguerite Mooers Marshall, "What the Salvation Army girl Sees," *World Magazine*, June 27, 1909, 5.

84. Ibid.

85. "Now Rose Livingston Works in Chinatown," *NYT*, December, 1912. "Cadet" was the common term for the young man responsible for ensnaring a young woman into white slavery.

86. Willard Travell, MD, "Physician's Report," July 1, 1912, Series IV. White Slavery, Folder 92 Correspondences, July–Dec, 1912, Harriet Wright (Burton) Laidlaw Papers, Schlesinger Library.

87. Police Commissioner to Robert Adamson, Secretary to the Mayor, May 21, 1912, Box GWJ-54, Mayors' Papers.

88. Mayor William J. Gaynor to Mary Beard, June 11, 1912, Box GWJ-92, Mayors' Papers.

89. Established by prominent New York businessmen in 1900, the Committee of Fifteen sought to expose and eradicate the city's vice activities, in particular gambling and prostitution. Like their fellow Progressives, members of this nonpartisan committee acted under the belief that the city's Tammany Hall-controlled politicians and police force did not adequately perform their duties to suppress vice activities and saw that it was their civic duty to instigate reform.

90. Report of J. Mayers, July 12, 1901; Report from J. Reiswirth, July 13, 1901, Box 5, Committee of Fifteen Papers.

91. "Warn White Women to Leave Chinatown," *NYT*, June 1, 1909; and "Chinese Merchants Ask for Protection," *NYT*, July 4, 1909.

92. "Blue Days for Chop Suey Town and Fantan Land," *World*, July 11, 1909, third news section.

93. "Trace Yung Dat in Sigel Mystery," *NYH*, July 5, 1909.

94. "Chinese to Fight for Girl's Return," *NYH*, July 25, 1909.

95. *Fifth Annual Report of the Chinatown and Bowery Rescue Settlement for Girls* (1908–1909), 5.

96. Passed in 1896, the Raines Law was originally meant to restrict working-class saloons from operating on Sundays by allowing only hotels with ten or more beds to serve alcohol. Instead, the legislation inadvertently worked to entrench further prostitution in working-class saloons. Saloon keepers subdivided their rear rooms or upper floors into small "bedrooms" in order to qualify as hotels under the Raines Law and often rented these spare lodgings to prostitutes in the neighborhood. Committee of Fifteen, *The Social Evil: With Special Reference to Conditions Existing in the City of New York* (New York: G. P. Putnam's Sons, 1902), 159–168.

97. Report by Stockdale to G. W. Hooke, August 12, 1910, Box 28, Committee of Fourteen Papers.

98. "Information. Arranged According to Streets," 37, Committee of Fourteen Papers.

99. Charles Doelger to Hooke, September 24, 1910, Box 17, Committee of Fourteen Papers.

100. Letter from Lee Chung to the Committee of Fourteen, September 27, 1910, Box 17, Committee of Fourteen Papers.

101. For example, Patrick Sullivan, a saloon proprietor also signed a pledge agreeing "to serve no women in my saloon at #6 Mott Street and will immediately have signs posted in the rear room to that effect." Patrick Sullivan to Committee of Fourteen, no date, Box 17, Committee of Fourteen Papers.

102. Report of Patrolman John F. Dennin and Michael W. Murphy, April 29, 1911. Box GWJ-34, Mayors' Papers.

103. "More 'Elsie' Letters Found in Chinatown," *NY Tribune*, June 21, 1909.

104. "No Chinatown Trip for Popular Girls," *NYH*, July 17, 1909.

105. "First Vice Attack made on Chinatown," *NYT*, October 24, 1910.

106. Ibid.

107. "Sight-seeing Autos to Shun Chinatown," *NYT*, October 25, 1910.

108. "First Vice Attack made on Chinatown"; "Raids by Driscoll Fill Night Court," *NYT*, October 26, 1910.

109. Committee of Fourteen, *The Social Evil in New York City: A Study of Law Enforcement* (New York: Andrew H. Kellogg Co., 1910), 1–22, 137–138.

110. "Lights out in Chinatown," *NYT*, October 27, 1910.

111. This is most likely Lee B. Lok, an associate of the store Quong Yueng Shing, at 32 Mott Street. Lee B. Lok arrived in New York in 1887 and became proficient in English after studying at high school evening classes for several years; "Chinese Petition Driscoll," *NYT*, November 1, 1910.

Chapter Two
Beyond Chinatown

1. "Leon's Tracks Followed Out," *Newark Evening News*, June 30, 1909.

2. "White Woman in Opium Den," *NYT*, June 22, 1909.

3. "White Girl Had Opium Pipe," *NYT*, June 23, 1909.

4. "Information. Arranged According to Streets," Box 28, Committee of Fourteen Papers.

5. The following census information comes from the 1910 Federal Census, Supervisor's District 1, Enumeration District #47.

6. Henry Tom, "Colonia Incognita: The Formation of Chinatown, New York City, 1850–1890" (master's thesis, University of Maryland, 1975), 57–59, 66. For discussions on white labor and the anti-Chinese movement, see Alexander Saxton, *The Indispensable Enemy: Labor and the Anti-Chinese Movement in California* (Berkeley: University of California Press, 1971).

7. Tom, 62.

8. Wong Ching Foo, "The Chinese in New York," *Cosmopolitan* 5 (June 1888): 297. For a discussion on the early history of Chinese hand laundries in

New York City, see Renqiu Yu, *To Save China, To Save Ourselves: The Chinese Hand Laundry Alliance of New York* (Philadelphia: Temple University Press, 1992), 8–30. For more on the life and career of Wong Ching Foo, see Qingsong Zhang, "The Origins of the Chinese Americanization Movement: Wong Chin Foo and the Chinese Equal Rights League," in *Claiming America: Constructing Chinese American Identities during the Exclusion Era,* eds. Sucheng Chan and K. Scott Wong (Philadelphia: Temple University Press, 1998), 41–63.

9. Foo, 297.

10. Beck, 12.

11. Tom, 68–69.

12. Ibid., 68. For a more detailed study of Chinese laundry workers in a U.S. city, see Paul C. P. Siu, *The Chinese Laundryman: A Study of Social Isolation* (New York: New York University Press, 1987), ed. John Kuo Wei Tchen; and Yu, *To Save China.*

13. Mary Ting Yi Lui, "Groceries, Letters, and Community: The Local Store in Chinatown's 'Bachelor Society,'" *BuGaoBan,* 8 (1991): 1. Warner M. Van Norden, *Who's Who of the Chinese in New York* (New York: Warner Van Norden, 1918), 47.

14. Lui, "Groceries, Letters, and Community," 1, 3.

15. *People vs. John J. Corcoran,* Court of General Sessions of the Peace for the City and County of New York (1881): 2–5.

16. *Year Book of St. Bartholomew's Parish* (1901): 97.

17. Lee Chew, "The Story of a Chinaman," in *The Life Stories of Undistinguished Americans As Told by Themselves,* ed. Hamilton Holt (New York: Routledge, 1990), 181. This "life story" was originally published in the *Independent,* September 21, 1905. The topic of laundry vandalism had become so familiar by the turn-of-the-century that it was used to comedic effect in a 1903 short film titled *A Boomerang.*

18. "Slaying of Chinese Restaurant Proprietors,"*New York Police Department Annual Report* (1912): 16.

19. *Yearbook of St. Bartholomew's Parish* (1900): 93. For a more in-depth discussion of the Chinese Guild, see chapter 4.

20. For discussions on the CCBA's role in regulating internal and external community relations, see Yu, *To Save China,* 16–19, 31–36; Peter Kwong, *Chinatown, N.Y. Labor & Politics, 1930–1950* (New York: Monthly Review Press, 1979), 38–44.

21. Captain William Clinchy to Superintendent George W. Walling, February 14, 1884, Box EF-12, Mayors' Papers.

22. Case No. 28205 *People vs. Li Hong,* New York County - District Attorney's Office - Record of Cases.

23. Case No. 33352 *People vs. Lee Kee Song, Li Ying Wah, Lee Ching, and Lee Gang alias, Walter Lee,* February 26, 1901. See also Case No. 6463 *People vs. Charley Sing,* New York County - District Attorney's Office - Record of Cases.

24. Letter from William C. Timm to William Travers Jerome, D.A., dated March 4, 1908 in Case No. 65075 *People vs. Yong Fong Yee,* March 3, 1908, New York County - District Attorney's Office - Record of Cases.

25. Geary Act of 1892 (Chap 60, 5 May 1892), 27 United States Statutes at Large, 25–26.

26. *An Appeal of the Chinese Equal Rights League to the People of the United States for Equality of Manhood* (New York: 1892), 2.

27. The literature on the role of commercialized leisure and entertainment in incorporating and assimilating the immigrant working class into American urban industrial society is vast. For example, see Peiss, *Cheap Amusements*; Kasson, *Amusing the Million*; Lewis Erenberg, *Steppin' Out: New York Nightlife and the Transformation of American Culture* (Chicago: University of Chicago Press, 1984).

28. John Stewart Burgess, "A Study of the Characteristics of the Cantonese Merchants in Chinatown, New York, as Shown by their Use of Leisure Time" (master's thesis, Columbia University, 1909), 32, 36–38.

29. Ibid., 29, 36, 43.

30. William Wood Register, Jr., "New York's Gigantic Toy," in *Inventing Times Square: Commerce and Culture at the Crossroads of the World*, ed. by William R. Taylor (Baltimore: Johns Hopkins University Press, 1991), 243–270.

31. Burgess, 28–29.

32. In contrast to Chinatown's many village or family associations that were based on geographical origin or kinship ties, "tongs" were fraternal organizations where members made "blood oaths" to brotherhood. According to historian Sucheng Chan, tongs were popular among Chinese immigrants "because they provided alternative, antiestablishment social organizations with which people, especially the declasse within the immigrant population, could affiliate." During this period, Hip Sing Tong's largest rival in New York City's Chinatown was the On Leong Tong. Chan, *Asian Americans*, 67. See also Peter Kwong, *The New Chinatown* (New York: Noonday Press, 1987), 97–100. An in-depth history of tong activity in New York City Chinatown has yet to be written, though contemporary accounts are numerous. Such activities were frequently the topics of city newspaper articles. For an example of the colorful stories around Mock Duck and Tom Lee's respective tong activities and rivalry, see Herbert Asbury's *Gangs of New York: An Infernal History of the Underworld*, 303–308. See also "Claws of the Dragon Losing Grip on New York's Famous Chinatown," *Sun*, June 15, 1913, section 4.

33. Numerous reports discuss the openness of streetwalkers' solicitations in the area. See, for example, any number of reports submitted to G. W. Hooke by Stockdale in 1910, Box 28, Committee of Fourteen Papers.

34. "Report on 12 Chatham Sq., dive," submitted by A. E. Wilson, no date, Box 4, Committee of Fifteen Papers.

35. Statement from Quan Yick Nam, dated February 19, 1901, Box 4, Committee of Fifteen Papers. A year earlier, an *Evening Post* journalist made similar charges that at least sixteen gambling dens could be found along Mott, Pell, and Doyers streets and that each club paid $10 per week to the police for protection, totaling up to an annual amount of $35,000 ("$35,000 from Chinatown," *The Evening Post*, April 28, 1900).

36. Report to W. G. Hooke, March, 28, 1913, Box 28, Committee of Fourteen Papers. Kevin Mumford found similar examples of Asian male participation in Chicago's dance halls. Although Mumford's discussion is more focused on

Filipino workers, he also noted participation by Chinese men. Kevin Mumford, *Interzones: Black/White Sex Districts in Chicago and New York in the Early Twentieth Century* (New York: Columbia University Press, 1997), 53–71.

37. Forman, 626.

38. Beck, 146.

39. According to Lewis Erenberg, the city's commercial vice district shifted location in the latter half of the nineteenth century, growing from its mid-century location at the Bowery to the Tenderloin (Sixth Avenue between Twenty-fourth and Fortieth streets) and Coney Island by the 1870s and 1880s. Erenberg, 21.

40. Report of W. C. Steele, Jr., March 20, 1901, Box 21, Committee of Fifteen Papers.

41. "1905 File on Resorts," Box 91, Lillian Wald Papers, Rare Book and Manuscript Library, Columbia University.

42. Statement from Quan Yick Nam, February 19, 1901, Box 4, Committee of Fifteen Papers.

43. Letter from S. Robinson to J. H. Hooke, March 23, 1911, Box 1, Committee of Fourteen Papers.

44. See "Take Girls from a Laundry" and "White Woman in Opium Den" *NYT*, June 22, 1909; "White Girl Had Opium Pipe," *NYT*, June 23, 1909; "Chinaman and Girl Caught," *BDE*, June 28, 1909.

45. The Chinese-owned businesses included: Sam Lee's cigar store at 554 1/2 Seventh Avenue, Wah Lung's Laundry at 157 West Twenty-eighth Street, Charles Sing's Laundry at 225 West Thirty-second Street, and Young's Laundry at 310 West Thirty-fifth Street. J. H. Brown, "Reinspection of houses reported as containing prostitutes and places reported as resorts of prostitutes," May 17, 1901, Box 20, Committee of Fifteen Papers.

46. "Houses and Resorts of Prostitution in the City of New York," February 1, 1912, 8, Box 28, Committee of Fourteen Papers.

47. Tom, 78.

48. The directory separated out Chinese-owned laundries under the heading of "Chinese." *Trow Business Directory of New York City*, vol. 1 (New York, 1897), 573–577.

49. Business directories from this period list laundries throughout neighborhoods in the city. According to historian Olivier Zunz, the number of people employed in the clerical profession began to increase dramatically after 1870, growing from 1 percent of the working population to 3 percent by 1900. "But it was in the first decade of the century that the growth in the number of clerks reached its highest level for any ten-year period: 127 percent." Olivier Zunz, *Making America Corporate, 1870–1920* (Chicago: University of Chicago Press, 1992), 126–127.

50. See for example, "The 'Leprous Heathen,'" *NYT*, May 10, 1883; "A New Charge," *NYT*, May 13, 1883; and "The Asiatic Hordes," *NYT*, May 18, 1883. I am grateful to Timothy Gilfoyle for pointing out this reference.

51. "April 5—(Case No. 64,217)," NYSPCC, *Annual Report* (December 31, 1892): 30. The annual reports of the NYSPCC noted a number of cases involving charges of Chinese laundry workers luring young girls to their laundries. In "Feb. 25," NYSPCC, *Annual Report* (December 31, 1884): 39; "May 27—(Case No. 23,647)" and "July 9—(Case No. 24,357)" NYSPCC, *Annual Report* (December 31, 1886): 32, 35; "Feb. 14—(Case No. 33,599)," NYSPCC, *Annual*

Report (December 31, 1888): 24. It is unclear, however, how often the cases brought by the NYSPCC were warranted. On several occasions, cases mounted by the NYSPCC were dismissed in court. See for example, Case No. 51161-2 *People vs. Sam Sing*; and Case No. 121840 *People vs. Robert Kee*, New York County - District Attorney's Office-Record of Cases.

52. "July 9—(Case No. 24,357)" NYSPCC, *Annual Report* (December 31, 1886): 35.

53. April 5—(Case No. 64,217), NYSPCC, *Annual Report* (December 31, 1892): 30–31.

54. *People of the State of New York vs. Sing Lee*, April 28, 1898, Case No. 18219, New York Supreme Court Case Files, NYCMA.

55. Unfortunately, the surviving case file does not provide any clues as to why Ling Ong was acquitted. Case No. 22086 *The People vs. Ling Ong*, filed June 2, 1898; Case No. 22087 *The People vs. Ling Ong*, filed June 2, 1898, New York County - District Attorney's Office - Record of Cases.

56. Case No. 51161-2 *People vs. Sam Sing*, New York County - District Attorney's Office - Record of Cases.

57. Society for the Prevention of Cruelty to Children, "The Crime Wave," no date, 5, Box MGB-87, Mayors' Papers.

58. Case No. 97738 *People vs. Song Lee*, January 16, 1914, New York County - District Attorney's Office - Record of Cases.

59. Mary Heaton Vorse, "Mrs. McClanahan, the Chinese Laundry, and Beller," *McClure's Magazine* 30 (February 1908): 482.

60. *In a Chinese Laundry*, American Mutoscope Company, 1897; *New Chinese Laundry*, distributed by S. Lubin, 1903. The Chinese laundry was a familiar setting in this period's film depictions of Chinese people. Some other films include: *Chinese Rubbernecks*, American Mutoscope and Biograph Company, 1900; *Chinese Laundry*, distributed by S. Lubin, 1903; and *A Boomerang*, American Mutoscope and Biograph Company, 1903.

61. "Yellowface" is a particular genre of racial performances whereby white actors transformed themselves into "Oriental" characters through the use of makeup, costumes, gestures, or accented "pidgin" speech. Tchen, *New York before Chinatown*, 127–128; Robert Lee, *Orientals: Asian Americans in Popular Culture* (Philadelphia: Temple University Press, 1999), 43.

62. *The Heathen Chinese and the Sunday School Teachers*, American Mutoscope and Biograph Company, 1904.

63. *A Raid on a Chinese Opium Joint*, American Mutoscope and Biograph Company, 1900. *Secret Sin*, Jesse L. Laskey Feature Play Company, 1915.

64. I am cautioning against our too ready acceptance of Paul Siu's claim of social isolation for Chinese immigrant laborers in his Chicago study, *The Chinese Laundryman*. By looking at the New York example, it becomes clear that Chinese laborers and their workplaces were not so separated from the neighborhoods in which they were situated. It is possible of course that the lives of Chicago laundry workers studied by Siu had become more isolated by the 1920s and 1930s. But even in his book he notes several ways in which the workers participated in the neighborhood life around them, such as the activity of commercial prostitution.

65. Riis, 78.

66. Descriptions of secret tunnels have been a major trope in many nineteenth- and twentieth-century American writers' stories about Chinatown. For example, see Chester Bailey Fernald, *Chinatown Stories* (London: William Heinemann, 1900); Arnold Genthe and Will Irwin, *Old Chinatown* (New York: Mitchell Kennerley, 1913). Herbert Asbury, kept these stories alive in his descriptions of tong violence in New York City at the turn of the century (312). Secret tunnels also figured prominently in films supposedly set in Chinatown or involving Chinese characters. The climax to the film *The Secret Sin* (1915), about a white female opium addict, depicts a chase scene through subterranean tunnels in Chinatown that are accessed through a trap door in an opium den. In *The Mission of Mr. Foo* (1915), the film's Chinese character has an underground apartment located beneath a Chinese laundry. This theme is picked up once again in the musical *Thoroughly Modern Millie* (1967), where Chinese white slavers abduct single white women through the use of underground tunnels.

67. "Elsie Sigel, in Fear of Chinese Sweetheart, Sought to Banish Him," *World*, June 20, 1909.

68. "Girl Missionary Strangled, Body Packed in Trunk: The Victim Was a Granddaughter of General Sigel."

69. "Elsie Sigel, in Fear of Chinese Sweetheart."

70. This characterization of Leon Ling bears a remarkable resemblance to the character of Haka Arakau, the ruthless Japanese ivory merchant who attempts to ensnare a white socialite through usury in Cecile B. DeMille's 1915 classic, *The Cheat*. Given the notoriety of the Sigel murder, it's possible that DeMille used these descriptions of Leon Ling to model the character of the westernized Japanese merchant.

71. "Chinaman and Girl Caught," *BDE*, June, 28, 1909.

72. "New Clew to Slayer," *Washington Post*, June 29, 1909.

73. "Clue in Sigel Murder in Harlem Laundry," *NYT*, June 29, 1909.

74. *In re Opinion of the Justices*, 207 Mass. 601, 94 N.E. 558. See also *Chinese Daily Paper*, April 1, 1910 and May 5, 1910.

75. Yee Kin Wah also went by the name of Yee Foon. "Body Believed to be Leon Ling's," *Boston Globe*, July 2, 1909, morning edition.

76. *In re Opinion of the Justices*, 207 Mass. 601, 94 N.E. 558.

77. Ibid.; "Prohibited by Constitution," *Boston Globe*, March 23, 1911.

78. Nelson Harding, "Converted!" *BDE*, June 25, 1909.

79. "Women in Saloons" *Boston Globe*, April 29, 1910.

CHAPTER THREE
POLICING URBAN GIRLS' AND WOMEN'S MOBILITY AND DESIRES

1. "Take Girls from a Laundry"; "Three Young Girls Arrested in Laundry," *BDE*, June 21, 1909; "Three Chinamen Discharged," *BDE*, June 22, 1909.

2. "Three Chinamen Discharged."

3. Walter Campbell, *A Night in Chinatown*, 1905, 54. The play was also copyrighted in 1901 as "The Heart of Chinatown." All page numbers refer to the 1905 version.

4. Joanne Meyerowitz, *Women Adrift: Independent Wage Earners in Chicago, 1880–1930* (Chicago: The University of Chicago Press, 1988), 44–64; Barbara Hobson, *Uneasy Virtue: The Politics of Prostitution and the American Reform Tradition* (New York: Basic Books, 1987), 56–61, 70–76; and Regina Kunzel, *Fallen Women, Problem Girls: Unmarried Mothers and the Professionalization of Social Work, 1890–1945* (New Haven: Yale University Press, 1993), 19–25.

5. Michael Denning, *Mechanic Accents: Dime Novels and Working-Class Culture in America* (London: Verso, 1987), 190–193.

6. For a similar depiction, see "Celestial Fascinations" in Alfred Trumble, *The Heathen Chinee at Home and Abroad* (New York, 1882), 8–9. A sketch of a seduction scene shows a Chinese man holding the hand of a young white woman. He smiles lasciviously as her head is turned away and downward to reveal a more demure disposition. In the background an older white man looks upon the scene with great alarm. To emphasize his racial difference, the artist has darkened his face in contrast to the whiteness of the woman's face.

7. Campbell, *A Night in Chinatown*, 22.

8. Following Spain's surrender of the Philippines to the United States, another war occurred between Filipino forces against the U.S. occupying troops; the war ended in 1902. Stuart Creighton Miller, *Benevolent Assimilation: The American Conquest of the Philippines*, 1899-1903 (New Haven: Yale University Press, 1982); and Henry F. Graff, ed., *American Imperialism and the Philippine Insurrection* (Boston: Little, Brown, 1969).

9. Campbell, *A Night in Chinatown*, 19–20.

10. Images of white womanhood under assault were common in nineteenth-century popular culture. As African American historians have pointed out, images of sexually aggressive black men attacking white women were widespread and clearly not limited to depictions of Chinese men and white women. See for example, Jacquelyn Dowd Hall, "'The Mind that Burns in Each Body': Women, Rape, and Racial Violence," in *Desire: The Politics of Sexuality*, ed. by Ann Snitown, Christine Stansell, and Sharon Thompson (London: Virago Press Ltd., 1984), 339–347.

11. "Two Kid Slippers, Size 3 1/2: Fickle Fannie May Wear Them When She Weds Her Chinaman," *World*, July 29, 1891.

12. Meyerowitz, 61. See also Ruth Rosen, *The Lost Sisterhood: Prostitution in America, 1900–1918* (Baltimore: Johns Hopkins University Press, 1982), 46–50.

13. "Two Kid Slippers."

14. Norr, 4.

15. Ibid., 72.

16. Ibid., 57–58.

17. Ibid., 69.

18. Case No. 37839 *People vs. Chu Lem and Jennie Hall*, New York County - District Attorney's Office - Records of Cases.

19. Christine Stansell, *City of Women: Sex and Class in New York, 1789–1860* (Urbana: University of Illinois Press, 1987), 203.

20. David Nasaw, *Children of the City: At Work & At Play* (New York: Oxford University Press, 1985), 17–38.

21. Peiss, *Cheap Amusements*, 115–138. Erenberg, 21–22. Susan A. Glenn, *Daughters of the Shtetl: Life and Labor in the Immigrant Generation* (Ithaca: Cornell University Press, 1990), 159–166; Elizabeth Ewen, *Immigrant Women in the Land of Dollars: Life and Culture on the Lower East Side, 1890–1925* (New York: Monthly Review Press, 1985).

22. Emma Brace, ed., *The Life of Charles Loring Brace . . . Edited By His Daughter* (New York, 1894); Boyer, 94–112.

23. Nicola Beisel, *Imperiled Innocents: Anthony Comstock and Family Reproduction in Victorian America* (Princeton: Princeton University Press, 1997), 53–75.

24. Stansell, 215.

25. The three reformatories established by the Women's Prison Association included: the Hudson House of Refuge (1887), the Western House of Refuge at Albion (1893), and the New York State Reformatory for Women at Bedford Hills (1901). In 1903, the Hudson House of Refuge was reorganized to work with girls under the age of sixteen. Ruth Alexander, *The "Girl Problem": Female Sexual Delinquency in New York, 1900–1930* (Ithaca: Cornell University Press, 1995) 34–36.

26. Case No. 24271, Inmate Case Histories, 1824–1935, New York House of Refuge Papers, NYSA.

27. Case No. 24528, Inmate Case Histories, 1824–1935, New York House of Refuge Papers.

28. Rosen, 20. Mary E. Odem, *Delinquent Daughters: Protecting and Policing Adolescent Female Sexuality in the United States, 1885–1920* (Chapel Hill: The University of North Carolina Press, 1995), 1–4, 95–127.

29. Alexander, 20–21, 59.

30. The New York House of Refuge, operated by the Society for the Reformation of Juvenile Delinquents in the City of New York, was the first juvenile reformatory in the United States. Opened in 1825, the institution received male and female juveniles. By the turn of the century, the Female Division was later transferred to the new House of Refuge for Women in Bedford.

31. Leslie Woodcock Tentler, *Wage-Earning Women: Industrial Work and Family Life in the United States, 1900–1930* (New York: Oxford University Press, 1979), 62–69. Peiss, *Cheap Amusements*, 63. Alexander, 22–23. Nasaw, 104–114.

32. Case No. 24187, Inmate Case Histories, 1824–1935, New York House of Refuge Papers.

33. Case No. 24191, Inmate Case Histories, 1824–1935, New York House of Refuge Papers.

34. "Jan. 2—(Case No. 39,499)," NYSPCC, *Annual Report* (December 31, 1889): 15.

35. Report dated October 19, 1910. Hattie Rose Correspondence, Folder 89, Series IV "White Slavery," Harriet Wright (Burton) Laidlaw Papers.

36. "Oct. 1—(Case No. 44,797)," NYSPCC, *Annual Report* (December 31, 1889): 15. In the report published by the NYSPCC, Corman's age is listed as

seventeen. According to the marriage registry of the Five Points Mission, however, she stated that she was eighteen years old. Baptism and Marriage Registry
of the Five Points Mission, 366–367, Five Points Mission Collection, Methodist
Library, Drew University.

37. "Oct. 1—(Case No. 44,797)," 15.

38. Ibid.

39. "Dec. 12—(Case No. 45,933)," NYSPCC, *Annual Report* (December 31,
1889): 58.

40. Reports for May 15, 1910 and November 29, 1910, Hattie Rose
Correspondence, Folder 89, Series IV "White Slavery," Harriet Wright (Burton)
Laidlaw Papers.

41. During this period, women's factory wages did not provide a living wage
that would guarantee economic independence. Tentler, 14. David Katzman,
Seven Days a Week: Women and Domestic Service in Industrializing America
(New York: Oxford University Press, 1978), 226–232.

42. Domestic work actually offered little independence for the worker. Susan
Strasser, *Never Done: A History of American Housework* (New York: Pantheon
Books, 1982), 162–179; Katzman, 109–117.

43. Case Nos. 13380-3 *People vs. Lee Woh, Lilly Miller, Leni Loy, Charlie
Lee, Lee Sen*, District Attorney's Office-Records of Cases.

44. Report for February 25, 1910, Hattie Rose Correspondence, Folder 89,
Series IV "White Slavery," Harriet Wright (Burton) Laidlaw Papers.

45. Another version of this incident was also described in the reports of
Hattie Rose, a prison missionary who worked in the city's streets and hospitals.
The author of the report claimed to have seen the woman who induced Elbert to
come to Chinatown "bargaining with 4 Chinamen as to which one would buy
her. This took place at 16 Doyer Street. Just passed in time to hear some
one sobbing, went in, and demanded the girl." Reports dated February 29,
1910 and May 11, 1910, Hattie Rose Correspondence, Folder 89, Series IV
"White Slavery," Harriet Wright (Burton) Laidlaw Papers. *A New York Times*
article, however, stated that this was only Rose Livingston's version of the
story. Rather, the article stated that police detectives Brickley and Reilly of the
Elizabeth Street police station investigated the complaint and found no evidence
to support Livingston's story. Instead they found that Elsie Lee had taken Elbert
to a restaurant in Doyers Street and bought her supper, and then attempted
to help Elbert find the friend who had written her the letter. It was at that
point that they encountered Livingston and Elsie Lee decided to place Elbert
in her care. Livingston's more sensational version of the story suggests the
possibility that some claims of white slavery in Chinatown could have been
exaggerated by social reformers. "Save Young Girls from Chinatown," *NYT*,
September 8, 1909.

46. Historian Kathy Peiss's examination of the Committee of Fourteen's
investigators' reports points to how middle-class reformers' failure to interpret
correctly working-class women's styles of dress often led to mistaken assumptions about their morality. Peiss, *Cheap Amusements*, 98.

47. Report by Stockdale to G. W. Hooke, June 29, 1912, 3, Box, 28, Committee
of Fourteen Papers.

48. Peiss, *Cheap Amusements*, 6.

49. Ibid., 33.

50. According to historian Regina Kunzel, until the mid-1910s maternity homes working with unwed mothers "viewed marriage as the ultimate guarantor of redemption." Whenever possible, workers urged the unwed mother to secure marriage with the father of her child. When that was not possible, any marriage was encouraged. Some maternity home matrons even went as far as to urge women to change their names and gave out wedding rings before releasing their inmates from the maternity home. Kunzel, 32.

51. Case No. 1621 *People vs. Jung Hing*, Roll No. 208, October 28, 1912, 113, JJCA.

52. People against *George Tow impleaded with Louie Way and Yee Toy*, Case No. 598, Roll No. 96, October 1, 1906, 576, JJCA.

53. Ibid., 384–387.

54. Margaret Wing had been arrested for selling opium at her husband's store that sold cigars, slippers, teas, and other Chinese goods. Ibid., 396. Large numbers of Chinese storekeepers were arrested for selling opium because a few products carried in their stores contained opium and were not properly labeled. For some of these 1897 cases see Case No. 18,670 *People vs. Wong Wo Tie*; Case No. 18,671 *People vs. On Hing*; District Attorney's Office - Records of Cases. In these two cases, Wong Wo Tie, who was said to be in "groceries" and On Hing, who was in the "segars" business, were arrested for selling a "shell of opium paste containing more than two grains of opium to an ounce." Wong Wo Tie was acquitted while On Hing was found guilty and fined $30. The outcome of *People vs. On Hing* is described separately in the Supreme Court Case File. See Case no. 18671 *People vs. On Hing*, New York Supreme Court Case Files.

55. *People against George Tow impleaded with Louie Way and Yee Toy*, 574.

56. *People vs. Jung Hing*, 90–91, 132–139, 173–178, 599–606.

57. Ibid., 606.

58. Ibid., 10–11. The "streetwalker" was considered the lowest position of the prostitution hierarchy. See Rosen, 107.

59. *People vs. Jung Hing*, 5.

60. Ibid., 633.

61. Campbell, *Darkness and Daylight*, 558.

62. Case No. 1659 *People vs. Lee Dock, Eng Hing*, January 10, 1913, Roll No. 213, 416–418, 442–445, JJCA.

63. According to the baptism registry at the Church of the Transfiguration, Rosina Hup, the two-year-old daughter of John Hup and Maud Shoeffer, was baptized on March 8, 1912. Arcangela Casale served as the child's godmother. Baptism Registry, Church of the Transfiguration (March 1911 to April 1912): 90.

64. *People vs. Lee Dock, Eng Hing*, 517.

65. Chinatown Rescue Settlement and Recreation Room, *First Annual Report of the Society for Neighborhood Work Among Erring Girls* (1905): 3, 5–6; "Among the American Girls of Chinatown," *Charities* 12 (July 16, 1904): 739.

66. See Ruth Hutchinson Crocker, *Social Work and Social Order: The Settlement Movement in Two Industrial Cities, 1889–1930* (Urbana: University of Illinois Press, 1992).

67. Peiss, *Cheap Amusements*, 163–184.

68. *First Annual Report of the Society for Neighborhood Work Among Erring Girls*, 4.

69. Ibid.

70. *Sixth Annual Report of the Chinatown and Bowery Rescue Settlement for Girls* (1910): 4.

71. *First Annual Report of the Society for Neighborhood Work Among Erring Girls*, 3, 6. The figure of 1,469 visits noted most likely refers to multiple visits per visitor rather than individual visitors.

72. Ibid., 14–15.

73. *Second Annual Report of the Chinatown and Bowery Rescue Settlement for Girls* (1906): 7.

74. Kenneth L. Ames, *Death in the Dining Room & Other Tales of Victorian Culture* (Philadelphia: Temple University Press, 1992), 150–184. Ames's study of nineteenth-century material culture, focusing specifically on household furnishings, provides an interesting way to look at the popular attitudes and social aspirations of the Victorian middle class.

75. *Fifth Annual Report of the Chinatown and Bowery Rescue Settlement for Girls* (1908–1909): 6.

76. *Seventh Annual Report of the Chinatown and Bowery Rescue Settlement for Girls* (1911): 3, 8.

77. *First Annual Report of the Society for Neighborhood Work Among Erring Girls*, 6–7.

78. *Second Annual Report of the Chinatown and Bowery Rescue Settlement for Girls*, 9.

79. *First Annual Report of the Society for Neighborhood Work Among Erring Girls*, 3, 5.

80. Ibid., 10.

81. *Fifth Annual Report of the Chinatown and Bowery Rescue Settlement for Girls*, 8.

82. *Seventh Annual Report of the Chinatown and Bowery Rescue Settlement for Girls*, 2–3. All three examples came from this report.

83. Ibid., 4.

84. Report for January 22, 1910, Hattie Rose Correspondence, Folder 89, Series IV "White Slavery," Harriet Wright (Burton) Laidlaw Papers.

85. The negative publicity surrounding the Elsie Sigel murder may have partially contributed to the settlement house's temporary closing in 1909. According to the annual report for 1908–1909, the CBRSG had to suspend operation in spring 1909 "on account of lack of means to carry it on." The settlement house apparently remained closed during the height of the murder investigation, as it did not reopen until October 1909. *Fifth Annual Report of the Chinatown and Bowery Rescue Settlement for Girls*, 5.

86. Lawrence Burt, "Woman's Love of the Exotic," *Munsey's Magazine* 41 (September 9, 1909): 831–832.

CHAPTER FOUR
PLAYING THE "MISSIONARY GAME"

1. Editorial, "The Murder of Elsie Sigel," *Newark Star*, June 23, 1909.
2. "Elsie Sigel, in Fear of Chinese Sweetheart, Sought to Banish Him." Quotes are as they appear in the original newspaper article.
3. Editorial, "Let Men Teach the Chinese," *NYT*, June 21, 1909.
4. "Shocking and Dangerous," *NY Tribune*, June 22, 1909.
5. "'Extras' in Chinese Tell of Death of the American Girl," *World*, June 21, 1909.
6. See Carroll Smith-Rosenberg, "The New Woman as Androgyne: Social Disorder and Gender Crisis, 1870–1936," in *Disorderly Conduct: Visions of Gender in Victorian America*, ed. by Carroll Smith-Rosenberg (New York: Alfred Knopf, 1985).
7. "Blow to Mission Work," *NYH*, June 25, 1909. T. G. Hom, president of the Chinese Y.M.C.A., and Fung Y. Mow, of the Morning Star Mission, made similar statements to the press. T. G. Hom, Editorial "A Unique Crime," *NYT*, June 28, 1909; and "His Society Hides Leon," *NY Tribune*, June 22, 1909.
8. For more on the history of the U.S. foreign missionary movement in China, see John K. Fairbank, ed., *The Misionary Enterprise in China and America* (Cambridge: Harvard University Press, 1974).
9. The numbers of members and workers differ from one denomination to the next. By 1895, for example, the various Methodist women's missionary societies together had over 150,000 members. In 1910 membership grew to 267,000 and nearly doubled in 1920 to 500,000. Patricia Hill, *Their World Their Household: The American Woman's Foreign Mission Movement and Cultural Transformation, 1870–1920* (Ann Arbor: University of Michigan Press, 1985), 8–9, 48–49.
10. Ibid., 3–5. See also Barbara Welter, "She Hath Done What She Could: Protestant Women's Missionary Careers in Nineteenth-Century America," in *Women in American Religion*, ed. Janet Wilson James, (Philadelphia: University of Pennsylvania Press, 1976), 111–125.
11. Mary Ryan, "A Women's Awakening: Evangelical Religion and the Families of Utica, New York, 1800–1840," in ibid., 102.
12. Jane Hunter, *The Gospel of Gentility: American Women Missionaries in Turn-of-the-Century China* (New Haven: Yale University Press, 1984), 52–53.
13. Welter, in James ed., 120–125.
14. Gail Bederman, "'The Women Have Had Charge of the Church Work Long Enough': The Men and Religion Forward Movement of 1911–1912 and the Masculinization of Middle-Class Protestantism," in *A Mighty Baptism: Race, Gender, and the Creation of American Protestantism*, eds. Susan Juster and Lisa MacFarlane (Ithaca: Cornell University Press, 1996), 107–140. See also Lears, 97–139.
15. Peggy Pascoe, *Relations of Rescue: The Search for Female Moral Authority in the American West, 1874–1939* (New York: Oxford University Press, 1990), 13–17.

16. *"Report of the Superintendent for 1865," Five Points Monthly Record* 8 (April 1866): 205.

17. "The Chinese," *Five Points Monthly Record* 16 (November 1872): 111. William F. Bernard, *Forty Years at the Five Points* (New York, 1893), 41–45.

18. *Thirty-fifth Annual Report of the New York Ladies' Home Missionary Society* (1879): 9.

19. Ibid., 15.

20. *Annual Report of the New York Bible Society, October* 1879 (1879): 12.

21. *Annual Report of the New York Bible Society, October 1880* (1880): 12; *Annual Report of the New York Bible Society, September 1883* (1883): 16–17; *Annual Report of the New York Bible Society, September 1884* (1884): 12–13.

22. *Members of the Fifth Avenue Presbyterian Church for One Hundred Years*, Box "Letters of Transfer Mixed Names & Index," Fifth Avenue Presbyterian Church Collection, NYHS.

23. Huie Kin first arrived in San Francisco from Guangdong province in 1868. Kin, 24, 36, 46–50.

24. The report was dated May 10, 1886. *Records of the New York Presbytery*, No. 12, 1883–1888, 324. Presbyterian Historical Society Archives.

25. Kin, 55–58.

26. "Chinese School," *Year Book of the Presbyterian Church on University Place, New York 1888–9* (1889): 25.

27. *Records of the New York Presbytery*, No. 15, January 13, 1893 to December 10, 1894, 301–302. The report was dated May 7, 1894. Presbyterian Historical Society Archives.

28. *Records of the New York Presbytery*, No. 16, January 14, 1895 to December 28, 1896, 222–223, 228. Presbyterian Historical Society Archives. With the aid of their American friends and contributions from the Chinese community, the couple worked together to turn the mission into the First Chinese Presbyterian Church of New York City, which was duly incorporated on December 18, 1910. Kin, 77–82.

29. Chinese Sabbath School Association of New York, *Statistics of the Chinese Churches, Missions, Schools and Institutions of North America* (New York: 1892), 15. The list of states and territories include: California, Colorado, Connecticut, Delaware, District of Columbia, Florida, Georgia, Illinois, Indiana, Iowa, Kentucky, Louisiana, Maine, Maryland, Massachusetts, Minnesota, Missouri, Montana, Nebraska, New Hampshire, New Jersey, New York, Ohio, Oregon, Pennsylvania, Rhode Island, South Carolina, Texas, Utah, Virginia, Washington, and Wyoming. The eleven denominations include: Baptist, Presbyterian, Congregational, Methodist, Protestant Episcopal, Christian, Reformed Presbyterian, Lutheran, United Brethren, United Presbyterian, and Reformed Dutch.

30. Annie S. Dodge, *A Glimpse at Our Chinese Immigrants* (Boston: Woman's American Baptist Home Mission Society, 1904), 12.

31. "Miscellaneous Reports" *Year-book of the Fifth Avenue Presbyterian Church*, 1887 (1888): 31.

32. Similar sentiments were expressed by Baptist missionaries. "Home and foreign missions here blend into one. Christian converts have come from China

to America, and Christian Chinese, converted in America, have gone back home to preach the gospel and maintain churches." "The Chinese in America," *Home Mission Monthly* 26 (December 1904): 449.

33. "That Chinese Sunday-School," *World*, September 21, 1891.

34. *Eleventh Annual Report of the Baptist City Mission* (1881): 12.

35. "That Chinese Sunday-School." Some contemporary examples of the Chinese coolie as labor competition include: Hinton R. Helper, *The Land of Gold: Reality Versus Fiction* (Baltimore, 1855): Edwin R. Meade, *The Chinese Question* (New York: Arhur & Bonnell, 1877); George F. Seward, *Chinese Immigration, in Its Social and Economical Aspects* (New York: Charles Scribner's Sons, 1881); and Esther E. Baldwin, *Must the Chinese Go: An Examination of the Chinese Question*, Third Edition (New York: H. B. Elkins, 1890).

36. *Year-book of the Fifth Avenue Presbyterian Church 1887* (1889): 31. "Grateful Chinamen," *BDE*, February 10, 1892. *Thirteenth Annual Report of the Baptist City Mission* (1883): 7–8.

37. "Chinese Sunday School," *Work in New York: Being the 63rd Annual Report of the New York City Mission and Tract Society* (1890): 48.

38. "Chinese Hospital Association," *NYT*, October 27, 1891.

39. Helen F. Clark, "The Morning Star Mission," *Home Mission Monthly* 16 (November 1894): 450.

40. Chief Clerk of the Police Department of the City of New York to John Jeroloman, July 29, 1896. Box SWL-46, Mayors' Papers.

41. Frank F. Ellinwood to George Alexander, June 18, 1896, Box 1 "NYU, MacKenize College, Union College/Emmanuel Chapel," George Alexander Papers, NYHS.

42. E. Tipple to Mayor Hugh Grant, February 3, 1892, Box GHJ-39, Mayors' Papers.

43. Captain Donald Grant to William Murray, February 17, 1892, Box GHJ-41, Mayors' Papers.

44. E. J. Taylor to Assistant District Attorney Osborn, no date, Case No. 35344 *The People vs. Wah Sing*, New York County - District Attorney's Office - Record of Cases.

45. Letter to O. H. Platt from Moses G. White, M.D., February 21, 1887, Box 1, RG85, Chinese Exclusion Files Cases 3358d, NA.

46. Petition to Daniel Manning, Secretary of the Treasury, February 1, 1887, Box 1, RG85, Chinese Exclusion Files 3358d.

47. Letter from Secretary of the Treasury to M.C. White, March 1, 1887, Box 1, RG85, Chinese Exclusion Files 3358d. Note that this is a draft of a letter to be sent to M. C. White.

48. Mrs. L. S. Davis to U.S. Secretary of the Treasury, May 19, 1888, Box 1, RG85, Chinese Exclusion Files 3358d. Other examples of such letters can be found in the National Archives. Mrs. John Lucas, a Sunday school teacher, wrote similar letters for the Chinese laborers and merchants that attended her school in Philadelphia. Draft of Letter to Mrs. John Lucas, April 17, 1891; and Letter from Mrs. John Lucas to A. B. Nettleton, Acting Secretary of Treasury, April 8, 1891, Box 4, RG85, Chinese Exclusion Files 3358d.

49. Lee Num to James G. Blaine, March 17, 1891, Box 4, RG85, Chinese Exclusion Files 3358d.

50. Letter from George E. Rees to Secretary of Treasury, May 26, 1891, Box 4, RG85, Chinese Exclusion Files 3358d. This part of the sentence was underlined in the original letter.

51. In 1890 Dack Shing, a Chinese man who had lived in New York City since 1875, wrote to Secretary James G. Blaine stating that he wished to make a return visit to China, but wanted to be able to reenter the United States. He received the same reply, stating that he could return as long as he was not a laborer. Letter from Dack Shing to James G. Blaine, April 24, 1889; Letter from Assistant Secretary to Dack Shing, May 1, 1889, Box 4, RG85, Chinese Exclusion Files 3358d. In response to George Rees's request, the letter stated that it included "a copy of Departments Circular #44 of July, 1890, from which you will see that if the Chinese person you mention is a laborer, he is absolutely debarred from relanding in the United States should he leave this country for a visit to China." Letter from Assistant Secretary of the Treasury to George E. Rees, May 29, 1891, Box, 4, RG85, Chinese Exclusion Files 3358d.

52. *Year Book of St. Bartholomew's Church, New York City, 1889* (1889): 49.

53. *Year Book of St. Bartholomew's Church, New York City, 1890* (1890): 75–76.

54. John Thorne, "Report of the St. Bartholomew's Chinese Guild," *Year Book of St. Bartholomew's Church, New York City, 1889*, 52–53.

55. *Year Book of St. Bartholomew's Parish, New York City, 1913* (1913): 97.

56. Ibid.

57. Lucien Bianco, *Origins of the Chinese Revolution, 1915–1949* (Stanford: Stanford University Press, 1971), 27–44. For a discussion on the effects of China's modernization movement on San Francisco's Chinese immigrant community at the turn of the century, see also Yong Chen, *Chinese San Francisco, 1850–1943: A Trans-Pacific Community* (Stanford: Stanford University Press, 2000).

58. *Year Book of St. Bartholomew's Parish, New York City, 1913*, 98.

59. *Year Book of St. Bartholomew's Church, New York City, 1889*, 50.

60. *Year Book of St. Bartholomew's Church, New York City, 1891* (1891): 71.

61. *Year Book of St. Bartholomew's Church, New York City, 1895* (1895): 61–62.

62. *Year Book of St. Bartholomew's Parish, New York City, Christmas, 1900* (1900): 95.

63. *Year Book of St. Bartholomew's Church, New York City, 1889*, 51–52.

64. *Year Book of St. Bartholomew's Church, New York City, 1891*, 69–70.

65. *Year Book of St. Bartholomew's Church, New York City, 1890*, 81.

66. *Year Book of St. Bartholomew's Church, New York City, 1889*, 56.

67. Ibid., 54.

68. "Many Chinese Approve," *NYT*, April 12, 1893.

69. *Fong Yue Ting v. U.S.*, 149 U.S. 698 (1893), May 15, 1893.

70. "Ready for the Supreme Court," *NYT*, May 7, 1893.

71. *Year Book of St. Bartholomew's Church, New York City, 1895*, 73–77.

72. *Year Book of St. Bartholomew's Church, New York City, 1895*, 77.

73. *Year Book of St. Bartholomew's Parish, New York City, 1901* (1901): 97.

74. Guy Maine, "Report of the Chinese Guild," *Year Book of St. Bartholomew's Parish, 1909* (1909): 56.

75. Guy Maine, "Report of the Chinese Guild," *Year Book of St. Bartholomew's Parish, 1910* (1910): 97, 99. Over the Guild's twenty-year existence, its Sunday school and overall attendance figures declined steadily. Maine attributed this decline to the effect of the Chinese Exclusion Acts, especially the Geary Act in rounding up and deporting Chinese residents.

76. Martha Hodes, "Sex across the Color Line: White Women and Black Men in the Nineteenth Century American South," (Ph.D. diss., Princeton University, 1991), 148–149.

77. Martha Hodes, *White Women, Black Men: Illicit Sex in the Nineteenth-Century South* (New Haven: Yale University Press, 1997), 144–145. Historians have attributed the coining of the term "miscegenation" to this incident.

78. "Wedded to her Chinese Pupil," *NY Tribune*, November 27, 1890. See also "Married Her Chinese Pupil," *NYT*, November 27, 1890. The *Times* article refers to the same couple as Miss Rowley and Wong Sing.

79. Robert S. MacArthur, *History of Calvary Baptist Church New York* (New York, 1890), 84.

80. "Too Fond of the Heathen," *World*, September 20, 1891.

81. "Trouble over Chinaman," *NYT*, September 19, 1891.

82. "One Side Will Have to Go," *NYT*, September 20, 1891.

83. "Too Fond of the Heathen."

84. *Fourteenth Annual Report of the Baptist City Mission* (1884): 9.

85. *Thirteenth Annual Report of the Baptist City Mission* (1883): 8.

86. *Sixteenth Annual Report of the Baptist City Mission* (1886): 9.

87. Pascoe, *Relations of Rescue*, 59–60, 69, 102–103. Pascoe specifically identifies the women's deployment of an ideology of "female moral authority" in their work that allowed women to undertake the role of "moral maternalists reaching out to desperate, powerless women." Although Augusta Carto and most of Chinatown's missionaries worked with Chinese men and not women, I would argue that this same sense of maternalism was in operation. Instead of young women these missionaries sought to protect and nurture their Chinese male pupils, whom they saw as children.

88. Rev. V. A. Lewis, "Converting Chinamen," *BDE*, December 13, 1891.

89. Ibid.

90. *Tenth Annual Report of the Baptist City Mission* (New York: 1880): 11.

91. "Chinese Pupils," *BDE*, December 14, 1891.

92. "Chinese in the Sunday Schools," *BDE*, December 15, 1891.

93. Editorial, *BDE*, February 3, 1892.

94. "Hire a Hall," *BDE*, December 28, 1891. The letter was printed in its entirety. Though these men were clearly acculturated Christian converts, the article nonetheless referred to them as "Disciples of Confucius."

95. "Defending the Chinese," *NY Tribune*, December 30, 1891.

96. "Sharp Replies," *BDE*, December 30, 1891.

97. Ibid.

98. "Chinese in the Sunday Schools."

99. Rev. V. A. Lewis to the editor, "Converting Chinamen," *BDE*, December 13, 1891.

100. "Three New Chinese Converts, *NYT*, January 8, 1892.

101. See editorial, *BDE*, February 3, 1892.

102. At the time, J. M. Singleton was affiliated with the Congregational Church in Brooklyn and was an interpreter in the Custom House at New York. His Chinese name was Chu Mon Sing but he seemed to have used his Americanized name in official correspondence and in matters with the American public. Warner Van Norden, 33.

103. "The Chinese Again a Subject of Discussion by the Brooklyn Presbytery," *BDE*, February 2, 1892.

104. W. D. Gleason to the editor, *BDE*, May 15, 1892.

105. "Chinaman Lee Wore Diamonds and Captivated Miss Grace French," *BDE*, May 13, 1892.

106. "Eloped with a Chinaman," *NYT*, May 14, 1892.

107. "Mr. French to Punish the Chinaman," *NYT*, May 20, 1892.

108. "She Is Pleased with Her Lot as a Chinaman's Wife," *BDE*, May 20, 1892.

109. "Mrs. Lee Talks" *BDE*, May 21, 1892.

110. "Chinese Picnic," *BDE*, June 20, 1892.

111. Ibid.

112. "Quite Bland," *BDE*, June 21, 1892, 4.

113. "Wants Blood," *BDE*, May 23, 1892.

114. "The Story Is Denied: No Chinaman Married to a White Woman at Pearsalls," *BDE*, July 20, 1891.

115. "Chinese Sunday Schools,"*NYT*, January 29, 1892.

116. "Chinamen Are Downhearted," *NYT*, July 7, 1893.

117. *Work in New York: Being the 67th Annual Report of the New York City Mission and Tract Society* (1894): 72–73.

118. *Work in New York: Being the 69th Annual Report of the New York City Mission and Tract Society* (1896): 35.

119. Letter from Helen F. Clark to *Century* Magazine editor [no name given], July 28, 1893, Box 19 "Clark, Eliz. - Coates," *Century* Collection, NYPL. *Century* did publish her article. See Helen F. Clark, "The Chinese of New York Contrasted with their Foreign Neighbors," *Century*, November, 1896.

120. *Home Mission Echo* 10 (June 1894): 12.

121. "Folly of White Girls Christianizing Chinese," *The Oakland Times*, June 30, 1909.

122. "Miss Clark Assails Mission's System," *NYH*, June 21, 1909.

123. "Pernicious System Slew Elsie Sigel, Says Miss Clark," *NYH*, June 27, 1909, third section.

124. Dodge, 12.

125. *Home Mission Echo* 10 (June 1894): cover.

126. Frances M. Schuyler, *Glimpses of Work with Chinese Women and Children in the United States* (Chicago: Woman's American Baptist Home Mission Society, 1909), 18–19.

127. *The Heathen Chinese and the Sunday School Teachers*, American Mutoscope and Biograph Company, 1904. See chapter 2 for a lengthy discussion of the film.

128. "A Plain Word About a Shocking Case," *BDE*, June 21, 1909.

CHAPTER FIVE
CHINESE AMERICAN INTERRACIAL COUPLES AND FAMILIES IN NEW YORK CITY

1. "White Wife for Leong Ti," *NYT*, July 3, 1909.
2. "Japanese Weds a Brooklyn Girl," *NYH*, July 11, 1909.
3. "Arrest Friend of Miss Sigel."
4. "Police Find 35 Love Letters from 'Elsie' in Suspect's Trunk."
5. Lee Chew, "The Life Story of a Chinaman," in Holt.
6. Historian John Kuo Wei Tchen, for example, has examined the history of New York City's port district from 1820 to 1870 and noted that about 25 percent of the resident Chinese seamen, peddlers, and cigar makers were married to women of Irish descent. John Kuo Wei Tchen, "New York Chinese: The Nineteenth-Century Pre-Chinatown Settlement," in *Chinese America: History and Perspectives* (San Francisco: Chinese Historical Society of America, 1990), 176–177. In his study of the 1903 Boston Chinatown raid, historian K. Scott Wong, also located a number of mixed-race couples in that community. K. Scott Wong, "'The Eagle Seeks a Helpless Quarry': Chinatown, the Police, and the Press. The 1903 Boston Chinatown Raid Revisited," *Amerasia Journal* 22 (1996): 89–92. Increasingly, Asian American historians have begun to document the existence of interracial couples and families in nineteenth-century American cities in the Northeast. Some studies of nineteenth- and twentieth-century interracial sexual relations in the South have also been published. See Lucy Cohen; Loewen; and Robert Seto Quan, *Lotus among the Magnolias: The Mississippi Chinese* (Jackson: University of Mississippi Press, 1982).
7. Riis, 81.
8. Ibid., 76.
9. For discussions of West Coast depictions of Chinese prostitutes see Shah, 78–88. See also George Anthony Peffer, "Forbidden Families: Emigration Experiences of Chinese Women under the Page Law, 1875–1882," *Journal of American Ethnic History* (Fall 1986): 28–46; Benson Tong, *Unsubmissive Women: Chinese Prostitutes in Nineteenth-Century San Francisco* (Norman: University of Oklahoma Press, 1994). I am not arguing that Chinese female prostitutes were absent on the East Coast, but I have found little in the court records to construct this history. Some tantalizing clues do appear, such as a 1905 case involving May May Soon, also known as May Moy Man Soon, who was arrested in Massachusetts on separate occasions on the charges of "fornication" and "vagrancy." Soon was arrested a third time in New York City's Chinatown, where she stabbed Louis Yuen after he had refused to provide her with cigarettes. Although it is unclear from the case records whether or not Soon had worked as a prostitute, her history suggests at the very least that not all Chinese women residing in Chinatown were the secluded merchant wives contemporary accounts have suggested. Case No. 52460 *People vs. May May Soon*, New York County - District Attorney's Office - Records of Cases.
10. Helen F. Campbell, 558.
11. Beck, 38.

12. The recognition of marriages performed under traditional Chinese custom also had legal ramifications in terms of merchants' wives seeking to immigrate to the United States. Sucheng Chan, "The Exclusion of Chinese Women, 1870–1943," in *Entry Denied*, ed. Sucheng Chan, 115–116. In her study of missionary activities in turn-of-the-century San Francisco, Peggy Pascoe noted that "Mission workers, who were horrified by the deceptions and conditioned by racial and cultural bias to believe that Chinese marriages weren't really marriages at all, did help many [Chinese] women secure annulments or divorces. In at least a handful of these cases, missionaries arranged for new husbands as well." Peggy Pascoe, "Gender Systems in Conflict: The Marriages of Mission-educated Chinese American Women, 1874–1939," *Journal of Social History* 22 (Summer 1989): 641.

13. Ryan, 157–162. Barbara Finkelstein, "Casting Networks of Good Influence: The Recreation of Childhood in the United States, 1790–1970," in *American Childhood: A Research Guide and Historical Handbook*, eds. Joseph M. Hawes and N. Ray Hiner (Westport, CT: Greenwood Press, 1985), 111–152.

14. Karin Calvert, *Children in the House: The Material Culture of Early Childhood: 1600–1900* (Boston: Northeastern University Press, 1992), 104–106.

15. "Our Chinese Colony," *Harper's Weekly* 34 (November 22, 1890): 910.

16. Beck, 37–38.

17. Ibid., 42.

18. "June 12—(Case No. 90,704)," NYSPCC, *Annual Report* 21 (December 31, 1895): 33–34. The report states the names of the parents as "Annie Glueckner, a white woman" and "Sing Lee, a Chinese laundryman, of No. 11 Pell Street."

19. For an example of these stories by Chinatown missionaries, see Helen F. Clark, *The Lady of the Lily Feet* (Philadelphia, 1900). For an example of these stories written by missionaries in China see Rev. J. A. Davis, *The Chinese Slave-Girl: A Story of Woman's Life in China* (Philadelphia 1880); Adele M. Fielde, *Chinese Nights' Entertainment* (New York, 1893) and *A Corner of Cathay* (New York, 1894).

20. Special Committee of the Board of Supervisors, "Chinatown: Startling Report of the Hideous and Disgusting Features of Chinatown," *San Francisco Daily Report*, July 21, 1885, supplement.

21. Hattie E. Genung, "Evenings with Missions," *The Chinese in America*, No. 5 (Boston, 1894), 5.

22. Harry B. Wilson, "Children of Chinatown," *NYT*, November 22, 1896, supplement.

23. For example in 1899, three-year-old Oliver Brush Finds, the son of John Finds or Jung Fot and Maggie Florence, traveled to China with his mother and two brothers. Unfortunately, Maggie Florence died a few years later while they were still abroad in Mow Bow Village. Oliver Brush Finds, Box 245, Folder 47/55 Oliver Brush Finds, RG 85, Chinese Exclusion Files, NA-NY. For other examples where non-Chinese wives accompanied their husbands or families on return visits to China, see the following case files in RG 85, Chinese Exclusion Files, NA-NY: Box 6, Folder 6/2111 Wong Fung; Box 228, Folder 34/48 Mrs. Huie Kin; Box 230, Folder 4/171 Jing Hong Quon; Box 345, Folder 105/477

Thomas and James Harper Hill; and Box 351, Folder 105/860 Josephine Gee Leong.

24. Report from Amos P. Wilder, American Consul General in Hong Kong to Assistant Secretary of State, Washington, D.C., January 25, 1908 in RG 59, M862, Roll 803, Case No. 12205, NA-CP.

25. Letter from Amos P. Wilder, American Consul General, Hong Kong, to Assistant Secretary of State, Washington, D.C., July 20, 1908 in RG 59, Roll 932, Case No. 15302, NA.

26. Peffer, *If They Don't Bring Their Women Here*, 28–46. Chan, "The Exclusion of Chinese Women," 94–146. California State Legislature, "Chinese Immigration: Its Social, Moral and Political Effect," *Report to the California State Senate of Its Special Committee on Chinese Immigration* (Sacramento, California, 1878), 154.

27. The administration of the Chinese Exclusion Acts was originally housed in the Department of Treasury and its Customs Houses. In 1903 the Bureau of Immigration was transferred from the Treasury Department to the new Department of Commerce and Labor. Three years later, the Bureau was also placed in charge of naturalization and its name changed to the Bureau of Immigration and Naturalization.

28. Letter from Assistant Secretary of the Treasury to Lai Moon, alias John Lee, February 1, 1886; Letter from William A. Brown to Daniel Manning, Secretary of the Treasury, March 23, 1886. Both letters are housed in Box 1, RG 85, Chinese Exclusion Files 3358d.

29. "Chinaman Adopts a Boy," *NYT*, December 19, 1901.

30. The absence of anti-miscegenation laws does not suggest that such relationships escaped the attention of legislators. In 1913 Manhattan Democrat James J. Walker made the first attempt to introduce a bill into the state legislature to prohibit marriage between whites and blacks. The bill, however, did not move beyond the judiciary committee and never came to a vote. Attempts to pass such laws also occurred in the Midwest. In 1889, Illinois state senate considered passing laws that forbade marriages between blacks and whites as well as Chinese and whites. Sixteen years later, the House deliberated upon a bill that would invalidate the marriage between a white and a person with more than one-eighth African, Chinese, or Japanese ancestry. The Michigan House in 1911 considered a similar bill, but the bill was later defeated in the senate. The 1913 marriage of a Chinese restaurant owner to a white woman in Detroit, further spurred that state's legislators to reconsider enacting such a bill. In 1905, shortly after the arrival of Filipino students at the University of Indiana, the state senate also reviewed a bill prohibiting white-Filipino marriages. In 1913 Ohio also considered a bill banning marriage of whites to "negroes, mulattoes, or with Chinamen." Though these Midwestern states decided against passing these bills into law, their deliberations suggest that organized and vocal public opposition to these marriages clearly existed. David H. Fowler, *Northern Attitudes Towards Interracial Marriage: Legislation and Public Opinion in the Middle Atlantic and the States of the Old Northwest, 1780–1930* (New York: Garland Publishing, Inc., 1987), 287–305.

31. See chapter 1.

32. Foo, 308.

33. It is difficult to say with certainty how many Chinese were counted by census takers as residing in the Sixth Ward at this time because two different enumerations were done showing some names to be repeated in both counts. If one were to just use the number provided in the second enumeration, it would clearly be around 35. 1870 Federal Census, New York City (Second Enumeration), Sixth Ward.

34. The following census information comes from the 1870 Federal Census, New York City (first enumeration), Sixth Ward, fifth election district.

35. The following census information comes from the 1880 Federal Census, New York City, Enumeration District 42.

36. The Department of the Interior was aware of potential enumeration problems and took steps to address them, because an accurate count of the Chinese population was necessary in order to assess the effectiveness of the administration of the Chinese Exclusion Acts. In 1880 and 1890, the Department of the Interior requested the Chinese Consul-General at San Francisco to distribute a proclamation written in Chinese directing all Chinese in the United States to comply with the census. Such a proclamation was probably also issued to the Chinese community of New York. Letter from A. F. Childs, Acting Superintendent of Census, The Secretary of the Interior to Secretary of State, April 23, 1890, Box 1, RG 48, Entry 286, NA-CP.

37. "Celebrating Chinese New Year Visiting and Indulging in Luxuries— Waiting to Name a Baby," *NY Tribune*, February 15, 1885.

38. "A Chinese Romance," *NYT*, December 9, 1890.

39. The husbands' fears were not unfounded. During the 1890s several cases involving the immigration of Chinese wives of merchants called into question the validity of Chinese marriage customs. For example, see *In re Lum Lin Ying*, 59 Federal Reporter 682 (D. Ore. 1894).

40. The marriage registry of the Five Points Mission recorded these two marriages, but spelled the names differently. The record shows that on December 3, 1890, Chin Jen married Chong Fong and Chin Jian married Lin Fong. From my examination of the mission's available marriage records, these were the first two weddings between a Chinese bride and groom to be recorded in the mission's registry. Baptism and Marriage Registry of the Five Points Mission, 368–369, Five Points Mission Collection, Methodist Library, Drew University.

41. Because of a fire the 1890 census records for the New York City Chinatown area were destroyed. Thus I am relying on the marriage and baptism records of the Five Points Mission to show that weddings of interracial couples continued to occur during this period. Baptism and Marriage Register of the Five Points Mission, Five Points Mission Collection.

42. Ibid., 368–369. Both weddings are recorded on this page.

43. The following census information comes from the 1900 Federal Census, New York City, Enumeration District 34.

44. I do not want to overemphasize this point for these women could have been third generation Irish American. Unfortunately, the census only lists the individual's and parents' birthplaces.

45. For Adaline Archung, see 336–337; L. Archung, see 346–347; Edward Low Chung, see 348–349, Baptism and Marriage Register of the Five Points Mission, Five Points Mission Collection.

46. The *In re Ah Quan* decision in 1884 and the *Cheong Ah Moy v. United States* decision in 1885 established this protocol in dealing with the wives of Chinese laborers. Sucheng Chan, "The Exclusion of Chinese Women," in *Entry Denied*, 94–146.

47. Interrogation transcript of Harry Fang, or Fong Hong, February 6, 1917, Box 253, Folder 56/15 Harry Fong, RG 85, Chinese Exclusion Files, NA-NY. Harry Fang's last name is spelled "Fang" and "Fong" throughout the transcript.

48. Letter from H. D. Baker, American Consul in Trinidad, B.W.I. to the Secretary of State, Washington, October 10, 1921, Box 13, Folder 6/529 Olga Claudine Chin & Carlton Chin, RG 85, Chinese Exclusion Files, NA-NY.

49. Compiled by author from 1910 Federal Census, New York City, Supervisor's District no. 1.

50. Three baptisms performed at the Church of the Transfiguration were found from the 1860s. See Baptism registry, Church of the Transfiguration (1861–1868): 123; and Baptism registry, Church of the Transfiguration (1861–1868): 193 and 285.

51. For a history of the Church of the Transfiguration, see *Transfiguration Church: A Church of Immigrants, 1827–1977* (New York: Park Publishing Company, 1977).

52. Ibid., 20–21. In 1874 several Chinese were baptized: thirty-year-old Peter Fang, thirty-six-year-old William Yong, thirty-seven-year-old John Le Chong, and thirty-seven-year-old John Aging. Baptism registry, Church of the Transfiguration (February 1868 to November 1881): 339, 345, 348.

53. See the following volumes of the Marriage Registry of the Church of the Transfiguration: June 1861–1881, May 1881–May 1895, 1895–1905, and 1905–1914. Not until the convening of Vatican II (1962–1965) and the resulting *Decree of Ecumenism* (1966) did the Church begin to reach out to other faiths and liberalize its views on marriage between Catholics and non-Catholics. *The HarperCollins Encyclopedia of Catholicism* (San Francisco: Harper SanFrancisco, 1989), 820; "Ritual for the Celebration of Marriage," *Catholic Almanac*, 1970, 318–319; Egon Mayer, *Love & Tradition: Marriage between Jews and Christians* (New York: Plenum Press, 1985), 49–50.

54. See the following volumes of the Marriage Registry of the Church of the Transfiguration: 1861–1868, February 1868–November 1881, November 1881–April 1887 (books 1 and 2), April 17, 1887–October 25, 1888, October 1888–November 1890, November 1890–February 1894, February 18, 1894–January 18, 1900, January 18, 1900–March 27, 1904, March 1904–June 30, 1904, March 21, 1905–December 31, 1906, January 1906–February 1908, February 1908–April 1908, April 19, 1908–April 29, 1909, April 24, 1909–April 3, 1910, April 10, 1910–March 23, 1911.

55. Marriage Registry, Church of the Transfiguration (1895–1905): 211; 1910 Federal Census, New York City, Enumeration District 48.

56. Although there were few Chinese-Italian marriages recorded, the Youngs were not alone. Down the street at 22 Mott Street Ching Hung resided with his wife Lilla. In their building a number of Chinese and working-class Italian American families also resided. Bertulla Gauzza, a street cleaner, who lived with his wife Maria and four children next door at 20 Mott Street, also became the

godparents of the Ching's daughter, Marian. 1910 Federal Census, New York City, Enumeration District 46; Marriage Registry, Church of the Transfiguration (January 18, 1900–March 27, 1904): 73.

57. Robert Orsi, *The Madonna of 115th Street: Faith and Community in Italian Harlem, 1880–1950* (New Haven: Yale University Press, 1985), xx, 114–149.

58. Samuel L. Bailey, *Immigrants in the Lands of Promise: Italians in Buenos Aires and New York City, 1870–1914* (Ithaca: Cornell University Press, 1999), 150–152.

59. Baptism and Marriage Register of the Five Points Mission, 344–347, Five Points Mission Collection.

60. Baptism Registry, Church of the Transfiguration (November 1881–April 1887), book two, 296.

61. Baptism Registry, Church of the Transfiguration (April 17, 1887–October 25, 1888): 15, 16, 65, 316.

62. Given the frequent use of the name "John" for Chinese men during this period, it's possible that John Chin Tin is actually either James or Charles Chin Tin. Thus, there would only be two Chin Tin families listed in the two combined registries as opposed to three. Without more information it would be difficult to rule out this possibility completely. However, it is certain that Charles and James Chin Tin were indeed two different people, since the registries list different last names for their wives. Charles Chin Tin was married to Elizabeth Smith and James Chin Tin was married to Elizabeth Holden.

63. The information in this paragraph comes from the 1900 Federal Census, New York City, Enumeration Districts 34 and 37. The addresses of buildings where at least four Chinese families resided included: 13 Mott Street with four families, 21 Mott Street with six families, 32 Mott Street with eight families and 43 Mott Street with twelve families. The addresses of buildings where at least four interracial families resided included: 11 Mott Street with four families, 15 Mott Street with four families, 15 1/2 Mott Street with nine families, 19 Doyers Street with four families, 9 Pell Street with eleven families, 11 Pell Street with nine families and 12–14 Pell Street with ten families.

64. 1900 Federal Census, New York City, Enumeration District 37.

65. 1870 Federal Census, New York City (Second Enumeration), Ward 6. John's surname was listed as "Aloon" in the 1870 census.

66. Information regarding Josephine Toy's family background comes from an interview conducted with her sister, Mary Lee, by the Immigration and Naturalization Service in 1938. During her interview Mary Lee presented her baptismal certificate, stating that she was born on July 28, 1881 and baptized the following month at the Church of St. Peter, a Roman Catholic Church located on Barclay Street in New York City. Similar to her sister, Josephine was most likely also a baptized Catholic. Interrogation transcript with Mary Lee, Box 527, Folder 170/459 Raymond Axson Lee, RG 85, Chinese Exclusion Files, NA-NY.

67. The 1900 federal census lists the head of the Mon Ki family as a twenty-eight-year-old widow named "Mon Ki." The name, "Cynthia," does not appear as one of the family members listed as residing at the address. She is most likely Cynthia Mon Ki. According to the interview transcript of John A. Looan or Lum, his eldest daughter was named Cynthia. Interrogation transcript of

John A. Looan, December 31, 1910, Box 156, Folder 24/698, RG 85, Chinese Exclusion Files, NA-NY.

68. According to the 1900 census, the Mon Ki children—Sarah, Kung Poi, and Ellen, were ten, five, and three respectively; the Toy children—Mammie, Frances, and Fred—were eight, six, and one respectively; and the Bock children—Josephine, Lawrence, and Adolpho were fourteen, six, and two respectively.

69. A daughter, Anna, was also born on October 27, 1885 and later baptized at the Five Points Mission. Baptist and Marriage Register of the Five Points Mission, 348–349, Five Points Mission Collection.

70. Interrogation transcript of Henry Wing, March 5, 1908, 1–2, Box 198, Folder 27/279 Henry Wing, RG 85, Chinese Exclusion Files, NA-NY.

71. The marriage took place on February 2, 1916. Marriage Registry, Church of the Transfiguration (1913–1916): 485.

72. The following information comes from the 1910 Federal Census, New York City, Enumeration District 46.

73. Letter from W. W. Sibray, Assistant Commissioner General to Mrs. J. C. Ing, March 22, 1923; Interrogation transcript with Julia C. Ing, August 21, 1924; Interrogation transcript with Arthur Gun Ing, May 31, 1932. The above documents are in Box 292, Folder 61/170 Arthur Gun Ing, RG 85, Chinese Exclusion Files, NA-NY.

74. Hsu, 90–123.

75. 1900 Federal Census, New York City, Enumeration District 34.

76. Interrogation transcript with Wing Kwong Lang, December 16, 1912, Box 320, Folder 75/375 Wing Kwong Lang, RG 85, Chinese Exclusion Files, NA-NY.

77. Wing Kwong Lang served in the U.S. Navy during World War I. He continued to live in Chinatown at 32 Mott Street and found work as a postal clerk. He did not have an opportunity to visit his family again until 1931. Interrogation transcript with Wing Kwong Lang, March 14, 1931, Box 320, Folder 75/375 Wing Kwong Lang, RG 85, Chinese Exclusion Files, NA-NY.

78. Harry Joe and Bertha Koster were married on December 27, 1920. He was twenty-eight and she was twenty-five. Letter from Marks Rosen to Inspector in Charge, Chinese Division, October 17, 1935; Interrogation transcript with Joe Fook, September 4, 1935; Interrogation transcript with Harry Joe, September 4, 1935; Interrogation transcript with Caroline Lee Wah, September 11, 1935, Box 493, Folder 168/618 Joe Fook, RG 85, Chinese Exclusion Files, NA-NY.

79. Letter from Mabel Tie to Rose Livingston, December 19, 1912; Letter from Mrs. Sarah T. Ring to Rose Livingston, January 1, 1913, Hattie Rose Correspondence, Folder 92. Correspondences, July–Dec, 1912, Series IV. White Slavery, Harriet Wright (Burton) Laidlaw Papers.

80. Interrogation with Gurli Dohn Kirk Beardsley, September 15, 1930; Interrogation transcript with Clara Boyer, September 15, 1930; Letter from Mrs. S. R. Beardsley to Hopewell Society of Brooklyn, September 29, 1930, Box 403, Folder 132/551 Elliot Chan Kirk, RG 85, Chinese Exclusion Files, NA-NY.

81. Interrogation transcript of Margaret Hanratty, July 12, 1923; Interrogation transcript of Lee Du, July 12, 1923, Box 253, Folder 56/7 Tom Lee, RG 85, Chinese Exclusion Files, NA-NY.

82. Interrogation transcript of Margaret Hanratty, July 12, 1923.

83. Letter from P. A. Donhaue to Inspector in Charge, New York, July 23, 1923, Box 253, Folder 56/7 Tom Lee, RG 85, Chinese Exclusion Files, NA-NY.

84. Letter from Ernest K. Coulter to A. W. Brough, August 9, 1923, Box 253, Folder 56/7 Tom Lee, RG 85, Chinese Exclusion Files, NA-NY.

85. Charles Sing's birth and arrival dates are recorded in his naturalization papers from the Commonwealth of Massachusetts. I thank Edward Rhoads for sharing this piece of information on Charles Sing and his research on the Chinese shoemakers in North Adams. The remaining biographical information on Charles Sing comes from the transcript of his interrogation by U.S. immigration authorities in 1902. Interrogation transcript of Charles T. Sing, ca. 1902, Box 55, Folder 12/499 George D. Sing, RG 85, Chinese Exclusion Files, NA-NY.

86. Faced with erratic and costly work stoppages, Sampson contracted the Chinese laborers to discipline the striking white laborers who were predominantly Irish American and members of the Knights of Crispin. The name of Charles Sing appears as the witness for the contract between C. T. Sampson and Ah Young and Ah Yan of San Francisco dated May 26, 1870. "Chinese Contracts and Wages," *Adams Transcript*, August 18, 1870. For more on the history of Chinese laborers in North Adams, see Frederick Rudolph, "Chinamen in Yankeedom: Anti-Unionism in Massachusetts in 1870," *American Historical Review* 53 (October 1947): 1–29; Andrew Gyory, *Closing the Gate: Race, Politics, and the Chinese Exclusion Act* (Chapel Hill: University of North Carolina Press, 1998).

87. "The Treatment of the Chinese," *Adams Transcript*, March 27, 1873.

88. "The Celestials in Sunday-School," *New York Scribner's* (March 1871): 556–559.

89. For examples on New Year's celebrations, see *Adams Transcript*, February 19, 1874; February 12, 1880.

90. *Adams Transcript*, August 29, 1872; February 13, 1873; February 20, 1873; February 6, 1879. See also *Adams Transcript*, October 4, 1877.

91. An article in the *Adams Transcript* estimated that most of the Chinese workers found the work to be profitable. "Departure of the Chinese," *Adams Transcript*, September 16, 1880.

92. It is difficult to ascertain exactly which position Charles Sing held in the factory. See "Death of John Thomas," *Adams Transcript*, February 6, 1879. In another article, he is named foreman while in others he is called business agent. If he was indeed the foreman, he would have earned more than his fellow workers. According to the terms of the 1870 contract, Sing would have earned "$60 per month for overseeing 75 men." In addition, the foreman was to receive 50¢ per additional man hired past seventy-five. In contrast, workmen and cooks received $23 per month for the first year and $26 per month for the second and third years. *Adams Transcript*, August 18, 1870.

93. In one incident, workers blamed Sing for Sampson's decision to discharge a small group of workers who had engaged in strikes and work stoppages in the past. *Adams Transcript*, October 30, 1873.

94. Even after he moved away from North Adams, his activities continued to be reported in the local paper. *Adams Transcript*, June 14, 1883.

95. Years later, his son, George, explained to immigration officials that Charles Sing never expressed a desire to return to China: "He does not like China either. He is an American citizen all his life nearly." Interrogation transcript of George Sing, February 7, 1902, in George T. Sing case file, RG 85, NA-SB.

96. *Adams Transcript*, December 19, 1878. Although Chinese were barred from becoming citizens by the "free, white persons" qualification established by the 1790 uniform rule of naturalization, a small number of Chinese managed to obtain citizenship. In 1878, fifteen Chinese were granted citizenship in New York. Chan, *Asian Americans*, 47. It is unclear, however, whether or not Charles Sing retained his citizenship privileges following the passage of the Chinese Exclusion Acts.

97. *Adams Transcript*, October 26, 1876. Sing also regularly advertised in *Adams Transcript*. For example, see *Adams Transcript*, January 17, 1878.

98. *Adams Transcript*, November 23, 1876. The listing of his store in the 1879–1880 *Directory of North Adams* suggests that Sing continued to promote his store as an American dry goods store and compete directly with the other general stores in town, stating that his stock included "choice family groceries, provisions, teas, coffees, etc. at the lowest prices in town." *Directory of North Adams, 1879–1880* (Albany, 1879), 86.

99. "Births," *Adams Transcript*, May 22, 1879.

100. *Adams Transcript*, June 19, 1879. This one month old birthday celebration has long been an important cultural practice for Chinese families from Guangdong Province. A translation of a 1936 account of such an occasion celebrated in Pu Ning County describes the event in this manner: "A family in better circumstances gives a party when the baby completes one month of life. A cook is hired to prepare an elaborate dinner for friends and neighbors called 'the feast after one full month.'" "Birth Customs," in *Chinese Civilization and Society: A Sourcebook*, ed. Patricia Buckley Ebrey (New York: The Free Press, 1981), 303.

101. *Directory of North Adams, 1881–1882* (Albany, 1881): 27. The new proprietor, A. Wilburn, may have been a relation of his wife, Ida Wilburn.

102. According to the *Adams Transcript*, the Chinese workers in North Adams did not stay beyond 1880. "Departure of the Chinese," *Adams Transcript*, September 16, 1880. A few years later, another group of Chinese workers began to settle in the area—hand laundry workers. In 1885, Quong Wing Wah and Wing Wong Wah opened the town's first Chinese hand laundry at 31 Eagle Street. *North Adams General Directory, 1885–1886* (Albany, 1885), 150.

103. Affidavit of Marvin Oakley, September 29, 1897, in George T. Sing case file, RG 85, NA-SB.

104. Aside from Herbert and George, the names of the other three surviving children were Robert, Rosina, and Lulu.

105. Yung, 126.

106. *United States vs. Wong Kim Ark* established that a child of Chinese parentage born in the United States is an American citizen. Nonetheless this did not mean that American-born Chinese enjoyed the same privileges as native-born whites. In the case of traveling abroad, all U.S.-born Chinese still had to apply for

a special citizen's return certificate, Form 430, to allow for their reentry into the United States. Certificates were granted only after satisfactory investigation and interrogation of the applicant, family members, and white witnesses. The failure to apply for the proper return certificate could result in the denial for reentry. See for example, John Hayes, Jr. case file in Box 90, Folder 14/888 John Hayes, Jr. (Wong), RG 85, Chinese Exclusion Files, NA-NY. On the *Wong Kim Ark* case, see Charles J. McClain and Laurene Wu McClain, "The Chinese Contribution to the Development of American Law," in *Entry Denied*, ed. Sucheng Chan, 20–21.

107. Letter from Alfred Anderson, Chinese Inspector, to The Collector Customs, N.Y., February 18, 1902; Affidavit of Sylvester Johnson, September 24, 1897; Affidavit of Marvin Oakley, September 29, 1897; George T. Sing case file, RG 85, NA-SB.

108. The following biographical information about George D. Sing is from the interrogation transcript of George D. Sing, April 11, 1923, Box 55, Folder 12/499 George D. Sing, RG 85, Chinese Exclusion Files, NA-NY. George Sing's experience was certainly not unique, as similar cases of American-born Chinese being raised in the United States could be found. In 1899 Oliver Brush Finds traveled with his mother, Maggie Florence, and two brothers to China. Because Oliver did not return to the United States until he was seventeen years old, he became more fluent in Chinese than English. At the age of twenty, he returned to China for a second time and married Chew She. He stayed for about three years, long enough to see his wife give birth to a daughter, Fung Wah, and a son, George Jung. He didn't return to China again until 1930. Box 245, Folder 47/55 Oliver Brush Finds, RG 85, Chinese Exclusion Files, NA-NY.

109. Arnold Irving Chong also went by the name of Harry Irving Hong. His Chinese names were Chong Oy Wing and Chong Gow Kow. Interrogation transcript with Arnold Irving Chong, September 3, 1912; Affidavit of Chung Hong, April 26, 1902, Box 318, Folder 75/162 Arnold Irving Chong, RG 85, Chinese Exclusion Files, NA-NY. Baptism Registry, Church of the Transfiguration (February 18, 1894 to January 18, 1900): 18.

110. The baptism records for the Church of the Transfiguration also listed Alice Chung born on May 17, 1897 and Cecilia Chung born on February 2, 1900. Baptism Registry, Church of the Transfiguration (February 18, 1894– January 18, 1900): 234; (January 18, 1900–March 27, 1904): 10. Another daughter, Sadie was listed as two years old in the 1900 federal census, New York City, Enumeration District 34.

111. Interrogation transcript with Arnold Irving Chong, August 27, 1912, Box 318, Folder 75/162 Arnold Irving Chong, RG 85, Chinese Exclusion Files, NA-NY.

112. Interrogation transcript with Arnold Irving Chong, September 3, 1912, Box 318, Folder 75/162 Arnold Irving Chong, RG 85, Chinese Exclusion Files, NA-NY.

113. Among the men who testified were Chung Bing, a former partner at Quong Lung Yuen, and Jang Shaw, a partner at the firm of Quong Yick Wo, which later replaced Quong Lung Yuen at 22 Mott Street. Letter from Chinese Inspector to Chinese Inspector in Charge, District of New York and New Jersey, September 20, 1912, Box 318, Folder 75/162 Arnold Irving Chong, RG 85, Chinese Exclusion Files, NA-NY.

114. Interrogation transcript with Henry Lem, Jr., September 23, 1926; Interrogation transcript with Mrs. Henry Lem, September 23, 1926, Box 354, Folder 110/164 Henry Lem Jr., RG 85, Chinese Exclusion Files, NA-NY.

115. Baptism and Marriage Register of the Five Points Mission, 372, Five Points Mission Collection; 1900 Federal Census, New York City, Enumeration District 34; 1910 Federal Census, New York City, Enumeration District 46.

116. Interrogation transcript with Annie Toro, September 23, 1926, Box 354, Folder 110/164 Henry Lem, Jr., RG 85, Chinese Exclusion Files, NA-NY.

117. For example, Harvard's name was "Ah Nom." Interrogation transcript with Harvard Lem, January 22, 1943, Box 576, Folder 174/982 Harvard Lem, RG 85, Chinese Exclusion Files, NA-NY.

118. As an adult Henry Jr. told immigration officials that he could only speak "one or two words" in Chinese. Although it is possible that he chose to hide his Chinese language ability to ensure that his application for a return certificate as a citizen would be granted, it seems unlikely since Henry had sufficient documentation—birth certificate and affidavits of white witnesses—to prove his citizenship. More likely the Lems spoke little Chinese in the home because Emma herself was probably not fluent in Chinese since her mother, Elizabeth, was an Englishwoman. See interrogation transcript with Henry Lem, Jr., September 23, 1926, 3, Box 354, Folder 110/164 Henry Lem Jr., RG 85, Chinese Exclusion Files, NA-NY.

119. Ibid.

120. Interrogation transcript with Emma Lem, September 23, 1926, Box 354, Folder 110/164 Henry Lem Jr., RG 85, Chinese Exclusion Files, NA-NY.

121. Another daughter, Henrietta, had died at a young age. Interrogation transcript with Harvard Lem, January 22, 1943, Box 576, Folder 174/982 Harvard Lem, RG 85, Chinese Exclusion Files, NA-NY.

122. Interrogation transcript with Emma Lem, January 22, 1943, Box 576, Folder 174/982 Harvard Lem, RG 85, Chinese Exclusion Files, NA-NY.

123. For more on the CCC see John A. Salmond, *The Civilian Conservation Corps, 1933–1942: A New Deal Case Study* (Durham: Duke University Press, 1967).

124. Interrogation with Harvard Lem, January 22, 1943, Box 576, Folder 174/982 Harvard Lem, RG 85, Chinese Exclusion Files, NA-NY.

125. At the time of the interview, Rosie, who also went by the name of Eva, was engaged as a drill press operator. Interrogation with Rosie Lem, January 22, 1943, Box 576, Folder 174/982 Harvard Lem, RG 85, Chinese Exclusion Files, NA-NY.

126. Rosie was not alone, Chinese American women in San Francisco experienced similar job opportunities during the war. Yet, wartime employment gains for women and minorities were by no means secure and remained vulnerable to unions' and employers' visions of race and gender in the postwar industrial labor force. Yung, 260–277. See also Ruth Milkman, *Gender at Work: The Dynamics of Job Segregation by Sex During World War II* (Urbana: University of Illinois Press, 1987); William Harris, *The Harder We Run: Black Workers Since the Civil War* (New York: Oxford University Press, 1982), 113–122.

CHAPTER SIX
"THE MOST REMARKABLE GET-AWAY IN POLICE HISTORY"

1. "New Witnesses Found Here," *NYT*, June 22, 1909.
2. *World*, June 29, 1909.
3. "Chong Saw Ling Kill Sigel Girl," *NYT*, June 23, 1909.
4. "Chong Admits Lying about Sigel Murder," *NYT*, June 24, 1909.
5. "Take Chong Sing to Murder Scene,"*NYT*, June 25, 1909.
6. "Warn White Women to Leave Chinatown"; "Chinatown Withering," *NY Tribune*, July 5, 1909.
7. "Arrest Friend of Miss Sigel."
8. Gilfoyle, 92–116.
9. The article, however, did not offer any evidence to support this rumor. "His Society Hides Leon," *NY Tribune*, June 22, 1909
10. Helper, 86–88.
11. Robert G. Lee, 83–105; 89–90; Gary Okihiro, *Common Ground: Reimagining American History* (Princeton: Princeton University Press, 2001), 76–78.
12. For a fuller discussion on popular narratives of interracial sexual relations between Chinese and whites, see chapter 3.
13. Hoganson, *Fighting for American Manhood: How Gender Politics Provoked the Spanish-American and Philippine-American Wars* (New Haven: Yale University Press, 1998), 143–145.
14. John Kasson, *Houdini, Tarzan, and the Perfect Man: The White Male Body and the Challenge of Modernity in America* (New York: Hill and Wang, 2001), 8.
15. Ibid., 87.
16. *World*, June 20, 1909.
17. "Arrest Friend of Miss Sigel."
18. "Chong Saw Ling Kill Sigel Girl."
19. "Chinese Suspect Examined Here," *Orange Country Times-Press*, June 22, 1909; "Claims that Chinese Murderer Passed through Binghamton Last Evening," *The Binghamton Press and Leader*, June 21, 1909, evening edition.
20. "Elsie Sigel's Suspected Murderer is Arrested in Schenectady," *Albany Evening Journal*, June 21, 1909.
21 "Orientals' Reward for Arrest of Murderer," *Albany Evening Journal*, June 22, 1909; "Fails to Identify Chu Hop," *NYT*, June 23, 1909.
22. Editorial, *The Utica Observer*, June 22, 1909.
23. "Leon Not in Boston," *Boston Globe*, June 20, 1909, morning edition.
24. "Worcester Chinese Questioned," *Boston Globe*, June 23, 1909, evening edition.
25. "Body Believed to be Leon Ling's," *Boston Globe*, July 2, 1909, morning edition. For more on Yee Kin Wah's arrest, see chapter 3.
26. "Find Miss Sigel Dead in Trunk."
27. "Girl Here with Murder Suspect," *Washington Post*, June 20, 1909.
28. "Leong Sent Message," *Washington Post*, June 21, 1909.
29. "Chinatown is Stirred," *Washington Post*, June 20, 1909; "Leong Reported in Baltimore" *Washington Post*, June 22, 1909.

30. "Celestial Is Nabbed," *Washington Post*, June 26, 1909.

31. "Chinaman Resembles Leon," *Washington Post*, June 27, 1909.

32. "Police Search for Murderer," *San Francisco Chronicle*, June 23, 1909.

33. "Search Big Steamer for Chinese Murderer," *San Francisco Chronicle*, June 25, 1909; "Police Search for Slayer of Sigel Girl," *San Francisco Chronicle*, June 24, 1909.

34. *Chinese Daily Paper*, June 30, 1909, 3; and *Chinese Daily Paper*, July 12, 1909, 2. "Search Chiyo Maru for Chinese Slayer," *Oakland Tribune*, June 29, 1909, evening edition.

35. *Chinese Daily Paper*, June 24, 1909, 3.

36. *Chinese Daily Paper*, June 25, 1909, 3.

37. *Chinese Daily Paper*, June 28, 1909, 2.

38. *Chinese Daily Paper*, June 29, 1909, 3.

39. "Leon in Johnstown?" *Pittsburg Dispatch*, June 23, 1909.

40. "Chong Admits Lying about Sigel Murder."

41. "Leon was in Newark," *NY Tribune*, June 27, 1909.

42. "Another Leong Ling Seen," *Washington Post*, June 27, 1909.

43. "Seek Leon in Disguise as a Chinese Woman," *BDE*, June 23, 1909.

44. "New York Police at Sea over the Sigel Murder," *Daily Picayune-New Orleans*, June 28, 1909; "Gulfport Chinaman Released," *Daily Picayune-New Orleans*, June 29, 1909. The suspect's name is listed as "Fung Ling" in this article. The man's name was also referred to as Laung Yin in other newspapers.

45. "Think They Have Leon Ling," *NYT*, September 14, 1909.

46. "Clew Given Here in Sigel Murder."

47. "Sigel Murderer Caught in West?" *Chicago Daily Tribune*, June 22, 1909.

48. "Recognized in Philadelphia," *NYT*, June 21, 1909.

49. "Leon Gets New Start," *NY Tribune*, July 3, 1909.

50. "Tracking a Murderer," *NYT*, June 27, 1909, Part V.

51. "Mistaken for William Leon," *Chicago Daily Tribune*, June 25, 1909.

52. "Chinese Chased in Newark," *NYT*, June 29, 1909.

53. "Thought They Had Leon," *Newark Evening News*, July 7, 1909.

54. "Chong Admits Lying about Sigel Murder."

55. "Sigel Murderer Caught in West?"

56. "Elsie's Body Traced," *Washington Post*, June 30, 1909; "Chinamen Saw Ling Send Trunk Away," *NYT*, June 30, 1909.

57. "Clue in Sigel Murder in Harlem Laundry"; "Says Ling Escaped in Cousin's Wagon," *NYT*, July 6, 1909.

58. "Leon Not Aboard the Minnesota," *NYH*, July 8, 1909.

59. "Now Think Ling Sailed," *NYT*, July 7, 1909.

60. "Leon Ling in Budapest?"*BDE*, July 12, 1909.

61. "Leon Ling in London an American Says," *NYT*, July 17, 1909. The English authorities were most likely already familiar with the Sigel murder and the hunt for the missing suspect because the British press had also published accounts of the murder investigation. See "Murder in New York," *The Times*, June 21, 1909; "A Girl Mission Worker's Fate," *The Manchester Guardian*, June 21, 1909.

62. "We Want Leon Ling If London Gets Him," *NYT*, July 18, 1909, Part III.

63. American Vice Consul General Stuart J. Fuller to Assistant Secretary of State, July 7, 1909, RG 59, M862, Roll 1090, Case 20559, NA-CP.

64. "New York Trunk Mystery," *The Morning Post*, July 7, 1909.

65. Wilbur J. Carr to Stuart J. Fuller, August 16, 1909, RG59, M862, Roll 1090, Case 20559, NA-CP.

66. Telegram from Robert H. Fuller, Secretary to the Governor of New York to Secretary of State, July 16, 1909. In the telegram, Fuller quotes an earlier telegram sent on July 15 by William Travers Jerome, District Attorney to George Curtis Treadwell, Acting Secretary to the Governor. RG 59, M862, Roll 1090, Case 20559, NA-CP.

67. Telegram from American Ambassador Leishman to U.S. State Department, July 14, 1909; Telegram from Huntington Wilson to governor of New York, July 14, 1909; Telegram from Huntington Wilson to Ambassador Leishman, July 15, 1909. RG 59, M862, Roll 1090, Case 20559, NA-CP.

68. U.S. Ambassador Reid to secretary of state, July 16, 1909; U.S. Ambassador David J. Hill (Berlin) to Secretary of State P. C. Knox, July 24, 1909. RG 59, M862, Roll 1090, Case 20559, NA-CP.

69. For example, see Hy. Mayer, "A Raid in Chinatown Puzzle Find the Guilty One," *NYT*, April 30, 1905.

70. "Ling Rode in Cab with Body in Trunk," *NYT*, June 27, 1909, Part II.

71. "Many Chinamen Arrested," *NYT*, June 22, 1909.

72. "New Clew to Slayer," *Washington Post*, June 29, 1909; "Take Another Jap as Sigel Slayer," *Newark Star*, July 2, 1909.

73. "Investigating at Birmingham," *Daily Picayune-New Orleans*, June 25, 1909.

74. According to Eleanor Gluck's study of U.S. Census statistics, the 1910 Japanese immigrant and American-born population of New York City numbered 1,037. Slightly more than 75 percent of the Japanese immigrant population resided in the borough of Manhattan. Eleanor Alther Gluck, "An Ecological Study of the Japanese in New York City" (master's thesis, Columbia University, 1940), 22, 31.

75. "Miss Sigel's Body May Go to Potter's Field," *NY Tribune*, June 20, 1909.

76. "Many Chinamen Arrested."

77. "Japanese Clerk Arrested," *NYH*, June 26, 1909. See also "Killed Girl in a Rage," *NY Tribune*, June 26, 1909.

78. W. K. Igawa to Mayor McClellan, October 11, 1909, Box MGB-76, Mayors' Papers.

79. The Bertillon system, developed by Alphonse Bertillon in France in 1883, combined bone length measurements and physical descriptions to affix a person's identity. In 1883 Theodore Roosevelt instituted the Bertillon system as part of his reforms as police commissioner of New York City. Although fingerprinting began to be employed in 1905, the police department limited its use to specific crimes such as burglary. In 1909 the Bertillon system was still the primary identification system in place. See Simon A. Cole, *Suspect Identities: A History of Fingerprinting and Criminal Investigation* (Cambridge: Harvard University Press, 2001), 32–59.

80. Thomas Carroll, Secretary to Police Commissioner, to W. K. Igawa, September 24, 1909. This letter is quoted in full by Igawa in his letter to the

mayor. W. K. Igawa to Mayor McClellan, October 11, 1909, Box MGB-76, Mayors' Papers.

81. Ibid.

82. "Story of Ling's Visit Here All Nonsense, Says Koshiwa," *New Orleans Item*, June 25, 1909.

83. Kitty Calavita, "The Paradoxes of Race, Class, Identity, and 'Passing': Enforcing the Chinese Exclusion Acts, 1882–1910," *Law and Social Inquiry* 25 (Winter 2000): 1–40; Cole, 122–127. See also Erika Lee, *At American's Gates: Chinese Immigration During the Exclusion Era, 1882–1943* (Chapel Hill: University of North Carolina Press, 2003).

84. Mitziko Sawada, *Tokyo Life, New York Dreams: Urban Japanese Visions of America, 1890–1924* (Berkeley: University of California Press, 1996), 13–16.

85. "Foreign Colonel Victim of Fancied Resemblance," *New Orleans Daily Picayune*, June 30, 1909.

86. "Sigel Witnesses Identify Sing," *NYT*, July 1, 1909.

87. Lucy M. Cohen, 138.

88. Ibid., 52–62. See also Moon-Ho Jung, "'Coolies' and Cane: Race, Labor, and Sugar Production in Louisiana, 1852–1877," (Ph.D. diss., Cornell University, 2000).

89. Lucy M. Cohen, 154.

90. "Love-Mad Convert Kills Mission Girl," *New Orleans Item*, June 19, 1909.

91. "New Letter for Ling," *Washington Post*, June 24, 1909, 2.

92. For example, see James Weldon Johnson's *The Autobiography of an Ex-Colored Man* (New York: Dover, 1995), or Nella Larsen's *Passing* (New York: Penguin Books, 1997)

93. *In re Halladjian et al., Circuit Court, D. Massachusetts.* December 24, 1909. See also Helen Hatab Samhan, "Not Quite White: Race Classification and the Arab-American Experience," *Arabs in America: Building a New Future*, ed. Michael W. Suleiman (Philadelphia: Temple University Press, 1999), 209–226.

94. "Thinks He Has Leon Out in Illinois," *NY Herald*, July 17, 1909.

95. Editorial, "The Chinese Murder," *NYT*, August 4, 1909.

96. Riis, 80.

97. "Clue in Sigel Murder in Harlem Laundry."

98. "Leon Ling Known in Pittsburg," *NYT*, June 20, 1909.

99. "Suspect Is Released Here," *Chicago Daily Tribune*, June 23, 1909.

100. "Chicago Chinese Hunt Leon," *Chicago Tribune*, June 24, 1909.

101. Editorial, "A Chance for the Chinese," *NYT*, June 29, 1909.

102. "Tells of Missing Leon Ling" *NYT*, June 30, 1910.

CHAPTER SEVEN
"DISGRACE ON THE WHOLE BODY OF OUR PEOPLE"

1. "Arrest Friend of Miss Sigel."

2. "Father Now Identifies Girl."

3. "Murdered Girl False to Both Chinese Lovers," *The World*, June 25, 1909.

4. "Take Chong Sing to Murder Scene."

5. "Chong Saw Ling Kill Sigel Girl."

6. "Arrest Friend of Miss Sigel."

7. "Take Chong Sing to Murder Scene."

8. "Chong Saw Ling Kill Sigel Girl."

9. "Chong Now Admits Hearing a Quarrel," *NYT*, June 26, 1909.

10. This account comes from the article "Roommate of Sigel Girl's Slayer Held in Amsterdam," *Amsterdam Evening Recorder and Daily Democrat*, June 21, 1909, evening edition.

11. Ibid.

12. Ibid.

13. Ibid.

14. "Sigel Girl's Friend Back in New York," *Amsterdam Evening Recorder and Daily Democrat*, June 22, 1909, evening edition.

15. "Chong Saw Ling Kill Sigel Girl."

16. "Chong Admits Lying about Sigel Murder."

17. *Ibid.* The name "Quen Yick Nam" appears under the list of "Court Interpreters" in Warner M. Van Norden's *Who's Who of the Chinese in New York*, 86. Quan Yick Nam also appeared as an interpreter or a witness for the prosecution in a number of cases in the Court of General Sessions throughout the late nineteenth and early twentieth centuries. See for example, Case No. 7765 *The People vs. Wong Sang*, filed June 30, 1896; Case No. 43241 *The People vs. Ja Fong*, filed June 29, 1903; Case No. 43242 *The People vs. Sing Lee*, dated June 29, 1903. New York County - District Attorney's Office - Records of Cases, NYCMA.

18. During 1901, for example, Quan Yick Nam wrote several letters and reports on gambling, opium smoking, and prostitution in New York City's Chinatown to George Wilson Morgan, Assistant Secretary of the Committee of Fifteen. The Committee of Fifteen was temporarily formed to look for evidence linking Tammany Hall to police corruption. Report from Quan Yick Nam, February 19, 1901, Box 4, Folder Precinct 6 - 12 Chatham Square - 32 Mott St., Subfolder 12 Chatham Square "Dive," Subfolder 7 Mott St. "Prostitution"; Quan Yick Nam to George Morgan, February 25, 1901. Box 1, Folder Letters Received, 1900–1901, "N-Q"; Quan Yick Nam to George W. Morgan, April 12, 1901, Box 4, Folder Precinct 6 - 100 Mott St. - 119 Mulberry St., Subfolder Mott & Pell Streets (Quan Yick Nam); Report from Quan Yick Nam to George Morgan, May 27, 1901, Box 5, Folder Precinct 6 - 9 Pell St. - 34 Pell St.; Report from Quan Yick Nam to George Morgan, June 7, 1901, Box 5, Folder Precinct 6 - 9 Pell St. - 34 Pell St.; Committee of Fifteen Papers.

19. "Take Chong Sing to Murder Scene."

20. "Chong Now Admits Hearing a Quarrel."

21. "Police Theory Upset in the Sigel Murder," *NYT*, June 28, 1909.

22. Acting District Attorney Nathan A. Smyth to Elmer C. Miller, n. d., Roll 43, M.N. 11494, New York County-District Attorney's Papers, NYCMA.

23. William T. Smith, Editorial, "Torture to Force Confession," *NYT*, June 26, 1909.

24. Thomas F. Millard, "'The Third Degree' and Justice in China," *NYT*, July 4, 1909, Part V.

25. "Might Hold Sing for Life," *NYT*, August 4, 1909.

26. "Chong Sing out on Bail," *NYT*, September 10, 1909.

27. "Charged with Sigel Murder," *NYT*, September 25, 1909.

28. "Raves about Sigel Murder," *Boston Globe*, June 29, 1909, morning edition.

29. "Sigel Case Prompts Swindle," *NYT*, July 17, 1909.

30. Case No. 72915 *People vs. John Brown*, alias Patrick O'Hara, New York County-District Attorney's Office-Records of Cases. The complaint was filed on June 27, 1909; "Sigel Case Prompts Swindle."

31. "Sigel Murder Has Driven Off Chinese," *NYH*, June 25, 1909.

32. "More 'Elsie' Letters Found in Chinatown," *NY Tribune*, June 21, 1909.

33. "Chinese Merchants Ask for Protection."

34. "Chinese Accuse Police," *NYT*, July 6, 1909.

35. *Chinese Daily Paper*, July 8, 1909, 2. The entire handbill was reprinted in this issue.

36. This is a pin yin transliteration of the Chinese characters in this man's name. A *New York Times* article named the murder victim as "Ung Yow, an 'Americanized' Chinaman." The man was found murdered on the morning of July 1. Police at first assumed that the murder was connected to the Sigel case, believing that Ung Yow may have been an accomplice of Leon Ling's. However, they later concluded that there was probably no connection. "Drowned Chinaman May Be Leon Ling," *NYT*, July 2, 1909.

37. Although the spelling of the name is different, this is the same person named in the CCBA's handbill.

38. Memorandum from the Imperial Chinese Legation to the U.S. State Department, July 3, 1909, RG 59, M862, Roll 1086, Case 20418, NA-CP.

39. For an example of articles discussing the need for a saner Fourth of July, see *NYT*, July 5, 1909. For an interesting class analysis on the struggle over Fourth of July celebrations in Worcester, Massachusetts, see Roy Rosenzweig, *Eight Hours for What We Will* (Cambridge: Cambridge University Press, 1983). The draft rioters initially vented their anger against a revised federal draft law on government and military buildings, but eventually burned down the Colored Orphan Asylum on Fifth Avenue as well as lynched several black men. For a history of the riots, see Iver Bernstein, *The New York City Draft Riots: Their Significance for American Society and Politics in the Age of the Civil War* (New York: Oxford University Press, 1990). For more on nineteenth century race riots in New York City, see Roediger, 100–110; and Paul A. Gilje, *The Road to Mobocracy: Popular Disorder in New York City, 1763–1834* (Chapel Hill: University of North Carolina Press, 1987).

40. In addition, many Chinese communities throughout the United States had also suffered numerous mob attacks such as the famous incident at Rock Springs, Wyoming in 1885. Sucheng Chan, *Asian Americans*, 48–51.

41. Confidential Telegram from Huntington Wilson, acting secretary of state, to Charles E. Hughes, governor of New York, July 3, 1909, RG 59, M862, Roll 1086, Case 20418, NA-CP.

42. Telegram from Charles Hughes to secretary of state, July 4, 1909. RG 59, M862, Roll 1086, Case 20418, NA-CP. Telegram from Charles E. Hughes to Mayor McClellan, received July 4, 1909, Box MGB-76, Mayors' Papers. Telegram from Charles E. Hughes to secretary of state, July 4, 1909. RG 59, M862, Roll 1086, Case 20418, NA-CP.

43. Memo from the Department of State to the Chinese Legation, July 7, 1909, RG 59, M862, Roll 1086, Case 20418, NA-CP.

44. Acting Mayor Patrick F. McGowan to Governor Charles Hughes, July 6, 1910, Box MGB-110, Mayors' Papers.

45. Mayor George McClellan to Charles E. Hughes, July 12, 1909, Box MGB-76, Mayors' Papers.

46. "Extra Police Out; Fear Tong Feud," *NYH*, July 6, 1909.

47. "Look to Chinamen to Catch Leon Ling," *NYT*, July 5, 1909.

48. "On Leongs Celebrate," *NY Tribune*, July 6, 1909.

49. "Washington Gets US to Set Guard on Chinatown," *World*, July 6, 1909.

50. Editorial, "A Chance for the Chinese," *NYT*, June 29, 1909.

51. "Oriental Club Offers $500 Reward for Arrest of Murderer,"*BDE*, June 22, 1909.

52. "New Witnesses Found Here," *NYT*, June 22, 1909.

53. This is a pin yin spelling of the name of the tong. *Chinese Daily Paper*, June 26, 1909, 2. American newspapers also carried news of the rewards. See "Chinese Here Offer Reward," *Chicago Tribune*, June 26, 1909; "Killed Girl in a Rage," *NY Tribune*, June 26, 1909. The American newspapers, however, did not mention the contribution by the Hong Xun Tong.

54. *Chinese Daily Paper*, July 13, 1909, 2. Interestingly, the *Chinese Daily Paper* made a point of correcting the American newspapers' statement that the reward was $500. See for example, "San Francisco Chinese Offer $500 Reward for Arrest of Leon," *NYH*, July 12, 1909.

55. "Woman Says She Can Locate Leon," *NYH*, July 12, 1909. It is unlikely that Leon Ling had an American wife, as Stewart alleged, since no other reports confirmed her claim.

56. *NYT*, June 27, 1909, Part V.

57. "Chinese Consul Lends Aid," *NYT*, June 24, 1909. The *New York Times* printed a translation of the consul's memorial for its readers. Ou Shou Tchun's name was also transliterated as Ng Shau Chan.

58. *Chinese Daily Paper*, July 1, 1909, 2; "Chinese Minister Urges Search for Ling," *The Oakland Times*, July 2, 1909.

59. "Chinese Aiding Police," *Washington Post*, June 23, 1909.

60. *Chinese Daily Paper*, June 29, 1909, 3.

61. "Chinese Here Offer Reward," *Chicago Tribune*, June 26, 1909.

62. *Chinese Daily Paper*, June 28, 1909, 2.

63. "Minister Wu Joins Hunt," *NYT*, June 23, 1909.

64. "Sigel Witnesses Identify Sing,"*NYT*, July 1, 1909.

65. Letter from W. Jerome to Robert L. Park, July 7, 1909, Roll 43, M.N. 11494, New York County-District Attorney's Papers. Park most likely learned of District Attorney Jerome's request from an article published in the *San Francisco Chronicle*. See "Says Chung Sin Is Accomplice to Leon Ling," *San Francisco Chronicle*, July 1, 1909.

66. T. G. Hom, Editorial, "A Unique Crime," *NYT*, June 28, 1909.

67. "Chinese Freemasons," *NYT*, July 4, 1909; Lue J. Frank, *BDE*, July 4, 1909.

68. For example, the *New York Times* reported a rumor that came from Wing Lee, "who is practically boss of Denver's Chinese colony," regarding a

bulletin issued by the Chinese government on the Sigel murder claiming that the Chinese Consul in New York had declared the murder a suicide and Leon Ling fled the city out of fear of being charged with her death. In addition the article alleged that the bulletin contained orders from the Chinese Masons, sanctioned by Peking, to Chinese all over the world to protect Leon Ling. See "China Won't Shield Ling," *NYT*, July 15, 1909. The Chinese Legation, however, denied that the statement attributed to Denver's Chinese community was correct. "Legation Discredits Story," *BDE*, July 14, 1909.

69. Chinese Minister Wu Ting Fang estimated that there were approximately five hundred Chinese students studying in the United States around this period. Wu Ting Fang, L.L.D., "Chinese Students in America," *The World's Chinese Students' Journal* 3 (July–August, 1908): 9. For more on the history of Chinese students in the United States, see Y. C. Wang, *Chinese Intellectuals and the West, 1872–1949* (Chapel Hill: University of North Carolina Press, 1966).

70. Po Heng Lum, *NYT*, July 3, 1909. Lum was referring to a statement made in another letter to the editor. See "A Chance for the Chinese."

71. Vi Kyuin Wellington Koo was born in China on January 29, 1888. He completed his advanced degree in political science in 1912 and published his thesis, "The Status of Aliens in China." Koo then embarked on a career in the newly established Republic of China as the English secretary to the president. William L. Tung, *V. K. Wellington Koo and China's Diplomacy* (New York: Center of Asian Studies, St. John's University, 1977), 5–6. While in New York, Koo received some recognition in the local press for his skills and talents. In an article about Chinese students in America, he was held up as exemplary of his cohorts. "V. K. Wellington Koo, for instance, now of Columbia Law School, has been elected to the student board of representatives of Columbia, has been secretary of the popular social organization, King's Crown, was admitted to the exclusive senior society of nacoms, and has been editor in chief of the Columbia daily, *The Spectator*." "Chinese Students in American Schools," *BDE*, July 25, 1909.

72. V. K. Wellington Koo, "Protest of a Chinese Student," *NY Tribune*, July 8, 1909.

73. Koo had actually met Theodore Roosevelt a year earlier when the overseas student community selected Koo to be their spokesman at a special event held in honor of T'ang Shao-i's visit to Washington, D.C. T'ang Shao-i had been sent by the Chinese Imperial Court as a special envoy to visit with the president. Tung, 6. For more on Progressivism see Richard Hofstadter, *The Age of Reform* (New York: Vintage Books, 1955), 131–328.

74. Since the 1890s a number of well-publicized investigations, such as the Lexow committee inquiry into Tammany Hall and police corruption, have occupied the New York City political landscape. See David C. Hammack, *Power and Society: Greater New York at the Turn of the Century* (New York: Columbia University Press, 1982); Jay Stuart Berman, *Police Administration and Progressive Reform: Theodore Roosevelt as Police Commissioner of New York* (New York: Greenwood Press, 1987). Special interest Progressive groups, such as the Society for the Prevention of Crime and the Committee of Fifteen, were organized by white, middle-class businessmen and civic leaders to investigate charges of police and municipal corruption. See "Introduction by the President, Charles

H. Parkhurst," *Report of the Society for the Prevention of Crime* (New York, 1896), 6.

75. See Lui-Ngau Chang, "Working for China's Welfare Abroad," *Chinese Students' Monthly* 5 (June 1910): 546. S. H. Kee, "The Chinese: A Social Entity in America, *Chinese Students' Monthly* 7 (May 1912): Part II, 607–608.

76. I have decided not to offer an English translation of the organization. A rough translation of the words *Shen Gong Li Hui* would be an organization for the purposes of redress.

77. *Chinese Daily Paper*, July 15, 1909, 3.

78. *Chinese Daily Paper*, July 20, 1909, 3.

79. *Chinese Daily Paper*, July 20, 1909, 1.

80. See article 7 of the group's by-laws. *Chinese Daily Paper*, July 15, 1909, 3.

81. *Chinese Daily Paper*, July 20, 1909, 1.

82. *Chinese Daily Paper*, July 27, 1909, 2; *Chinese Daily Paper*, July 31, 1909, 3; *Chinese Daily Paper*, August 2, 1909, 3; *Chinese Daily Paper*, August 5, 1909, 3; *Chinese Daily Paper*, August 14, 1909, 3; *Chinese Daily Paper*, August 25, 1909, 2; *Chinese Daily Paper*, August 26, 1909, 2.

83. *Chinese Daily Paper*, July 17, 1909, 2.

84. For example the list of contributions showed donors from Fresno, Oakland, Vancouver, Portland, and other cities. *Chinese Daily Paper*, July 26, 1909, 3.

85. See, for example, *Chinese Daily Paper*, July 15, 1909, 3; *Chinese Daily Paper*, July 17, 1909, 2; and *Chinese Daily Paper*, July 20, 1909, 3.

86. *Chinese Daily Paper*, August 2, 1909, 3.

87. *Chinese Daily Paper*, August 10, 1909, 2.

88. *Chinese Daily Paper*, July 15, 1909, 3.

89. *Chinese Daily Paper*, July 19, 1909, 9.

90. *Chinese Daily Paper*, August 5, 1909, 2; and *Chinese Daily Paper*, August 6, 1909, 2.

91. *Chinese Daily Paper*, July 24, 1909, 1–2.

92. *Chinese Daily Paper*, July 19, 1909, 2; and *Chinese Daily Paper*, August 3, 1909, 2.

93. *Chinese Daily Paper*, August 25, 1909, 2; and *Chinese Daily Paper*, August 26, 1909, 2.

94. "Bayonne Ban on Sigel Pictures," *NYT*, July 7, 1909; "Sigel Pictures Barred," *Newark Star*, July 7, 1909.

95. *Chinese Daily Paper*, August 3, 1910, 2.

96. Petition to William Jay Gaynor, August 4, 1910. Box GWJ-100, Mayors' Papers. The Columbia students who signed were V. K. Wellington Koo, Chen Huanchang, Zan Chee Zia, Chen Shao Kwan, Li Chien Luan, Huang Chen Sheng, Hua Yü, Peng, and Y. Y. Chan.

97. William Jay Gaynor to F. H. Burgher, Acting Police Commissioner, August 5, 1910, Box GWJ-176, Mayor's Papers. See also letter from Police Commissioner Baker to William Jay Gaynor, August 10, 1910, Box GWJ-16, Mayors' Papers.

98. *Chinese Daily Paper*, August 18, 1910, 2.

99. *Chinese Daily Paper*, August 30, 1910, 3.

100. "Trouble Again for Chinese in America," *Chinese Students' Monthly* 6 (February 10, 1911): Part I, 420.

101. *Chinese Daily Paper*, August 22, 1910, 2.

102. *Chinese Daily Paper*, August 25, 1910, 2.

103. The *Chinese Daily Paper* reported on the play's opening in cities throughout the country. For Worcester, Massachusetts see November 23, 1910, 2; December 15, 1910, 3; Spokane, Washington see December 23, 1910, 3; Portland, Oregon, January 11, 1911, 2. The play also made an appearance at the Clunie Theatre in Sacramento, California on January 28. See advertisement, *Sacramento Bee*, January 25, 1911.

104. "The Chinatown Trunk Mystery," *Oregon Journal*, January 8, 1911, Section 4s.

105. *Chinese Daily Paper*, January 11, 1909, 2; *Chinese Daily Paper*, January 12, 1911, 3; and *Chinese Daily Paper*, January 13, 1911, 2.

106. "Lurid Melodrama Will be Housed at Princess," *San Francisco Chronicle*, February 12, 1911; "Trouble Again for Chinese in America," 420.

107. *Chinese Daily Paper*, January 21, 1911, 2; and *Chinese Daily Paper*, January 25, 1911, 3.

108. *Chinese Daily Paper*, January 24, 1911, 2.

109. Advertisement, *Oregon Journal*, January 8, 1911, section 4.

110. "Lurid Melodrama Will be Housed at Princess."

111. "'Mystery' at Bungalow," *Daily News Portland*, January 7, 1911.

112. "Melodrama for Princess," *San Francisco Chronicle*, February 9, 1911.

113. "The Chinatown Trunk Mystery."

114. "Melodrama for Princess."

EPILOGUE

1. "May Be Sigel Murder Clue," *NYT*, May 12, 1913. Another odd link to the Sigel murder occurred in 1928. Thirty-seven-year-old Willis Albert Wolfe, an escaped mental patient suspected of killing a female college student, confessed to having killed Elsie Sigel. Police, however, did not take his statement seriously. "Woman Student Waylaid and Slain," *NYT*, August 9, 1928.

2. "See Murder Linked to Sigel Slaying," *NYT*, July 14, 1935; and "Two Get 180 Years for Killing Lang," *NYT*, August 9, 1935.

3. "Mrs. Dunkel Admits Seeing Lang Slain," *NYT*, July 16, 1935; "Two Get 180 Years for Killing Lang."

4. Batterberry, 218. Even in cases where the murder is properly situated in midtown Manhattan, the links to Chinatown remain. For example, an account by Meyer Berger mentioned the murder as part of his historical account of police activities of the West Forty-seventh Precinct, but he also maintained the belief that Elsie Sigel was a Chinatown missionary. Meyer Berger, *The Eight Million: Journal of a New York Correspondent* (New York: Simon and Schuster, 1942), 136–137.

5. In 1912, *The Great Chinatown Trunk Mystery*, another play about the Elsie Sigel murder appeared in New York City. As with the first play, *The*

Chinatown Trunk Mystery, a letter of protest sent to the mayor's office led Mayor William Jay Gaynor to request Police Commissioner William Baker to authorize a police investigation of the performance. Police commissioner to James Matthews, executive secretary, City Hall, May 29, 1912, GWJ-54, Mayors' Papers.

6. The 1920s marked the establishment of the University of Chicago's sociology department under the direction of Robert Park and the growth of sociology as an accepted academic discipline in America. Park and his students were particularly interested in the social adjustment and assimilation of racial and ethnic groups in modern American society. In terms of Asian Americans, a number of scholars undertook research on the social experiences of Chinese Americans and Japanese Americans. A good number of Park's students have become familiar to Asian American scholars. Many of these Chicago graduates later conducted and published research on Asian American communities. Among the more familiar names are Romanzo Adams, Emory Bogardus, Jesse Frederick Steiner, William Carlson Smith, R. D. McKenzie, Andrew Lind, Rose Hum Lee, Frank Miyamoto, and Paul Siu. See Henry Yu, *Thinking Orientals: Migration, Contact, and Exoticism in Modern America* (New York: Oxford University Press, 2001).

7. See for example, William Carlson Smith, *The Second Generation Oriental in America* (Honolulu: University of Hawaii Press, 1927) and *Americans in Process: A Study of Our Citizens of Oriental Ancestry* (Ann Arbor: Edwards Brothers, 1937). See also Charles S. Johnson and J. Masuoka, eds., *Orientals and their Cultural Adjustments: Interviews, Life Histories and Social Adjustment Experiences of Chinese and Japanese of Varying Backgrounds and Length of Residence in the United States* (Nashville: Social Science Institute Fisk University, 1946).

8. Works ranging from Mary Coolidge's *Chinese Immigration* to Gunther Barth's *Bitter Strength* show the degree to which this conceptualization of Chinatowns as insular, socially isolated ethnic communities easily dominated studies of Chinese American urban life in the first half of the twentieth century. Mary Roberts Coolidge, *Chinese Immigration* (New York: Henry Holt and company, 1909); Barth's work described Chinatowns as insular "bachelor societies" and created a historical narrative that implied ethnic and racial homogeneity and solidarity formed the basis of community life for San Francisco's Chinese immigrants. Gunther Barth, *Bitter strength: A History of the Chinese in the United States, 1850–1870* (Cambridge: Harvard University Press, 1964). Some key texts in Asian American Studies looking at the social relations that make Chinatown an ethnic community include: Victor Nee and Brett deBary Nee's *Longtime Californ': A Documentary Study of an American Chinatown* (New York: Pantheon Books, 1972); Chia–Ling Kuo, *Social and Political Change in New York's Chinatown: The Role of Voluntary Associations* (New York: Preager, 1977); Bernard P. Wong, *Patronage, Brokerage, Entrepreneurship and the Chinese Community of New York* (New York: AMS Press, 1988); Min Zhou, *Chinatown: The Socioeconomic Potential of an Urban Enclave* (Philadelphia: Temple University Press, 1992); Yong Chen, *Chinese San Francisco, 1850–1943: A Trans-Pacific Community* (Stanford: Stanford University Press, 2000).

9. I am essentially advocating a more careful examination of how the processes of racial formation and spatial formation are intrinsically linked. The work of Henri Lefebvre has been particularly useful for seeing the ways in which the historical production of space as lived and perceived by people is intrinsically connected to their everyday social and cultural practices. As Lefebvre states, "(social) space is a (social) product." Henri Lefebvre, *The Production of Space*, trans. Donald Nicholson-Smith (Oxford: Blackwell Publishers, 1991). See also Dolores Hayden, *The Power of Place: Urban Landscapes as Public History* (Boston: MIT Press, 1997), 2–43; and Michael Omi and Howard Winant, *Racial Formations in the United States from the 1960s to the 1990s* (New York: Routledge, 1994).

10. For example, see John Kasson, *Amusing the Million: Coney Island at the Turn of the Century* (New York: Hill & Wang, 1978); Kathy Peiss, *Cheap Amusements: Working Women and Leisure in Turn-of-the-Century New York* (Philadelphia: Temple University Press, 1986); Lewis Erenberg, *Steppin' Out: New York Nightlife and the Transformation of American Culture, 1890-1930* (Westport, Connecticut: Greenwood Press, 1981); Kevin Mumford, *Interzones: Black/White Sex Districts in Chicago and New York in the Early Twentieth Century* (New York: Columbia University Press, 1997); William R. Taylor, ed., *Inventing Times Square: Commerce and Culture at the Crossroads of the World* (Baltimore: Johns Hopkins University Press, 1991).

11. This approach is also taken by a number of recent works in Asian American studies that combine cultural and social history. See for example, John Kuo Wei Tchen, *New York before Chinatown* (Baltimore: The Johns Hopkins University Press, 1999); Nayan Shah, *Contagious Divides: Epidemics and Race in San Francisco's Chinatown* (Berkeley: University of California Press, 2001); and Kay Anderson, *Vancouver's Chinatown: Racial Discourse in Canada, 1875–1980* (London: McGill-Queen's University Press, 1991). Another important work examining the deployment of "Oriental" images in American popular culture is Robert G. Lee's *Orientals: Asian Americans in Popular Culture:* (Philadelphia: Temple University Press, 1999).

12. See Gary Okihiro, *Margins and Mainstreams: Asians in American History and Culture* (Seattle: University of Washington Press, 1994), 64–92; Sylvia Yanagisako, "Transforming Orientalism: Gender, Nationality and Class in Asian American Studies," in *Naturalizing Power: Essays in Feminist Cultural Analysis*, eds. Carol Delancy and Sylvia Yanagisako (New York: Routledge, 1995), 275–298. Several important recent works attempting to address the absence of women in Asian American historiography include: Judy Yung, *Unbound Feet: A Social History of Chinese Women in San Francisco* (Berkeley: University of California Press, 1995); Evelyn Nakano Glenn, *Issei, Nisei, War Bride: Three Generations of Japanese American Women in Domestic Service* (Philadelphia: Temple University Press, 1986); Dorothy B. Fujita Rony, *American Workers, Colonial Power: Philippine Seattle and the Transpacific West, 1919–1941* (Berkeley: University of California Press, 2003); Catherine Ceniza Choy, *Empire of Care: Nursing and Migration in Filipino American History* (Durham: Duke University Press, 2003).

Bibliography

ARCHIVES

American Baptist–Samuel Colgate Historical Library, Rochester, New York
   Minutes of the Twenty-third Street Baptist Church in the City of New York.
John Jay College Library (JJCA), New York City
   New York Supreme Court Cases (microfilm).
Library of Congress, Prints and Photographs Division, Washington, D.C.
   George Grantham Bain Collection.
   New York World-Telegram and Sun Newspaper Photograph Collection
   (NYWTS).
National Archives–College Park (NA-CP), Maryland
   Record Group 48 (RG 48), Department of the Interior.
   Record Group 59 (RG 59), M862, Numerical and Minor Files of the Depart-
   ment of State (microfilm).
National Archives–Northeast Region (NA-NY), New York City
   Record Group 85 (RG 85), Chinese Exclusion Case Files.
National Archives–Pacific Northwest Region (NA-SB), San Bruno, California
   Record Group 85 (RG 85), Chinese Exclusion Case Files.
National Archives (NA), Washington, D.C.
   Record Group 85 (RG 85), Chinese Exclusion Files 3358d.
New York City Municipal Archives (NYCMA), New York City
   Mayors' Papers.
   New York Supreme Court Case Files.
   New York County-District Attorney's Office-Records of Cases.
   New York County-District Attorney's Papers (microfilm).
New York Historical Society (NYHS), New York City
   Reverend George Alexander Papers.
   Fifth Avenue Presbyterian Church Papers.
New York Public Library (NYPL), New York City
   Century Papers.
   Committee of Fifteen Papers.
   Committee of Fourteen Papers.
New York State Archives (NYSA), Albany, New York
   New York House of Refuge Papers.
Presbyterian Historical Society, Philadelphia, Pennsylvania
   Records of the New York Presbytery.
Schlesinger Library, Radcliffe Institute, Harvard University, Cambridge,
   Massachusetts
   Harriet Wright (Burton) Laidlaw Papers (microfilm).
United Methodist Archives Center, Drew University, Madison, New Jersey
   Five Points Mission Collection.

FEDERAL CENSUS SCHEDULES (NEW YORK CITY)

1870.

1880.

1900.

1910.

1920.

FILMS

A Boomerang, American Mutoscope and Biograph Company, 1903.
Chinese Laundry, Edison Company, 1894.
Deceived Slumming Party, American Mutoscope and Biograph Company, 1908.
The Fatal Hour, American Mutoscope and Biograph Company, 1908.
The Heathen Chinese and the Sunday School Teachers, American Mutoscope and Biograph Company, 1904.
The Mission of Mr. Foo, Edison Company, 1915.
Scene in a Chinese Restaurant, American Mutoscope & Biograph Company, 1903.
The Secret Sin, Jesse L. Lasky Feature Play Co., 1915.

NEWSPAPERS

Chinese Language Newspapers
Chinese Daily Paper (Chung Sai Yat Pao).

New York City Newspapers
Brooklyn Daily Eagle (BDE).
Independent.
New York Evening Journal.
New York Evening Post.
New York Herald (NYH).
New York Times (NYT).
New York Tribune (NY Tribune).
Sun.
World.

New York State Newspapers
Albany Evening Journal.
Amsterdam Evening Recorder and Daily Democrat.
The Binghamton Press and Leader.
Ithaca Daily Journal.
Orange County Times-Press.
The Utica Observer.

Other U.S. Newspapers

Adams Transcript.
Boston Globe.
Chicago Daily Tribune.
Daily News Portland.
New Orleans Daily Picayune.
New Orleans Item.
Newark Evening News.
Newark Star.
Oakland Times.
Oakland Tribune.
Oregon Journal.
Pittsburg Dispatch.
Sacramento Bee.
San Francisco Chronicle.
San Francisco Examiner.
San Francisco Daily Report.
St. Louis-Post Dispatch.
Washington Post.

Foreign Newspapers

The Manchester Guardian.
The Morning Post.
South China Morning Post.
The Times.

ORGANIZATIONAL REPORTS

Annual Report of the Baptist City Mission (New York).
Annual Report of the Chinatown and Bowery Rescue Settlement for Girls and
   *First Annual Report of the Society for Neighborhood Work Among Erring
   Girls* (New York).
Annual Report of the Free Home for Destitute Young Girls (New York).
Annual Report of the New York Bible Society (New York).
Annual Report of the New York Ladies' Home Missionary Society (New York).
Five Points Monthly Record (New York).
Home Mission Echo and *Home Mission Echoes*
Home Mission Monthly
New York Police Department Annual Report (New York).
New York Society for the Prevention of Cruelty to Children (NYSPCC), *Annual
   Report.*
Report of the Society for the Prevention of Crime (New York).
Work in New York: Report of the New York City Mission and Tract Society
   (New York).
Year Book of the Presbyterian Church on University Place (New York).
Yearbook of St. Bartholomew's Parish (New York).

PERIODICALS

Arena.

Century.

Charities.

Chinese Students' Monthly.

Cosmopolitan.

Frank Leslie's Illustrated.

Harper's Weekly.

McClure's.

Munsey's Magazine.

New York Scribner's.

The Wasp.

PUBLICATIONS

"A Glimpse of New York's Chinatown," *Seen by the Spectator: Being a Selection of Rambling Papers First Printed in The Outlook.* New York: The Outlook Company, 1902, 193–206.

Abelson, Elaine S. *When Ladies Go A-Thieving: Middle-Class Shoplifters in the Victorian Department Store.* New York: Oxford University Press, 1989.

Addams, Jane, ed. *The Child, the Clinic, and the Court.* New York: New Republic, Inc., 1925.

Alexander, Ruth M. *"The Girl Problem": Female Sexual Delinquency in New York, 1900–1930.* Ithaca: Cornell University Press, 1995.

Ames, Kenneth L. *Death in the Dining Room & Other Tales of .Victorian Culture.* Philadelphia: Temple University Press, 1992.

An Appeal of the Chinese Equal Rights League to the People of the United States for Equality of Manhood. New York, 1892.

Anderson, Kay. *Vancouver's Chinatown: Racial Discourse in Canada, 1875–1980.* London: McGill-Queen's University Press, 1991.

Appleton's Dictionary of New York and Vicinity. New York, 1879.

Asbury, Herbert. *Gangs of New York: An Infernal History of the Underworld.* New York: Blue Ribbon Books, 1939.

Bailey, Samuel L. *Immigrants in the Lands of Promise: Italians in Buenos Aires and New York City, 1870–1914.* Ithaca: Cornell University Press, 1999.

Baldwin, Esther E. *Must the Chinese Go: An Examination of the Chinese Question.* Third Edition. New York, 1890.

Barth, Gunther. *Bitter Strength: A History of the Chinese in the United States, 1850–1870.* Cambridge: Harvard University Press, 1964.

Batterberry, Michael and Ariane. *On the Town in New York*. New York: Routledge, 1999.

Bayor, Ronald H. and Timothy Meagher, eds. *New York Irish, 1625–1990*. Baltimore: Johns Hopkins University Press, 1995.

Beck, Louis J. *New York's Chinatown: An Historical Presentation of Its People and Places*. New York, 1898.

Bederman, Gail. *Manliness and Civilization: A Cultural History of Gender and Race in the United States, 1880–1917*. Chicago: University of Chicago Press, 1995.

Beisel, Nicola. *Imperiled Innocents: Anthony Comstock and Family Reproduction in Victorian America*. Princeton: Princeton University Press, 1997.

Benson, Susan Porter. *Counter Cultures: Saleswomen, Managers, and Customers in American Department Stores, 1890–1940*. Urbana: University of Illinois Press, 1986.

Berger, Meyer. *The Eight Million: Journal of a New York Correspondent*. New York: Simon and Schuster, 1942.

Berman, Jay Stuart. *Police Administration and Progressive Reform: Theodore Roosevelt as Police Commissioner of New York*. New York: Greenwood Press, 1987.

Bernard, William F. *Forty Years at the Five Points*. New York, 1893.

Bernstein, Iver. *The New York City Draft Riots: Their Significance for American Society and Politics in the Age of the Civil War*. New York: Oxford University Press, 1990.

Bianco, Lucien. *Origins of the Chinese Revolution, 1915–1949*. Stanford: Stanford University Press, 1971.

Blackmar, Elizabeth. *Manhattan for Rent, 1785–1850*. Ithaca: Cornell University Press, 1989.

Booth, Commissioner & Mrs. Ballington. *New York's Inferno Explored*. New York, 1891.

Boyer, Paul. *Urban Masses and Moral Order in America, 1820–1920*. Cambridge: Harvard University Press, 1978.

Brace, Emma, ed. *The Life of Charles Loring Brace . . . Edited By His Daughter*. New York, 1894.

Brumberg, Joan Jacobs. *The Body Project: An Intimate History of American Girls*. New York: Random House, 1997.

Buckley, Patricia, ed. *Chinese Civilization and Society: A Sourcebook*. New York: The Free Press, 1981.

Burgess, John Stewart. "A Study of the Characteristics of the Cantonese Merchants in Chinatown, New York, as Shown by their Use of Leisure Time." Master's thesis, Columbia University, 1909.

Calavita, Kitty. "The Paradoxes of Race, Class, Identity, and 'Passing': Enforcing the Chinese Exclusion Acts, 1882–1910." *Law and Social Inquiry* 25 (Winter 2000).

California State Legislature. "Chinese Immigration: Its Social, Moral and Political Effect." *Report to the California State Senate of Its Special Committee on Chinese Immigration*. Sacramento, 1878.

Calvert, Karin. *Children in the House: The Material Culture of Early Childhood: 1600–1900*. Boston: Northeastern University Press, 1992.

Campbell, Helen F., Thomas W. Knox, and Thomas Byrnes. *Darkness and Day-light or Lights and Shadows of New York Life*. Hartford, CT, 1895.

Campbell, Walter. *A Night in Chinatown*. New York, 1905.

Chan, Sucheng. *Asian Americans: An Interpretive History*. Boston: Twayne Publishers, 1991.

_____. "Asian American Historiography." *Pacific Historical Review* 65, no. 3 (August 1996): 363–399.

_____. ed. *Entry Denied: Exclusion and the Chinese Community in America, 1882–1943*. Philadelphia: Temple University Press, 1991.

_____. "The Writing of Asian American History." *Organization of American Historians Magazine of History* (Summer 1996).

Chan, Sucheng and K. Scott Wong, eds. *Claiming America: Constructing Chinese American Identities during the Exclusion Era*. Philadelphia: Temple University Press, 1998.

Chauncey, George. *Gay New York: Gender, Urban Culture, and the Making of the Gay Male World, 1890–1940*. New York: BasicBooks, 1994.

Chen, Yong. *Chinese San Francisco, 1850–1943: A Trans-Pacific Community*. Stanford: Stanford University Press, 2000.

Chinese Sabbath School Association of New York. *Statistics of the Chinese Churches, Missions, Schools and Institutions of North America*. New York, 1892.

Choy, Catherine Ceniza, *Empire of Care: Nursing and Migration in Filipino American History*. Durham: Duke University Press, 2003.

Choy, Philip P., Lorraine Dong, and Marlon K. Hom, eds. *Coming Man: Nineteenth Century American Perceptions of the Chinese*. Seattle: University of Washington Press, 1994.

Clark, Helen F. *The Lady of the Lily Feet*. Philadelphia: The Griffith & Rowland Press, 1900.

Cohen, Lucy M. *Chinese in the Post–Civil War South: A People without a History*. Baton Rouge: Louisiana State University Press, 1984.

Cohen, Miriam. *Workshop to Office: Two Generations of Italian Women in New York City, 1900–1950*. Ithaca: Cornell University Press, 1992.

Cohen, Patricia Cline. *The Murder of Helen Jewett*. New York: Vintage Books, 1998.

Cole, Simon. *Suspect Identities: A History of Fingerprinting and Criminal Identification*. Cambridge: Harvard University Press, 2001.

Committee of Fifteen. *The Social Evil: With Special Reference to Conditions Existing in the City of New York*. New York: G. P. Putnam's Sons, 1902.

Committee of Fourteen. *The Social Evil in New York City: A Study of Law Enforcement*. New York: Andrew H. Kellogg Co., 1910.

Connors, Chuck. *Bowery Life*. New York: Richard K. Fox, 1904.

Coolidge, Mary Roberts. *Chinese Immigration*. New York: Henry Holt and Company, 1909.

Costello, A. E. *Our Police Protectors: History of the New York Police from the Earliest Period to the Present Time*. New York, 1884.

Cott, Nancy. *The Bonds of Womanhood*. New Haven: Yale University Press, 1977.

Cott, Nancy and Elizabeth H. Pleck, eds. *A Heritage of Her Own: Toward a New Social History of American Women*. New York: Simon and Schuster, 1979.

Crocker, Ruth Hutchinson. *Social Work and Social Order: The Settlement Movement in Two Industrial Cities, 1889–1930*. Urbana: University of Illinois Press, 1992.

Culin, Stewart. "China in America: A Study in the Social Life of the Chinese in the Eastern Cities of the United States." Paper presented before the Section of Anthropology, American Association for the Advancement of Science, New York, 1887.

Davis, J. A. *The Chinese Slave-Girl: A Story of Woman's Life in China*. Philadelphia, 1880.

Davis, Natalie Zemon. *The Return of Martin Guerre*. Cambridge: Harvard University Press, 1984.

Dear, Michael and Jennifer Wolch, eds. *The Power of Geography: How Territory Shapes Social Life*. Boston: Unwin Hyman, 1989.

Delaney, Carol and Sylvia Yanagisako, eds. *Naturalizing Power: Essays in Feminist Cultural Analysis*. New York: Routledge, 1995.

D'Emilio, John and Estelle Freedman. *Intimate Matters: A History of Sexuality in America*. New York: HarperCollins, 1998.

Denning, Michael. *Mechanic Accents: Dime Novels and Working-Class Culture in America*. London: Verso, 1987.

Dickens, Charles. *American Notes*. 1842. Reprint, Middlesex, England: Penguin Books, 1972.

Diner, Hasia R. *Erin's Daughters in America: Irish Immigrant Women in the Nineteenth Century*. Baltimore: Johns Hopkins University Press, 1984.

_____. *Lower East Side Memories: A Jewish Place in America*. Princeton: Princeton University Press, 2000.

Directory of North Adams, 1879–1880. Albany, 1879; and *North Adams General Directory, 1885–1886*. Albany, 1885.

Dodge, Annie S. *A Glimpse at Our Chinese Immigrants*. Boston: Woman's American Baptist Home Mission Society, 1904.

Domosh, Mona. *Invented Cities: The Creation of Landscape in Nineteenth Century New York and Boston*. New Haven: Yale University Press, 1996.

Duncan, James and David Ley, eds. *Place/Culture/Representation*. London: Routledge, 1993.

Dye, Nancy S. and Noralee Frankel, eds. *Gender, Class, Race, and Reform in the Progressive Era*. Lexington: University of Kentucky Press, 1991.

Ebrey, Patricia Buckley, ed. *Chinese Civilization and Society: A Sourcebook*. New York: The Free Press, 1981.

Engle, Stephen D. *Yankee Dutchman: The Life of Franz Sigel*. Fayetteville: The University of Arkansas Press, 1993.

Erenberg, Lewis. *Steppin' Out: New York Nightlife and the Transformation of American Culture, 1890–1930*. Westport, CT: Greenwood Press, 1981.

Ewen, Elizabeth. *Immigrant Women in the Land of Dollars: Life and Culture on the Lower East Side, 1890–1925*. New York: Monthly Review Press, 1985.

Fairbank, John K., ed. *The Missionary Enterprise in China and America*. Cambridge: Harvard University Press, 1974.

Fang, Wu Ting. "Chinese Students in America." *The World's Chinese Students' Journal* 3 (July–August, 1908).

Far, Sui Sin. *Mrs. Spring Fragrance*. Chicago: A. C. McClurg & Co., 1912.

Fernald, Chester Bailey. *Chinatown Stories*. London: William Heinemann, 1900.

Fielde, Adele M. *Chinese Nights' Entertainment*. New York, 1893.

_____. *A Corner of Cathay*. New York, 1894.

Fields, Barbara J. "Ideology and Race in American History." In *Region, Race, and Reconstruction: Essays in Honor of C. Vann Woodward*. J. Morgan Kousser and James M. McPherson, eds. New York: Oxford University Press, 1982.

Forman, Alan. "Celestial Gotham" Arena (April 1893).

Foucault, Michel. *Discipline and Punish: The Birth of the Prison*. New York: Vintage Books, 1979.

_____. *History of Sexuality: An Introduction, Volume I*. New York: Vintage Books, 1990.

_____. "Of Other Spaces." *Diacritics* 16 (Spring 1986), 22–27.

Fowler, David F. *Northern Attitudes Towards Interracial Marriage: Legislation and Public Opinion in the Middle Atlantic and the States of the Old Northwest, 1780–1930*. New York: Garland Publishing, Inc., 1987.

Fox, Richard Wrightman and T. J. Jackson Lears, eds. *The Culture of Consumption: Critical Essays in American History, 1880–1980*. New York: Pantheon Books, 1983.

Gabaccia, Donna. *From Sicily to Elizabeth Street: Housing and Social Change among Italian Immigrants, 1880–1930*. Albany: State University of New York Press, 1984.

Gates, Jr., Henry Louis. *"Race," Writing, and Difference*. Chicago: University of Chicago Press, 1985.

Genthe, Arnold and Will Irwin. *Old Chinatown*. New York: Mitchell Kennerley, 1913.

Genung, Hattie E. "Evenings with Missions." *The Chinese in America*. No. 5. Boston, 1894.

Gilfoyle, Timothy. *City of Eros: New York City, Prostitution, and the Commercialization of Sex, 1790–1920*. New York: W. W. Norton & Company, 1992.

Gilje, Paul. *The Road to Mobocracy: Popular Disorder in New York City, 1763–1834*. Chapel Hill: University of North Carolina Press, 1987.

Glenn, Evelyn Nakano. *Issei, Nisei, War Bride: Three Generations of Japanese American Women in Domestic Service*. Philadelphia: Temple University Press, 1986.

Glenn, Susan A. *Daughters of the Shtetl: Life and Labor in the Immigrant Generation*. Ithaca: Cornell University Press, 1990.

Gluck, Eleanor Alther, "An Ecological Study of the Japanese in New York City." Master's thesis, Columbia University, 1940.

Gorn, Elliot J. *The Manly Art: Bare-Knuckle Prize Fighting in America*. Ithaca: Cornell University Press, 1986.

Graff, Henry F., ed. *American Imperialism and the Philippine Insurrection*. Boston: Little, Brown, 1969.

Grossberg, Michael. *Governing the Hearth: Law and Family in Nineteenth-Century America*. Chapel Hill: University of North Carolina Press, 1985.

Gyory, Andrew. *Closing the Gate: Race, Politics, and the Chinese Exclusion Act*. Chapel Hill: University of North Carolina, 1998.

Hammack, David C. *Power and Society: Greater New York at the Turn of the Century*. New York: Columbia University Press, 1982.

Hapgood, Hutchins. *Types from City Streets*. New York: Funk & Wagnalls Company, 1910.

Harlow, Alvin F. *Old Bowery Days: The Chronicles of a Famous Street*. New York: D. Appleton and Company, 1931.

The HarperCollins Encyclopedia of Catholicism. San Francisco: Harper San Francisco, 1989.

Harris, William. *The Harder We Run: Black Workers Since the Civil War*. New York: Oxford University Press, 1982.

Hawes, Joseph M. and N. Ray Hiner, eds. *American Childhood: A Research Guide and Historical Handbook*. Westport, CT: Greenwood Press, 1985.

Hayden, Dolores. *The Power of Place: Urban Landscapes as Public History*. Boston: MIT Press, 1997.

Helper, Hinton R. *Land of Gold: Reality vs. Fiction*. Baltimore, 1855.

Hill, Patricia. *Their World Their Household: The American Woman's Foreign Mission Movement and Cultural Transformation, 1870–1920*. Ann Arbor: University of Michigan Press, 1985.

Hobson, Barbara Meil. *Uneasy Virtue: The Politics of Prostitution and the American Reform Tradition*. New York: Basic Books, Inc., 1987.

Hodes, Martha. "Sex across the Color Line: White Women and Black Men in the Nineteenth Century American South." Ph.D. diss., Princeton University, 1991.

_____, ed. *Sex, Love, Race: Crossing Boundaries in North American History*. New York: New York University Press, 1999.

_____. *White Women, Black Men: Illicit Sex in the Nineteenth-Century South*. New Haven: Yale University Press, 1997.

Hofstadter, Richard. *The Age of Reform*. New York: Vintage Books, 1955.

Hoganson, Kristin L. *Fighting for American Manhood: How Gender Politics Provoked the Spanish-American and Philippine-American Wars*. New Haven: Yale University Press, 1998.

Holt, Hamilton, ed. *The Life Stories of Undistinguished Americans As Told by Themselves*. New York: Routledge, 1990.

Homberger, Eric. *Scenes from the Life of a City: Corruption and Conscience in Old New York*. New Haven: Yale University Press, 1994.

_____. *The Historical Atlas of New York City: A Visual Celebration of Nearly 400 Years of New York City's History*. New York: Henry Holt & Company, 1998.

Horowitz, Helen Lefkowitz and Kathy Peiss, eds. *Love across the Color Line: The Letters of Alice Hanley to Channing Lewis*. Amherst: University of Massachusetts Press, 1996.

Howe, Wirt. *New York at the Turn of the Century, 1899–1916*. Toronto (privately printed), 1946.

Hsu, Madeline Y. *Dreaming of Gold, Dreaming of Home: Transnationalism and Migration between the United States and South China, 1882–1943*. Stanford: Stanford University Press, 2000.

Hunter, Jane. *The Gospel of Gentility: American Women Missionaries in Turn-of-the-Century China*. New Haven: Yale University Press, 1984.

In re Opinion of the Justices, 207 Mass. 601, 94 N.E. 558.

Incorporation of the Five Points House of Industry: Articles of Incorporation, By-Laws, and Addresses of the Trustees and Superintendent. New York, 1854.

Inness, Sherrie A., ed. *Delinquents and Debutantes: Twentieth-Century American Girls' Cultures*. New York: New York University Press, 1998.

Jackson, Kenneth T., ed. *The Encyclopedia of New York City*. New Haven: Yale University Press, 1995.

Jacobson, Matthew Frye. *Whiteness of a Different Color: European Immigrants and the Alchemy of Race*. Cambridge: Harvard University Press, 1999.

James, Janet Wilson, ed. *Women in American Religion*. Philadelphia: University of Pennsylvania Press, 1976.

Johnson, Charles S. and J. Masuoka, eds. *Orientals and their Cultural Adjustments: Interviews, Life Histories, and Social Adjustment Experiences of Chinese and Japanese of Varying Backgrounds and Length of Residence in the United States*. Nashville: Social Science Institute Fisk University, 1946.

Johnson, James Weldon. *The Autobiography of an Ex-Colored Man*. New York: Dover Thrift Editions, 1995.

Jung, Moon-Ho. "'Coolies' and Cane: Race, Labor, and Sugar Production in Louisiana, 1852–1877." Ph.D. diss., Cornell University, 2000.

Juster, Susan and Lisa MacFarlane, eds. *A Mighty Baptism: Race, Gender, and the Creation of American Protestantism*. Ithaca: Cornell University Press, 1996.

Kasson, John F. *Amusing the Million: Coney Island at the Turn of the Century*. New York: Hill and Wang, 1978.

———. *Houdini, Tarzan, and the Perfect Man: The White Male Body and the Challenge of Modernity in America*. New York: Hill and Wang, 2001.

———. *Rudeness and Civility: Manners in Nineteenth-Century Urban America*. New York: Hill and Wang, 1990.

Katzman, David. *Seven Days a Week: Women and Domestic Service in Industrializing America*. New York: Oxford University Press, 1978.

Kessler-Harris, Alice. *Out to Work: A History of Wage-Earning Women in the United States*. New York: Oxford University Press, 1982.

Kin, Huie. *Reminiscences*. Beijing: San Yu Press, 1932.

Kunzel, Regina. *Fallen Women, Problem Girls: Unmarried Mothers and the Professionalization of Social Work, 1890–1945*. New Haven: Yale University Press, 1993.

Kuo, Chia-ling. *Social and Political Change in New York's Chinatown: The Role of Voluntary Association*. New York: Praeger, 1977.

Kwong, Peter. *Chinatown, N.Y.: Labor & Politics, 1930–1950*. New York: Monthly Review Press, 1979.

———. *The New Chinatown*. New York: Noonday Press, 1987.

Larsen, Nella. *Passing*. New York: Penguin Books, 1997.

Lears, Jackson T. *No Place of Grace: Antimodernism and the Transformation of American Culture, 1880–1920*. New York: Pantheon Books, 1981.

Lee, Anthony W. *Picturing Chinatown: Art and Orientalism in San Francisco*. Berkeley: University of California Press, 2001.

Lee, Erika. *At America's Gates: Chinese Immigration During the Exclusion Era, 1882–1943*. Chapel Hill: University of North Carolina Press, 2003.

Lee, Robert G. *Orientals: Asian Americans in Popular Culture*. Philadelphia: Temple University Press, 1999.

Lefebvre, Henri. *The Production of Space*. Trans. Donald Nicholson-Smith. Oxford: Blackwell Publishers, 1991.

Leonard, Karen Isaksen. *Making Ethnic Choices: California's Punjabi Mexican Americans*. Philadelphia: Temple University Press, 1992.

Light, Ivan. "From Vice District to Tourist Attraction: The Moral Career of American Chinatowns, 1880–1940." *Pacific Historical Review* 43 (August 1974).

Loewen, James. *The Mississippi Chinese: Between Black and White*. Cambridge: Harvard University Press, 1971.

Lowe, Lisa. *Immigrant Acts: On Asian American Cultural Politics*. Durham: Duke University Press, 1996.

Lubove, Roy. *The Progressives and the Slums: Tenement House Reform in New York City, 1890–1917*. Pittsburgh: University of Pittsburgh Press, 1962.

Lui, Mary Ting Yi. "Chinatown Trunk Mystery: The Elsie Sigel Murder Case and the Policing of Interracial Sexual Relations in New York City's Chinatown, 1880–1915." Ph.D. diss., Cornell University, 2000.

———. "Groceries, Letters, and Community: The Local Store in Chinatown's 'Bachelor Society.'" *BuGaoBan* 8 (1991).

———. "'The Real Yellow Peril': Mapping Racial and Gender Boundaries in New York City's Chinatown, 1870–1910." *Hitting Critical Mass* 5 (Spring 1998).

MacArthur, Robert S. *History of Calvary Baptist Church New York*. New York, 1890.

MacCannell, Dean. *The Tourist: A New Theory of the Leisure Class*. New York: Schocken Books, 1989.

Mangan, J. A. and James Walvin, eds. *Manliness and Morality: Middle-class Masculinity in Britain and America, 1800–1940*. New York: St. Martin's Press, 1987.

Marchetti, Gina. *Romancing the "Yellow Peril": Race, Sex, and Discursive Strategies in Hollywood Fiction*. Berkeley: University of California Press, 1994.

Mayer, Egon. *Love & Tradition: Marriage between Jews and Christians*. New York: Plenum Press, 1985.

McCabe, James Jr. *Lights and Shadows of New York Life*. 1872. Reprint, New York: Farrar, Straus and Giroux, 1970.

Meade, Edwin R. *The Chinese Question*. New York, 1877.

Meyerowitz, Joanne. *Women Adrift: Independent Wage Earners in Chicago, 1880–1930*. Chicago: The University of Chicago Press, 1988.

Milkman, Ruth. *Gender at Work: The Dynamics of Job Segregation by Sex during World War II*. Urbana: University of Illinois Press, 1987.

Miller, Stuart Creighton. *Benevolent Assimilation: The American Conquest of the Philippines, 1899–1903*. New Haven: Yale University Press, 1982.

———. *The Unwelcome Immigrant: The American Image of the Chinese, 1785–1882*. Berkeley: University of California Press, 1969.

Milligan, Barry. *Pleasures and Pains: Opium and the Orient in Nineteenth-Century British Culture*. Charlottesville: University of Virginia Press, 1995.

Mills, William Wirt. *New York's Chinatown: Ancient Pekin Seen at "Old Bowery" Gate*. New York: King's Booklets, 1904.

Mjaglcij, Nina and Margaret Spratt, eds. *Men and Women Adrift: The YMCA and the YWCA in the City*. New York: New York University Press, 1997.

Mollenkopf, John, ed. *Power, Culture, and Place*. New York: Russell Sage Foundation, 1988.

Moy, James. *Marginal Sights: Staging the Chinese in America*. Iowa City: University of Iowa Press, 1993.

Mumford, Kevin. *Interzones: Black/White Sex Districts in Chicago and New York in the Early Twentieth Century*. New York: Columbia University Press, 1997.

Musto, David. *The American Disease: Origins of Narcotic Control*. New Haven: Yale University Press, 1973.

Nasaw, David. *Children of the City At Work & At Play*. New York: Oxford University Press, 1985.

Nee, Victor and Brett de Bary Nee. *Longtime Californ': A Documentary Study of an American Chinatown*. New York: Pantheon Books, 1972.

Ngai, Mae. "The Architecture of Race in American Immigration Law: A Reexamination of the Immigration Act of 1924." *Journal of American History* 86 (June 1999).

Norr, William. *Stories of Chinatown: Sketches from Life in the Chinese Colony*. New York, 1892.

Odem, Mary E. *Delinquent Daughters: Protecting and Policing Adolescent Female Sexuality in the United States, 1885–1920*. Chapel Hill: The University of North Carolina Press, 1995.

Okihiro, Gary. *Common Ground: Reimagining American History* (Princeton: Princeton University Press, 2001.

––––––. *The Columbia Guide to Asian American History*. New York: Columbia University Press, 2001.

––––––. *Margins and Mainstreams: Asians in American History and Culture*. Seattle: University of Washington Press, 1994.

Omi, Michael and Howard Winant. *Racial Formations in the United States from the 1960s to the 1990s*. New York: Routledge, 1994.

Orsi, Robert. *The Madonna of 115th Street: Faith and Community in Italian Harlem, 1880–1950*. New Haven: Yale University Press, 1985.

Pascoe, Peggy. "Gender Systems in Conflict: The Marriages of Mission-educated Chinese American Women, 1874–1939." *Journal of Social History* 22 (Summer 1989).

––––––. "Miscegenation Law, Court Cases, and Ideologies of 'Race' in Twentieth-Century America." *Journal of American History* 83 (June 1996).

––––––. "Race, Gender, and Intercultural Relations: The Case of Interracial Marriage," *Frontiers* 12 (1991).

––––––. *Relations of Rescue: The Search for Female Moral Authority in the American West, 1874–1939*. New York: Oxford University Press, 1990.

Peffer, George Anthony. "Forbidden Families: Emigration Experiences of Chinese Women under the Page Law, 1875–1882." *Journal of American Ethnic History* (Fall 1986).

————. *If They Don't Bring Their Women Here: Chinese Female Immigration before Exclusion.* Urbana: University of Illinois Press, 1999.

Peiss, Kathy. *Cheap Amusements: Working Women and Leisure in Turn-of-the-Century New York.* Philadelphia: Temple University Press, 1986.

Peiss, Kathy and Christina Simmons, eds. *Passion and Power: Sexuality and History.* Philadelphia: Temple University Press, 1989.

Pernicone, Carol Groneman. "'The Bloody Ould Sixth': A Social Analysis of a New York City Working-Class Community in the Mid-Nineteenth Century." Ph. D. diss., University of Rochester, 1973.

Petrik, Paula and Elliott West, eds. *Small Worlds: Children and Adolescents in America, 1850–1910.* Lawrence: University of Kansas Press, 1992.

Plunz, Richard. *A History of Housing in New York City: Dwelling Type and Social Change in the American Metropolis.* New York: Columbia University Press, 1990.

Posadas, Barbara M. "Crossed Boundaries in Interracial Chicago: Pilipino American Families since 1925." *Amerasia Journal* 8 (1981).

Quan, Robert Seto. *Lotus among the Magnolias: The Mississippi Chinese.* Jackson: University of Mississippi Press, 1982.

The Real New York. New York: The Smart Set Publishing Company, 1904.

Rhoads, Edward J. M. "Asian Pioneers in the Eastern United States: Chinese Cutlery Workers in Beaver Falls, Pennsylvania in the 1870s." *Journal of Asian American Studies* 2 (June 1999).

Riis, Jacob. *How the Other Half Lives: Studies among the Tenements of New York.* 1890. Reprint, New York: Penguin Books, 1997.

Roediger, David. *The Wages of Whiteness: Race and the Making of the American Working Class.* New York: Verso, 1991.

Rony, Dorothy B. Fujita. *American Workers, Colonial Power: Philippine Seattle and the Transpacific West, 1919–1941.* Berkeley: University of California Press, 2003.

Root, Maria P., ed. *Racially Mixed People in America.* Newbury Park, CA: Sage, 1992.

Rosen, Ruth. *The Lost Sisterhood: Prostitution in America, 1900–1918.* Baltimore: Johns Hopkins University Press, 1982.

Rosenberg, Charles. *The Cholera Years: The United States in 1832, 1849 and 1866.* Chicago: University of Chicago Press, 1962.

Rosenzweig, Roy. *Eight Hours for What We Will.* Cambridge: Cambridge University Press, 1983.

Rosenzweig, Roy and Elizabeth Blackmar. *The Park and the People: A History of Central Park.* Ithaca: Cornell University Press, 1992.

Rudolph, Frederick. "Chinamen in Yankeedom: Anti-Unionism in Massachusetts in 1870." *American Historical Review* 53 (October 1947).

Ryan, Mary P. *Cradle of the Middle Class: The Family in Oneida County, New York, 1790–1865.* Cambridge: Cambridge University Press, 1981.

Salmond, John A. *The Civilian Conservation Corps, 1933–1942: A New Deal Case Study*. Durham: Duke University Press, 1967.

Salyer, Lucy. *Laws Harsh as Tigers: Chinese Immigrants and the Shaping of Modern Immigration Law*. Chapel Hill: University of North Carolina Press, 1995.

Sante, Luc. *Low Life: Lures and Snares of Old New York*. New York: Vintage Books, 1991.

Sawada, Mitziko. *Tokyo Life, New York Dreams: Urban Japanese Visions of America, 1890–1924*. Berkeley: University of California Press, 1996.

Saxton, Alexander. *The Indispensable Enemy: Labor and the Anti-Chinese Movement in California*. Berkeley: University of California Press, 1971.

Scherzer, Kenneth. *The Unbounded Community: Neighborhood Life and Social Structure in New York City, 1830–1875*. Durham: Duke University Press, 1992.

Schuyler, Frances M. *Glimpses of Work with Chinese Women and Children in the United States*. Chicago: Woman's American Baptist Home Mission Society, 1909.

Scott, Joan. *Gender and the Politics of History*. New York: Columbia University Press, 1988.

Searman, Samuel A., A.M., *Annals of New York Methodism Being a History of the Methodist Episcopal Church in the City of New York from A.D. 1766 to A.D. 1890*. New York, 1892.

Seeing Chinatown. New York: Bignew Publishing Company, 1906.

Seward, George F. *Chinese Immigration, in Its Social and Economical Aspects*. New York, 1881.

Shah, Nayan. *Contagious Divides: Epidemics and Race in San Francisco's Chinatown*. Berkeley: University of California Press, 2001.

Sharpe, William and Leonard Wallock, eds. *Visions of the Modern City: Essays in History, Art, and Literature*. Baltimore: Johns Hopkins University Press, 1987.

Simons, Sarah E. "Social Assimilation." Part I. *The American Journal of Sociology* 7 (November 1901).

————. "Social Assimilation." Part II. *The American Journal of Sociology* 7 (January 1902).

Siu, Paul C. P. *The Chinese Laundryman: A Study of Social Isolation*. Edited by John Kuo Wei Tchen. New York: New York University Press, 1987.

Sklar, Katherine Kish. *Catherine Beecher*. New Haven: Yale University Press, 1973.

Smith, William Carlson. *Americans in Process: A Study of Our Citizens of Oriental Ancestry*. Ann Arbor: Edwards Brothers, 1937.

————. *The Second Generation Oriental in America*. Honolulu: University of Hawaii Press, 1927.

Smith-Rosenberg, Carroll. *Disorderly Conduct: Visions of Gender in Victorian America*. New York: Alfred A. Knopf, 1985.

Snitow, Ann, Christine Stansell, and Sharon Thompson, eds. *Desire: the Politics of Sexuality*. London: Virago Press Ltd., 1984.

Soja, Edward J. *Postmodern Geographies: The Reassertion of Space in Critical Social Theory*. London: Verso, 1989.

Spain, Daphne. *Gendered Spaces*. Chapel Hill: University of North Carolina Press, 1992.

Spickard, Paul R. *Mixed Blood: Intermarriage and Ethnic Identity in Twentieth-Century America*. Madison: University of Wisconsin Press, 1989.

Srebnick, Amy Gilman. *The Mysterious Death of Mary Roges: Sex and Death in Nineteenth Century New York*. New York: Oxford University Press, 1995.

Stansell, Christine. *City of Women: Sex and Class in New York, 1789–1860*. Urbana: University of Illinois Press, 1987.

Strasser, Susan. *Never Done: A History of American Housework*. New York: Pantheon Books, 1982.

Suleiman, Michael A., ed. *Arabs in America: Building a New Future*. Philadelphia: Temple University Press, 1999.

Susman, Warren. *Culture as History: The Transformation of American Society in the Twentieth Century*. New York: Pantheon Books, 1973.

Takaki, Ronald. *Strangers from a Different Shore: A History of Asian Americans*. New York: Penguin Books, 1989.

Taylor, William R., ed. *Inventing Times Square: Commerce and Culture at the Crossroads of the World*. Baltimore: Johns Hopkins University Press, 1991.

Tchen, John Kuo Wei. *Genthe's Photographs of San Francisco's Old Chinatown*. New York: Dover Publications, 1980.

_____. "Modernizing White Patriarchy: Re-viewing D. W. Griffith's *Broken Blossoms*." In *Moving the Image: Independent Asian Pacific American Media Arts*, edited by Russell Leong. Los Angeles: UCLA Asian American Studies Center and Visual Communications, 1991.

_____. *New York before Chinatown: Orientalism and the Shaping of American Culture, 1776–1882*. Baltimore: The Johns Hopkins University Press, 1999.

_____. "New York Chinese: The Nineteenth-Century Pre-Chinatown Settlement." In *Chinese America: History and Perspectives*. San Francisco: Chinese Historical Society of America, 1990.

Tentler, Leslie Woodcock. *Wage-Earning Women: Industrial Work and Family Life in the United States, 1900–1930*. New York: Oxford University Press, 1979.

Thompson, Richard. *Yellow Peril, 1890–1924*. New York: Arno Press, 1978.

Tom, Henry. "Colonia Incognita: The Formation of Chinatown, New York City, 1850–1890." Master's thesis, University of Maryland, 1975.

Tong, Benson. *Unsubmissive Women: Chinese Prostitutes in Nineteenth-Century San Francisco*. Norman: University of Oklahoma Press, 1994.

Trachtenberg, Alan. *The Incorporation of America: Culture and Society in the Gilded Age*. New York: Hill and Wang, 1982.

Transfiguration Church: A Church of Immigrants, 1827–1977. New York: Park Publishing Company, 1977.

Trow Business Directory of New York City. New York, 1893.

Trow Business Directory of New York City. vol. 1. New York, 1897.

Trumble, Arthur. *The "Heathen Chinee" at Home and Abroad*. New York: Richard K. Fox, Publishers, 1882.

Tung, William L. *V. K. Wellington Koo and China's Diplomacy*. New York: Center of Asian Studies, St. John's University, 1977.

Van Norden, Warner M. *Who's Who of the Chinese in New York*. New York: Warner Van Norden, 1918.

Walkowitz, Judith. *The City of Dreadful Delight: Narratives of Sexual Danger in Late-Victorian London*. Chicago: University of Chicago Press, 1992.

Wang, Y. C. *Chinese Intellectuals and the West, 1872–1949*. Chapel Hill: University of North Carolina Press, 1966.

Ward, David. *Cities and Immigrants: A Geography of Change in Nineteenth-Century America*. New York: Oxford University Press, 1971.

Ward, David and Olivier Zunz, eds. *The Landscape of Modernity: Essays on New York City, 1900–1940*. New York: Russell Sage Foundation, 1992.

Ware, Norman J. *The Labor Movement in the United States, 1860–1895: A Study in Democracy*. New York: Vintage Books, 1964.

Wiebe, Robert. *The Search for Order, 1877–1920*. New York: Hill and Wang, 1967.

Williams, Allen S. *The Demon of the Orient, and His Satellite Fiends of the Joints: Our Opium Smokers as They Are in Tartar Hells and American Paradises*. New York, 1883.

Wing, Yung. *My Life in China and America*. 1909. Reprint, New York: Arno Press, 1978.

Wollenberg, Charles M. *All Deliberate Speed: Segregation and Exclusion in California Schools, 1855–1975*. Berkeley: University of California Press, 1976.

Wong, Bernard P. *Patronage, Brokerage, Entrepreneurship and the Chinese Community of New York*. New York: AMS Press, 1988.

Wong, K. Scott. "Chinatown: Conflicting Images, Contested Terrain." *Melus* 20 (Spring 1995).

———. "'The Eagle Seeks a Helpless Quarry:' Chinatown, the Police, and the Press. The 1903 Boston Chinatown Raid Revisited." *Amerasia Journal* 22 (1996).

Wong, Sau-ling Cynthia. *Reading Asian American Literature: From Necessity to Extravagance*. Princeton: Princeton University Press, 1993.

Wood, Clement. *The Truth about New York's Chinatown*. Edited by E. Haldeman-Julius. Girard, KS: Haldeman-Julius Company, 1926.

Wright, Hamilton. "Report on the International Opium Commission and on the Opium Problem as Seen within the United States and Its Possessions." *Opium Problem*. 61st Congress, 2nd Session, February 21, 1910.

Yu, Henry. *Thinking Orientals: Migration, Contact, and Exoticism in Modern America*. New York: Oxford University Press, 2002.

Yu, Renqiu. *To Save China, To Save Ourselves: The Chinese Hand Laundry Alliance of New York*. Philadelphia: Temple University Press, 1992.

Yung, Judy. *Unbound Feet: A Social History of Chinese Women in San Francisco*. Berkeley: University of California Press, 1995.

Zhou, Min. *Chinatown: The Socioeconomic Potential of an Urban Enclave*. Philadelphia: Temple University Press, 1992.

Zunz, Olivier. *Making America Corporate, 1870–1920*. Chicago: University of Chicago Press, 1992.

Index

adolescent girls: and Chinatown visits, 93–94; and interracial marriage, 94–95; and rebellion, 89–90, 91–93, 95–96, 107, 109; sexuality of, 89–94; and state control, 91–96, 109; victimization of, 96–97

adoption, 149, 153

African Americans: in Chinatown, 38, 99, 234n.69; and draft riots, 207, 269n.39; and marriages to Chinese, 156, 161; and prostitution, 65; sexual stereotypes of, 242n.10

Alexander, George, 119, 120, 123

American Baptist Home Mission Society, 140–41

American Bible Society, 118

Anderson, Kay, 227n.10

anti-miscegenation laws, 10, 153, 174, 255n.30

Asian American studies, 224, 226, 253n.6, 275nn.11 and 12

Bao Niang Hui. See Chinese Guild, The

Barth, Gunther, 228n.32, 274n.8

Beck, Louis J.: and descriptions of New York City's Chinatown, 25–26, 27, 32, 34, 35, 38, 64; and discussions on interracial families, 146–47

Bertillon system, 190, 266n.79

Bowery, 38, 40 f., 47, 90, 103, 239n.39. *See also* Bowery boys

Bowery boys, 40–42. *See also* Connors, George Washington "Chuck"

Brace, Charles Loring, 91

Burgess, John Stewart, 62–63

Calvary Baptist Church, 122, 129–30

Campbell, Walter, 82–85

Catholicism, 257n.53. *See also* Church of the Transfiguration

census, 256nn.36 and 41. *See also* Chinese Americans, New York City population of Chicago: Chinese missions, 13–14; Sigel murder investigation, *see* manhunt, Illinois

children: Progressive reforms targeting, 90–91, 243n.25; views on mixed-race, 87, 147, 150. *See also* interracial families

Children's Aid Society, 91

Chinatown: association of Sigel murder with, 6, 17, 73–75; and bachelor society, 11, 37, 56, 59, 223, 274n.8; discursive formation of, 225–26; as ethnically and racially diverse neighborhood, 33–37; family images of, 147, 148 f., 150–51; gendered representations of, 6–7, 18–20, 37–46, 51, 109–10, *see also* opium smoking; impact of Sigel murder on, 47, 49, 205–7; maps of, 23 m., 53 m.; and masculine space, 37–46; odors, 27–28, 32, *see also* opium smoking; pre-modern image of, 24, 25, 231n.25; racial segregation of, 32, 50–51, 75; racial stereotypes of, 5, 17–18, 73–75; removal of white women from, 36–37, 47, 49–51, 99; raids, *see* New York City Police Department, Chinatown campaigns; rise of, 26–27, 33; secret tunnels under, 74, 241n.66; as sexual danger, 6, 18–20, 44 f., 86, *see also* opium smoking; sightseeing in, 206, *see also* tourist guidebooks; social center of, 56, 59; spatial boundaries of, 15, 54–55, 223–26; and Sunday laws, 34–36; as "terra incognita," 17, 195, 229n.3; vice district, 5, 63–64, 65, 176, *see also* prostitution, in Chinatown, charges of

Chinatown and Bowery Rescue Settlement for Girls, 103–9; and links to Sigel murder, 108 f., 109; Sigel murder's effect on, 246n.85

Chinatown Rescue Settlement and Recreation Room, 103. *See also* Chinatown and Bowery Rescue Settlement for Girls

Chinatown Trunk Mystery, The, 17, 217–21, 273n.103. See also *Great Chinatown Trunk Mystery, The*

Chinese Americans: and accusations of conspiracy, 73–74, 195–96, 270n.68; gendered depictions of, 178–79; impact

Chinese Americans (*continued*)
of Sigel murder on, 12–13, 52–53,
76–77, 204–10, 269n.36, *see also* manhunt; and labor, 55–56, 121, 231n.36;
male mobility, 52, 54–67, 78–80,
196–97; New York City population
of, 26–27, 55, 56, 256n.33; protests
against harassment, 15, 50–51, 206–7;
racial stereotypes of, 63, 75, 176, 188,
189 f., 178–79, 195, 203–4; use of legal
system by, 61; views of Sigel murder by,
217; violence against, 59–60, 269n.40.
See also Chinese exclusion; Chinese
Guild, The; citizenship; Shen Gong
Li Hui
Chinese Christians, depictions of, 137,
115 f., 181 f.
Chinese Consolidated Benevolent Association, 27, 60, 122; response to *The
Chinatown Trunk Mystery*, 218, 219;
response to Sigel murder, 207, 210, 216
Chinese Daily Paper. See Shen Gong Li Hui
Chinese Equal Rights League, 61–62
Chinese exclusion, 5, 25,145; and
American-born Chinese, 169, 170, 172,
173, 261n.106, 263n.118; bureaucratic
administration of, 255n.27; family migration of exempted classes under, 153,
157, 256n.39; female immigration
under, 152, 157; and identification of
Chinese, 191–92; impact of Sigel murder
on, 221; and interracial marriage, 153,
156–57; limits of, 197; marriage practices under, 254n.12, 256n.40; migration
of laborers and their families under,
123–24, 250n.51, 257n.46. *See also*
citizenship; *individual exclusion acts*
Chinese Exclusion Act, 5, 11, 152
Chinese Guild, The (*Bao Niang Hui*),
59–60, 124–29; and difference from
Chinese missions, 125–26; membership,
127, 251n.75; social services provided
by, 127–29. *See also* Maine, Guy
Chinese Legation: and *The Chinatown
Trunk Mystery*, 218–19; and Chinese
missions controversy, 139; protection of
Chinese Americans, 207–9; and Sigel
murder, 210–11
Chinese Missions: acceptance of interracial
marriage, 119, 129–30; assistance to
Chinese immigrants, 122–24, 254n.12;
and Brooklyn controversy, 131–39; in

Chicago, 13–14; Chinese American
participation in, 121–22; fears of miscegenation in, 9, 111–13, 121, 129–39;
film depictions of, 141–42; foreign missionary imperative of, 120–21, 124,
248n.32; likened to Chinatown, 45 f.,
116, 141–42; national distribution of,
120; New York City, rise of, 118–19;
in Pittsburgh, 14–15; racial divisions
in, 141; socializing in, 121–22, 130,
138–39; women's roles in, 9, 111–13,
121, 131–39. *See also* Chinese Guild,
The; Chinese Sabbath School Association; *individual churches*
Chinese Sabbath School Association, 120,
248n.29
Chinese Students' Alliance of Eastern
States. See *Chinese Students' Monthly*
Chinese Students' Monthly, 213–14. *See
also* Koo, V. K. Wellington
Chinese Theatre, 8, 35–36, 107, 122
Chinese World. See Shen Gong Li Hui
Chong Sing: arrest of, 200–201; disappearance of, 2; interrogation of, 201–4;
photograph of, 177 f.; release of, 204,
217; wanted circular, 178
chop suey joints, 1, 32, 54, 55; targeted by
police, 49, 50, 65–66, 75, 77
Chu Gain, 9, 10, 198–200
Chung Sai Yat Po. See Shen Gong Li Hui
Church of the Transfiguration: baptisms,
158–62, 169, 245n.63, 257n.50; history,
158; marriages, 158, 257n.53; school,
170
citizenship: American-born Chinese, 165,
169, 170, 172, 173, 261n.106,
263n.118; Chinese petitions for, 153,
167, 168, *see also* Chinese Equal Rights
League; and *In Re Ah Yup*, 232n.45;
and racial classifications and ineligibility,
194, 261n.96; and *U.S. vs. Wong Kim
Ark*, 261n.106
Clark, Helen, 134–35, 139–41; and response to Sigel murder, 140–41
class: and impact of Sigel murder on exempted classes, 212–13; and interracial
marriage, 153–57
commercial leisure, Chinese participation
in, 54, 62–65
Committee of Fifteen, 235n.89, 271n.74;
investigations in Chinatown, 46–47,
268n.18; investigations citywide, 65

Committee of Fourteen, 47–48, 64, 65, 66, 98, 244n.46
Comstock, Anthony, 91
Coney Island, 24, 54, 90; Chinese visits to, 62; female participation in, 91
Connors, George Washington "Chuck," 40–42, 234n.78
consumption: of Chineseness, 24; of exoticness, 109. See also slumming; tourist guidebooks
Coolidge, Mary Roberts, 228n.32, 274n.8
coroner, 1; and Sigel murder verdict, 204

Da Tong Ri Bao. See Shen Gong Li Hui
dance halls, 38, 48, 78, 98, 103, 234n.70, 238n.36
dandy, Chinese men as, 12, 137, 178
darkness/daylight, 6, 67, 74
Denning, Michael, 83
dime novels, 83
domestic ideology, 103, 145; in missionary movement, 117, 139–40; and child-rearing, 147

Fifth Avenue Presbyterian Church, 118–19, 120
Five Points, 21–23, 230n.14
Five Points House of industry, 118
Five Points Mission, 118; baptisms, 159; marriages, 94, 95, 155, 171, 243n.36, 256nn.40 and 41
Fong Yue Ting vs. U.S. See Geary Act, Chinese American challenge to
foreign missionary movement: rise of, 116; women's roles in, 116–18, 247n.9. See also Chinese missions
foreign students, Chinese, 12, 213–14, 218, 271n.69. See also Koo, V. K. Wellington
Fourth of July, 207–9
French, Grace. See Lee, Grace
Fung Y. Mow, 141, 210

gambling: in Chinatown, 21, 32, 36, 62, 64, 238n.35; as racial characteristic of Chinese, 64, 78, 79
Geary Act, 61, 139; Chinese American challenge to, 61–62, 127–28
geography, 15–16, 24, 33, 78, 224–25. See also darkness/daylight; race, space
Gibson, Otis, 27, 150

Great Chinatown Trunk Mystery, The, 273n.5. See also Chinatown Trunk Mystery, The
Great Depression, 173

Hapgood, Hutchins, 25
Harding, Nelson, 78, 79 f., 181 f.
Hayakawa, Sessue, 72
heathen chinee, 227n.6
Heathen Chinese and the Sunday School Teachers, The, 71–72, 141–42
Houdini, Harry, 179, 197
Hughes, Charles Evans, 187, 208
Huie Kin, 36, 119–20, 122–23, 136, 248nn.23 and 28; and response to Sigel murder, 113, 116

interracial families, 11–12, 55; childbirth practices, 171–72; in Chinatown, 33–34, 37, and chapter 5; effects of Chinese exclusion on, 162–63; and family celebrations, 168; immigration to New York City, 157, 171; impact of Sigel murder on, 143–44; and merchant class, 166–71; popular depictions of, 147–49, 150; residential patterns of, 160–61, 258n.63; and social networks, 159–66, 169–71; taking in boarders by, 154–55, 162; and travel to China, 162–63, 164–65, 168–69, 170, 254n.23, 262n.108
interracial marriage, 10–12, 153–54, 157–58; in Asian American historiography, 226, 228n.28; Chinese American views on, 144, 153; class composition of, 152–57; court opinions on, 94–95, 102; desertion in, 150, 151–52; ethnoracial composition of, 26, 154–57, 253n.6, 256n.44; popular depictions of, 19–20, 102, 137–39, 143–44, 146–47; teenage girls and, 94–95. See also anti-miscegenation laws; interracial families; interracial sex; miscegenation
interracial sex, 10–11; and cohabitation, 37, 46, 100–101, 146–47, 164–65; court opinions on, 99–102; and "fallen women" and redemption, 20, 87, 98, 106–7, 245n.50; popular depictions of, 85–89, 178–79; and prostitution, 65–66, 101; social pollution from, 87; theatrical depictions of, 82–85. See also anti-miscegenation laws; interracial families;

interracial sex (*continued*)
  interracial marriage; miscegenation;
    opium smoking
Irish Americans, 26, 68, 69, 158, 231n.35;
  and marriages to Chinese, 26, 154, 155,
  156, 164, 228n.28, 253n.6, 256n.44;
  stereotypes of, 83, 88
Italian Americans, 68, 158; and marriages
  to Chinese, 158–59, 257n.56

Japanese Americans: and interracial marriage, 94–95, 143; mistaken for Chinese,
  188–92; New York City population of,
  189, 192, 266n.74; protests by, 190–92

Kasson, John, 179
Koo, V. K. Wellington, 213–14, 218,
  271nn.71 and 73, 272n.96

laundry, Chinese-owned: cartoon depictions of, 78, 79 f.; and danger to children, 67–71, 93; and danger to white
  women, 52–53, 71–72, 76, 78–79, 81;
  and gendered space, 67; film depictions
  of, 71–72, 237n.17, 240n.60; literary
  depictions of, 70–71; New York City
  distribution of, 55–56, 58 m.; police
  surveillance of, 76, 81, 93; racialization
  of, 66; rise of, 66; social isolation of,
  67, 240n.64; as social menace, 67;
  vandalism of, 59, 60, 128, 237n.17
Lee, Edward. *See* Lee, Grace
Lee, Grace, 137–38
Lee, Tom ("Mayor of Chinatown"),
  63–64, 206
Leon Ling: alias William Leon, 12,
  177–78, 180, 182; Americanized qualities of, 12, 75, 176–78, 180–82; and
  Chineseness, 74–75; as Christian convert, 111, 113–16, 181 f.; and class,
  180; as dandy, 12, 178; and description
  of apartment, 73–75; disappearance of,
  3, *and chapter* 6; masculinity of,
  178–79; and relationships with white
  women, 74–75, 180; and sexuality, 178,
  180; sightings of, 13, 181–86, 188–90,
  192–94, 197; and sport, 12, 178;
  wanted circular, 12, 175, 176–78, 180;
  and whiteness, 179–80, 196
Leon, William. *See* Leon Ling, alias
  William Leon

Lewis, Valentine A., 131–36
Livingston, Rose, 46, 97, 244n.45
love letters: between Chu Gain and Elsie
  Sigel, 9, 198–99; between Leon Ling and
  Elsie Sigel, 1, 8, 144

Maine, Guy, 36, 136. *See also* Chinese
  Guild, The
manhunt, 175; in Alabama, 184, 188–89;
  in California, 183, *see also* Shen Gong Li
  Hui; in Canada, 186; Chinese American
  cooperation with, 211–12; in Europe,
  186, 187, 265n.61; in Hong Kong, 187;
  in Illinois, 184, 185, 194, 195–96; in
  Japan, 186; in Louisiana, 184, 192–93;
  in Massachusetts, 77, 182, 204; in
  Mexico, 186; in Mississippi, 184; and
  mistaken arrests, 13, 175–76, 180,
  182–86, 190–93, 194, 195; in New
  Jersey, 13, 52, 185, 188, 195; in
  New York State, 13, 180, 182, 200–201;
  newspaper coverage of, 12, 177–78,
  179–80, 184–85; in Oklahoma, 184; in
  Pennsylvania, 183–84, 195, 210; and reward offers, 210; and searches on ships,
  183, 186; in Tennessee, 184; in Texas,
  184; and vigilantism, 185; in Virginia,
  193; in Washington, D.C., 182–83, 188
Massachusetts: North Adams, 166–68,
  260nn.86, 91, 92, and 93, 262nn.98 and
  102; State Legislature of, 77–80. *See also*
  manhunt, in Massachusetts
Methodist Episcopal Church of the City
  of New York, 119
miscegenation, 129, 251n.77; threat of,
  84–85. *See also* anti-miscegenation laws;
  interracial marriage; interracial sex
missionaries: discussions of Chinese female
  oppression, 150; matron figure of, 131,
  251n.87. *See also* Chinese missions;
  Clark, Helen; foreign missionary
  movement
Morning Star Mission, 69; and competition with Chinese Theatre, 122; and race
  and gender policy, 140–41. *See also*
  Clark, Helen; Fung Y. Mow
Moy Jin Fuey (Jin Fuey Moy), 19. *See also*
  Chinese Guild, The

Nee, Victor, 228n.32
New York Bible Society, 118

New York City, 20, 22–24; corporate growth in, 239n.49; and draft riots, 207; homicides in, 4; immigration, 33; multiethnic port district of, 26; and public transportation, 56–57; vice districts in, 239n.39

New York City Baptist Mission Society, 131

New York City Police Department: abuses by, 205–6, 214; Chinatown campaigns, 11, 36–37, 49–51, 99; corruption charges against, 63–64, 195, 238n.35, 271n.74; criticisms of, 195, 203–4; and detention of Chinese Americans, 199–200, see also Chong Sing; and surveillance of Chinese Americans, 52–54, 208–9. See also Bertillon system; manhunt

New York District Attorney's Office: and attitudes toward Chinese witnesses, 203; Chinese American petitions to, 219

New York House of Refuge, 92, 93, 243nn.25 and 30

New York Ladies' Home Missionary Society. See Five Points Mission

New York Society for the Prevention of Cruelty to Children: and Chinatown raids, 95; and Chinese American children, 149, 165; and investigations of Chinese laundries, 68, 70; and interracial marriage, 94–95

New York Society for the Suppression of Vice, 91

newspapers: and Chinatown reporting, 2; and Sigel murder coverage and manhunt, 2, 13, 184–85; and yellow journalism, 4, 213

Ng Poon Chew, 215–16. See also Shen Gong Li Hui

Night in Chinatown, A, 82–85

nightclubs. See dance halls; saloons

Norr, William, 25, 87–89

opium: arrests for sale of, 245n.54; in candy, 68; medicinal uses of, 30. See also opium smoking

opium smoking: arrests for, 52–53; cartoon depictions of, 29 f., 78, 79 f., 181 f.; and danger to white womanhood, 19 f., 28–32, 72, 83, 85, 88; film depictions of, 72, 241n.66; and opium dens (opium joints), 30–32, 49, 64, 106, 220; as specific to Chinese, 27–32, 64, 181 f.

Page Law, 5, 11, 152

Park, Robert, 274n.6

Pascoe, Peggy, 251n.87, 254n.12

Peiss, Kathy, 98, 244n.46

Pittsburgh, Chinese Missions in, 14–15

Port Arthur restaurant, 9, 38, 198, 199, 234n.74

Progressive reformers, 20; and anti-vice campaigns, 63–64, 202, 268n.18; and female sexuality, 92. See also individual organizations

Progressivism, Chinese appeals to, 214.

prostitution: in Chinatown, charges of, 36–37, 46–47, 64, 90; and Chinese-owned businesses, 65–66, 239n.45; among Chinese women in New York City, 253n.9; identification of, 97–98; in San Francisco, 146, 150; social pollution from, 87; and streetwalkers, 245n.58. See also Raines Law

Quan Yick Nam, 65, 202, 238n.35, 268nn.17 and 18

race: identification of Chinese, 188, 189 f., 191–93, 194; indeterminacy of, 176, 191–95, 196; and narcotics, 232n.47; passing, 193–94, 196; and social science, 32, 194, 274n.6; urban geography of, 33, 78. See also citizenship

racial formation: of Chinese Americans, 176–80, 196–97. See also whiteness and Chinatown

Raines Law, 48, 235n.96

rape. See seduction

reform institutions, 243n.25. See also Progressive reformers; individual agencies

restaurants, in Chinatown, 34, 38–39, 234n.75. See also Port Arthur restaurant

Riis, Jacob, 28, 30, 73, 145–46, 195

Roosevelt, Theodore, 179, 214, 271n.73

saloons: in Bowery and Chinatown, 38, 41, 43–44, 46, 47–49, 98, 236n.101; as masculine space, 48, 98; unaccompanied women in, 98. See also Raines Law

Salvation Army, 30, 43–44, 46

seduction, 75, 92, 109–10, 242n.6; as plot device, 83–84, 88–89

settlement houses. See Chinatown and Bowery Rescue Settlement for Girls

Shah, Nayan, 227n.10
Shen Gong Li Hui, 215–17, 219, 272n.76
Sigel, Elsie: burial, 175; commercialization of, 217–21; disappearance of, 1; discovery of body of, 1; identification of body of, 1–2; missionary rumors of, 2, 7–8,108 f., 113–16, 142; and relationship with Chu Gain, 9–10, 198–99; and relationship with Leon Ling, 10, 198–99
Sigel family, 1, 7–8, 175, 182. See also Sigel, Franz
Sigel, Franz, 7, 227n.12
Sigel murder, later accounts of, 222–23, 273nn.1 and 4
sightseeing. See slumming; tourist guidebooks
Sing, Charles, 166–69, 260nn.85, 86, 92, 93, and 94, 261nn.95, 96, 97, 98, and 101
Singleton, J. M., 136, 138, 252n.102
Siu, Paul, 240n.64
slumming, 18, 49–50. See also Bowery boys; Connors, George Washington "Chuck"
social science, 32, 194, 223–24, 233n.50, 274nn.6 and 7
Society for the Prevention of Crime, 36, 271n.74
space: and race and gender, 224–25; and racial formation, 274n.9; Henri Lefebvre, 274n.9. See also Chinatown, laundry; geography
sporting male, 178
St. Bartholomew's Protestant Episcopal Church. See Chinese Guild, The
street life: Chinese participation in, 73; working-class formation of, 90; female participation in, 92
Sunday laws, 34–36
Sunday schools. See Chinese missions

Tchen, John Kuo Wei, 26, 153, 228n.28, 253n.6
Tenderloin, 74, 90, 239n.39
Tenement House Law, 50
Thoms, J. C., 36, 133, 134, 136, 138
Times Square, 54, 74; Chinese visits to, 63
tongs, 122, 238n.32; and commercial vice, 63–64; and depictions of Chinese, 78, 241n.66; feuds among, 8, 40, 101,
205–6, 208–9; and Sigel murder, 183, 205–6, 208–9, 210, 212
tourist guidebooks, 21–22, 30–32, 39–40, 42 f., 230n.12; and depictions of Chinese families, 151 f.
transnational households, 11, 162–63, 169

U.S.-Philippines War, 84, 242n.8
United States State Department: and Chinese immigration, 163; and hunt for Leon Ling, 187; and protection of Chinese Americans, 206–9, 219
University Place Presbyterian Church. See Alexander, George

Van Arnam, Louise. See also Huie Kin
vice: Chinese participation in commercial vice, 63–64. See also Chinatown, as vice district; gambling; prostitution
Vorse, Mary Heaton, 70–71

white slavery, 235n.85, 244n.45
white women, 16: and consumer culture and heterosexuality, 98; and consumption and interracial sex, 18, 83, 85, 87–89, 109; and "fallen women" and redemption, 20, 85, 87, 98, 106–7, 245n.50; legislation against mobility of, 77–80; and "New Women," 113; working-class culture of, 92; Progressive reforms, 90–91, 243n.25; sexual agency of, 81–82, 86–87, 91, 98, 109–10. See also Chinatown and Bowery Rescue Settlement for Girls; interracial families; interracial marriage; interracial sex; missionaries; opium smoking
whiteness, 193–94, 196; and masculinity, 179–80
Wilder, Amos P., 151–52
Woman's American Baptist Home Mission Society, 120
Wong Ching Foo, 55, 62, 153
working-class families: depictions of, 88–89, 148 f.; discipline in, 92–93; economy and labor of, 92; and women's wages, 244n.41
World War I, 259n.77
World War II, 173, 263n.126

yellowface, 71, 240n.61
Young Women's Christian Association, 91

Zhou, Min, 229n.32

CPSIA information can be obtained at www.ICGtesting.com
Printed in the USA
BVOW08s0057081215

429677BV00003B/133/P